Kevin Warner
(1996)

£5

THE ROAD TO WAR

THE ROAD TO WAR

Richard Overy

with Andrew Wheatcroft

BBC BOOKS

First published 1989 by
MACMILLAN LONDON LIMITED
4 Little Essex Street London WC2R 3LF
and Basingstoke and BBC BOOKS a division
of BBC Enterprises Ltd, Woodlands,
80 Wood Lane London W12 0TT

Associated companies in Auckland, Delhi, Dublin, Gaborone,
Hamburg, Harare, Hong Kong, Johannesburg, Kuala Lumpur,
Lagos, Manzini, Melbourne, Mexico City, Nairobi, New York,
Singapore and Tokyo

A CIP catalogue record for this book is available from the British Library.

ISBN 0-563-20827-9 (BBC Books)
ISBN 0-333-44182-6 (Macmillan)

Typeset by Wyvern Typesetting Ltd, Bristol
Printed in Great Britain
by Butler and Tanner Ltd,
Frome and London.

CONTENTS

ACKNOWLEDGEMENTS

In the course of writing this book we have accumulated a great variety of debts which more than deserve our acknowledgement. We owe a very great deal to Gill Coleridge, whose enthusiasm for the project from the outset sustained us through its treacherous foothills and beyond. Our editor, Adam Sisman, has shown the same enthusiasm and a keen editorial eye, and the book is the better for his gently proffered recommendations. Malcolm Porter drew the maps under great pressure of time, for which we are very grateful. The book has grown side by side, in a happy symbiosis, with the documentary series, which bears the same name and carries the same structure as the book. A special acknowledgement must be given to the BBC team on *The Road to War* who have turned a complex academic conception into very watchable television; in particular Tim Gardam and Peter Pagnamenta for launching the series, and Hugh Purcell, Denys Blakeway, Chris Warren, Bill Jones, Richard Vaughan, Angus MacQueen, Marisa Apugliese and Sally-Ann Kleibel for bringing it to fruition. We have argued points backwards and forwards and the book has benefited a great deal from the exercise. Any faults that remain are our own. *The Road to War* is written with the co-operation of the BBC production team but the views expressed in it are those of the authors. We are grateful to the many agencies and archives who have assisted us with the images for this book, but in particular, to Jane Carmichael, Keeper of Photographs and her staff at the Imperial War Museum, London, Mona Adams of the BBC and the staff of the Still Pictures Division of the National Archives, Washington DC. We have sought permission to use all the copyright images that we have reproduced here, but if any copyright holder has not been acknowledged, we offer our apology and would ask them to contact us via our publisher. Last, but not least, our families have been more than patient: a final thank you.

The work was divided on lines that followed our particular expertise. Richard Overy wrote chapters 1, 2, 3, 5, 7 and the introduction and conclusion; Andrew Wheatcroft wrote chapter 6 and selected and captioned the pictures and maps; chapter 4 was written jointly.

Richard Overy
Andrew Wheatcroft

LIST OF MAPS

Note

The maps have been compiled using the place names as standardised by *The Times* from 1926 to 1939. This reflects a usage familiar to contemporaries. In a few cases where there is a choice of place name we have sought to apply one consistently throughout the maps. The dates given in the title refer to the beginning and end of the period covered by each map.

PREFACE

Twenty years ago, Professor Fritz Fischer published his *War of Illusions*.[1] His attempt, spread over many years, through a series of books and articles, to reinterpret the origins of the First World War produced an impassioned reaction. That debate continues, some of its arguments unresolved and its personal animosities still bitter. But now the focus has shifted from the First to the Second World War, inevitably perhaps, with the fiftieth anniversary of the outbreak of war in Europe now upon us. The parallels with the Fischer dispute are uncomfortable. There is a 'conventional wisdom', sanctified by the work of almost two generations of fine scholarship beginning with that most eminent of non-academic historians, Winston Churchill. But as historians have begun to mine the documentary resources, this traditional picture has been weakened at some points and strengthened in others. Only one major attempt – by A. J. P. Taylor – has questioned the basic assumptions of the tradition. He asked awkward questions. This book aims to ask different questions, but, the authors hope, equally awkward.

What is the traditional view? It has two aspects – the popular and the scholarly. The popular view is a morality tale of Good and Evil. One supremely evil madman Adolf Hitler captured the German nation and drove the world remorselessly towards war. Only two nations, France and Britain, stood against him, and then only after a shameful period of pandering to the dictator. That shame – appeasement – was redeemed by the two nations fighting in defence of freedom. One nation was beaten (France), the other fought on alone, inspired by one great man, Winston Churchill. And, eventually, the United States entered the war to create, with the Soviet Union and Britain, a great allied coalition which won ultimate victory over the powers of darkness. The final act was retribution, when at Nuremberg and Tokyo, the authors of the war were tried and executed.

The scholarly version tells roughly the same tale, less highly coloured, but with the same basic assumptions. It focuses a very great deal on Europe, and the struggle there between Britain, France and Germany. It accepts that cowardice and moral weakness among the Western powers allowed Nazi power to flourish, and it condemns the politicians of the West as 'appeasers', a word which they themselves chose to describe their activity.

But the evidence begins to tell a different tale. Firstly, each of the nations eventually involved in the war had complex motives for their policy in the years between the wars. Secondly, as the documents of the time make clear beyond ambiguity, there was a much larger cast of actors in the drama of international relations than the traditionalist's three-hander: Britain, France and Germany. The shaping of policy looks very different when viewed from the perspective of Washington, Moscow, Rome or Tokyo rather than exclusively from London, Paris or Berlin. Each government, in a world still made up of nation states, felt the immediate pressures of national or domestic preoccupations. So US policy was framed in a context where a President had to seek re-election every four years; Britain and France were not just European states, but felt the daily burden of sustaining and defending their worldwide empires.

The aim of this book is to retell the story of the twenty years between the wars without the benefit of hindsight, without the knowledge that there was going to be a war, in which the West would eventually triumph. For the basic problem with the traditional view is that the reader knows the end of the story: that the events of the 1920s and 1930s led to war in 1939. To the participants, the picture was more uncertain, and other possibilities seemed more likely.

One part of the traditional picture does not change. Hitler was certainly not mad, but he was an evil and ruthless man, determined to enforce his will in a way which even those who had read his treatise *Mein Kampf* could scarcely credit. He stood outside the normal Western pattern of discussion, debate and compromise: such a creature was beyond the understanding of most of the statesmen who faced him. They had built an international system based on reason, or at the very least on the principles of political horse-trading. Hitler in Germany, and those who followed the 'war path' in Japan and Italy, were not traders but hunters, belonging in a sense to an earlier stage of human history. In the context of the 1930s they were radical, violent states seeking a new order at home and abroad. A strategy to confront these forces was difficult to formulate. There was no easy answer to the challenge.

We have tried to tell a long and complex story in a confined space. We seek to focus on the politics of the era in terms understood at the time, within the nations themselves. Each of the major actors has a chapter to itself; we could have extended the book to include many more. We have organised the chapters by the order in which the nations went to war, beginning with Poland and ending with the

United States. The principle we have sought to follow throughout is that international relations are made by countries and statesmen who have their own unique perception of events. The relationship between this perception and the wider forces at play in the system help to build up, stone by stone, the Road to War.

INTRODUCTION

'WHO WILL DIE FOR DANZIG?'

On the Baltic coastline, at the mouth of the Vistula river, stands the chief port of modern Poland, Gdansk. It was given to Poland at the end of the Second World War as part of the post-war settlement of Eastern Europe. Until then it was known by its German name, Danzig. In 1939 a conflict between Poland and Germany over the future of the city led to open warfare. On the morning of 1 September, German troops invaded Poland on a broad front. The war for Danzig eventually engulfed the whole world and brought the death of fifty million people. Yet – to answer Marcel Déat's question of May 1939 – hardly any of the victims died for Danzig. Like the Sarajevo assassination in 1914, Danzig became the trigger that set off a conflict already in the making, over issues far deeper and more dangerous than the fate of a Prussian port.

Danzig was ideal for such a role. Some kind of conflict over its future was almost certain when the victorious powers severed the city from Germany at the end of the First World War and gave it independent status as a 'free city'. Since the eighteenth century Danzig had been part of Prussia. It was an ancient Germanic trading city, the rows of high-gabled merchant houses dating back three centuries or more to the time when Danzig was one of the most prosperous ports of Northern Europe. When Prussia absorbed the city in 1793 it was already in decline, as economic power shifted to the western seaboard of Europe. In 1871 it became part of the new German empire created by Bismarck. Up to the war of 1914 it remained a thoroughly provincial city, not sharing in the great burst of industrial expansion in the other major cities of the empire.[1] It was only by chance that Danzig became, at the end of the war, in 1919, an international issue.

It was geography that gave Danzig its new prominence. The victor powers intended to create an independent Poland. The commitment was enshrined, inauspiciously, in the thirteenth of American President Woodrow Wilson's 'Fourteen Points' for peace. To make the new state viable the powers promised 'free and secure access to the sea'. Without an outlet on the Baltic Poland would remain landlocked, at the mercy of the German populations that lay between her and the shore. Danzig was the obvious answer. An Allied commission awarded the port and its hinterland, and a 'corridor' of territory through Prussia, to the Poles. There were loud protests from the German population involved. The Allies fell out among themselves over an issue that violated so clearly the principle of self-determination of peoples to which they were ostensibly committed. It was realised at the time that it might be a cause of real weakness for Poland to be faced with a sulky, resistant German minority across her main trade route. A second commission sat under the chairmanship of a British historian, J. Headlam-Morley. Searching Danzig's ancient but more independent past, he was struck by an apposite compromise: Poland should keep the Corridor but Danzig would become a free city, neither part of Germany nor part of Poland, under the general supervision of an international committee of the new League of Nations. The Poles were given guarantees for their trade into and out of Danzig, the German population was given self-government. The settlement was agreed and was included in the Versailles Treaty signed on 28 June 1919.[2]

The outcome satisfied neither Germans nor Poles. It was a compromise that barely satisfied the draftsmen at Versailles. Danzig would remain, thought Lloyd George, 'a hostile and alien element'. The new Polish state won its outlet to the sea, but only at the cost of an arrangement that stood as a permanent challenge to German national pride. Poland's first premier, the pianist Ignace Paderewski, warned his countrymen prophetically that Danzig 'ultimately will return' to Germany. German nationalists hailed Danzig as the 'open wound' in the east.[3] No German government, whatever its political complexion, would accept the Danzig solution as a permanent one. Berlin maintained close contacts with Danzig, supporting and subsidising its economy, reproducing in miniature the politics of the German party system in Danzig's parliament, keeping alive the flame of irredentism. Poland used Danzig only for what had been intended, the flow of Polish trade. In the 1920s almost all Poland's exports to the outside world passed through the port. Yet to guard against the day when Germany might reclaim the city, the Polish authorities embarked on an unforeseen solution. The small fishing village of Gdynia, a few miles from Danzig, situated in what was now Polish territory in the Corridor, was rapidly transformed into a bustling port to rival Danzig. A new harbour was constructed which by the 1930s handled only a little less of Polish trade than its rival. Danzigers viewed the new development with alarm. During the 1920s their nationalism had abated. Fear of Poland and commercial good sense combined to produce a resigned

Poland's fear of Russia proved amply justified.

acceptance of the status quo. The success of Gdynia was bought at Danzig's expense. The diversion of trade challenged the viability of the Free City and provoked renewed nationalism among the town's predominantly German population. In May 1933 the Danzig Nazi Party assumed power, winning 38 out of the 72 seats in the city assembly.

The Danzig solution was a typical outcome of the Versailles peace. A rational compromise between the liberal peacemakers of the West became another fiery ingredient in the cauldron of East European nationalism. From the view of Pole and German alike the problem was not solved, but simply postponed. Danzig was bound up in the whole network of national jealousies, political irredentism and hopes of vengeance that scarred the new post-war order in Eastern Europe. Poland knew this. Danzig mattered to her not just as an economic lifeline to the sea, important though that was, but because the survival of the Free City was, in the words of Marshal Pilsudski, 'always the barometer of Polish–German relations'.[4] Polish leaders realised that the loss of Danzig to Germany would compromise the rest of Poland's gains in 1919 and might mean the slow economic strangulation of Poland. From the outset Danzig was an issue never distinct from the issue of Polish independence.

Poland's own international position was just as precarious as Danzig's. The new Polish state was carved out of the Polish territories of the three empires, German, Russian and Austrian, that collapsed at the end of the First World War. Polish leaders had no illusion that the independence of the new state was barely tolerated by the two major powers, Germany and the Soviet Union, on either side. Russia was only prevented from overrunning the infant state in 1920 by the Poles' fierce defence of their newly won freedom and the military skills of Marshal Pilsudski, whose Polish legionnaires defeated the Red Army as it approached the suburbs of Warsaw. Almost twenty years later Soviet politicians were still eagerly awaiting 'the time of reckoning' with Poland.[5] German leaders in the 1920s made no attempt to disguise their bitter hostility to the Poles. Many echoed General von Seeckt's view that 'Poland's existence is unbearable. . . . It must disappear. . . . Russia and Germany must re-establish the frontiers of 1914.'[6] Polish foreign policy boiled down to the simple equation of keeping a balance between the two threats. The 'Doctrine of the Two Enemies' was engraved in Polish strategy; every effort was made to keep an equilibrium between Moscow and Berlin, never making a move towards one that would alienate the other. In the 1920s this was relatively easy; Poland was more heavily armed than disarmed Germany, and the Soviet Union withdrew into socialist isolation. Under Marshal Pilsudski, whose military coup in 1926 brought the army to the centre of Poland's political stage, the Polish economy recovered and domestic politics stabilised at the expense of the fragile democracy established in 1919. Poland began to see herself as one of the major powers of Europe.

The unreal situation in Europe, with Germany weakened and the Soviet Union in abstention, fuelled such delusions. In the small pond of Eastern Europe Poland was a big fish. Efforts were made to expand Polish military strength; by the mid-1930s over half of all government expenditure went on defence. A military effort of this size weakened Poland's fragile economy, which was dominated still by an inefficient and numerous peasantry. Two-thirds of Poland's population lived on the land. During the 1930s the state tried to speed up the industrial modernisation of Poland, pumping money into a new Central Industrial Region set in the geographical heart of Poland away from the threat of German or Soviet forces. The cost of the effort to become a major military power and a modern economy in a mainly agrarian state, at a time of serious world recession, was permanent financial insecurity and low living standards. Poverty and unemployment provoked regular social unrest, industrial protest and peasant 'strikes'. By the mid-1930s political conflict and social instability pushed the army into assuming virtual military control behind a political front organisation, the Camp of National Unity. This loose alliance of conservative and radical nationalist groups dominated Polish politics up to the war. They were united by a fierce anti-communism and a powerful Polish nationalism that demanded 'Poland for the Poles'.[7]

The Polish nationalism of the 1930s was a reflection of the fact that Poland was herself a multi-national state. Beside the two-thirds of the population who were ethnic Poles, there were Germans, Jews, Ukrainians, Russians, Lithuanians, Czechs and Byelorussians. Friction between Poles and the non-Polish minorities was another source of weakness for the new state. Ukrainians looked to the formation of a Greater Ukraine, which alienated Poland's powerful Soviet neighbour. Germans looked to the Reich, which they wanted to rejoin; Polish anti-German feeling alienated her powerful western neighbour. The issue of minority rights did not make Poland ungovernable, but it sharpened nationalist feelings on both sides and created a permanent source of tension in a state already weak economically and socially divided. Only anti-Semitism united the different races in Poland. During the 1930s Polish Jews found themselves like their German cousins excluded from professional life and business, subject to special restrictions and deliberately pauperised through state policy. By 1938 one-third of Poland's Jews lived on government relief, thousands emigrated. It was the Poles, not the Nazis, who first suggested Madagascar as a place of exile for Europe's Jews.[8]

Political conflict and economic weakness made Poland an unattractive prospect as an ally, but did little to blunt Polish pretensions to greatness. Pilsudski himself declared that 'Poland will be a Great Power or she will not exist.'[9] Pilsudski's spirit lived on after his death in 1934. Poland deliberately pursued an independent course to give weight to this claim. Non-aggression pacts were signed with the Soviet Union in 1932 and with Hitler's Germany in 1934. Polish dependence on Western goodwill was seen as a sign of weakness and the links with France, and French interests in Eastern Europe, formalised in a Treaty of Friendship in 1921, were deliberately attenuated. Poland distanced herself from the League of Nations; she was among the first powers to recognise the Italian conquest of Ethiopia and Japan's puppet state, Manchukuo, set up after the seizure of Chinese Manchuria, both outlawed by the League. Poland counted herself among the revisionist powers, with dreams of a southward advance, even a Polish presence on the Black Sea. The victim of the revisionist claims of others, she did not see the Versailles frontiers as fixed either. In 1938 when the Czech state was dismembered at the Munich conference, Poland issued an ultimatum to Prague of her own, demanding the cession of the Teschen region; the Czech government was powerless to resist. While Hitler was building a new German empire, Josef Beck, Poland's Foreign Minister, had hopes of making Poland the heart of a 'Third Europe', a bloc of independent non-aligned states stretching from the Baltic to the Mediterranean, a counterweight to the German and Soviet colossi.[10] The Third Europe never materialised; other states had a more sober assessment of Polish strength. Polish pursuit of an independent line led not to greater power, but to isolation.

It was at this point that Danzig re-entered the European stage. On 24 October 1938, a few weeks after digesting the German-speaking areas of Czechoslovakia handed to Germany at Munich, the German Foreign Minister, Joachim von Ribbentrop, invited the Polish Ambassador, Josef Lipski, to call on him in Hitler's Bavarian retreat at Berchtesgaden. In the course of the conversation Ribbentrop told him that the time had come to resolve the outstanding issues between Poland and Germany in a single, general settlement. Danzig, he said, should return to the German Reich; Germany should also have an extraterritorial rail and Autobahn link across the Corridor to join East Prussia once again to the homeland. The talks were conducted in a friendly way. Ever since Hitler had come to power in Germany in 1933 relations between the two states had steadily improved. Nazi leaders always maintained that at some point the issue of Danzig would have to be resolved, and made this clear to Warsaw; but they also indicated that it was an issue that could be settled by agreement. German leaders hoped that Poland, in the front line of states hostile to communism, would eventually end the strategy of equilibrium and join the German bloc as a junior partner. For German 'protection' Poland would be compelled to give up the areas assigned to her by Versailles which had once been German, and to become an economic satellite of the Reich. Little of this was communicated directly to the Poles; relations were marked by a cordial exchange of expressions of goodwill and endless promises of German good behaviour. The other major powers took all this at face value, and assumed that the Poles had sold themselves to their powerful Nazi neighbour. Polish support for German aims at Munich, and the seizure of Teschen, confirmed for them where Polish sympathies lay. In fact the Polish government made no genuine move towards Germany during the 1930s, though they welcomed the abandonment of the fierce anti-Polish nationalism of the pre-Hitler days. The 'Doctrine of the Two Enemies' was not forgotten.

With Ribbentrop's request for Danzig, the doctrine was rapidly rejuvenated. Lipski detected in the German demands, coming so soon after the dismemberment of Czechoslovakia, the beginning of a German desire to bring Poland firmly under German influence, even domination. He told Ribbentrop that the loss of the Free City to Germany was not possible; Polish public opinion would not tolerate it.[11] Beck confirmed his Ambassador's instinctive reaction. The German proposals were flatly rejected. Beck was not even sure that Hitler himself knew what Ribbentrop was up to. He did not think the disagreement would lead to anything more than a 'war of nerves'.

Beck instead sent proposals of his own: the League administration of the Free City should be eliminated and a joint Polish–German agreement arrived at over the future of the city which safeguarded the interests of both states. The return of Danzig to the Reich would 'inevitably lead to conflict'.[12] Unknown to Beck, on 24 November, five days after his formal refusal was communicated to Berlin, Hitler instructed his armed forces to draw up plans for a surprise seizure of Danzig by force. German leaders still clung to the view that Poland would willy-nilly be compelled to come into the German camp on their terms. Beck was invited to come to meet Hitler in person. On 5 January 1939 a state visit was arranged; every courtesy was extended to the Polish Foreign Minister. But the meeting with Hitler marked a turning point. He was no longer friendly towards his Polish

Josef Beck, from a 1938 cartoon. He thought he knew how to deal with Hitler's 'Austrian mentality'.

guest. 'There were', Beck later wrote, 'new tones in Hitler's words.'[13] Hitler insisted that Beck should seize the opportunity to embark with Germany on new solutions in Europe, forgetting the 'old patterns'. He hinted at joint action over the Jewish question, even colonies. But he insisted that Danzig 'will sooner or later become part of Germany'.[14] Ribbentrop repeated the demand for Danzig on a return visit to Warsaw three weeks later. Beck remained adamant.

German leaders were nonplussed. Ribbentrop regarded his proposals as very moderate and was surprised by Polish intransigence. In March the pressure was increased. Lipski was brusquely informed of Hitler's disappointment. The proposals were turned into demands and Beck's presence was requested in Berlin to thrash out the issue with Hitler. Beck did not come to Berlin; nor did Lipski speak with either Hitler or Ribbentrop again until 31 August, the eve of the German invasion. On 25 March the armed forces were instructed by Hitler to prepare not just to seize Danzig by force but for all-out war with Poland if she could be isolated politically and refused to see sense. On 3 April Hitler gave a direct order to prepare for war against the Poles under the codename 'Case White'. War would 'root out the threat' from Poland 'for all future time'; but it was an essential precondition that she should be isolated: 'to limit the war to Poland'.[15] The armed forces were directed to prepare a surprise assault and to make every effort to camouflage the preparations and final mobilisation. Hitler concluded that isolation was certainly possible, with France facing internal turmoil for the foreseeable future, Britain unlikely to fight with a weakened France, and Soviet help for the Poles ruled out by Poland's fierce anti-bolshevism. On 28 April the Polish–German non-aggression pact of 1934 was renounced publicly by Hitler. By force, or through fear, Poland was to be subdued during 1939.

Hitler's assessment of the Poles' meagre chances of assistance was solidly based. Of all the new states created at Versailles Poland was almost certainly the most disliked and her Foreign Minister the most distrusted. Poland's pursuit of an independent line left her bereft of any close friends by the end of 1938; to the outside world, Germany seemed the closest. The Western powers saw Poland as a greedy revisionist power, illiberal, anti-Semitic, pro-German; Beck was 'a menace', 'arrogant and treacherous'.[16] The West, anxious enough to avoid war themselves at Munich by giving away the Sudetenland, pilloried Poland for taking her share of the spoils. The French Prime Minister, Daladier, told the American Ambassador in Paris that 'he hoped to live long enough to pay Poland for her cormorant attitude in the present crisis by proposing a new partition. . . .'[17] British diplomats attributed Poland's delusions of grandeur to the fact that Beck was 'full of vanity', consumed with 'ambition to pose as a leading statesman'. The Polish ambassadors in London and Paris found after Munich that their hosts were 'cold and hostile', showing 'such obvious ill-will' that prospects of support in the face of German power seemed remote. The French Ambassador to Warsaw, Léon Noël, advised Paris in October 1938 to terminate once and for all any remaining agreements with Poland.[18]

The Soviet Union was so hostile to Poland over Munich that there was a real prospect that war between the two states might erupt quite separate from the wider conflict over Czechoslovakia. The Soviet premier, Molotov, denounced the Poles as 'Hitler's jackals'. Beck made conciliatory noises in Moscow and the affair cooled. In November 1938 Poland and the Soviet Union issued a joint declaration reaffirming the stance of mutual non-aggression and tidying up minor points of dispute, but neither side did anything to suggest that the Soviet Union would ever be a factor in restraining German demands on Poland.[19] The smaller states of Central Europe were no more sympathetic. Hungary even promised Berlin that she would apply pressure in Warsaw to get the Poles to abandon not only Danzig, but the Corridor as well. Roumania, Poland's other neighbour, was now too alarmed by German strength to risk siding with the weaker Poles. Poland entered the contest with Hitler's Reich almost entirely friendless.

Nor was the issue of Danzig likely to arouse much sympathy. Beck himself already considered the city a 'lost post' in 1938, though he would never say so publicly. The League of Nations Commissioner, the Swiss historian Carl Burckhardt, whose task it was to maintain the integrity of the Free City, was far from committed to its independent survival. Lord Halifax, the British Foreign Secretary from February 1938, thought the status of Danzig and the Corridor 'a most foolish provision of the Treaty of Versailles'.[20] Moreover the city whose independence was to provoke a general European war was, by 1938, a Nazi city. The Nazi Party had taken control of the Danzig parliament in May 1933; the process of Nazification was carried on energetically under the Nazi Gauleiter, Albert Forster. Despite League objections the Nazi Party by 1936 had established virtual one-party rule and had imported the repressive apparatus of the parent model. The full range of Nazi organisations and institutions was reproduced in Danzig, where the Party won the active support of many of the craftsmen and officials, shopkeepers and farmers that made up Danzig's strongly nationalist population. From 1937 onwards an official anti-Semitic policy was pursued, again in defiance of the League. In November 1938 the notorious Nuremberg Laws, applied in the Third Reich against Jews since 1935, were promulgated in Danzig. Jews were forced into emigration, or made to accept impoverishment and loss of status at home. Most of Danzig's Jewish population escaped to Palestine or Britain or Poland. In 1939 the Gauleiter succeeded in getting himself approved as the head of state in Danzig, the Danzigers' *Führer*.[21]

Without firm allies, Poland's chances of persuading other powers to help her safeguard a Nazified Danzig against a predatory Germany seemed remote. Hitler had not chosen his moment idly. Poland was isolated and shunned, Danzig a Nazi outpost abandoned by the League. Two things transformed the situation: the Polish decision that they would fight rather than abandon the Free City, and the British decision to side with Poland if it came to a fight. Poland's decision came first; from the start of negotiations with Germany Polish leaders made it clear that any unilateral German threat to Danzig was a cause of war. There was never any doubt in Beck's mind that this was the right course. 'If they touch Danzig,' he told the Roumanian Foreign Minister, 'it means war. . . . I am not the man to bow to the storm.'[22] Beck was a committed patriot. He had fought on the German side in the First World War against tsarist armies, in the famous Polish Legions. He was a central figure in the contest to establish an independent Poland in 1919 and was a confidant of Pilsudski. He was not a popular minister in Warsaw, but was grudgingly respected. By 1939 he was the longest-serving foreign minister of any major power, a career that fed his confident optimism that he understood from experience how to handle foreign statesmen. He was certain that he had the measure of Hitler: 'only firmness can be envisaged as the basis of our policy.' Beck was the first man in Europe to stand up to Hitler; this in itself encouraged him to think that the German reaction would be surprised withdrawal. Nor did he count Hitler as a real German, but as an Austrian. He claimed to understand 'the Austrian mentality' which 'knew how to deal with weakness but became undecided when faced with the necessity of dealing with strength'.[23]

Beck gambled that when Hitler saw the real risk of war he would stand back. He was dismissive of German strength, 'the common exaggeration of German military power', conquering Europe bloodlessly with 'nine divisions'.[24] In his turn he greatly exaggerated Polish strength and was encouraged in that by the military circles in Warsaw. Polish military thinking was still dominated by the experience of the First World War on the Eastern Front. Poland's cavalry was numerous, brave and obsolete. Her thirty infantry divisions simply lacked sufficient modern military equipment to fight either of her powerful neighbours effectively. Poland's generals counted on other qualities: the courage and strategic skills of the officer corps, and the patriotic determination of the rank and file. In March 1939 Beck finally made the decision to fight if Germany would not back down. On 24 March he told his colleagues that the Danzig issue, 'regardless of what [it] is worth as an object', had become 'a symbol' which Poland was determined to stand and defend by force.[25] A few days later the Polish General Staff drew up Poland's war plan. Polish armies would fight a defensive withdrawal in the face of Germany's initial assault to prepared positions on the main rivers of Poland where they would regroup and defend Warsaw until the winter rains or Western help brought the German offensive to a halt. They anticipated two weeks of military uncertainty, even chaos, to be followed by a stubborn defence.[26]

There was an element of the hopelessly heroic in Poland's stand. Up to the very outbreak of war the Polish leaders clung to the belief that Poland's cause was not a lost one. This was not mere perversity. Beck recognised clearly that Danzig was not really the issue at all:

'these matters only served as a pretext.'[27] The Poles had watched as Germany advanced into Austria, then Czechoslovakia, carefully preparing each step, starting with modest issues that turned inexorably into an ultimatum. After Munich they were well aware of the pressure put by Germany on the rump Czech state and the tactic of playing off one race against another, first Sudeten German against Czech, then Czech against Slovak. Beck needed no special insight to grasp that the 'general settlement' proposed by Ribbentrop in October 1938 was the likely prelude to a real challenge to Poland's independence. Even if Beck had been willing to make concessions to Germany, Polish public opinion was overwhelmingly hostile to appeasement. Whatever else divided Poles, they were agreed on the fact that they did not want to be ruled by anyone else, German or Russian. When the American journalist, William Shirer, talked to Polish workers in Gdynia later in 1939 he found a strong resolution: 'We're ready. We will fight. We were born under German rule in this neighbourhood and we'd rather be dead than go through it again.'[28] During the course of German–Polish negotiations Polish nationalism erupted in violence. In Danzig German students fought Polish. In February anti-German demonstrations took place in all Poland's main cities, Warsaw, Poznan, Lvov, Cracow. Polish authorities began to arrest German nationalists; from May German schools and businesses were closed down. Thousands of Germans fled from Poland to the Reich. Public opinion in Poland was solidly opposed to making concessions. Throughout the period up to the actual outbreak of war the Polish government made no departure from the stand declared by Beck in March. The choice was simply a question of Polish independence or 'reduction to the role of a German vassal'.[29]

The British decision to fight for Poland was for the most part taken independently of the Polish one. Until April the British did not even know clearly what was at issue between Poland and Germany, nor of the decisions taken by the Polish government and armed forces. The British view was governed not by the question of Danzig or Poland at all, but by the behaviour of Germany. Until March 1939 relations between Britain and Poland remained cool. But when Germany invaded and occupied the remainder of the Czech state on 15 March in defiance of the Munich agreement, the British government were determined to find an issue that would let them state clearly to Hitler that he would no longer be able to expand in Europe on his own terms. Ministers had already begun to think in terms of some general Eastern pact which would include both Poland and Russia, a tactic that indicated how little the British understood Polish politics.

The Poles indicated their hostility to any agreement that included Russia, but since it seemed that Poland might be Hitler's next intended victim, the British arrived instead at the idea of a unilateral guarantee of Poland's independence. The Prime Minister, Neville Chamberlain, announced the guarantee in Parliament on 31 March. It was intended to quiet domestic critics of British policy, as the Polish Ambassador in Paris pointed out to Warsaw; and it was intended to show Hitler that Britain would tolerate no more.

The Polish reaction to the guarantee was wary. The Polish Ambassador in London admitted in his memoirs that he had had virtually nothing to do with acquiring it, despite the congratulations that poured in. The fear in Warsaw was that acceptance of the guarantee would make war more certain, and would tie Poland too closely to the policies of a foreign power after all her efforts at independence. There was a subsidiary fear, that Britain was not in earnest and that Poland's future was simply a plaything again in the political squabbles of the great powers. Beck took the guarantee, he told the Roumanian Foreign Minister, as a 'reinsurance', in the hope that firm Western ties would constitute a further and powerful deterrence to German ambitions.[30] But to avoid the appearance of mere dependence on Western goodwill, Beck insisted on making the agreement a mutual one between equal partners, Poland in return guaranteeing the frontiers of Western Europe against aggression. A similar agreement was reached with a much less enthusiastic France, who only agreed to follow the British line on condition that Britain also guarantee Roumania and begin peacetime conscription.

Poland's sceptical view of Western assistance never entirely evaporated, but as the crisis with Germany deepened it became clearer that Britain was committed to her pledge in Eastern Europe. The Poles remained convinced that if it came to war the West would actively intervene. Staff talks were undertaken between the two sides. In May the French promised to begin an offensive against Germany on the fifteenth day after a German attack on Poland 'with the bulk of her forces'. Both Britain and France promised to begin bombing attacks on Germany immediately war broke out to weaken German morale.[31] But in practice the West had no intention of giving Poland serious assistance. Even before the guarantee was given Halifax admitted that 'there was probably no way in which France and ourselves could prevent Poland from being overrun.'[32] The promise to bomb Germany was ruled out by the agreement between Britain and France to avoid provoking aerial counter-attacks on their own populations. The Royal Navy was needed elsewhere, Poland was told, to safeguard imperial sea routes. The agreement in May to start a French offensive was never formally accepted in Paris. Secret Anglo-French planning for war with Germany was based on the assumption of a long war in which Poland could only be saved after final victory over Germany. In July the two allies agreed that 'the fate of Poland' would 'depend upon the ultimate outcome of the war . . . and not on our ability to relieve pressure on Poland at the outset'.[33] As a result the Polish requests for financial help and military equipment were either turned down or substantially reduced. Instead of a credit of £50 million requested by the Poles to buy goods in Britain, the British government gave only £8 million. Not until 7 September, a week after the German attack, did Britain finally agree to make cash sums available, and by then it was too late.[34]

The failure to provide any real assistance to Poland, and the dishonesty of the Anglo-French strategic promises to the Poles, indicated how little Poland mattered in herself in the calculations of the great powers. Poland was buoyed up with promises of aid to prevent her from reaching a separate agreement with Hitler. Polish forces, which were regarded in the West favourably enough, were important to the extent that they contributed to the bargaining power of the Western powers as they tried to deter Hitler into compromise during 1939. Danzig mattered even less. Not until July did the British and French agree half-heartedly that a German seizure of Danzig alone was even a cause for war. The guarantees had talked only of the 'independence' of Poland, which the West viewed as a commitment which could be treated flexibly. During the whole period of crisis the Western powers assumed that a negotiated settlement of the Danzig problem on its own was a possibility. What the Western states would not tolerate was unilateral and violent action by German forces anywhere else in Europe; not because Poland was worth saving but because German expansion meant a fundamental threat to their interests, a challenge to the existing international order which they felt compelled to confront, or risk decline to the rank of second-class powers. The Western powers would have fought Germany for any other state in 1939; Polish interests were entirely subordinate to their own.

Like Beck, Chamberlain and Daladier, the French premier, hoped that a firm stand over Poland would force Hitler to retreat and make war unnecessary. This meant forcing Hitler to discuss Danzig and the Corridor within a framework of negotiation acceptable to the Western powers and Poland. But confident of Western support, the Poles remained rigidly opposed to any discussion except on the terms Hitler had rejected in 1938. The British Ambassador in Berlin was sure that this would contribute to conflict: 'I have held from the beginning that the Poles were utterly foolish and unwise.'[35] Even Halifax, an enthusiast for the guarantee in March, began to wonder by August whether it had been a sensible move after all. The French remained convinced that it was a mistake. They had no particular love for the Poles; it was the French view that the only sensible course was an alliance with the Soviet Union, whose very great military and economic strength really would stop Hitler in Eastern Europe. But once the commitment had been made to Poland, it proved almost impossible to reach an agreement in Moscow, for the other issue on which all Poles were united was their unremitting hostility to the Soviet Union.

The Poles knew that France would prefer a Russian alliance. They also knew that such an alliance made military sense only if they allowed Soviet troops to enter Poland to fight Germany. Poland was utterly opposed to such a course. The Poles understood all too well that the Soviet Union had never been reconciled to the existence of an independent Poland; Polish history was overshadowed by the entry of Russian forces in the eighteenth century, which had led to its forced partition. The French Ambassador in Warsaw warned Paris of his hosts' conviction that once Russian troops 'had entered a country they would never leave it'. Beck refused all French requests to agree to the passage of Soviet troops: 'we saw two imperialisms,' he wrote later, 'tsarist imperialism and communist imperialism.'[36] During the summer months French and British negotiators tried to secure a political and military agreement in Moscow, but the stumbling block proved to be Polish anti-Soviet feeling. The Poles doubted Soviet goodwill, and when on 22 August it was announced that the Soviet Union was signing a non-aggression pact with Germany instead, their position was vindicated. The French and British asserted gloomily that the Russian alliance was overrated, and that the Polish army was after all in better strength and more prepared for war than the Red Army. In mid-July General Ironside, Inspector-General of British Overseas Troops, visited Warsaw and telegraphed back to London that the Polish military effort was 'prodigious' and that 'the Poles are strong enough to resist'.[37] In the final days of August the Western powers returned to the assumption that thirty-seven Polish divisions, four British and 110 French would deter anyone.

Hitler was not deterred. He won a Russian alliance that instead encircled Poland. In a secret protocol Stalin and Hitler divided up Poland between them; the issue for them both in August 1939 was another partition, not the status of Danzig. Hitler had said as much to his generals in May: 'It is not Danzig that is at stake. For us it is a matter of expanding our living space in the east and making food supplies secure.'[38] Hitler was as certain that the West would back down as Beck was confident of Western assistance. Hitler failed to see that for the West too it was not Danzig that was at stake. Ribbentrop argued that 'If 100 Englishmen or Frenchmen were asked, 99 would concede without hesitation that the reincorporation of Danzig . . . was a natural German demand.'[39] During the summer of 1939 there was much less of a war atmosphere in Germany than there was in Britain, France or Poland. In Danzig in August Shirer found the German population confident of peace: 'They have a blind faith in Hitler that he will effect their return to the Reich without war.'[40] In Germany the long run of successes had blunted the popular fear of war. The population shared their leaders' conviction that the West would not seriously fight for Poland, let alone Danzig, which they regarded as an issue on which right was clearly on the German side.

By August battle-lines were drawn up. Britain and France spent the summer preparing mobilisation and evacuation plans and co-ordinating their military preparations. Poland did the same. German forces planned in detail the local war with Poland. The Soviet Union awaited the moment to acquire its share of the spoils agreed with Germany; the United States remained a distant neutral observer. Beck recognised that he could expect little from America, 'too remote from the scene of European difficulties to assume other than a neutral role . . ..'[41] From President Roosevelt came messages to all sides counselling peace. The Pope appealed to Poland's Catholics to hand over Danzig and the Corridor and save peace. Beck rejected every appeal. He was convinced that Hitler would in the end back down, but was anxiously searching for a way of saving face. Hitler was convinced that the West would make 'theatrical gestures' and abandon Poland as they had abandoned the Czechs. The Western powers hoped that Hitler would be deterred and brought back to the conference table.

In Danzig tension was coming to a head. Forster followed the line that whatever the Poles conceded 'it is intended to increase the claims further, in order to make accord impossible.'[42] In the city itself there were German military personnel everywhere; roadblocks and anti-tank traps lay across every Polish road into Danzig. Arms were stockpiled, smuggled in from East Prussia. On 6 August German authorities in Danzig told the Poles that their customs officials could no longer work in the port. The Polish government presented an ultimatum demanding their reinstatement. The

Danzig government denied the charge. In the German press a furious propaganda campaign against Poland was unleashed. On 17 August Poland asked Britain to make the guarantee into a formal alliance. A draft was drawn up and signed on the 25th. Unknown to the West Hitler intended to attack Poland on the following day. The German training ship *Schleswig-Holstein* had arrived in Danzig harbour on a 'goodwill' visit. The German Foreign Ministry prepared to send the codeword 'Fishing' to the Danzig authorities to indicate that war had begun. The Polish–British alliance contributed to Hitler's decision to postpone the attack for five days. He sent appeals to London and Paris to keep out of the Danzig affair; to the British he promised the guarantee of the empire in return; to the French a promise of goodwill. German leaders made every effort to persuade the Poles that the West would sell them out, and to detach Britain from France. But throughout the final days of crisis the convictions that governed the choices made earlier in the year only hardened.

The only hope of peace was continued discussion between Britain and Germany. British leaders gave Germany the opportunity of reaching an agreement on Danzig that satisfied both sides and left Poland genuinely protected. On 28 August Britain offered to mediate between the two sides formally but only on terms of complete parity for both sides and an international guarantee of the outcome. Hitler was happy to string out negotiations for as long as necessary in the belief that Britain was simply looking for a way of extricating herself from an awkward commitment. Poland agreed to direct negotiations under British protection. But time was short. German troop movements could be observed on all frontiers. On 29 August Hitler demanded that a Polish plenipotentiary be sent to Berlin on the following day to begin direct negotiations. This was not what Britain intended. Poland refused to send a plenipotentiary under conditions that amounted to an ultimatum. Ribbentrop drew up sixteen demands for the settlement of the Polish dispute, but refused to hand them to either the British or the Polish Ambassador. On the evening of 31 August the proposals were broadcast over the German radio. At 4.45 a.m. the following morning German forces launched the assault on Poland; 'Fishing' had begun. The *Schleswig-Holstein* turned its guns on Polish installations. SS troops in Danzig machine-gunned the Polish frontier guards and seized the Polish post office. Burckhardt, the League High Commissioner, was bundled into a car and sent off in the direction of Lithuania. The swastika flag was raised over the League building.[43] Polish resistance was quashed, and Danzig returned *Heim ins Reich*, home to the Reich.

POLAND UNDER ATTACK, 1939

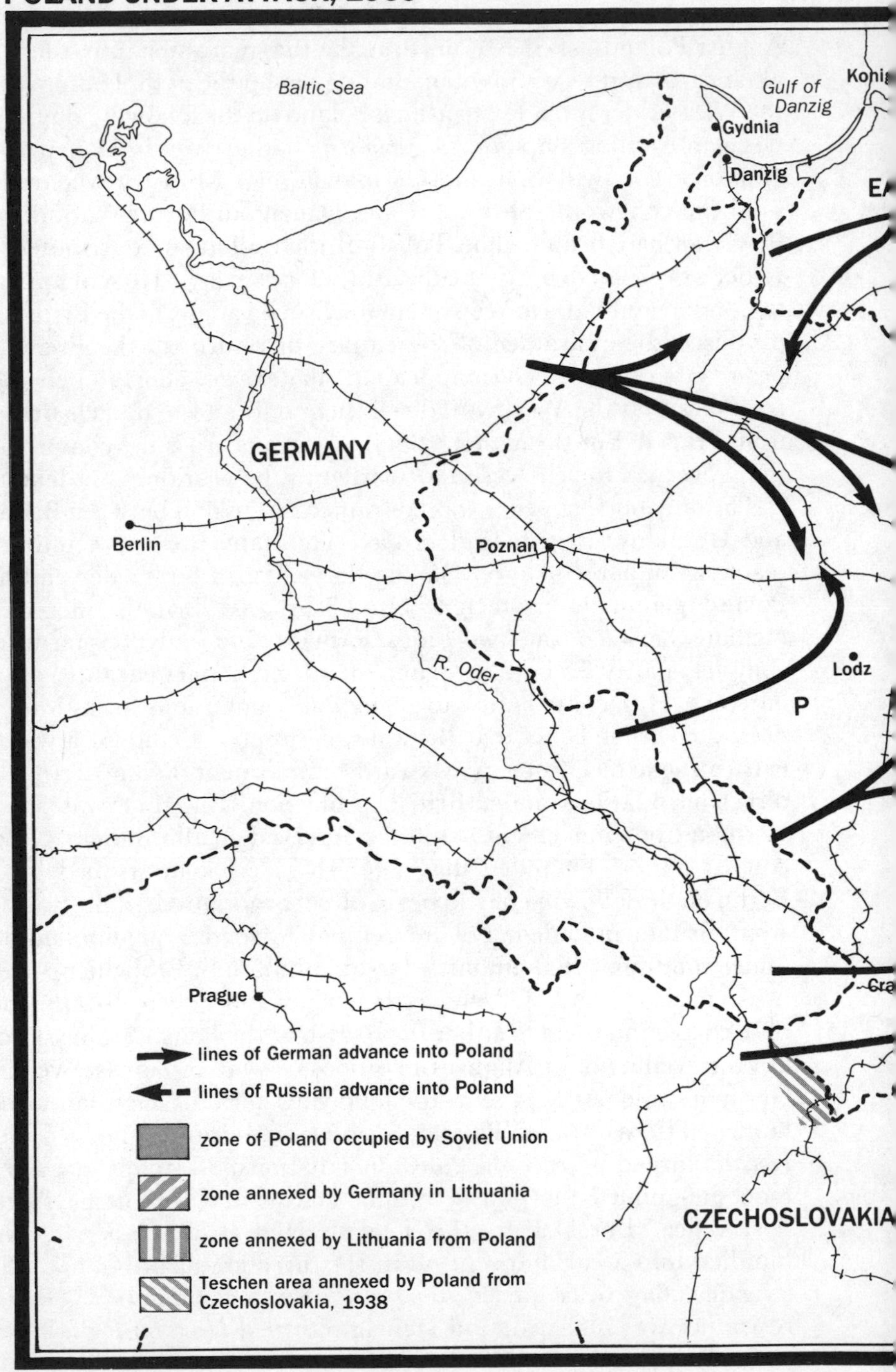

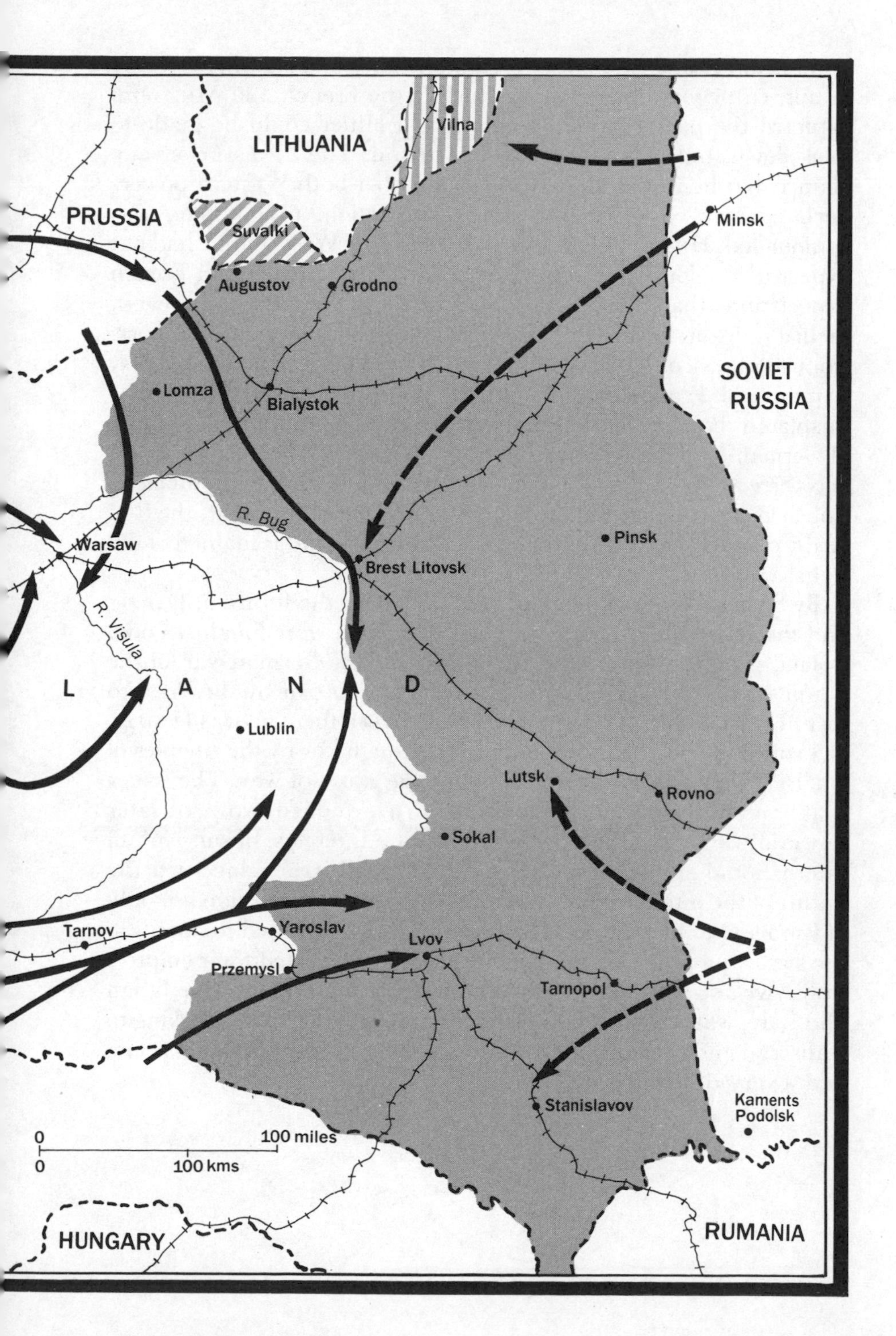

LITHUANIA
Vilna
PRUSSIA
Suvalki
Augustov
Grodno
Minsk
Lomza
Bialystok
SOVIET
RUSSIA
R. Bug
Warsaw
Brest Litovsk
Pinsk
R. Visula
L
A
N
D
Lublin
Lutsk
Rovno
Sokal
Tarnov
Yaroslav
Lvov
Przemysl
Tarnopol
Stanislavov
Kaments
Podolsk
0
100 miles
0
100 kms
HUNGARY
RUMANIA

Britain and France did not immediately fight for Poland. Two days of hurried negotiations continued while the French and Mussolini explored the prospects of a conference if Hitler could be made to back down and withdraw from Polish soil. There was never any chance that he would do so. On 3 September both Western powers declared war on Germany. Every conviction, except one, was confounded. Hitler was faced with a war in the West that he had not expected; the local war could not be localised. British and French expectations that Hitler would back down or face domestic revolt, fuelled right up to the very outbreak of war by exaggerated reports from Berlin, collapsed completely. The Polish conviction that Britain and France would fight for them also turned out to be misplaced. Poland was defeated in two weeks; there was no bombing of Germany, no French invasion from the west. Only one conviction was correct: Polish distrust of the Soviet Union. On 17 September, as Polish forces collapsed in the face of the German onslaught, the Red Army crossed the eastern frontier and overran what remained of the Polish state.

By September 1939 the issue was no longer the future of Danzig and the safety of Poland. Three separate wars were fought as one: Poland's war to maintain her independence; the German war for the domination of Eastern Europe; and the war fought by the West to restore the balance of power. The link between them all was Danzig, a Nazified city whose independence was fought for by the enemies of Nazism. Danzig was the occasion not the cause of war. The issues that brought the powers to the brink in 1939 and led two years later to world war were issues perceived as vital interests, of survival, of international status, of morality. The central issue concerned the nature of the international system, the political complexion not only of Europe, but of the world. Britain and France wanted to maintain the status quo, the existing structure which permitted their empires to survive and their way of life to be preserved. Germany, like Japan and Italy, was a radical power in the context of the 1930s, seeking to transcend and overturn the old order in favour of new, rising powers, and a very different way of life.

CHAPTER ONE
GERMANY

> Strong, healthy and flourishing nations increase in numbers. From a given moment they require a continual expansion of their frontiers, they require new territory for the accommodation of their surplus population. Since almost every part of the globe is inhabited, new territory must, as a rule, be obtained at the cost of its possessors – that is to say, by conquest, which thus becomes a law of necessity.
>
> (General Friedrich von Bernhardi, 1912)

> We must once and for all time create the politically and biologically eternally valid foundations of a German Europe. . . . But our true object is to set up our rule for all time. . . . Today we are faced with the iron necessity of creating a *new social order*. Only if we succeed in this shall we solve the great historical task which has been set our people.
>
> (Adolf Hitler, 1932)

In early March in the last year of the First World War peace was signed between Germany and Russia at Brest-Litovsk. The terms of the treaty were devastating. German troops and their allies were to occupy and control the whole of western Russia, reaching almost to Petrograd in the north and the Volga river in the south. German forces crossed the Black Sea to reach beyond the Caucasus mountains to the rich oilfields of Baku and Batum. The Kaiser's forces brought the German Empire farther into Russia than Hitler's armies reached a generation later. Several weeks after Brest-Litovsk, on 21 March, the German army began the great offensive on the Western Front to bring about the final defeat of Britain and France and secure for Germany the mastery of Europe and half Asia.

Germany's new empire lasted only six months. Undermined by months of economic blockade, overwhelmed by sheer numbers at the front, Germany's leaders sued for an armistice. Within a year she was the victim in her turn of a punitive peace settlement at Versailles that stripped her of territory, all her shipping, her overseas colonies, and imposed disarmament and a vast war indemnity. Internationally isolated, with no fleet and her great armed might disbanded, German power in Europe was shattered. The Bismarckian Reich, founded fifty years before, had brought industrial prosperity and national pride to two generations of Germans and brought

Germany to the forefront of the great powers. Now the allies forced Germany to confess openly her sole responsibility for the Armageddon of 1914. 'Our entire national existence to be condemned as guilty and erroneous', complained the novelist, Thomas Mann.[1] Germany became the pariah of Europe; the German people were forced to adjust to a very different post-war world of political uncertainty and economic stagnation. The expectations of 1914 were rudely dispelled; a powerful sense of injustice scarred a whole generation of Germans.

The desire to reverse the judgement of Versailles, to restore German national honour, to return to the steady upward trajectory of German power lost in 1919, sank deep roots in German society. Before 1914 there was something natural, almost irresistible, about the gradual dominance of Germany in Europe. It was recognised by conquered and conqueror alike that in the long run this was a situation almost impossible to reverse. The question remained whether that dominance could be achieved, and could be accepted, within a framework of co-operation with the rest of Europe. This was a question not answered until 1939. By that date Hitler had restored German power to a point where it could not remotely be contained within the existing international order, led as it was by the most embittered and radical veterans of German collapse in 1918.

When the German delegation set out from Berlin to the Peace Conference at Versailles in April 1919 it was in the firm belief that the settlement would be a negotiated one. The German Foreign Minister, Graf Ulrich von Brockdorff-Rantzau, carried with him a list of concessions that the German government were prepared to accept. These included the transfer of Alsace-Lorraine to France, and small territorial concessions to Denmark and the new state of Poland, but only after a plebiscite had determined the wishes of the populations concerned; a promise to disarm to the same extent as Germany's neighbours; and an undertaking to pay reparations for damage to civilian property. In return the German delegation was empowered to demand the return of German colonies captured by the Allies and the restitution of the German merchant fleet. It was the German view that the Armistice signed on 11 November 1918 was a truce not a surrender.

The reality faced by the German delegation in France exceeded even the most pessimistic expectations. The envoys were placed in an isolated hotel surrounded by barbed wire. They were brought to the conference as a defeated and guilty enemy. The Allied delegates sat; the Germans were made to stand. 'The hour has struck', said

Georges Clemenceau, head of the French delegation, 'for the weighty settlement of our account.'[2] It was an account no German could believe. Germany was to be almost completely disarmed, confined to a 100,000-man army for internal police responsibilities, denied the use of tanks, warplanes and submarines, the great German General Staff disbanded. The German Empire was to be dismembered; the colonies were taken over by the newly formed League of Nations and distributed to Britain, France and Japan as mandates; in Europe one-eighth of German territory was distributed to France and Belgium in the west, Denmark in the north and Poland and Czechoslovakia in the east. The Polish settlement was a bitter blow. The Allies agreed to allow Poland a 'corridor' of territory to the sea carved out of West Prussia, dividing the old heartland of the Reich and leaving a vulnerable rump of East Prussia surrounded by Polish territory, cut off from the rest of Germany. The transferred territories in the east and west included much of the coal and iron-ore resources of the pre-war Reich; the Saar basin was placed under international control, rendering Germany's economy yet more anaemic. The Rhineland was permanently demilitarised. The final humiliation was the Allied insistence that Germany admit its war guilt formally, in the terms of the Treaty; and that having done so the German government should undertake to pay in reparation any sum agreed by her victors. The final sum amounted to 132 billion gold marks; the schedule of payments drawn up in 1921 would have burdened the German economy until 1988.

The German government was told that there was no room for negotiation. Politicians of all parties in Berlin counselled rejection. The Allies replied with an ultimatum: either the German government accepted the Treaty within one week or Germany would be invaded and occupied. A week of frantic activity followed. Only hours before the ultimatum was due to expire did the High Command of the army finally admit that there was no effective way Germany could resist. The Treaty was accepted in word but not in spirit; for the West it was a peace settlement, in Germany it was the *Diktat*, the dictated, imposed settlement. The socialist politicians who had called for the Armistice and signed the Treaty became in the eyes of German nationalists betrayers of Germany, the 'November criminals', who had 'stabbed Germany in the back'. Even Germans of more moderate opinions could not be reconciled to war guilt and reparations, which together placed Germany in a permanent state of moral inferiority and economic subjection for a conflict that was not solely of Germany's making. It was this profound sense of injustice that infused all Germany's foreign policy during the

DANZIG: THE FLASHPOINT, 1939

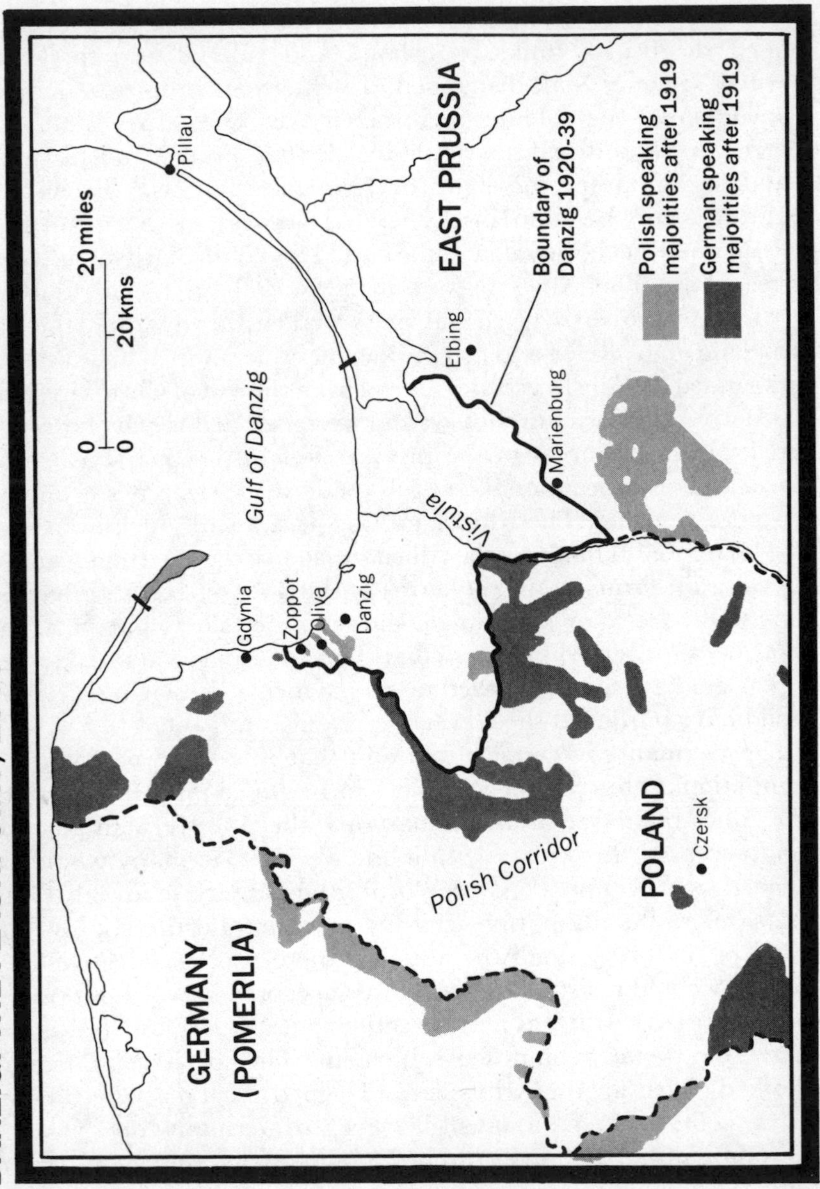

0 20 miles
0 20kms
Pillau
EAST PRUSSIA
Gulf of Danzig
Elbing
Boundary of Danzig 1920-39
Marienburg
Vistula
Gdynia
Zoppot
Oliva
Danzig
GERMANY (POMERLIA)
Polish Corridor
POLAND
Czersk
Polish speaking majorities after 1919
German speaking majorities after 1919

years that followed. This was not only a German view. There were powerful critics of the peace terms on the Allied side who saw the deliberate emasculation of Germany as a shortsighted and vengeful solution, which would weaken Europe's economy and encourage political extremism.

The evidence from Germany confirmed these fears. The German military collapse in November 1918 plunged Germany into political chaos. The government was assumed by an alliance of moderate and radical socialists for the first time. The radical left saw the end of the war as an opportunity to repeat what had happened in Russia in 1917, and in January 1919 they declared a revolution; in Bavaria a soviet regime was established; in the Ruhr workers' committees took over the running of factories. The moderate left had no other course but to call on the army to help restore order. In months of patchy, vicious conflicts, the revolution was suppressed. Prodded by the watchful Allies, German politicians arrived at a constitutional solution which the bulk of the population accepted. At Weimar a National Assembly was established which ushered in a new democratic constitution, turning Germany from a semi-authoritarian monarchy into a full parliamentary state. It was an unhappy birth. Attacked from the extreme right and extreme left, the political system remained weak and vulnerable. Street violence and assassination became endemic. Among its prominent victims was Matthias Erzberger, the Catholic politician who had signed the Armistice and argued in parliament for signature of the Versailles Treaty.

Political crisis went hand in hand with economic catastrophe. Weakened by the loss of territory and resources, saddled with massive war debts and escalating government deficits, the German currency collapsed. By 1923 Germany was gripped by hyper-inflation. The government blamed reparations and the economic vindictiveness of the Allies, but the real cause was the impossibility of paying for the massive war effort and reconstruction from an economy so reduced in size and power by the aftermath of war. By December the German mark had collapsed completely; political conflict resurfaced violently. In Hamburg and Saxony communist coups were mounted; in Munich General Ludendorff, the soldier who sought the Armistice in 1918, attempted to overthrow the Bavarian state government by a clumsy street protest in alliance with a young populist agitator, Adolf Hitler. Order was restored at home by the army and the police, but economic order could only be brought from outside. Four years after Versailles, the victor powers once again sat to consider the fate of Germany. The currency was restored on a stable footing, and a new schedule, the Dawes Plan, was set up for reparations payments, adjusted more realistically to what Germany could pay. In return German finances were placed under the supervision of commissioners appointed by the victor states.

The impact of hyper-inflation was felt most keenly by the middle classes. The value of their savings was wiped out; it was they, in the end, who had to bear the full cost of Germany's war effort when government war bonds became worthless. Anyone whose income derived from shares or investment was ruined; all those on fixed incomes were destitute. The private wealth generated by German industrial progress before 1914 was wiped out. The psychological and material shock could not be erased. The inflation left Germany's middle classes vulnerable and politically defensive, more hostile than ever to the Allies, whose actions were held responsible for the disaster, and increasingly alienated from a parliamentary system which had failed to protect them from ruin. In the background stood German communism, which had almost triumphed in 1919 and reared up again in the crisis of 1923; middle-class anxiety about communism became a recurrent theme. The post-war years had brought three great shocks to the established social and political order: a humiliating treaty, social revolution and economic crisis. No German was unaffected, but those with most to lose were affected most. Four years of terrible war and four years of post-war confusion weakened allegiance to the state and sharpened social antagonisms and cultural prejudices. Germany's national fortunes were unpredictable but bleak. 'We are an object', noted Gustav Stresemann, 'in the policies of others.'[3]

By 1924 there was a universal desire in Germany for a period of peace and stability, for a licking of wounds. No man symbolised this longing more than Stresemann, Foreign Minister from 1923 to his death in 1929. Though far from a convinced republican, and deeply resentful at Germany's treatment after 1918, he saw the necessity for respite. He encouraged even the most disillusioned Germans to become what he called 'republicans of the head, not the heart', to accept that for better or worse democracy was there to stay and should be worked with, not resisted. He preached a foreign policy of fulfilment of the Treaty. This was the only way, he argued, that Germany could be accepted back into the international arena. He pursued a strategy of accommodation with the Western powers. Foreign loans were provided to rebuild Germany's weak economy; in 1925 Germany signed the Locarno Agreement with Britain and France, guaranteeing the western frontiers agreed at Versailles; in

The first shots of the war in Europe, 1 September 1939: the German training ship *Schleswig-Holstein* shells the Polish installations on the Westerplatte, close to Danzig.

Crowds in Danzig's Lange Markt demonstrate, demanding the right to join Hitler's Reich, 23 June 1939.

Under the watchful eye of Adolf Hitler, Admiral von Trotha explains to an audience in Danzig the part the city will play in the new Germany. By 1939 the whole apparatus of Nazidom had been introduced into Danzig.

Two ways of war. (*Above*) German: a Heinkel 111 releases its bombs over Poland, September 1939. The Polish campaign seemed to confirm the view that the bomber was the key to modern war. (*Below*) Polish: Poland's eleven cavalry brigades found themselves in the front line against German tanks and aircraft. Here Polish lancers cross a river during the campaign.

Hitler and his generals outside the German army HQ in Poland after the German victory. This was the war he planned to fight in 1939, not the war with Britain and France.

The first meeting between German and Soviet staff officers at Bialystok after the occupation of Poland. They settled the remaining questions of partition, agreed in principle in the Nazi-Soviet Pact. The Soviet Union renounced Warsaw in return for a dominant position in Lithuania.

German military might, displayed at the Nuremberg Party Rally in September 1938. The public propaganda image was of overwhelming air power matched by armoured divisions on the ground; in practice German rearmament was less advanced than its enemies supposed.

On 6 October 1938 Hitler was greeted rapturously by the German inhabitants of the Sudetenland. These areas, granted to Czechoslovakia in 1919, were reintegrated into Germany through the decision of the Munich Conference. Hitler's 'bloodless victory' was popular throughout Germany; for the Czechs it spelt disaster.

Anschluss, March 1938. Hitler drives through Vienna and addresses a wildly enthusiastic crowd in the Heldenplatz shortly after his native Austria had been forcibly reunited with the Reich.

Keeping the West at bay. Hitler is inspecting the German *Westwall* in the final stages of construction, May 1939; the fortifications matched the French Maginot Line, but in the war of movement in 1940 they proved redundant for both sides.

German forces rest during the advance into Poland, September 1939. Like all the armies of 1939–40, German mobility depended on the horse as much as on motor transport. Only six of the sixty German divisions were motorised.

1926 Germany won the right to sit in the League of Nations. As the war receded into the past, some of the more minor or petty provisions of the Treaty were removed. Stresemann was right to assume that this was a quicker route to rehabilitation. But on one issue neither he nor any other German statesman would budge; he was determined that the settlement in the east would one day be revised. In 1925, the year of Locarno, he privately admitted his ambition to achieve 'the readjustment of our eastern frontiers; the recovery of Danzig, the Polish Corridor'.[4]

In the mid-1920s such ambitions could not possibly be realised; they were publicly voiced only by the most extreme wing of German nationalism. To the outside world Germany was no longer the outcast, but had learned her lesson. A modest economic recuperation brought a brief period of political stability. Democracy was taking root. 'Americanisation' followed the influx of American loans. German industry began to rationalise along American lines. Berliners danced to Western jazz; the wealthy drove cars made by Ford and General Motors in the Ruhr. German artists and writers courted the avant-garde. An aggressive modernism began to permeate German life; it was the age of Brecht and the *Bauhaus*. Political life was dominated by big business and the labour unions, both of which had survived the period of inflation more successfully than the rest of German society. In Parliament the social democrats represented organised labour; the centre parties drew their funds from large-scale industry. In the climate of revival and economic renewal the social fissure began to heal. The Weimar system encouraged the progressive forces in German life, and urged on the modernisation of German society.

Weimar's liberal credentials were real enough, but they masked another, very different Germany. For all those Germans who genuinely embraced democracy and the modern age, there were those whose experience of the 1920s pointed to a deep national and cultural crisis, a social malaise for which 'fulfilment' offered no way out. This other Germany was deeply nationalist. It was sentimentally attached to the golden age of pre-war Germany, the days of order and prosperity. But support for this other Germany was widely scattered, socially diverse, politically weak. At the heart of the nationalist movement was the old ruling class whose world fell apart in 1919. The loss of the monarchy and aristocratic dominance was bad enough; the loss of a great army, the traditional power-base, was disastrous. The old elite retreated to the *Herrenklub* in Berlin or sulked on their estates, sniping at the republic from the wings. Then in 1925, following the death of the social-democrat President,

Friedrich Ebert, one of the most famous of their number, Field Marshal Paul von Hindenburg, was elected President. He was seen by many German voters as a political father-figure who would help to unite an unhappy people. Slowly but surely the old elite began to gather its strength again around the figure of the ageing war-hero. While Stresemann pursued fulfilment, they encouraged strategies of defiance. In 1922 Germany and the Soviet Union had signed a pact renouncing their mutual war claims at Rapallo. Now the conservatives around Hindenburg demanded a strengthening of ties with this unlikely ally. In 1926 the Treaty of Berlin was signed promising mutual assistance, but, more important, offering the disarmed German forces the opportunity to develop prohibited weapons and train German soldiers and airmen on Soviet soil. In Germany the Defence Ministry became the centre for military planning and strategic thinking for the day when Germany could once again rearm without restriction.

The slow revival in the fortunes of the old conservative classes was not matched by the other groups alienated from the Weimar republic. The traditional nationalism of general and landowner was joined in the 1920s by a powerful new popular nationalism that drew its strength from social hardship and economic decline. It was a movement still too socially diverse and politically unskilled to co-ordinate its hostility to the new age. There were peasants heavily in debt, resentful at foreign competition, hostile to the growing dominance of city culture and industrial politics. There were craftsmen and small businessmen unshielded from the fierce winds of competition, frightened of the working class, envious of the rich. There were the schoolteacher and the bureaucrat, their incomes lower than in 1914, their savings gone, their status under threat from the rise of new industrial white-collar classes, their memories of an age when they were valued and the nation was strong. Linking them all together was an intellectual elite which articulated the widespread sense of decline and disorder, which expressed a fierce anti-Marxism, which gave voice to the call for moral renewal in the face of modern decadence, and, most important, pronounced that Germany's day would come. Exposed to internal decay and external humiliation, the authors of Germany's *fin de siècle* predicted that Germany would rise again as the old world order crumbled away. 'It is the German people's providential mission', announced Edgar Jung, 'to rebuild the West.' The Germans would show the way between the extremes of capitalism and socialism, to build what the writer Möller van den Bruck called 'The Third Way', the way of the 'Third Reich'.[5]

All these groups shared to some extent a yearning for authority and hostility to the parliamentary regime. They resented the new politics of party and interest group because it left them powerless and marginal. They did not embrace the liberal, Western system, with enthusiasm. They saw it as yet another product of defeat. These groups were ill adapted to the new pressures of economic liberalism and political individualism imported from the West. This was a point that Western governments consistently failed to grasp in their dealings with Germany. It was always assumed that generous doses of modernisation and political liberty would cure Germany of her unfortunate past. The opposite was the case. Broad sections of the German community shared very different values: a strong state, economic justice, social order, cultural intolerance. It was difficult to build this into a broad political movement. German populism bubbled beneath the surface of republican politics. As long as the economy continued to grow, the democratic system and its modernising core were tolerated. But when this system itself began to collapse in the world depression that came in 1929, German populism and nationalism burst, boiling, through the weak veil of German democracy.

The slump of 1929 hit Germany with exceptional force. It was the worst economic depression in German history. For many Germans it was the final straw after a decade of repeated catastrophe. Even those Germans who supported the Weimar system lost confidence in the survival of German capitalism. The figures reveal a grim catalogue of economic decline. In 1929 two million Germans were already unemployed; by 1931 almost five million; by 1932 there were eight million fewer Germans employed than in 1928, one in every three of the working population. The income of German farmers, already low, was halved; the earnings of shops and small businesses fell by more than half. Industrial production, which had just returned to the levels achieved by 1914, fell back to 58 per cent of that level in 1932. Foreign capital, which had buoyed up the reviving economy in the mid-1920s, now fled to safety. Terrified of a repeat of the inflation the German government pursued rigidly orthodox financial policies, dragging the economy down still further through tough deflation. The social impact was indiscriminate. There had been widespread poverty and low incomes during the fragile economic revival; now recession brought real hardship to all sections of the community, industrial worker, craftsman and farmer alike.[6]

The political impact of economic collapse after the high hopes of national revival was explosive. Angry workers turned once again to

German election poster, 1932: Hitler delivered his promise to the unemployed.

communism. By 1932 the German Communist Party had almost doubled its number of seats in the Reichstag. Parliamentary coalition government fell apart as the parties squabbled over economic priorities. By 1930, when the Catholic Party leader, Heinrich Brüning, became Chancellor, parliamentary rule was effectively replaced by rule through emergency presidential decree. This placed more power in the hands of the conservative coterie around the almost senile President. Democracy was on shaky ground. For the conservative masses the depression cut them adrift from the system and revived the terrifying spectre of communism. They had read their Marx: the collapse of capitalism would bring the harsh rule of the proletariat. Caught between the collapsing parliamentary system, economic misery and the threat of social overthrow, they searched for a way out.

Millions of Germans found that escape in National Socialism. In 1928 the Nazi Party was a small, fringe group that had campaigned unsuccessfully to win the factory working class away from socialism. It polled a tiny proportion of votes, and elected a mere twelve deputies in 1928. The Party was led by a young, populist demagogue, an Austrian who had hovered on the edges of radical right-wing politics in the early 1920s and had launched the abortive coup with Ludendorff in 1923. For this Hitler was imprisoned. On his release the Party began the slow task of rebuilding. But little in its history suggested the extraordinary surge of electoral success that was to follow. The key to that success was its recognition of a large and anxious body of conservative voters, radicalised by fear of the left and social decline, for whom Hitler and the Nazi leadership provided the authentic voice of protest.

The rise of Nazi electoral success was a marriage of convenience. The Party needed a mass base in order to achieve power; the masses in the villages and small towns of Germany longed for a movement that would give political voice to their social anxieties and yearning for order. The rise of Hitler had something almost messianic about it. As the Party organisation smothered the country with Party officials and propaganda it mobilised the broad populist community on the promise that Hitler alone held the key to German revival and social peace. Hitler, like them, was a 'small man', a man of the people. He gave expression to their prejudices. He shared their desire for strong government and social order. He led a movement actively fighting the menace of communism on the streets. More important, Hitler was all too obviously free of the taint of parliamentary politics, neither a product of the corrupt party system, nor a pawn of the old Prussian elite. His strategy was a straightforward one. He promised 'Bread and Work' and national revival; modernism and decadence would be replaced by the German way. He mobilised a powerful nationalist rebellion against the post-war order, drawing on the rediscovered bitterness towards the victorious Allies, memories of German humiliation and defeat. In the charged atmosphere of the crisis years the message seemed to make sense: order could only come with a return of German power and independence. For the disgruntled and desperate middle classes the Nazi message was difficult to resist. What drew the young Albert Speer to the Party in 1931 was 'the sight of discipline in a time of chaos, the impression of energy in an atmosphere of universal hopelessness'.[7] The bandwagon rolled on; in 1932 Hitler challenged Hindenburg for the Presidency. He polled thirteen million votes; only the votes of communists, switched to Hindenburg on the second ballot, prevented victory.

Many Germans did resist the nationalist backlash. If the movement was tailor-made for embittered villagers and *declassé* bourgeois, its fierce anti-Marxism alienated the organised working classes and the unhealthy aroma of street politics and crude anti-Semitism repelled wealthier or more responsible Germans. The Nazi rise to power was not inevitable. Even at its height the Nazi movement secured only just over one-third of the electorate. Its violent, volatile character made it difficult to find parliamentary allies. In the end the Nazi movement came to power in Germany not entirely through its own efforts but through a tactical alliance with the old nationalists around Hindenburg. They were eclipsed by the rising tide of popular nationalism, but were anxious to retain their influence. The Nazi movement promised a mass base for them, and would, they believed, be tamed by office. 'I had always maintained', wrote their chief spokesman, Franz von Papen, in his memoirs, 'that it could only be neutralised by saddling it with its full share of public responsibility.'[8] In January 1933 the President was finally, and reluctantly, persuaded to call Hitler to the Chancellorship. He instinctively disliked the commoner, Hitler, and was completely out of touch with the new nationalism of the masses; he agreed, to avoid anything worse and on condition that only three Nazis join the government. On 30 January Hitler became Chancellor of Germany, his adopted land.

Informed opinion at home and abroad was divided on what effect Hitler's victory would have. A view commonly held was that the movement would burn itself out, and Hitler would fall disgraced, or be forced to take a back seat to his artful and experienced conservative colleagues in government. What few reckoned with was the rapid and almost complete destruction of the old system and the great wave of revolutionary violence unleashed by the movement throughout the year. The conservatives gave Hitler a foot in the door; they did not expect him to beat it down and ransack the house. But the movement was almost uncontrollable. In 1933 the young men of the Party, brought up on street violence, suddenly found the law on their side. They took revenge on all the enemies of the 'new Germany'; on trade union officials and communists; on moderate socialists and Catholics; on artists and writers of the avant-garde; and on the Jews. By the end of the summer Germany was a one-party state, the trade unions were destroyed, democratic government replaced by the authority of the *Führer*, the leader. The conservatives had powerfully misjudged Hitler; he could not be tamed.

Hitler's triumph transformed Germany's international position. Even before 1933, the British Foreign Office complained that Germany was 'getting quite incurably tactless and voracious'.[9] Whether Hitler had come to power in 1933 or not, fulfilment was a dead letter. But Hitler had openly campaigned before 1933 for the repudiation of Versailles and the rearmament of Germany; he was the author of *Mein Kampf*, a rambling geopolitical tract that urged

Germany to overturn the existing world order. It was clear from the start that the Western powers would no longer be able to compel Germany through economic pressure and military threats to work within the Western system. In 1932 the powers had agreed at a conference in Lausanne to ease the burden of reparations on Germany. From 1933 Hitler's government refused to pay another mark. The secret rearmament begun in the 1920s was expanded, though only slowly, during the course of the year. In October 1933 Germany withdrew from the Disarmament Conference in permanent session at Geneva, in protest at the failure of the other powers either to disarm or to allow Germany parity.

The change in German attitudes carried some risk. In 1933 wild rumours circulated in Berlin of an imminent Polish attack on East Prussia. The army gloomily predicted a Polish victory. Hitler favoured a cautious approach. An active foreign policy was too risky as long as Germany was militarily feeble and economically prostrate. The first priority was to solve the economic crisis; without economic recovery the regime would not become secure politically. Nazi survival could not be taken for granted in 1933 with six million still unemployed. Hitler had no economic blueprint for Germany, but he knew what he wanted. In 1933 he recruited experts to do the job for him; he provided the political will and the full power of the state. Some kind of recovery from the trough of the depression would have occurred automatically. The intervention of the state accelerated and sustained it. Money was provided for public works and road-building; the unions were abolished and wages pegged; the banking system was supervised by the state; foreign trade was brought under close government control. The new regime gave a growing confidence that recovery was really possible through Germany's own efforts. By 1936 unemployment was reduced to one million and industrial production was higher than it had been in the last prosperous years of the Republic.

The regime made the most of its successes. Propaganda played on the theme of 'Bread and Work' for all it was worth. There is no doubt that the economic revival won grudging support for the regime even from those hostile to Nazism in 1933. The social crisis that threatened to engulf Germany in the depression retreated. The peasantry was given tariffs and subsidies; small business rode on the back of the public works and rearmament boom where it could; the urban workforce found steadier employment. Living standards remained low, but by the frightening standards of the depression, they were bearable. Economic revival encouraged political stability. This mattered even in a one-party state committed to violent repression. Businessmen were won over by the promise of a stable economic environment; the army supported any regime that offered rearmament; the enemies of the regime were isolated and pilloried as enemies of Germany. The greatest threat came not from Hitler's opponents, who were forced into Germany's first concentration camps or fled to exile, but from within the Party. The wave of revolutionary enthusiasm unleashed in 1933 was difficult even for Hitler to control. By 1934 there was talk of a 'second revolution' among the leaders of the Nazi private army, the SA. On 30 June 1934 Hitler purged the Party of its dissident elements in a night of summary executions and assassination. He took the opportunity to settle accounts with other political enemies. After the 'Night of the Long Knives' no one inside or outside Germany was in any doubt about the nature of the regime. Any remaining political opposition went underground where it was hunted down by Heinrich Himmler's secret police.

During the years of economic recovery and political stabilisation German foreign policy remained restrained and circumspect. The Foreign Ministry was one of the few areas of the state not brought under Nazi influence. The Minister, Constantin Freiherr von Neurath, was a career diplomat of the old school. The diplomatic service was still dominated by the old ruling class, closely linked with the leadership of the armed forces. This ruling class was strongly nationalist. It shared with many Germans the strong desire to revise the Versailles Treaty, and saw in Hitler an opportunity to revive German fortunes with his protection and approval. Revisionism was not a Nazi strategy alone, but was rooted in the widespread resentment in the 1920s at what many Germans perceived as an unjust and unequal world order. The conservative agenda differed little from the demands of popular nationalism. German rearmament was generally approved on grounds of parity; the failure of other powers to disarm entitled Germany to seek effective means for her own protection. The overturning of Versailles, already begun before 1933, was a central ambition. Almost all Germans agreed that some kind of territorial revision was long overdue, and they looked particularly to the east. Conservatives were anxious to get back German colonies too. Germany had been forced by Versailles to assume the role of one of the 'have-not' powers, her access to world markets and raw materials allegedly restricted by the loss of empire. Colonies were assumed to be a source of strength and economic protection. In the social-darwinist atmosphere of the 1930s empire still seemed to matter. But if overseas colonies were denied, there was another nationalist solution widely promoted even before the

First World War, the creation of a Central European economic bloc, *Mitteleuropa*, with Germany at its core.

There was little here for Hitler to fault. During the early years of the regime there was a consensus that Germany, without running undue risks, should transcend the limitations imposed on her by the Allies fifteen years before. In October 1933 Germany withdrew from the League of Nations, in symbolic repudiation of the Versailles system. In 1935 Hitler publicly announced German remilitarisation, and signed a bilateral Naval Agreement with Britain which effectively gave qualified approval to German rearmament. The same year the Saarland returned to Germany after a plebiscite showed 90 per cent of the population in favour. The next logical step was to restore full German sovereignty in the Rhineland, which under the terms of Versailles was to remain indefinitely demilitarised. This was an altogether riskier undertaking, for it touched on an issue of vital concern to France. Hitler took the risk after watching the British and French respond feebly and in disagreement to the Italian attack on Ethiopia in October 1935. On 7 March 1936 German troops crossed the Rhine bridges with orders not to shoot if they met opposition. Only two squadrons of aircraft could be mobilised, and only ten of the planes were armed. As they flew from aerodrome to aerodrome their markings were changed to give the impression that German air strength was much greater than it really was.[10] Hitler waited on board a special train bound for Munich tense for news of foreign reaction. The first news arrived from London indicating that Britain would not use force: 'At last!' Hitler exclaimed, 'the King of England will not intervene. That means it can all go well.' He had judged the situation correctly; neither Britain nor France was prepared to carry the political and military risks of reoccupying Germany. Hitler later argued that the reoccupation of the Rhineland was the first and greatest risk he took. 'If the French had taken any action,' he told Speer, 'we would have been easily defeated; our resistance would have been over in a few days.'[11]

The Rhineland coup was a turning point. From 1936 Hitler began to take foreign policy more into his own hands. Success in the Rhineland fed his distorted belief that he had a pact with destiny. The bloodless victories fuelled nationalist enthusiasm and eroded the tactics of restraint. Neurath and the conservatives became anxious that what had so far been gained might be squandered by an excess of Nazi hubris. A gap began to widen between the nationalism of traditional Germany and the ambitions of the radicals in the Party for whom revisionism was not the end but the means. As Hitler's star rose, his personal vision of the German future began to trespass obtrusively into the opportunistic and conventional nationalism of the old elite.

Hitler's aims were not simply opportunistic. They embraced the revisionism of other German nationalists, and the more extensive hopes of the pan-Germans for German domination in Central Europe. Hitler shared all these lesser goals, but his view of the world was fundamentally different from that of the hard-headed nationalists at the Foreign Ministry. Hitler was very much a product of the political underworld of pre-war Austria where he spent his intellectual apprenticeship. Here he picked up an idealist, irrational justification for the crude pan-Germanism, anti-Marxism and anti-Semitism that was the stock-in-trade of Vienna's anxious petty-bourgeoisie in the declining years of the Habsburg Empire. For Hitler it was not class struggle or national rivalry that explained the course of history but racial struggle. Only races that retained their biological purity and cultural virility would survive in the endless 'struggle of peoples' that mirrored the struggles of the natural world. Racial struggle involved a fight for territory and space; this conflict, too, could only be won by a people sure of its racial identity, toughened by military experience, led by men of tenacity and willpower who would shrink from nothing to achieve the prize of world mastery.

None of this irrational, fantastic and fundamentally unworldly vision would have mattered if Hitler had remained a political nonentity in his native Vienna. It mattered when, against all reasonable expectations, he became the leader of one of Europe's most powerful states, with a great military tradition and a restless, intensely nationalistic population. As he drew power more firmly into his hands, so his muddled dreams of racial victory became more dangerously real. Germany was not the end but the means, an instrument to demonstrate the certainty of Hitler's view of life, to prove something inherently unprovable.

This vision of world destiny mingled uneasily with a personality that Speer found thoroughly 'provincial'. An early follower described him as 'obsequious and insecure, yet at the same time often abrasive'.[12] Others from Hitler's inner, intimate circle attested to the contrast between the petty-bourgeois, stultifying atmosphere of Hitler's daily routine, and the bouts of furious temper and uncontrollable, self-centred anxiety which punctuated it. His reputation as a frothing madman who chewed carpets in a rage was based on nothing more than a mistranslation of the German word *Teppichfresser*, someone who paces up and down a carpet, not someone who chews it. But there were plenty of witnesses to the fierce, paranoid reaction to anything that crossed him. These contradictions in Hitler's personality and behaviour were recollected by Walther Schellenberg, a high-ranking security officer, who had plenty of opportunity to observe Hitler at close quarters:

> Hitler's knowledge was on the one hand sound and on the other completely superficial and dilettante. He had highly developed political instincts which were combined with a complete lack of moral scruples; he was governed by the most inexplicable hallucinatory conceptions and *petit-bourgeois* inhibitions. But his one dominant and dominating characteristic was that he felt himself appointed by providence to do great things for the German people. This was his historic 'mission', in which he believed completely.[13]

This 1937 poster for an exhibition in Munich denounced the 'eternal Jew' who had sold Germany to Soviet bolshevism.

Hitler was a private person, and the more power he gained, the more he retreated into a self-imposed isolation. He disliked committee meetings, preferring to meet people face to face in what were often rather theatrical confrontations in which Hitler would speak at great length, and calculatedly. He had a conviction which grew with time that his provincial understanding, his self-taught and 'phenomenal memory', his position as a mere man of the people, socially anonymous, gave him a kind of wisdom that 'experts' lacked. He learned economic and technical data by heart to show up the ignorance of his senior officers and officials. His increasingly oracular pronouncements contributed to the manufactured 'myth of the *Führer*', of a leader whose insight and sympathy stood him apart from the ordinary world of Germans, and pandered to his self-delusions of simple genius.

Hitler did not produce a blueprint for Germany's future; there were broad commitments in *Mein Kampf* to racial conflict directed at the Jews, as the chief enemy of racial purity, and the Slavs who were historically destined for servitude. Germany comprised the *Herrenvolk*, the master-race, ordained to replace the declining empires of the West and reinvigorate European culture. Only when Hitler was in power did it gradually become clear how he saw the evolution of this destiny. There were three main stages. The first was to build up a strong German state, free from political conflicts, militarily strong, racially pure, a Germany 'healthy, rich and impregnable'.[14] This involved the isolation and forced emigration of Germany's Jewish population, set in motion with the Nuremberg Laws of 1935. Hitler regarded it as the Party's responsibility to bring about the internal transformation of Germany necessary before the master-race could assume its birthright, and the army's role to create a fighting force to defend and enlarge the Reich. The second stage was to construct a large pan-German area: 'Kindred blood', he wrote on the first page of *Mein Kampf*, 'should belong to a common empire.' This involved the destruction of the Versailles settlement. In the centre of the German Empire, he told Hermann Rauschning in 1934, 'I shall place the steely core of a Greater Germany wedded into an indissoluble unity. Then Austria, Bohemia, and Moravia, western Poland. A block of one hundred million, indestructible, without a flaw, without an alien element.'[15] The next stage was to turn Germany from a powerful racial state into the heart of a racial empire and a world power.

Central to this imperialism was the concept of *Lebensraum*, living-space. No country could become a world power, Hitler argued, if it lacked space for its surplus population and economic resources for the foundation of its power. He was in the habit of quoting from memory the ratio of land to people for all the major powers: China, America, Russia and the British Empire were all 'spatial formations having an area over ten times larger' than Germany.[16] Without space Germany would decline however strong her racial stock. 'We cannot,' he told Rauschning, 'like Bismarck, limit ourselves to national aims.' To be a master-race Germans needed somewhere to rule. 'In the east,' he continued, 'we must have the mastery as far as the Caucasus and Iran. In the west, we need the French coast. We need Flanders and Holland. . . . We must rule Europe or fall apart as a nation, fall back into the chaos of small states.'[17] This hegemony could only be achieved, he consistently maintained, by an alliance with Britain. As early as 1922 he arrived at the view that Germany should avoid treading on British toes if Germany wanted ascendancy on the continent. This done, Germany could attempt 'the destruction of Russia with the help of England', while England 'would not interrupt us in our reckoning with France'. But the crucial struggle was not in the West but in the East. The historic conflict between German and Slav could be postponed but not evaded. 'We alone can conquer the great continental space. . . . It will open to us the permanent mastery of the world.'[18]

It is easy to dismiss Hitler's geopolitics as flights of dictatorial fancy. German generals and diplomats told their younger colleagues when they first heard Hitler not to take him seriously. Yet the basic ideas and the strategic conception they gave rise to recur with persistent regularity in Hitler's private and public utterances throughout the 1930s and on into the war. They were imitated and enlarged by the radical Nazis who surrounded Hitler. There can be little doubt that the worldview outlined in *Mein Kampf* shaped in all kinds of ways the choices Hitler made only eight years later when he achieved power in Germany, and continued to do so when he later gambled on world conquest and annihilated Europe's Jews. From the middle of the 1930s he spent his few leisure hours endlessly discussing and criticising the giant plans for the rebuilding of Germany's cities which began even before the war at the Party centre in Nuremberg. Berlin was to become a world's capital, a place where the subjects of the new empire would come like visitors to ancient Rome, to marvel at the power that built such monuments.[19]

But Hitler had no illusions that his dream of empire could be realised effortlessly. His arguments were peppered with the words 'struggle', 'sacrifice', 'conflict'. War was for him a necessity, a natural outcome of the competition between races, and a school for social discipline and unity. Yet, if war was ultimately unavoidable, Hitler recognised the limits of German action in the 1930s. He was too good a politician not to be aware of the role of circumstances and opportunity in international affairs. His plans were seldom unalterable, until he was sure of his ground. He combined a general sense of the direction in which he was moving, with great tactical flexibility: 'In politics, there can be no sentimentality, but only cold-blooded calculation.'[20] If his basic ideas were not opportunistic, he was a supreme opportunist in their execution. 'I shall advance step by step. Never two steps at once,' he told the Nazi leader in Danzig.[21] His method of negotiation with other statesmen was unscrupulous and unconventional. His assertion that there was no lie he would not tell for Germany was elevated into a principle of international conduct. Other countries, like Germany, were merely a means to an end.

None of these plans could be realised as long as German military power remained limited. Rearmament on a large scale was unavoidable: 'Empires are made by the sword,' said Hitler. Yet German military revival was a formidable task. For not only was Germany virtually defenceless in 1933, but the economy had been temporarily reduced to the level of the 1890s. Hitler recognised the close relationship between military and economic strength. He was haunted by memories of 1918 and the collapse of the home economy. From the outset German rearmament was shaped by the idea of economic rearmament, the building of an economy that could withstand blockade, safeguard food supplies and win a war of material attrition. Here he was at one with his generals. During the 1920s German military leaders reflected on the lessons of the past war. They too arrived at the view that any future war between the major powers would be a total war. 'Modern war is no longer a clash of armies,' wrote Colonel Thomas, 'but a struggle for the existence of the peoples involved.' Soldier and war-worker fought the same battle. 'It is necessary', wrote General Groener in 1926, 'to organise the entire strength of the people for fighting and working.'[22] The military evolved a new strategic concept, *Wehrwirtschaft*, the defence-based economy, which symbolised the recent marriage between industrial power and military capacity.

When Hitler came to power rearmament in this broader sense was authorised immediately. On 9 February 1933 Hitler announced to his ministerial colleagues that 'billions of marks are necessary for German rearmament . . . the future of Germany depends exclusively and alone on the rebuilding of the armed forces. Every other task must take second place to rearmament. . . .'[23] The responsibility was handed over to the armed forces themselves. They set about the rebuilding of Germany's military structure with a vengeance. They had been waiting for this moment since 1919. All over Germany airfields were rebuilt, barracks constructed, training centres established. The 100,000-man army was trebled in size by 1935. German industry was recruited to the task of manufacturing equipment that was outlawed by Versailles. By 1936 Germany had made good much of the gap left by her compulsory disarming, and had reintroduced conscription. Yet the position by the time of the reoccupation of the Rhineland was still rudimentary. Most of the aircraft built, which so alarmed foreign observers, were trainer aircraft, almost two-thirds of all production between 1933 and 1937.[24] The first bomber fleets were made up of clumsy Junkers airliners rapidly converted for emergency use. Even this effort had strained the German economy. Food imports jostled with the import of strategic materials; consumer demands competed with military contracts. Germany faced a major balance-of-payments crisis. The army became more hesitant. The next stage of their plans called for an army three times bigger and military spending swollen to the largest amount in Germany's peacetime history, but they had no desire to achieve that at the cost of economic collapse and the prospect of social disorder.

The army recommended the militarisation of much of the economy in the hope that firm controls would stem the consumer boom. Hitler had a bolder plan. During August 1936 he retreated to his summer headquarters high in the Bavarian Alps at Berchtesgaden. When he came down from the mountain he carried a memorandum, one of the few that he ever drafted himself, that formed the basis of what became known as the Four Year Plan. The core of the plan was a commitment to 'autarky', economic self-sufficiency. In the face of rearmament elsewhere Hitler argued that Germany should fall back as far as possible on her own resources. Some such arguments were circulating in Party circles well before 1936. Hitler gave them a coherence and strategic purpose. The object was to make Germany as secure as possible in the long run against the sort of blockade France and Britain had mounted in the war, by reducing German dependence on overseas trade. At the same time it was necessary to extend controls over the German economy to prevent competition between civilian and military requirements, in favour of the latter. Consumer production was restricted, heavy industry encouraged. The strategy of autarky would not, it was recognised, make Germany independent entirely of outside sources of supply. Hence the importance of increasing German economic and political influence in Eastern and Central Europe where there were large resources of labour, land and raw materials.[25]

The Four Year Plan gave expression to Hitler's economic conception of strategy. It also signalled a clear shift in German politics, for instead of giving the plan to the army and industry he put in charge of it the flamboyant and ambitious head of the air force, Hermann Göring. He was a deliberate choice. Where the other ministers urged Hitler to slow down the pace of rearmament to what Germany could afford, Göring argued that the completion of rearmament was '*the* task of German politics'.* Hitler regarded Göring as the ideal politician for the job: 'a man of the greatest willpower, a man of decision who knows what is wanted and will get it done'.[26] Göring cut through every objection; within twelve months he extended state control over almost every area of economic life. He set in motion gigantic projects for the synthetic production of oil and rubber, for the exploitation of vital domestic iron ores, for the basic chemicals needed in wartime. For the next three years two-thirds of all industrial investment was diverted to the plan and the arms industry. The greatest industrial project of all was the state-owned Hermann Göring Works, which began in 1937 as a company to mine domestic German iron ores, and grew by 1940 into the largest industrial conglomerate in the world, employing 600,000 people and producing everything from bricks to tanks.[27]

From 1936 Germany was building the foundation for massive armed strength, transforming the economy of Central Europe as Stalin was transforming the Soviet Union. The change of tempo was too much for Hjalmar Schacht, the Minister of Economics who master-minded the early economic recovery, and a close collaborator of the army and big business. He had accepted rearmament in 1933 in order 'to put Germany back on the map'.[28] Now he fought a rearguard action to reverse the great drive for military power, which he feared would plunge Germany back into economic chaos. In November 1937 he was forced to resign. His business allies were brought into line with the threat of summary arrest for 'sabotage'. The army swallowed its fears, unable to gainsay a strategy which was ultimately of their own making. William Shirer, Berlin correspondent for CBS, was struck at the time by 'the complicated and revolutionary way in which the land is being mobilized for Total War'.[29]

The Four Year Plan did more than indicate a change in the pace of rearmament. It contained a secret instruction to prepare the economy and armed forces for war. This marked a decisive break with the strategy of the more cautious conservative nationalists, who

* Italics in original.

had assumed, naively as it turned out, that rearmament was designed only to restore Germany's defensive strength and re-establish her among the society of independent great powers. War for Hitler was a necessity; for many Germans it was a disaster to avoid. In 1936 the initiative passed to Hitler and his allies in the Party who favoured a more active and aggressive foreign policy.

The timing of this change had numerous causes. The radical imperialists in the Party were anxious for the *Führer* to quicken the pace now that economic recovery and internal security had been achieved. The threat of Russian rearmament loomed larger as Stalin's Five Year Plans transformed the Soviet economy. While many conservatives, with memories of the help Stalin gave to the German army in the 1920s, favoured some kind of accommodation with the Soviet Union, the Party leaders were fiercely antagonistic to the 'Jewish bolshevism' which they had fought with blood on German streets in the 1920s. Hitler's Four Year Plan was deliberately aimed at the growing menace in the East. Yet the most important cause lay not here, but in the West. Hitler saw plainly a window of opportunity opening up as the League system crumbled away. The Western powers, absorbed by economic crisis and political instability, their armaments reduced, unable to agree among themselves, presented a quite different picture from the avenging victors of the 1920s. America was deeply isolationist and showed no signs of stirring: she 'is not dangerous for us' was Hitler's comment.[30] For Hitler the international order resembled the feeble party system he had confronted in Germany in 1929, which collapsed in the face of his determined offensive.

The difficult question was how best to exploit the opportunity. Hitler's foreign policy programme was based on an assumed alliance with Britain which would free him for the drive to the east. Yet during 1936 relations between them cooled, while Germany drew closer to Britain's other potential enemies, Italy and Japan. This was in some respects a natural choice, for both were, like Germany, revisionist powers, keen to upset the international applecart themselves. Relations with Mussolini were initially poor. When the two fascist dictators met in June 1934 Hitler found him flamboyant and frivolous; Mussolini thought him vulgar and neurotic. They disagreed on the fate of Austria, which Nazis hoped to unite with the Reich. But when Mussolini himself ran foul of the Western powers in his war with Ethiopia and took Italy out of the League the natural affinities between the two regimes overcame the earlier coolness. The Spanish Civil War which broke out in July 1936 found both dictators supporting Franco's nationalists with military supplies and units. The Spanish intervention willy-nilly turned Germany and Italy in the eyes of the world into a fascist 'bloc'.

Relations with Japan were also slow to mature. The Foreign Ministry firmly favoured support for China where Germany had strong and traditional trading links. But the German Ambassador in Tokyo, Herbert von Dirksen, a keen supporter of the Nazi revolution, urged a German–Japanese link on the grounds that Japan was doing to Asia what Germany was doing in Europe: 'It seems to be both a psychological imperative and one dictated by reasons of state that these two powers, who are combating the status quo and promoting the dynamism of living forces, should reach common agreement.'[31] He was supported by the Party foreign affairs spokesman, Joachim von Ribbentrop, who sought during the summer months to find a way of formally linking the two states in some pact directed against the Soviet Union. Hitler acknowledged in his memorandum on the Four Year Plan that Japan, too, belonged to the circle of powers ideologically committed against communism: 'apart from Germany and Italy, only Japan can be regarded as a Power standing firm in the face of the world peril.'[32] On 25 November in Berlin the two states signed the Anti-Comintern Pact committing them in public to fight communism internationally, and in private to benevolent neutrality if either found themselves at war. A year later Italy joined the pact, completing the triangle of powers committed to the reordering of world affairs.

This still left unsolved the issue of Anglo-German relations. There is no doubt that Hitler saw Britain as the key. The choice was to be with her or against her. He later told Mussolini that he had always argued 'that Germany could either side with England against Russia or with Russia against England'. His preference was 'to co-operate with England, as long as England did not limit Germany's living space, especially towards the east'.[33] Yet by 1936 he had already begun to form a more unfavourable view of Britain: 'The modern Empire shows all the marks of decay and inexorable breakdown. . . . Britain will yet regret her softness. It will cost her her Empire.'[34] It is difficult to date the point exactly at which Hitler decided on the course of *ohne England*, without a British alliance. But during 1937 he came more under the influence of Ribbentrop, whose fruitless stay in London as Hitler's envoy to search for a British agreement in 1936 had left him an embittered, envious anglophobe. Hitler regarded his judgement on Britain as surer than his own. He regarded Ribbentrop, who could speak French and English fluently and had travelled widely on business for his family champagne company, as a man of the world. Other German diplomats regarded him as a fool and an ignoramus. Göring nicknamed him 'Germany's No.1 Parrot' for always repeating what he heard Hitler say. Ribbentrop confirmed the view Hitler already had of British decadence, but he added with force the argument that Britain not only did not want an agreement, but obstructed German ambitions at every turn. It was Ribbentrop's view that Britain could only be won round by confronting her with an alliance system so strong that she would be forced 'to seek a compromise'.[35] Either way Britain's ability or willingness to obstruct the German drive eastwards was no longer a serious threat.

There is a profound historical irony here. Historians of British appeasement policy have argued that this was just the stage at which efforts to give Germany what she wanted were at their height; yet in Germany it was exactly the point at which anti-British hostility became a significant factor, the point when Hitler began to perceive Britain as an enemy, not a friend. And he did so because on the substantive political issues that concerned German leaders, Britain did not make the concessions they wanted. By November 1937 Britain had become a 'hate-inspired antagonist'. Göring saw Britain becoming Germany's 'enemy-in-chief'.[36] German leaders found the reasons for this change difficult to grasp. In December Göring spoke openly and indiscreetly to a British visitor: 'You know of course what we are going to do. First we shall overrun Czechoslovakia, and then Danzig, and then we shall fight the Russians. What I can't understand is why you British should object to this.'[37] The truth was that Britain had sought some kind of settlement with Germany for some time and was willing to adjust the Versailles provisions on terms generally acceptable to the signatory powers, but had consistently failed to find points of contact between the two. The last attempt was made in November 1937 when the British statesman Lord Halifax visited Germany at Chamberlain's bidding to find out what Hitler wanted. Halifax came away profoundly convinced that the difference between the two systems was too great to be bridged. Hitler could not be contained within the limits of conventional diplomacy, which he thought 'totally unsuited to the rough world, constantly changing, in which we have to live'.[38]

What Halifax did not know was that Hitler a fortnight before had finally in secret session at the Chancellery announced his new foreign policy programme. On 5 November he called together the heads of the armed forces and the Foreign Minister to explain to them in a session lasting over four hours his irrevocable decision to begin German expansion. The problem was one of living-space. Germany could not be entirely self-sufficient, nor could she rely on world trade. The only answer was to expand territorially. This involved two separate stages: the first the occupation of Austria and Czechoslovakia; the second a major conflict with the great powers no later than 1943–5. The revision of Versailles Hitler expected to achieve without general war. Britain would not, he argued, seek another European war for two states she had already written off, and without Britain a French attack was 'hardly probable'. It only remained to choose the best opportunity to strike, when the other powers were distracted or divided.[39]

Hitler's long-term goals were widely known before November 1937; now he gave them a timetable and a tactical framework. He had already hinted to Goebbels earlier in the year that he expected the 'great world conflict' in five or six years time, a conflict that would only end by the early 1950s,[40] the date when Speer was to finish the victory buildings of Berlin. The timetable for the great war in the 1940s was built into the rearmament plans; not until then would the training and equipment of the troops be completed, nor the great steel, oil and chemical programmes. Neither could the economic rearmament of Germany be completed from the sources of the Reich alone; the first stage of expansion into Central Europe was to seize not just living-space but the industrial and agricultural resources of *Mitteleuropa*.

The plans for empire threw the Foreign Ministry and the army into confusion. They had been used to Hitler's lectures in the past, but the general direction of German economic and military policy showed that Hitler meant what he said this time. It soon became evident to Hitler that the old guard were hostile to or sceptical of the new course. Until 1937 the Treaty revisionism of the old nationalism and the new had lived side by side; the revelation of Hitler's true aims caused an open breach. The conservative nationalists, schooled in the traditions of Bismarck, could not bring themselves to gamble with Germany's future in such a reckless way only a few years after the great crises of the early 1930s. Hitler could see this and acted accordingly. In February 1938 the army was purged of those hostile to expansion; the Foreign Minister was sacked and replaced by Ribbentrop, and the foreign service brought for the first time under Party scrutiny. Hitler assumed supreme command of the armed forces for himself; Göring became the 'economic dictator' of Germany. Hitler was the victim of a growing isolation; surrounded only by those who uncritically echoed his views, absent for long periods from Berlin, his view of the outside world was increasingly wayward and impressionistic. Greater power than ever was concentrated in his hands; the constraints on using it responsibly were yielding.

The opportunity to strike against Austria came sooner than expected, and was not entirely of Hitler's making. The agitation of the Austrian Nazi movement, fuelled by money and advice from Berlin, brought Austria to the edge of political crisis early in 1938. Italy was embroiled in Spain and was anxiously watching France in the Mediterranean. France was in the midst of a government crisis. The British Foreign Secretary, Anthony Eden, had just resigned. British intervention could be discounted. Hitler presented the Austrian Chancellor, Kurt Schuschnigg, with an ultimatum to accept Nazis into the Austrian government and co-ordinate foreign and economic policy with the Reich. The ultimatum was rejected and Schuschnigg organised a national referendum on the issue of union with Germany. Though there was widespread support for union in Austria beyond the confines of the Nazi movement, it was not clear that the referendum would go Hitler's way. Faced with all the risks of occupying Austria by force under the eyes of the League powers Hitler experienced a sudden loss of nerve. It fell to Göring to communicate German threats and instructions to Vienna on the night of 11 March; faced with domestic chaos, isolated internationally, Schuschnigg gave in and 'invited' German troops to restore order. The *Anschluss* was a fact. For the first and last time a state was conquered by telephone.

The deed accomplished, Hitler found his nerve again. Like all pan-Germans, even more as an Austrian, he was overjoyed at the union of the two states. Austria was integrated into the Reich and the secret police and the Four Year Plan assumed their tasks of oppression and exploitation at once. The international response was muted; the opportunity was well judged. Austria opened the way to the German domination of Eastern Europe. The almost complete lack of resistance to union with Austria made a settlement of the Czech question an opportunity that could not be resisted. In the German areas of the Czech state ceded by Versailles the Nazi movement had its own organisation led by Konrad Henlein. This was used like the Austrian Nazi movement as a Trojan horse to achieve Hitler's aim of 'smashing' Czechoslovakia. At the end of March the Sudeten Germans were encouraged to escalate their demands of the Czech government in such a way that they would always be unacceptable. Then on 28 May Hitler held another meeting with ministers and soldiers at which he announced his intention of proceeding to destroy the Czech state by force in the near future, when a 'favourable moment' arrived. That moment appeared imminent; there was 'no danger of a preventive war by foreign states against Germany'.[41] The programme was on schedule;

protected by French weakness and British detachment the Central European bloc could be created without general war. The major war would still be fought in the 1940s against the great powers.

Over the summer of 1938 the Czech government dragged out the negotiations with its German minority while it sought assurances of support from abroad. German armed forces drew up their plans for 'Case Green', the attack on Czechoslovakia. Hitler was anxious for a military outcome to test the armed forces and to cement domestic support, and as a challenge to the rest of Eastern Europe, a signal of the shift in the balance of power. The Party, Göring told the Polish Ambassador, wanted a 'speedy action'.[42] But against expectations Britain did intervene. The Czech government were persuaded to accept an independent mission to adjudicate between Germans and Czechs. Henlein with Hitler's support continued to increase the stakes at each round of negotiation. Then on 15 September, following a fiery and bellicose speech from Hitler at the Nazi Party rally in Nuremberg four days before, Chamberlain flew to meet Hitler face to face. Hitler did not want to launch a general war over the crisis, for which German forces were far from prepared. Even if Britain and France abstained, Hitler was uncertain about Soviet intentions, and certainly wanted no risk of a war on two fronts. 'Berlin . . . bombarded us with countless enquiries about it,' recorded a junior German diplomat at the Embassy in Moscow. In September he made a journey to Odessa and could report 'no indication that they were preparing to move'.[43] But even secure in this intelligence, Hitler agreed to accept a negotiated settlement which would allow self-determination for the Sudetenland.

British intervention left Hitler in a quandary. Convinced on the one hand of British feebleness and pushed on by Ribbentrop to risk the war with Czechoslovakia, he was also under growing pressure from his military leaders and even from Göring to avoid a general war at all costs. Torn between these two courses, he stuck to willpower. When Chamberlain came back to see him at Bad Godesberg on 22 September he presented an ultimatum. German forces should occupy the Sudeten areas by 28 September by agreement, otherwise they would use force. After a protracted argument he changed the date to 1 October. Willpower was backed up by solid intelligence provided by the German secret services. There was no evidence of Soviet mobilisation to help the Czechs, despite a pact of mutual assistance; and there was a stream of evidence that London and Paris were putting every pressure on the Czech government to give way. Nevertheless the British Cabinet would not accept anything in the form of an ultimatum. By 27 September the position was deadlocked; France and Britain were committed to going to war if German forces crossed the Sudeten frontier. 'As the news got around,' wrote one witness, 'a wave of disappointment, indignation and panic spread through Germany . . . the fearful shock could be read plainly in people's faces.'[44]

Hitler became more agitated; he developed a nervous tic clearly evident to those who knew him well. On 27 September a military parade was organised through the streets of Berlin. Hitler stood on the balcony of the Chancellery to watch; the crowds beneath were thin and gloomy. There was no cheering. Hitler turned to Goebbels: 'I can't lead a war with such a people!'[45] The following morning Hitler was met by a delegation headed by Göring and Neurath counselling caution. Göring's argument won the day; the Sudetenland could be occupied by agreement with Britain, and the Czech state would become a virtual dependency of the swollen Reich. That afternoon a reply was sent to Chamberlain agreeing to a negotiated settlement. At Munich a four-power conference gave Hitler everything he had wanted through agreement, and without war.

There is no doubt that Hitler did not want a major war in 1938. 'Führer wants no war', noted his army adjutant in his diary on the 28th.[46] He hoped to achieve a local victory over the Czechs and counted on Western weakness. Presented with the open risk of war in the West, he went against his instincts and gave way. At Munich he was irritable and unsmiling. When Chamberlain left Munich on 30 September Hitler is alleged to have said: 'If ever that silly old man comes interfering here again with his umbrella, I'll kick him downstairs. . . .'[47] If Munich was a public defeat it was a private gain. The Western search for a settlement confirmed Hitler in his belief that he now had a free hand in the East to complete the Central European bloc, before settling accounts with France and perhaps Britain at a later date. Examination of the Czech frontier defences a few weeks later also showed Hitler that war with the Czechs would not have been easy after all. Without the defences the rump Czech state was powerless. 'What a marvellous starting position we have now,' he told Speer. 'We are over the mountains and already in the valleys of Bohemia.'[48]

German leaders began almost immediately to compromise what remained of Czech independence. Hitler promised Ribbentrop that he would march on Prague and smash 'the Czech remnants' as soon as he could. The Czechs were now, Göring said, 'even more at our mercy'.[49] He demanded economic agreements with the Czechs to help German rearmament and the right to build a motorway through Czech territory. Slovak separatists were courted, to play the role previously played by Austrian Nazis and Sudeten irredentists. Nevertheless Hitler could never escape the feeling that he had missed an opportunity at Munich. At the end of the war in 1945 he told his secretary, Martin Bormann, that if he had stuck to his guns in 1938 he could have had both Czechoslovakia and Poland without a major war:

> September 1938, that was the most favourable moment, where an attack carried the lowest risk for us. . . . Great Britain and France, surprised by the speed of our attack, would have done nothing, all the more so since we had world opinion on our side. . . . we could have settled the remaining territorial questions in Eastern Europe and the Balkans without fearing intervention from the Anglo-French powers. . . . We ourselves would have won the necessary time for our own moral and material rearmament and a second world war, even if it was altogether unavoidable, would have been postponed for years.[50]

*

'The successes of that year', Speer later wrote, 'encouraged Hitler to go on forcing the already accelerated pace.'[51] The bloodless victories so closely conformed with Hitler's stated programme that it is easy to see why he became convinced that his prognosis had been the right one. Once the initial humiliation was past, Munich turned into a victory. It secured for Germany the free hand in Central Europe Hitler wanted; and it brought into the Reich very real gains. The occupation of Austria secured £60 million of gold and the chance to exploit the Austrian 'Erzberg', the iron-ore mountain. The Sudetenland secured generous supplies of 'brown coal', the material needed to produce synthetic petrol for the air force and the motorised armies.

These resources were more vital than ever. In the wake of the Munich crisis Hitler ordered a final all-out rearmament drive to produce the weapons to fight the great war in four or five years' time. In 1938 Germany already consumed 17 per cent of her national product on the military, twice the level of Britain or France. In 1939 the figure was to double again. In October 1938 Hitler outlined to Göring 'a gigantic programme', trebling the level of arms output. In the summer he had already set up an explosives programme that exceeded by a wide margin what Germany had produced at the end of the First World War; the air force was to be increased fivefold in combat strength now that the training programme was near completion; and for the first time Hitler approved the building of a great battlefleet to challenge the Western navies. In January 1939 the navy 'Z-Plan' was given Hitler's go-ahead as a top priority.[52] By the mid-1940s Germany was to build a powerful force of battleships and ocean-going submarines. In 1939 Germany was well on the way to producing the first jet aircraft and the first rockets. Her aeronautical and military equipment was the most advanced in the world. In 1939 Hitler launched the bid for superpower status, to take him beyond the feeble Western powers in one leap.

This could not be achieved quickly or easily. The economic costs were enormous in an economy already heavily saddled with demands for defence. There was no question that Germany would be ready for a major war for another three or four years. Hitler was also aware of the political issues involved. He had watched the sullen crowds in September outside the Chancellery. 'These people still need enlightenment,' commented Goebbels.[53] There were secret reports from all over Germany to indicate the mood of the people. 'The local population . . .', ran one such report, 'hope most fervently for a solution that will avoid war.' In 1939 efforts were intensified on the propaganda front to prepare Germany, in Göring's words, 'spiritually for total war'. Otto Dietrich, Hitler's press chief, urged that 'The German people must be roused to a readiness for sacrifice and for maximum participation.'[54]

The irony was that support for Hitler increased after the Munich crisis not because people were eager for war but because they believed that Hitler's political skills would achieve what was needed internationally without bloodshed. 'The man in the street in Germany', wrote the diplomat Johann von Herwarth, 'considered Chamberlain a hero, for he did not want war. That same man in the street believed Hitler's affirmation that there would be no World War II.'[55] The long string of diplomatic victories brought a renewed confidence in Hitler after the crisis months of 1938. Politically the regime was increasingly secure. Even those Germans who were strongly anti-Nazi could find something in the regime to approve, or were too demoralised by years of state repression to resist. While Western populations prepared reluctantly but positively for war in 1939, the German population relaxed from the tensions of the previous summer. The economy boomed, even if consumer goods were beginning to disappear from the shops. 'In Berlin,' Goebbels wrote in April 1939, 'no one thinks of war.' Even in August Shirer found Berliners taking advantage of the hot August weather at the lakes around the city, 'oblivious of the threat of war'.[56]

The only serious political threat came from the generals and their upper-class allies, who had been forced since the spring of 1938 to take a back seat in German decision-making. Their worst fears had

GERMAN LOSSES, 1919-26

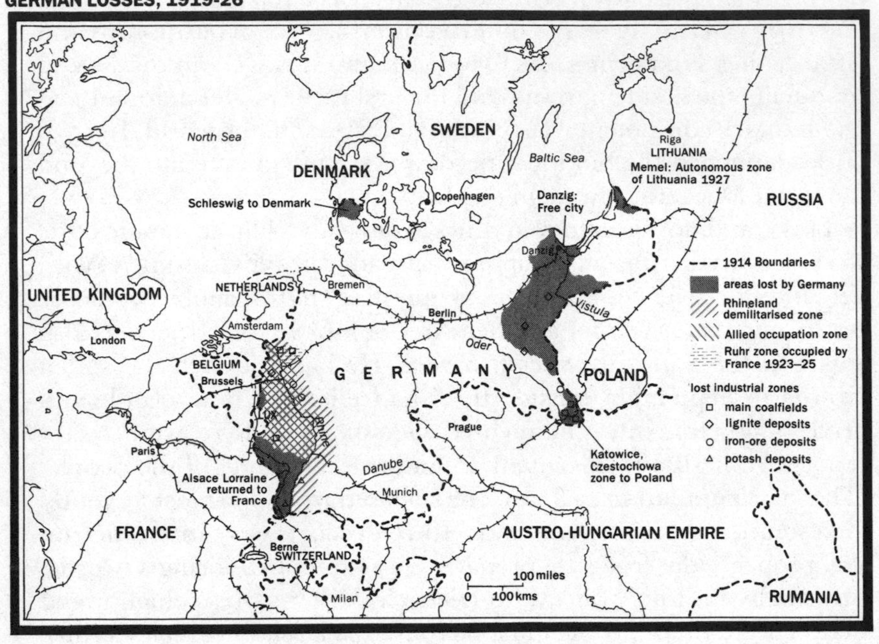

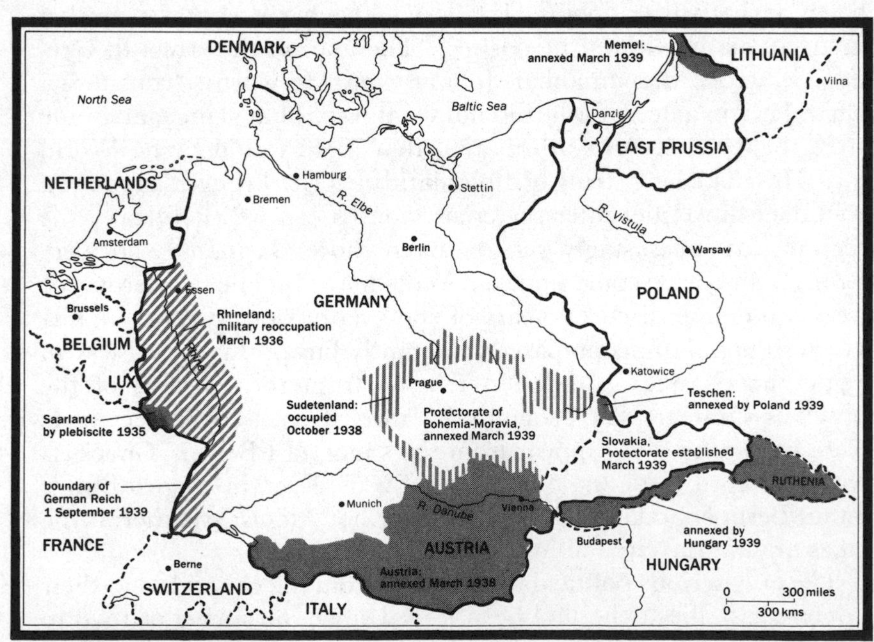

GERMAN EXPANSION 1933–39

not been completely fulfilled, for the Czech crisis passed off without war. But many of them, faced with the very real prospect of a general war which they thought would destroy Germany, had plotted to overthrow the Hitler government and install a moderate regime, possibly with Göring at its head, which could then lead Germany back to accommodation with the West on terms of full equality. The Munich agreement ended prospects of a coup because of the sudden increase in popular support for the regime. But during the winter of 1938–9 the conservative 'resistance' established secret contacts with the British government to encourage them to take a firm line against Hitler in the hope that this would lead to his overthrow. Their problem, as they saw it, was to choose a moment when popular opinion would be on their side. Yet in 1939 public confidence in Hitler was waxing; even the generals were affected by the scale of Hitler's success, and wondered, after all, if Hitler had not been right to take risks. A General Staff essay, purportedly by General Beck, one of the leading anti-Nazis in the military establishment, written before the occupation of Prague, highlighted this ambiguity. Against his expectations Hitler had exploited the irresistible power of 'self-determination' using 'military threats' with 'revolutionary methods' in Austria, the Sudetenland and Slovakia, and had turned the tables on the West. Versailles was overturned without war. 'The next blackmail operation will again end in the capitulation of the western states, for the western powers will only be willing to fight if assured of great superiority from the start.'[57] Beck could see that the dreams of the old pre-war nationalists in Germany might be achieved after all without general war. Most generals were agreed that Poland was an enemy worth fighting; they and their aristocratic cousins had lost out in the dismemberment of old Prussia in 1919. In 1939 moderate opinion was to play a much less conspicuous part than it played in the crisis of 1938 in restraining Hitler. Its effect was greater in London than Berlin, where intelligence from sources hostile to Hitler nourished the hope that British firmness might lead to political crisis and a palace revolution.

The forced pace in 1939 was soon in evidence. Rearmament made the economic conquest of Eastern Europe a necessity. German trade missions toured the Balkans offering generous credit and German machinery in return for the oil, bauxite and wheat needed to sustain the drive to war. In March 1939 Hitler sketched out his plan for the 'Great Economic Area': 'German dominion over Poland is necessary in order to guarantee the supply of agricultural products and coal for Germany. . . . Hungary and Roumania belong without question to the area essential for Germany's survival. . . . The same can be said of Yugoslavia. This is the plan, which shall be completed up to 1940.' The rump state of Czechoslovakia served the same goal, 'to increase German war potential'.[58] In March 1939 it was turned from a virtual dependency into a protectorate, on the spurious grounds that the Slovak minority sought self-determination. Rich resources were won. The Skoda armaments works, one of the largest in the world, was immediately transferred to German control. Czech industry supplied steel, coal and machine tools. Czech military supplies equipped fifteen infantry and four armoured divisions for Germany. This time the Western protests were vigorous and angry. Chamberlain denounced aggression and issued a powerful warning. Roosevelt put a heavy tax on German imports. They were not to be taken seriously, confided Goebbels to his diary, 'it is all just theatre.'[59]

The next step was Poland. This wish to return Danzig and the Corridor to German rule united all German nationalists. Even among his critics in the German army this was a popular issue. 'The idea of regaining Danzig and the Corridor', wrote Herwarth, 'was not unpopular in the German army . . . [it] reflected the feeling in Germany as a whole, particularly in the army, that both territories were properly Germany's.'[60] Hitler told his military adjutants on 1 October 1938, the day the army occupied the Sudetenland: 'The solution of the disputed questions with Poland had not gone away. At the given moment, when they were softened up, he would shoot the Poles.' Hitler was aware not only of Poland's strategic position and economic resources, but of the pursuit of the pan-German solution, the return of all Germans to the Reich. Polish 'Germans' were the last; with their return 'the whole Versailles Treaty is annulled'.[61] But there were several ways in which this return might be effected. Relations with Poland, so poor throughout the 1920s, had improved during the period since 1933. In 1934 a non-aggression pact was signed. Problems in Danzig, with a large and strongly pro-Nazi majority in control of the city's affairs, were resolved, when they arose, through direct negotiation. In 1938 Germany encouraged Poland to take its share of Czech territory at the time of Munich. As German power expanded Hitler and Ribbentrop expected Poland to come of necessity into the German orbit, and to make territorial revisions as she did so. There was no question of Polish resistance. Hitler told the Danzig Nazi, Rauschning, four years before that 'All our agreements with Poland have a purely temporary significance. I have no intention of maintaining a serious friendship with Poland.'[62] In October 1938 Ribbentrop opened the question of revision in Warsaw. For six months no progress was made; Poland was not prepared to concede a single acre. By March

Hitler was resolved to solve the Polish issue by force, if necessary, before the year was out.

It was at this juncture that Poland found herself the fortuitous object of a British territorial guarantee. Searching for a gesture after the occupation of rump Czechoslovakia, Chamberlain saw Poland as the obvious candidate for Hitler's next move. Armed with the guarantee Polish intransigence continued. The consequence was predictable; in April Hitler definitely resolved to attack Poland and bring the disputed territories, rich in coal and agricultural resources, into the Greater Reich by force. On 23 May he called the military together again to his study in the Chancellery. 'The Pole is not a fresh enemy,' he told them, 'Poland will always be on the side of our adversaries. . . . It is not Danzig that is at stake. For us it is a matter of expanding our living-space in the east and making food supplies secure.' But the crucial factor was to choose the moment carefully. 'Our task is to isolate Poland. . . . It must not come to a simultaneous showdown with the West.'[63]

The war could be isolated only, Hitler continued, as 'a matter of skilful politics'. His experience of Western appeasement in 1938 convinced him that neither Britain nor France would seriously fight for Poland. This conviction dominated Hitler's thinking throughout the crisis which led to war. The decision to attack Poland can only be understood in the light of this conviction. The war with the West, if it came to war, would come not in 1939, but in three or four years as planned, 'when the armaments programme will be completed'.[64] German leaders clung to this timetable uncritically. In May Ribbentrop told the Italian Foreign Minister, Count Ciano, that 'it is certain that within a few months not one Frenchman nor a single Englishman will go to war for Poland.' In August Hitler told Ciano the same thing: 'the conflict will be localised. . . . France and England will certainly make extremely theatrical anti-German gestures but will not go to war.'[65]

Why Hitler and the radical circle around him accepted and then clung to this conviction is a factor of decisive importance in any explanation for the outbreak of war in September. Hitler saw the contest with the West as a contest of wills: 'Our enemies have men who are below average. No personalities. No masters, men of action. . . . Our enemies are little worms. I saw them at Munich.'[66] Democracy had made the West soft. 'In Hitler's opinion,' explained General Keitel to a colleague in August 1939, 'the French were a degenerate, pacifist people, the English were much too decadent to provide real aid to the Poles. . . .'[67] These views were fuelled by the anglophobe Ribbentrop, who considered the British 'too snobby, after centuries of world domination and Oxford and Cambridge', to risk their empire over Poland.[68] In London the German Ambassador, the same Dirksen who so admired the Japanese, sent regular reports back to Berlin in the same vein: the empire was now too decrepit to risk a general war. Chamberlain, wrote Dirksen, realised 'that the social structure of Britain, even the conception of the British Empire, would not survive the chaos of even a victorious war'.[69]

But Hitler's conviction did not rest on intuition alone, important though that proved to be. German leaders saw the West burdened by the limitations of the democratic process. Western leaders lacked the same freedom of action; they were always conscious of the 'opposition within'. As the Polish crisis drew to a head Hitler was convinced that the governments in Paris and London would be overthrown. Western populations, Ribbentrop argued, would be unwilling to fight 'over so immoral an issue as Danzig'.[70] Nor did Hitler think it possible, as it was in Germany, to impose large armaments on an unwilling population. Throughout 1939 Hitler believed on the basis of the military intelligence he received, that both Western powers were still too weak militarily to risk a war. 'There is no actual rearmament in England,' he told his generals in August, 'just propaganda.' He knew that Britain had no serious army to send to the continent; intelligence estimated British aircraft production at less than half the true figure. In the German view British and French rearmament would not become a serious threat for another two or three years.[71] On the other hand Hitler was well aware of Germany's military achievements. During the summer and autumn of 1938 a great defensive line, the *Westwall*, was built on the German frontier facing France, eliminating the prospect of a French attack across the Rhine. During 1939 the defences were further strengthened by a bank of anti-aircraft defences 100 kilometres deep. Hitler intervened personally in the designing and construction of the fortifications, which at their peak consumed half the output of the entire German cement industry and employed 500,000 people. There was still much to be done before Germany was fully armed; but Hitler was confident that Germany was stronger than her enemies. 'We must be conscious', Hitler continued to his generals, 'of our great production. It is much bigger than 1914–1918.'[72]

If these arguments were not compelling enough, the international situation in 1939 developed, in Hitler's eyes, only in his favour, leaving Britain and France isolated and vulnerable. In May Mussolini offered Hitler a pact of mutual assistance, the 'Pact of Steel'. Japan would not be drawn by the invitation to sign a similar pact, but the threat in the Far East weakened the Western response in

Europe. The United States offered sympathy to the West but no promise of direct assistance. In the east and south-east of Europe the smaller states were either moving towards Germany or were too alarmed to obstruct her. Under such adverse circumstances Hitler could not understand why Britain continued to thwart Germany in Eastern Europe, and would not arrive at an agreement. During the summer of 1939, while German forces prepared for a local war against Poland, Hitler kept open lines of communication with London in the hope of a change of heart. The price for such agreement was a free hand against the Poles and absolute equality as world powers. Ribbentrop explained Hitler's view to an English acquaintance in July:

> Perhaps the British have dominated the world for too long to be able to admit that any other race should live beside them on terms of absolute equality. And on that absolute equality we must insist. Hitler would not agree to Britain having even 50.15% and Germany's having 49.85%: it must be absolutely 50/50. Britain has not made one single important concession to Germany during the last twenty years, only opposed, opposed, opposed, always trying to keep Germany down.[73]

Hitler remained convinced that over Poland Britain 'was only bluffing'.

There was only one nagging, insistent doubt: the fear of a revival of the old entente of the First World War between Britain, France and Russia. The war on two fronts was a conflict for which German resources were far from adequate in 1939. From March onwards German intelligence knew that Britain and France had begun to explore the possibility of isolating Germany politically by reaching an agreement with Stalin. A few weeks later the Soviet Union began to make limited approaches to Berlin on the possibility of reviving trading links, with hints of a possible political agreement. The difficulty for Nazi leaders was the fanatical anti-bolshevism of the movement which had been a barrier to better relations since Hitler came to power. For Hitler himself the problem was less acute. He never saw himself limited by ideological scruple. Rauschning recorded Hitler's comments to him in 1934: 'Perhaps I shall not be able to avoid an alliance with Russia. I shall keep that as a trump card. Perhaps it will be the decisive gamble of my life.' In utmost secrecy contacts with the Soviet Union were reciprocated. At the end of May the German Ambassador in Moscow was instructed that Berlin had 'decided to undertake definite negotiations with the Soviet Union'.[74]

Germany was in a strong position. The Soviet Union wanted the advanced machinery and military equipment that German trade would secure. Germany could offer neutrality in any European conflict; Britain and France could only offer the prospect of a dangerous peace at best, war with Germany at worst. Negotiations were nonetheless slow. Stalin could afford to play with Germany and the West to see who would bid the most, or force Germany into making major concessions in Eastern Europe from fear of encirclement. By mid-August the economic discussions were complete. Ribbentrop, who had entered the negotiations with the ideological enemy reluctantly, now became an enthusiast for a Russian agreement to add weight to his arguments about British abstention. On 12 August the Soviet Union finally indicated its willingness to arrive at a political agreement. Speed was of the essence; the invasion of Poland was scheduled for the 26th, before the autumn rains came, but after the harvest was in. On 16 August Ribbentrop agreed to almost all the points presented by the Soviet Foreign Minister, Molotov, as the basis for a pact and offered to go to Moscow to sign it in person. Speer noticed that Hitler was unusually tense. 'Perhaps something enormously important will happen soon,' Hitler told him, 'if need be I would even go myself. I am staking everything on this card.'[75]

By 19 August both sides had agreed a draft. Stalin agreed to accept Ribbentrop in Moscow by 26 August; Hitler could not wait that long. Overriding the Foreign Office he sent a personal appeal to Stalin to receive Ribbentrop on the 23rd. Stalin accepted this change; Germany's position was now much weaker as the necessity for agreement grew more urgent. Hitler agreed to everything Stalin asked for. Ribbentrop arrived on the 23rd and after a day of final discussions the pact was formally signed in the early hours of the 24th. Hitler was at dinner when confirmation was received; he read the telegram and then banged his fist on the table: 'I have them!' he exclaimed. The pact with the Soviet Union meant no repeat of 1914. Hitler was more convinced than ever that the collapse of Western efforts to encircle Germany spelt the end of serious efforts to help Poland. The West would make gestures of defiance, but they would not fight. 'The *Führer*', noted his adjutant, Gerhard Engel, in his diary, 'repeats that he now looks on developments more calmly than some months ago.'[76]

The armed forces were instructed on 21 August to prepare for limited economic mobilisation for a war only against Poland. The generals were more optimistic too, approaching 'the coming tasks with confidence'.[77] Their operational planning was directed in detail only at the local conflict. There was no Schlieffen plan like 1914 – no planning for general war in the autumn of 1939. Instead Hitler eagerly awaited news from London and Paris that the coup in Moscow had brought the downfall of the democratic governments. There was no news; instead on 25 August Chamberlain cemented the agreement to fight for Poland if Germany attacked. The same day Mussolini, whose views on British intentions were much less sanguine, extricated Italy from the obligation to fight if general war broke out. It was this news, rather than moves in London, that hit Hitler hardest; 'completely bowled over', recalled one witness.[78] Hitler hesitated, and postponed the attack on Poland until the end of the month. The unofficial contacts with London were now in the hands of Göring and a Swedish business acquaintance of his, Birger Dahlerus. Hitler instructed Göring to speed up efforts to 'eliminate British intervention'. A few days later Hitler once again appeared confident; Italy was a disappointment but not a disaster. Hitler hoped that Britain could be kept at bay by the prospects of negotiations while Poland was quickly defeated. The idea of general war was not seriously entertained.[79]

Faced with the prospect of war at last against Poland, Hitler became much more assured than he had been during the Rhineland crisis, the *Anschluss* or the Czech crisis. 'I have always accepted a great risk in the conviction that it may succeed,' he told the generals. 'Now it is also a great risk. Iron nerves, iron resolution.' Speer noted in Hitler a genuine 'self-assurance'.[80] Hitler was determined this time to take the risk he did not take a year before, confident that he had the measure of the timid, appeasing statesmen he confronted. Goebbels was hesitant; Göring warned Hitler, 'You cannot play *va banque*.' Yet that was exactly what Hitler wanted to do. 'He was like a roulette player,' Otto Dietrich later recalled, 'who cannot quit the tables because he thinks he has hit a system that will break the bank.'[81]

On 31 August German troops were in position. A border incident was fabricated to put the blame clumsily on Polish violence. In the early morning of 1 September German forces moved forward on a broad front into Poland. As Hitler had suspected, the West sent only angry letters. By 2 September there were strong signs that they were seeking a second Munich through the intervention of Italy. The strategy was falling into place. When finally on 3 September the British Ambassador, Nevile Henderson arrived at the German Foreign Ministry at nine o'clock in the morning to deliver a British ultimatum there was only Hitler's interpreter, Paul Schmidt, to meet him. He took the document over to the Chancellery where he found an anxious party of soldiers and officials waiting for news. He was shown into Hitler's study, and in the presence of Hitler and Ribbentrop slowly read out the ultimatum. 'When I finished,' wrote Schmidt, 'there was complete silence. Hitler sat immobile, gazing before him. . . . after an interval which seemed an age he turned to Ribbentrop, who had remained standing at the window. "What now?", asked Hitler with a savage look.'[82]

The war that broke out on 3 September left Hitler 'to begin with, at a loss'. He made no effort to disguise it. 'It was plain to see how stunned he was,' Dietrich recalled. It took time for Hitler to realise that for the first time since his charmed diplomatic life had begun in 1936 he had miscalculated. For a while he argued that the declarations were merely a sham to avoid losing face. 'There would be no fighting,' he told Speer.[83] When Poland was rapidly defeated he searched again for agreement with Britain, unsuccessfully. He could not grasp at any point in the summer and autumn of 1939 why the British wanted to fight for a country they could not save, on an issue which a year before they might have happily signed away. Hitler's eyes were fixed by 1939 on the future, on the great wars of the 1940s when he *would* risk Germany for the stakes of world power; on the victory parades through the giant avenues and stadia of the new German Empire.

The war in September brought Hitler face to face with international reality. Britain now obstructed a course she seemed the year before to have approved. There were perfectly rational grounds for supposing that the West would not fight. The invasion of Poland was not a simple gamble. Yet it became the wrong war, not the war Hitler expected. For most Germans, it was the wrong war too. 'Hardly anyone in Germany', wrote Dietrich, 'thought it possible that Hitler, who enjoyed the confidence of the people because he had so often proved his political adroitness, would fail to control the situation.'[84] Though most Germans were happy to take the gains when they came, to reverse the humiliating powerlessness of the 1920s, they did not welcome war. Hans Gisevius, a prominent member of the German resistance, could see no 'cheering masses' as he drove through the streets of Berlin on 31 August. All he saw were small groups of Germans standing silently, nervously, 'with faraway expressions'.[85] The nationalists who had cheered Hitler in 1933 and applauded the end of Versailles wanted a strong, independent Germany, dominant in Europe from sheer size and economic strength, but they did not want world war. The last war had spelt ruin for Germany; the new conflict would do the same. 'Germany can never win this war,' complained Papen, architect of Hitler's triumph in 1933, 'nothing will be left but ruins.'[86]

War was not inevitable in 1939. With Hitler at the helm war at some time almost certainly was. The problem that the majority of more moderate German nationalists faced in the 1930s was the difficulty of creating a domestic political environment that would restrain Hitler. The brutal methods which had revolutionised Germany in 1933 were institutionalised. As the regime became more confident, and repression more widespread and effective, the scope for the radical agenda of racism and war became fuller and more explosive. But what really permitted Hitler to go further, to 'accelerate the pace', was the fundamental weakness of the international structure into which he burst. The world order dominated by Britain and France could scarcely cope with colonial squabbles; a Germany lurching rapidly and unpredictably towards superpower status was quite beyond control. The radical nationalists and racists around Hitler could see this; they tied themselves to Hitler in the hope of profiting from the new German order. British and French power was swept aside in 1940; Soviet power was almost destroyed a year later. But the strength of the United States tipped the scales. Consistent to the last, Hitler reflected in the ruins of Berlin in 1945 that Germany had not been ready, after all, for world leadership. She had fought the racial struggle and lost; in war, as in nature, only the fittest survived.

CHAPTER TWO
GREAT BRITAIN

> However strong you may be, whether you are a man or a country, there is a point beyond which your strength will not go. It is courage and wisdom to exert that strength up to the limit to which you may attain; it is madness and ruin if you allow yourself to pass it.
>
> (Lord Salisbury, *c.* 1898)

> Again and again Canning lays it down that you should never menace unless you are in a position to carry out your threats.
>
> (Neville Chamberlain, September 1938)

On 12 May 1937 George VI was crowned in Westminster Abbey in front of an assembly of his subjects drawn from the four corners of the globe. Two days later the British Prime Minister, Stanley Baldwin, used the Coronation as the opportunity to convene an Imperial Conference. There were delegates from Canada, Australia, New Zealand, India, Ceylon, Burma and South Africa; the British delegation represented the rest of the British Empire, a necklace of colonies that circled four continents. The British Dominions and territories covered a quarter of the world's surface. It was the largest empire in the history of the world; its leaders sat solemnly contemplating its defence. The conference was an opportunity for mutual expressions of goodwill and solidarity. It was a reminder to the rest of the world that Britain's interests were truly global. No history of Britain's path to war in 1939 can ignore how greatly the interests of that Empire mattered to British statesmen. On 15 June the conference broke up with the words of Neville Chamberlain ringing in the delegates' ears: 'It is our belief that in Empire Unity lies the seat of our influence in the world. . . . We are raised from the status of a fourth-rate power to be the heart of an Empire which stands in the front of all the Powers of the World.'[1]

In truth the conference was far from united. The Dominions could agree neither a common foreign policy nor a common means of defence. If the Empire was a source of British strength, it was also the source of fundamental weakness. By the 1930s it was a structure almost impossible to defend adequately, even if Britain had enjoyed sufficient resources to attempt it. But Britain simply lacked the economic strength and military capacity to hold the Empire together in the face of serious threat. It was Chamberlain's private view that 'We are a rich and a very vulnerable empire and there are plenty of poor adventurers not very far away who look upon us with hungry eyes.'[2] This was a much more realistic assessment. Britain had obligations throughout the world in the 1930s; only the most radical British politicians were prepared to abandon them. Yet responsibility without power brought a heavy duty. The dilemma Britain faced throughout the years to 1939 was how to preserve economic strength and social progress at home, and at the same time provide a credible foreign policy to secure the Empire. Britain wanted an empire but baulked at the cost of maintaining it. Only in 1939 when the threat to the security of the Empire became profound was the dilemma confronted, though not solved. In September 1939 Britain embarked on her last great imperial war.

The defeat of Germany in 1918 brought British influence in the world to its zenith. The Empire had rallied to the cause of the mother country and had shared the sacrifices that brought final victory. The Treaty of Versailles gave to Britain the lion's share of German colonies, as mandated territories of the League of Nations. They were quickly painted red in British atlases. In the Middle East Britain and France divided the remnants of the Ottoman Empire between them. Britain assumed control of mandates in Palestine, Jordan and Iraq. During the 1920s a new 'Imperial vision' was promoted, of a united, liberal empire in which Britain, the industrial heartland, sent a stream of manufactures overseas while the Empire returned abundant food and raw materials. The Empire was Britain's *Lebensraum*, home to the surplus population and enterprise of the metropolis, a conduit for the liberal culture and political freedoms that the British enjoyed already. By the late 1920s almost two-thirds of Britain's overseas investments and almost half her trade went to the Empire, figures higher than ever before. Empire societies sprang up in Britain, propagating through endless films and lectures the virtues of the imperial ideal.

The Empire of the 1920s was a powerful vindication of the liberal belief in progress and civilisation, the end-product of a distinguished history. The British people, leaders and led, took the Empire for granted. Britain became a power committed to the status quo, a satiated power. 'We have got all that we want – perhaps more,' wrote Lord Chatfield in a candid moment. 'Our sole object is to keep what we have and to live in peace.'[3] The British position in the international order was by definition a defensive one; and challenge to that system, of whatever kind, inevitably impinged at some point on the interests of the Empire. 'Peace the first British interest' was a maxim born not merely of a moral view of foreign policy but of necessity. The preservation of world peace was the essential precondition for the survival of Britain's swollen world responsibilities.

For all the propaganda, the Empire promised a difficult stewardship. There was not a year in the 1920s when British forces were not in action at some corner of the Empire or even beyond, in Afghanistan, China or Persia. The illusion of imperial harmony and British moral ascendancy was transcended by a reality of civil war, nationalist resentments and tribal violence. At the moment of its fullest extent, the Empire was in the early throes of disintegration. Ireland was lost in 1922; in 1926 the white Dominions won virtual independence. Public opinion was much less wedded to the imperial ideal than the imperial classes would have liked. A stable world system was the only hope for the Empire's survival. 'We all agree – we want peace,' wrote a Chief of Staff in the 1930s, 'not only because we are a satisfied and therefore naturally a peaceful people; but because it is in our imperial interests, having an exceedingly vulnerable empire, not to go to war.'[4]

In the climate of the 1920s peaceableness, even peace from necessity, was an easy ambition to fulfil. After 1918 the dominant sentiment throughout Europe was 'never again'. Britain took her full part in constructing a liberal world order, in which collective security and moral suasion took the place of violence and alliance blocs. The 1920s saw the high-water mark of liberal diplomacy, the nineteenth-century conviction that the self-restraint and good sense of liberal statesmen, acting in concert, would resolve disputes and establish order. British foreign policy was a very moral foreign policy, but not an idealistic one. Issues had to be resolved on their merits, through co-operation, in a framework that was rational and just but which accorded, broadly, with British interests. It is doubtful if such a system ever existed even in the nineteenth-century heyday of Gladstonian liberal diplomacy; but in the context of the League of Nations and the general talk of disarmament and the pacific settlement of conflicts a liberal world order seemed a possibility. As the Prime Minister, Stanley Baldwin, told the House of Commons in 1923, 'It is to moralise the world that we all desire.'[5]

In practice Britain's commitment to collective security was always an ambiguous one. Though the belief in peace and international order was real enough, Britain took a global rather than a European view of her responsibilities. Britain's relationship with Europe, where collective security was most in demand, was, in the words of Austen Chamberlain, British Foreign Secretary under Baldwin, 'semi-detached'. Britain saw herself as a disinterested spectator of European affairs, a genial but aloof umpire, reasonable but not committed. 'For us', wrote Robert Vansittart at the Foreign Office, 'European politics are mostly other people's feuds and grievances. . . . Beyond a certain point, the quarrels of Europe are not our quarrels. . . .'[6] As a result Britain became increasingly isolated in the 1920s, returning to a diplomatic tradition which had been broken only by the growing world crisis before 1914. British politicians of all parties were reluctant to uphold the letter of the Versailles Treaty, which many found unreasonable and vindictive. Relations with France cooled rapidly after 1919. There were no formal ties to any other major power. The one alliance Britain did have, the 1902 Treaty with Japan, was allowed to lapse in 1922. Though Britain remained a clear defender of the status quo, she did so on her own terms, independently.

Peace and disarmament did more than reflect British strategic necessity and liberal inclinations; there were imperatives nearer home. British power before 1914 rested on British economic strength: financial stability at home, and a stable trading and investing environment abroad. War damaged British economic interests more than those of other powers because Britain lived on exports and overseas investment. The Great War damaged British trade abroad irretrievably; the cost of the war reduced British investments overseas by two-thirds, and threatened the stability of the home economy through inflation and war debts. Though some measure of stability was restored in the 1920s, the British economy never recovered the special position it had once enjoyed. British trade in 1921 was less than half the level of 1913; cotton exports, the core of British pre-war trade, fell by over half during the 1920s. Unemployment was well over a million for most of the decade; the government was saddled with a National Debt sixteen times greater in 1920 than it had been in 1910. A foreign policy of peaceful co-operation was essential to safeguard trade and to rebuild the foreign investment on which British economic influence had been based.

The search for balanced budgets and economic security inevitably affected defence policy too. Lower taxation and lower government spending could be gained only at the cost of the high levels of military expenditure at the end of the war. Independent of the League's injunction to disarm, British governments of right and left cut defence to the bone; in 1920 defence took £519 million, by 1929 £123 million. In July 1919 the Cabinet decided that 'the British Empire will not be involved in any large war over the next ten years. . . .'[7]

THE OLD EMPIRES, 1919-38

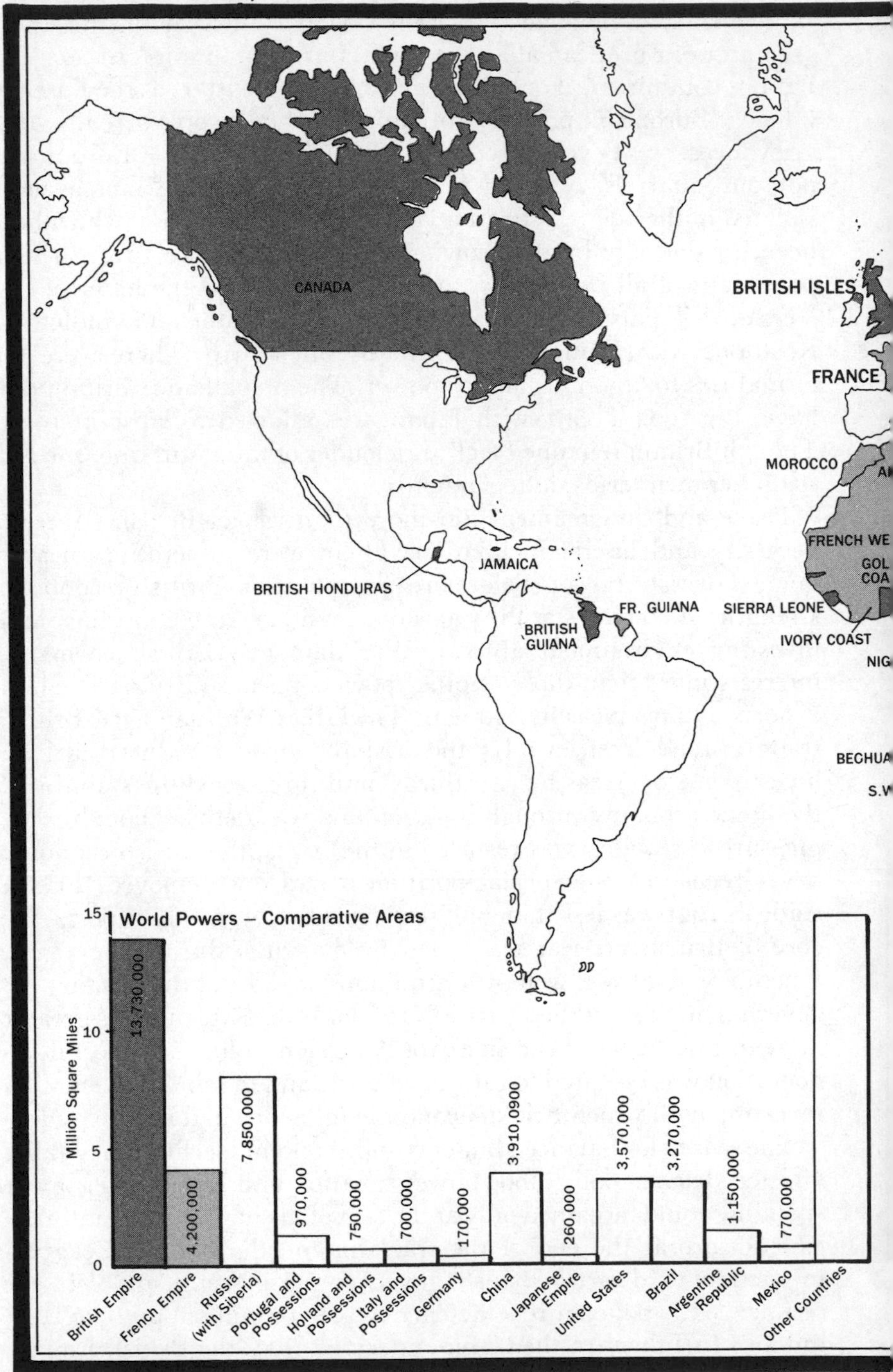

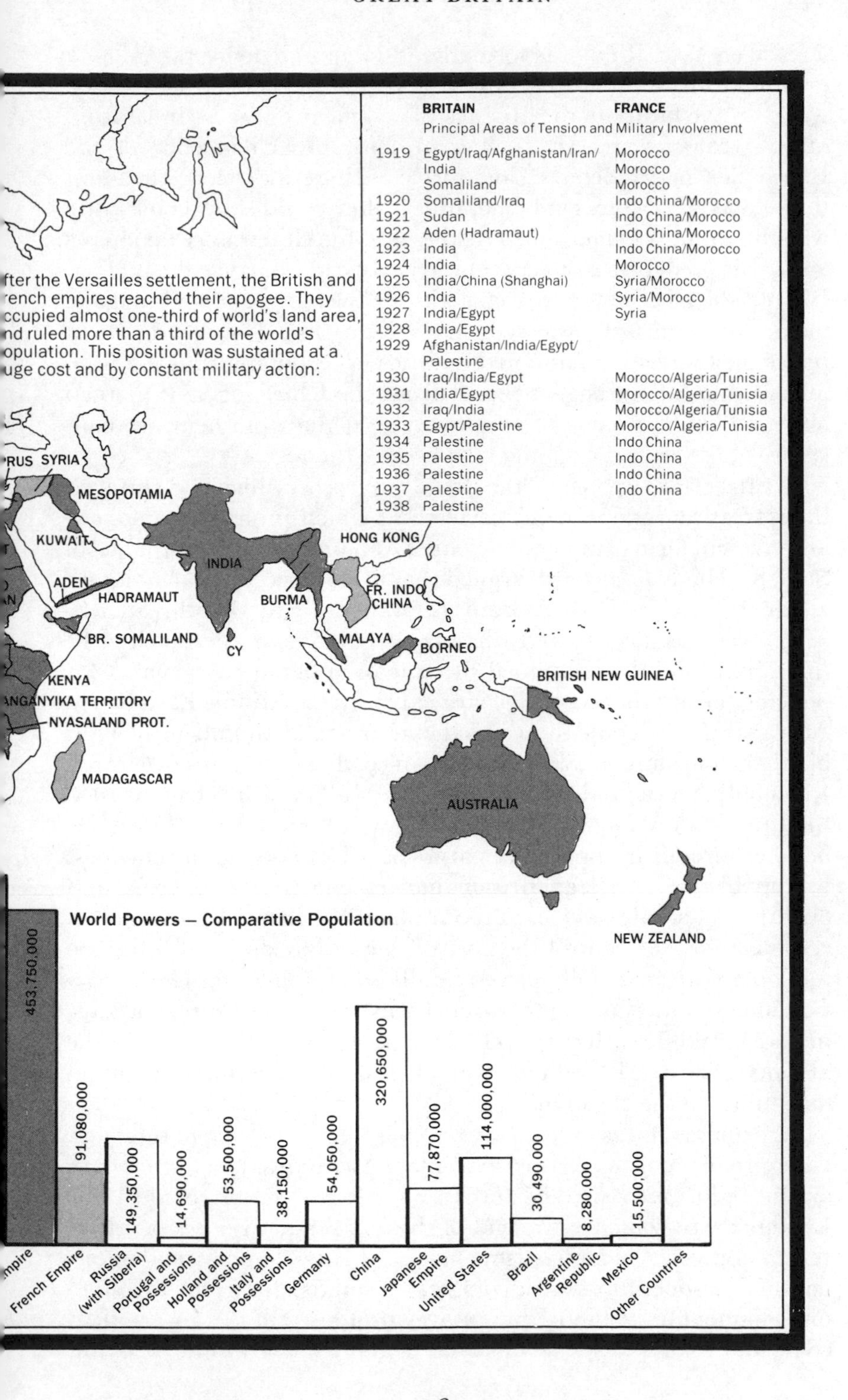

Principal Areas of Tension and Military Involvement

	BRITAIN	FRANCE
1919	Egypt/Iraq/Afghanistan/Iran/	Morocco
	India	Morocco
	Somaliland	Morocco
1920	Somaliland/Iraq	Indo China/Morocco
1921	Sudan	Indo China/Morocco
1922	Aden (Hadramaut)	Indo China/Morocco
1923	India	Indo China/Morocco
1924	India	Morocco
1925	India/China (Shanghai)	Syria/Morocco
1926	India	Syria/Morocco
1927	India/Egypt	Syria
1928	India/Egypt	
1929	Afghanistan/India/Egypt/ Palestine	
1930	Iraq/India/Egypt	Morocco/Algeria/Tunisia
1931	India/Egypt	Morocco/Algeria/Tunisia
1932	Iraq/India	Morocco/Algeria/Tunisia
1933	Egypt/Palestine	Morocco/Algeria/Tunisia
1934	Palestine	Indo China
1935	Palestine	Indo China
1936	Palestine	Indo China
1937	Palestine	Indo China
1938	Palestine	

This 'Ten Year Rule' was formally adopted in defence planning, a perennial assumption that military spending could be suppressed well into the future in the absence of any clear military threat from other great powers. In 1928 Churchill, the Chancellor of the Exchequer, persuaded the Committee of Imperial Defence to adopt the rule as their chief guideline, unless they could show good cause why the assumption no longer held true. Churchill was as anxious as any of his predecessors to cut military costs and balance the budget. He told the navy not to expect a war for twenty years, and to make major cuts. The army was reduced to a tiny force, designed to help police the Empire or maintain domestic peace, but quite incapable of intervention in Europe. A report from the Chiefs of Staff in 1926 observed that 'so far as commitments on the Continent are concerned, the Services can only take note of them. . . .'[8]

Greatest store was set by the Royal Air Force, which had survived the war as an independent service and which promised a modern and efficient form of imperial defence. At home, its energetic Chief of Staff, Sir Hugh Trenchard, argued that the air force should maintain an air striking force to attack any European enemy that threatened. Air power was a cheap and effective alternative to the trenches. In the Empire the RAF assumed the role of imperial policeman. 'Air policing' meant that control of large areas in the Middle East, North Africa or India could be carried out by small numbers of light bombers for punitive raids rather than costly expeditions over land. In Somaliland the activities of the 'Mad Mullah' which had plagued the British army there for twenty years were put to an end by a few bomber aircraft in three weeks at a cost of £70,000 – 'the cheapest war in history'. In Iraq Britain had 60,000 troops in 1920; and operations had already cost £100 million. When the RAF assumed responsibility for control the cost of operations dropped from £20 million a year to £6 million, and finally to £1.6 million.[9] Here was a way to maintain some kind of security in a restless empire, and save money for the British taxpayer at the same time. Air power, in the absence of any serious threat overseas, enabled Britain to maintain an empire on the cheap in the 1920s.

Disarmament was welcomed at home. There existed a natural and widespread revulsion against war, more pronounced on the left than on the right, but visible in both. The left, now represented by the Labour Party, which at the end of the war replaced the Liberals as the major voice of radicalism, favoured disarmament and international co-operation on ideological grounds; the right favoured disarmament on the more pragmatic grounds that the government could not afford to spend more, and that money would be better spent on social programmes to blunt the hostility of the newly political working class. The fear that rearmament would arouse the wrath of labour and destabilise the political system was ever present for Conservative leaders right up to 1939. In the 1920s the Chiefs of Staff kept troops at home in preference to overseas service in case of political unrest. The labour movement was still an unknown political actor; the conservative establishment could never be certain that labour would conduct foreign policy in the national interest or would not obstruct a more ambitious military and foreign policy. This class fear called for prudent, even conciliatory policies at home as well as abroad. Economic recovery and social stability were as much the key to imperial security as military strength. British post-war governments, as Baldwin later observed in 1936, 'had to choose between, on the one hand, a policy of disarmament, social reforms and ... financial rehabilitation, and on the other hand, a heavy expenditure on armaments. Under a powerful impulse for development every government of every party elected for the former.'[10]

Here already were all the ingredients of Britain's imperial dilemma: on the one hand an empire larger than ever, difficult to defend, punctuated by nationalist crisis; on the other, a growing isolation, a 'Little Englander' approach to world affairs, a reluctance to pay the full cost of imperial security and world-power status, made more acute by economic decline and social fears. The balancing act that this required was a difficult one under the best of circumstances; Neville Chamberlain recognised that it was 'one set of risks against another'.[11] In the 1920s the risks could be taken; Germany was disarmed, America isolationist, the Soviet Union inward turned, France controllable. The international economy boomed; war was unthinkable. But in 1929 the international economy collapsed, and with it the fragile security of the liberal order.

The Great Crash of 1929 and the three years of economic depression that followed profoundly affected the stability and security of the British Empire. Hopes that Britain's declining economic strength and international power could be arrested by a revival of world prosperity were shattered. The economic crisis was so severe that it aroused genuine fears of the collapse of Britain's global influence and social stability. British trade fell by 40 per cent over the depression and barely recovered for the rest of the decade; from 1931 began the long years of balance of payments crises. By 1932 over one-fifth of the insured workforce was unemployed. In 1931 Britain finally abandoned the gold standard, centrepiece of the nineteenth-century free-trade system, and devalued sterling. It was Labour's misfortune to have been in power when the crisis struck. In 1929 a minority Labour government under Ramsay MacDonald came to office; for fear of disapproval it clung firmly to orthodox economics, cutting government spending, balancing the budget. By 1931 a massive financial crisis loomed as confidence in sterling sagged and the world credit system ground to a standstill. To save the economy and his ailing political fortunes MacDonald split the Labour Party by joining forces with the opposition in a National Government. The new government was dominated by Conservatives pledged to stabilise British capitalism and secure economic recovery as the first priority.

Financial security and social revival eclipsed everything else in the years following the crisis of 1931, including foreign policy. Though no revolutionary threat did emerge as a result of the depression, Conservatives were convinced that the safety of the established order had been preserved by a narrow margin. Economic recovery was an essential means to social healing; National Government disguised the conservative character of the recovery years, and emphasised the general political consensus that domestic stability came first. British leaders would have preferred international co-operation to bring about world recovery, since the British economy was so dependent on world trade. But the depression encouraged all states to think primarily of themselves. Britain proved no exception. In order to protect her own industries and promote her own exports Britain abandoned the ark of the covenant, free trade, and turned to Empire protection. In 1932 at Ottawa a historic agreement was reached between Britain and the Dominions to establish an imperial economic bloc protected by quotas and tariffs. The Empire retreated into an economic isolation. By 1939 almost half of Britain's exports went to the Empire, in return for cheap foodstuffs which left British consumers with more money in their pockets to spend on Morris cars and Pye radios.

The Ottawa agreement confirmed a growing dependence on Empire and a retreat from collective action. States did not co-operate together but saved themselves. This was understandable enough; the shock to the international system of economic collapse loomed large in the political memory throughout the 1930s, inhibiting the pursuit of an active foreign policy until it was unavoidable. Between 1929 and 1932 financial crisis forced further cuts in military spending. MacDonald promoted the ideal of universal disarmament, and a Labour colleague, Arthur Henderson, chaired the first full Disarmament Conference convened at Geneva in February

1932. In March 1933 MacDonald himself presented the conference with a draft convention providing for substantial disarmament for a period of eight years. It was an effort doomed to failure. France and Germany could not be reconciled to disarm on equal terms, the more so after the arrival of Hitler in January 1933. Even Britain spent more on armaments in 1933 than in 1932, and there existed a powerful element in the National Government hostile to the whole idea, and deeply critical of the League. In October 1933 the conference adjourned *sine die*.

MacDonald, a radical idealist in foreign policy, was isolated among the Little Englanders and nationalists of the National Government. The recession made Britain more rather than less detached from Europe; more attached to Empire, but most concerned to preserve herself. 'Our foreign policy is quite clear,' wrote the Foreign Secretary, Sir John Simon, in 1934, 'we must keep out of troubles in Central Europe at all costs. July 20 years ago stands out as a dreadful warning.'[12] Armed with such attitudes, British leaders remained spectators rather than participants when the League system itself was violently challenged. The first shock came in the Far East, from Japan. In September 1931, while Europe was licking its financial wounds, Japanese armies occupied and secured the whole of Manchuria. The League condemned Japanese action but did nothing. But for the British Empire Japanese aggression signalled the end of an era. Until 1931 the assumptions of the Ten Year Rule still held good; there was no clear potential enemy, no military threat to the stable world system British interests needed. Japanese imperialism, not Hitler, overturned those assumptions entirely. In February 1932 the Chiefs of Staff reported with alarm that 'the whole of our territory in the Far East as well as the coastline of India and the Dominions and our vast trade and shipping lies open to attack. . . .'[13] But the government took no direct action for fear of endangering British economic interests in China. Neither did it support military spending to meet the threat; 'the very serious financial and economic situation' prompted caution. Neville Chamberlain, Chancellor of the Exchequer, was convinced that in 1932 'financial risks are greater than any other we can estimate.'[14]

There was much sense in this. Japan was a potential threat, but clearly not in the immediate future. Without financial security future defence programmes were put at risk. The rise of Hitler evoked a similar caution. It was appreciated that Germany was a revisionist power, but it was also evident that Hitler's priority was economic recovery and unemployment, as it was in Britain. Britain's financiers and industrialists hoped to profit from German recovery with increased opportunities for trade and investment. By 1937 more than 50 per cent of the international credit extended to Germany was British, double the level of 1933.[15] But by 1934 it was clear that Germany was not merely working for recovery and that Hitler was there to stay. In February 1934 a report from the recently formed Defence Requirements Committee concluded that 'We take Germany as the ultimate potential enemy against whom our long-range defensive policy must be directed.'[16] In March 1935 Hitler publicly declared German rearmament; a year later German forces reoccupied the Rhineland unopposed. Britain was in no position to resist Germany militarily, and most politicians in Britain assumed that Germany could not permanently be denied full access to her own territory. In two years Hitler undermined the security of Europe, as Japan had done in the Far East. In 1935 the Mediterranean followed, when Mussolini invaded Ethiopia. Italian imperialism was not of itself such a threat, and the British government was prepared to make substantial concessions to Italian claims in Africa. The real issue concerned the League, which at last thought it had found an occasion where something could be done. Economic sanctions were imposed on Italy, and Britain was reluctantly forced to comply. The result was a rapid estrangement between Britain and France on the one hand and Italy on the other. In the space of five years the strategic situation of the British Empire was transformed, its vulnerability conspicuously exposed.

By 1936 the British dilemma was no longer potential but real. It was in British interests to preserve the broad outlines of the status quo: 'We only want to keep what we have got and prevent others taking it away from us,' said the First Sea Lord.[17] But now the Empire was faced by threats not just from one quarter but in every major theatre. The 'All Red Route' to India through the Mediterranean could no longer be guaranteed, though it was the main artery linking the western and eastern empires. The Defence Requirements Committee pointed out the obvious lesson:

> It is a cardinal requirement of our national and Imperial security that our foreign policy should be so conducted as to avoid a possible development of a situation in which we might be confronted simultaneously with the hostility of Japan in the Far East, Germany in the West and any power on the main line of communication between the two.[18]

The important point was a simple one: British security was a global problem, not merely a German one. Until 1936 it was Japan and Italy, each with a substantial navy, that posed much the greater threat. In 1936 the threat from the Soviet Union against India could not be discounted. When the RAF drew up plans in that year for a long-range bomber it was with Soviet targets as much as German in mind. The problem of Empire defence was made more complex still by internal crisis, which reached a peak with the advent of external threat. In 1935 India was given a measure of self-government to still incipient nationalist revolt; in 1936 Egypt won almost complete autonomy and a share in the control of the Suez Canal. In Palestine the British army needed more soldiers to keep Arab and Jew apart than it kept for the defence of Britain. In the face of international crisis the Empire became less rather than more united.

The question that confronted British statesmen down to the outbreak of war in 1939 was quite simply how to regain the lost security of the Empire. The military's answer was an obvious one: 'So long as [the] position remains unresolved diplomatically, only very great military and financial strength can give the Empire security.'[19] British politicians knew this; but the answer was not straightforward at all. Financial strength could not be taken for granted. The economy was well on the way to recovery in 1936 but few politicians would have gambled with it, least of all Baldwin, now Prime Minister again, and Chamberlain, the Chancellor, who placed economic stability above all else. Britain was not militarily naked, but she certainly did not possess 'great military strength'. In 1934 Maurice Hankey, the Cabinet Secretary, was nearer the truth: 'We have but a façade of imperial defence. The whole structure is unsound.'[20] Nor was the diplomatic outlook more hopeful. The League system, in which British politicians had had little confidence, was universally recognised as bankrupt. Britain had no binding obligations in Europe; the United States, with whom Britain had most in common, was isolationist. British diplomacy had left her independent and flexible in the 1920s; in the 1930s it left her isolated and vulnerable. The policy of being '*sanely selfish*'* could no longer be justified.[21]

For want of any alternative, British foreign policy came to rely on the exercise of Britain's traditional diplomatic skills to disguise the very real weakness of the British position. These skills of arbitration and negotiation were widely respected, though not liked. Roosevelt complained that when he sat down with the British round a table they took 80 per cent and left everyone else 20. British officials and ministers were much more at home with diplomacy than force. This diplomacy was pragmatic, treating each problem as it arose, almost

* Italics in original.

in isolation. It gave British foreign policy an incoherent character, the appearance of drift and reaction rather than initiative. But there were some general principles at work throughout the inter-war years. British leaders were not averse to adjustments in the post-war settlement which did not threaten British interests directly. This allowed some room for manoeuvre in treating with potential enemies. There was room for colonial revision, though again not at Britain's expense. And almost all officials believed that even the most intractably hostile could be won over through economic collaboration and concession.

This strategy, if strategy is the right word, was called appeasement. It was a strategic conception with deep roots in British foreign policy, derived from the observable truth that it was better to resolve international disputes through negotiation and compromise, the rational adjustment of conflicting ends, than through balance-of-power politics and war. The first requirement was to find out what exactly was at issue. This was far from clear. Discussions with Japan elicited very little. 'It was always difficult to know what was going on inside the anthill,' complained Simon.[22] Britain's Commercial Consul in Peking warned that Japan would have to find an outlet somewhere as the tariff ring closed around her: 'The actions of an animal thrashing about to find an outlet from a net . . . are not predictable and reasonable, and Japan is in that position today.'[23] Discussions with Japanese statesmen ran aground on their determination not to forgo what they saw as essential gains in China. Mussolini was easier to understand, but no easier to conciliate. Until the war in Ethiopia relations between Italy and Britain were satisfactory. Mussolini was anxious about German ambitions in Austria and the Balkans, and Britain was happy to feed that anxiety to keep the two dictators apart. But from 1935 onwards it was clear that Mussolini wanted to secure more than this. Britain had very little to offer, for any substantial extension of Italian influence in Africa or the Balkans constituted an inevitable threat to British interests. Italian imperialism could not coexist with British without friction. In the Mediterranean the Italian navy greatly outnumbered the Royal Navy; in the Italian colony of Libya Italy kept six times as many men and aircraft as the British maintained in neighbouring Egypt. Though British leaders continued to court Mussolini down to 1939, they did so only to reduce their political risks, not to give anything substantial away.

Hitler's Germany was another matter altogether. It was evident that Germany wanted major revision of the Treaty of Versailles. Whether this extended beyond rearmament and an adjustment of the eastern frontiers to demands for the return of German colonies was less clear. In March 1935 Sir John Simon and Anthony Eden visited Hitler, who urged them to consider making colonial concessions in Africa. Simon privately suggested giving Germany Liberia.[24] In the same visit Hitler raised the prospect of an agreement on naval armaments, first raised by the German Commander-in-Chief of the navy the previous November. Since British intelligence were in some ignorance of German naval plans the offer of a fixed ratio of 35:100 in Britain's favour was too good to resist. Hitler sent Ribbentrop to negotiate the agreement, which was finally signed in June, despite what the British saw as an unfortunate arrogance and inflexibility in the German envoy. Economic agreements extending substantial credit to Germany existed from 1933; vital raw materials and food flowed from the Empire via London to German destinations. In return Britain bought advanced German machinery. Until 1937 Hitler's strategy still incorporated the possibility of agreement with Britain, and relations between the two states were better than German relations with any other Western government. But until 1936 Hitler did not ask for anything that the British were not, in the end, willing to concede. It was the decision to reoccupy the Rhineland in March of that year that began the slow estrangement between the two. But the breach was not an open one until much later. In 1936 Ribbentrop returned as German Ambassador; the landlord of his London flat was Neville Chamberlain.

The British approach to Germany was essentially pragmatic. It was not evident, as it was soon to become, that German ambitions were entirely open-ended and violent. But British leaders were not naive. The search for political solutions went hand in hand with a firm decision in 1934 to reverse the long decline in British military strength and to embark on an extensive rearmament. In November 1933 the Cabinet set up the Defence Requirements Committee to report on the long-term shape of Britain's defence effort. Though the sums of money proposed were trimmed back by an anxious Treasury, it was agreed to expand the navy, build a secure naval base at Singapore, and pour more resources into the RAF, with particular attention to air defences to meet the threat of the bomber. The army had to take third place, as it had throughout the 1920s. In 1935 military expenditure was a fifth higher than 1934, in 1936 two-thirds higher. But expenditure on the air force trebled in the same period. More important, military and civilian planners began to think not just in terms of finished armaments but in terms of war capacity as a whole. They knew that rearmament would take at least four or five years to complete. The lesson of 1914–18 was that war between major states was likely to be a long war, a war of attrition, in which the depth of economic resilience would be the deciding factor. This made it necessary to prepare industrial capacity and train labour in peacetime, 'to make sure that vital processes are not held up for want of necessary craftsmen'; it required the stockpiling of strategic materials; it called for detailed plans for economic mobilisation. Much of the economic rearmament effort was hidden from public view during its early stages. Its conception and development were much more broadbased than later critics of British rearmament supposed. British military leaders made educated, and as it turned out correct, guesses that the military threat to the Empire would not materialise for some years. Air plans were drawn up on the assumption of 'a war *with* Germany *in* 1939'. This prophetic timetable permitted a gradual expansion until the most modern equipment was ready, and avoided the temptation to put all the dearly won resources into large quantities of old-fashioned biplanes.[24]

This was, under the circumstances, the best that could be hoped for. Increased rearmament brought all kinds of political and economic difficulties of which the government was all too aware. The key issue revolved around whether military spending threatened the economic and financial stability which had been restored by the mid-1930s. This is not a fear we should regard lightly. Financial limitations were not placed on rearmament from ignorance or narrow-mindedness. The Treasury and most of the government were committed to orthodox finance, yet defence measures meant increased taxation or increased government debt. Either way, as Warren Fisher, permanent head of the Treasury, expressed it, 'We are in danger of smashing ourselves.'[25] Economic recovery was sustained but fragile; it was the Treasury view that high levels of rearmament were 'particularly dangerous to the capitalist states of Western Europe with their depressed incomes, their high taxation and their excessive national debts'.[26]

The survival of sound finances had a keen political edge to it. The National Government was well aware that there was no popular mandate for military spending. Extra arms meant sacrificing some other programme, housing, health or education. Yet these were exactly the policies that the National Government was committed to in its search for economic revival and social peace. In the 1935 general election Baldwin refused to emphasise the new rearmament plans for fear of losing popularity. The year before, the Peace Pledge Union had been founded to campaign against all war. Pacifism was at its height. The left was divided on the issue, but the parliamentary

BALLOT FORM.

If you have already answered these questions do not fill in this form.

Address..

Question 1. Should Great Britain remain a Member of the League of Nations?	Question 2. Are you in favour of an all-round reduction of armaments by international agreement?	Question 3. Are you in favour of the all-round abolition of national military and naval aircraft by international agreement?	Question 4. Should the manufacture and sale of armaments for private profit be prohibited by international agreement?	Question 5. Do you consider that if a nation insists on attacking another the other nations should combine to compel it to stop by (a) economic and non-military measures?	(b) if necessary military measures?	Signatures. All persons of 18 and over in your household are asked to fill in this form.

SPACE FOR COMMENTS. (If the space for comments is insufficient kindly attach further pages.)

No individual votes will be published; only totals.

The Peace Ballot, 1935, collected 11 million signatures.

Labour Party was wholly hostile to armaments. 'What is going to be the effect of all this expenditure on armaments, when the money has been spent?', asked Arthur Greenwood of the Commons; 'Social wreckage again and again.'[27] Nor were conservative forces much more friendly. Business leaders were opposed to greater state control which rearmament would bring; conservative voters favoured lower taxation, cheap credit, increased consumption. A new middle class was growing up in the areas of returning prosperity in the south and midlands; in the secure tree-lined new suburbs and the Garden Cities around London economic revival mattered just as much as it did to the government. Militarism had few champions; 'Never Again' was the middle class's motto too.

The National Government survived the election of 1935; but the political conflicts over armaments refused to subside. In 1936 Chamberlain introduced in the annual budget an extensive four-year plan for rearmament, which provided the framework for the military structure with which Britain entered the war in 1939. To pay for it the Chancellor placed a tax on, of all things, tea. Chamberlain defended the tax on the grounds that he 'wanted a tax which would be widespread', but it was widely denounced as an attack on working-class living standards. Chamberlain was forced to impose a levy on business to counteract the criticism, and brought a storm of protest from the wealthy as well. The increased rearmament was deplored by pacifist opinion too. Far from failing to rearm, the government was accused of rearming 'on a gigantic scale' and with 'such feverish haste'. Clement Attlee, the Labour leader, denounced Chamberlain for contemplating war 'not as a possibility, but as a certainty'.[28] The Labour Party remained committed to collective security, but opposed the rearmament necessary to make it effective, a contradiction that was unresolved up to the final outbreak of war. Chamberlain was very sensitive to the charges of warmongering: 'If only', he complained, 'it wasn't for Germany we would be having such a wonderful time just now. . . . What a frightful bill do we owe to Master Hitler, damn him!'[29]

It was not easy to persuade the British public that the defence of Britain's role as a world power was worth the loss in living standards. It was not easy to persuade the Treasury that financial risks were really necessary to preserve Britain's wider safety. It proved just as difficult to persuade the trade unions to co-operate in programmes of labour retraining and labour dilution in the industries that were to produce the new weapons. By mid-1937 Fisher gloomily predicted that Britain was 'rapidly drifting into chaos' even 'before the Boche feels it desirable to move'.[30] It was at this critical juncture, with British diplomacy adrift and incoherent, and the contradictions of rearmament unresolved, that Neville Chamberlain assumed the premiership.

When Chamberlain succeeded Baldwin he was already sixty-eight years old. He came to political life late, entering Parliament in 1918 when he was already nearly fifty, though his family was steeped in politics. His father, Joseph Chamberlain, was the spokesman for the liberal imperialists of the pre-war era; his half-brother, Austen, was British Foreign Secretary in the 1920s. Neville began life as a businessman and then graduated from municipal politics to the national stage. In the post-war governments he made his name as a social reformer, first in housing and slum clearance, then in pensions. He was a straightforward, practical politician who disliked rhetoric and politicking. He was wedded to the imperial ideal he borrowed from his father, but was no reactionary. He believed that social reforms would win the working classes away from socialism, which he detested, while prudent finance and economic growth would keep the loyalty of middle-class voters. His view of politics was a businessman's view: political conflicts had economic causes; social welfare and prosperity would quieten social confrontation at home; business and trade revival would damp down foreign crises. He believed profoundly that affairs of state could be settled like honest tradesmen, face to face, agreeing the price the market would bear.

He was a popular choice as Prime Minister. Few other ministers had as much experience in high office; he was widely respected in the Conservative Party and in Parliament. Baldwin, in ailing health, groomed him for the task. Chamberlain brought a very different personality to the role. His treatment of his colleagues could be high-handed and imperious. He was intolerant of those who disagreed with him, and impatient with anything or anybody that obstructed his path. He despised the French, deeply distrusted the 'half-Asiatic' Russians, scorned Americans and disliked the Germans, 'who are bullies by nature . . .'.[31] He was an easy man to respect, a difficult man to like. He interfered in the work of his colleagues, assumed their responsibilities without consultation, and told the Commons only what he wanted them to know. He was a strong Prime Minister who led from the front. His strength of purpose belied the wispy, almost feeble appearance, and the bleating voice.

He assumed office with a powerful purpose in mind, like a man, the Soviet Ambassador recorded, called 'to fulfil a sacred mission'.[32] That mission was to resolve the contradictions of British strategy, to solve the dilemma of responsibility without power abroad, to reconcile the claims of military revival and social stability at home. His overriding object was to avoid war: 'In war there are no winners, but all are losers.' The only means to avoid war was to pursue a Grand Settlement of all the outstanding grievances of the world. This was an immodest, but not, Chamberlain thought, an impossible ambition. He explained his purpose to Parliament in December 1937: it was to seek 'a general settlement, to arrive at a position in fact when reasonable grievances may be removed, when suspicions may be laid aside, and when confidence may again be restored'. He was determined to take a grip not only on the affairs of his country, but on the affairs of every state; 'We are not drifting; we have a definite objective in front of us. That objective is a general settlement of the grievances of the world without war.' This was more than mere appeasement; here was Metternich on a global stage.[33]

These were not delusions of grandeur. The idea of a 'general settlement' was circulating in government and Foreign Office circles well before Chamberlain became Prime Minister; Chamberlain gave the idea added force and coherence. But he had no illusions about how difficult a task he was faced with. He took what he saw as a very realistic approach to foreign affairs: 'You can lay down . . . general principles, but that is not a policy. Is not the real, practical question what action we can take in existing circumstances to carry the principle into effect?'[34] In July 1937 he explained to the Cabinet the impossibility of fighting Germany, Italy and Japan together: 'There were limits to our resources both physical and financial, and it was vain to contemplate fighting single-handed the three strongest Powers in combination.' The only solution was to find a way to separate these three powers by political means. Britain's military leaders agreed that the global defence of Empire was now beyond the country's means and urged the same solution: 'to reduce the number of our potential enemies and to gain the support of potential allies'. Chamberlain was prepared to explore the prospects of a settlement with each potential enemy in turn, to detach each from the aggressor bloc by an active examination of their grievances and the application of 'our common sense, our common humanity to the solution of these problems'. By a rather paradoxical route the general settlement was to be secured not through any general solution but through individual initiatives. When President Roosevelt suggested a world conference to Chamberlain late in 1937 he considered the idea to be 'drivel'.[35]

Chamberlain's first concern in 1937 was Continental rather than global: 'to bring peace and order into a disturbed Europe'.[36] He had long considered that Britain, because of her aloofness from European affairs, might have 'some special part to play as conciliator and mediator'.[37] He was no more in favour of fixed continental commitments than any of his predecessors, but he did recognise that Empire security and the maintenance of peace could not be achieved without British participation in European affairs. The Far East was not abandoned, but it was assumed by British policymakers that the United States would at least share the responsibility for security in the Pacific in the unlikely event of Japanese aggression. The return to Europe was a recognition of international realities, though it always carried the risk that Britain would become involved in war through the quarrels of others. Chamberlain recognised that the only way to reduce that risk was to make Britain stronger. Appeasement and rearmament were sides of the same coin. His aim was to negotiate eventually from strength. He was no man of war, but he understood the nature of deterrence: 'Fear of force is the only remedy.'[38] He was much influenced by the view of George Canning, the nineteenth-century Foreign Secretary, that threats are of no use without something to threaten with. While seeking political solutions, he hastened Britain's military revival.

It is easily forgotten that Chamberlain, man of peace that he was, did not exclude the possibility of war. 'Armed conflict between nations is a nightmare to me,' he told radio listeners later in 1938, 'but if I were convinced that any nation had made up its mind to dominate the world by fear of its force, I should feel that it must be resisted.'[39] Chamberlain as Chancellor of the Exchequer had played the leading part in the development of Britain's rearmament programme from 1933 onwards. In 1936 his budget proposals for the 'four-year plan' were denounced by the opposition as 'warmongering'. Though he recognised the financial and political constraints on higher levels of rearmament, he had endeavoured as Chancellor to strike a reasonable balance between the kind of risks Britain faced internationally and the level of military spending the economic recovery would permit. When he became Prime Minister rearmament was already well under way, though it was inevitably a slow process after years of military decline. The general aim in 1936 was to produce forces strong enough by 1939 to prevent defeat and deter the aggressor, but there was much argument between the services about how resources should be allocated to secure the object, and a more general confusion about what kind of war Britain should be preparing for. In the summer of 1937 Chamberlain determined to get a clearer view of future strategy and a firmer grip on rearmament. A Ministry for the Co-ordination of Defence had been set up in 1936 under Thomas Inskip. He was instructed to draw up a comprehensive survey of what had been achieved, and of what Britain needed to be able to fight a total war.

Chamberlain's view of war was an economic one. Industrial strength and financial stability, trade and blockade, were ingredients of strategy as surely as military force. A sound economy and secure finances were as important as aircraft and tanks for prosecuting a long war; indeed without them the aircraft and tanks could not be produced. In his report in December 1937 Inskip stressed that rearmament expenditure should be expanded only to a level which would not 'impair our stability, and our staying power in peace and war'. Chamberlain enlarged on these conclusions in Cabinet the same month: 'Seen in its true perspective, the maintenance of our economic stability would . . . accurately be described as an essential element in our defensive strength: one which can properly be regarded as a fourth arm of defence.'[40] The idea of the fourth arm ran through British war preparations throughout the 1930s. Britain faced great economic difficulties with rearmament; equipment and machinery had to be brought in from overseas; British industry was heavily dependent on overseas sources of raw materials; expanded military spending meant running the risk of a serious balance of payments crisis, or a run on the pound, both of which would undermine the ability to continue importing for rearmament. High levels of government spending on arms produced rising costs and the prospect of inflation, and serious shortages of skilled labour.[41] There was never a point at which high levels of military spending would not have distorted and damaged the economy. Churchill's view that the German threat could be met only by very high levels of current military expenditure ignored the constraints of industrial capacity, manpower and financial security, and underestimated the potential for a much more effective war effort three or four years hence. Large fleets of biplanes and light bombers in 1938 would have been unlikely to deter Hitler, or for that matter Japan and Italy, and would have sacrificed the resources needed for the new weapons in the pipeline. The British rearmament effort from its nature needed not money but time.

Chamberlain's object was to minimise the damage rearmament might do to the economy and social peace, to retain Britain's international economic security, and to ration military funds in such a way that optimum use could be made of the resources that were available. This meant an order of priorities. Discussions on the rationing of resources and effort went on through the winter of 1937–8. In February Inskip produced his final report. All were agreed that expenditure should be increased. In 1938 Britain spent four times as much on defence as in 1934, 38 per cent of all government expenditure. Plans for 1939 were higher still; a great effort of rearmament was set in motion to give real teeth to appeasement policy, without reaching levels that would produce economic collapse. First rank went to completing the air defence of Britain with radar and modern fighters; naval strength was expanded for the defence of Britain's vital trade routes; industrial mobilisation was speeded up with the so-called 'shadow factory' scheme, to build industrial capacity for war in peacetime. Only the army suffered; resources were slowly increased, but in the absence of any commitment to create a Continental army again, and with no very clear idea of what kind of war to prepare the army for, priority naturally went to those services which could directly protect Britain or the Empire from attack.

Neville Chamberlain, seen in this 1938 cartoon, was confident he could save the Empire.

The government recognised that it would be some time before Britain was secure from such a threat. The programmes would be complete or near completion in 1939 and 1940. Against this background Chamberlain embarked on his active efforts to settle the grievances of Europe. He did so, well aware that he faced more potential enemies than allies. He regarded France as feeble and socialistic, an unattractive prospect for friendship; he hoped for more from the United States, particularly economic assistance, but found an impermeable barrier of isolation and neutrality. This left Germany and Italy. He did not trust either Hitler or Mussolini. Both were capable of what the Foreign Office called a 'mad dog act'. But he was convinced, as were many of his colleagues, including Anthony Eden, whose phrase it was, that 'economic appeasement' would be understood even by dictators. 'Might not a great improvement in Germany's economic situation', Chamberlain asked, 'result in her being quieter and less interested in political adventures?'[42] Trade and financial agreements remained in operation until the outbreak of war. Chamberlain also shared with his colleagues the view that the Treaty of Versailles was not sacrosanct. This was a view held consistently almost since the Treaty was signed by politicians of all colours, including Churchill. In 1937 Chamberlain sent Lord Halifax to visit Hitler to find out what kind of revision the German leader wanted. Halifax hinted at 'possible changes in the European order'.[43] Chamberlain grasped not at Europe but at Africa as the key. Settlement of Germany's colonial claims was pushed to the forefront in the search for detente.

For Chamberlain the colonial question became a test of German goodwill and the possibility of general settlement. There was no question of handing back the mandated territories as a whole; Conservative imperialists were implacably opposed to such a course. Chamberlain proposed an unscrupulous solution: either Portugal or Belgium, or both, should be made to give up territory in Africa to compensate Germany. 'I have no doubt that Portugal would strongly object,' he wrote to his sister, but the Portuguese could be bought off by loans or territories elsewhere.[44] Nothing betrayed more clearly how much a figure of the nineteenth century Chamberlain was, when great powers carved up the world in their own interest. Nothing betrayed more clearly the real limitations to the concept of a general settlement, for German power was hardly to be restrained by half-hearted offers of someone else's empire. When the proposals were put to Berlin in March 1938 they were ridiculed.[45] 'The German Government', it was reported to the Cabinet, 'did not want to tie their hands by talks.' Nor was Chamberlain's approach to Italy any more successful. He initiated talks with Mussolini in January 1938 with a view to detaching him from the German camp which he had apparently joined the previous November when Italy signed the Anti-Comintern Pact. Italy, too, was to be bought off by sharing in an African settlement that would include recognition of the Italian conquest of Ethiopia, in return for a promise of withdrawal from the Spanish Civil War, in which Italian forces were fighting for the nationalist cause. The outcome of the talks was inconclusive. Mussolini, like Hitler, was not to be ensnared by a general settlement on British terms.

The Chamberlain initiative, on which he had placed such hopes, crumbled away almost before it had started. The British government needed signs of goodwill on the other side before the wider aspects of the general settlement could be promoted – disarmament, a return of Germany to the League, a Western non-aggression pact. With the failure of the exploratory talks Chamberlain did not bother to pursue the second stage further. The Foreign Office, and Eden, the Foreign Secretary, were sceptical of the chances of success from the outset. For all his realism, Chamberlain was hardly a man of the world. Officials and diplomats regarded the scheme as fanciful; Eden saw Chamberlain's actions as an unwarranted intervention in the responsibilities of his own office. On 20 February 1938 he resigned. In his place Chamberlain appointed his friend Edward, Lord Halifax. Halifax accepted the office with great reluctance: 'I have had enough obloquy for one lifetime.'[46] He knew how difficult his task would be for he had already acted as Chamberlain's intermediary with Hitler in November. In close session with the German leader he could see what a gulf separated Berlin from London: 'one had a feeling all the time that we had a totally different sense of values and were speaking a different language,' he recorded in his diary. Hitler made it clear to him that a general settlement 'offered no practical prospect of a solution of Europe's difficulties'.[47] Though he encouraged his leader's search for a solution, he had few illusions that a firm grip on diplomacy would be sufficient to hold the dictators back. His instinct was correct; on 12 March Hitler occupied Austria. Chamberlain faced the severest test of his new course.

The Austrian coup was not altogether unexpected, though British intelligence failed to give any advance warning when it happened. Chamberlain recognised that Britain could have done little to prevent it: 'Nothing short of an overwhelming show of force would have stopped it . . .', he told the Cabinet.[48] It was all too evident that in the spring of 1938 Britain did not possess such force, even had the defence of Austria seemed worth the battle. The risk of fighting Germany, as the Chiefs of Staff reminded the government, would almost certainly involve not only 'limited European war' but 'world war', as Italy and Japan took advantage of British distraction in Europe. Two years of rearmament had still not made the Empire more defensible. This was not, in Chamberlain's view, 'the moment to accept a challenge'. Yet there was every appearance now that Hitler would move on from Austria to Czechoslovakia. The problem of the Sudeten Germans was not new; Chamberlain had proposed some kind of concession to the minority as part of the general settlement in 1937. The whole Czech settlement had been, Churchill thought, 'an affront to self-determination'.[49] In March the British realised that the issue could no longer be ignored.

There were few defenders of the Czech state among British leaders. It was regarded as a 'highly artificial' creation, whose integrity was not a vital British interest. It was not an issue, remarked Alexander Cadogan, head of the Foreign Office, 'on which we would be on very strong ground for plunging Europe into war'.[50] Nor could the Czechs be given serious military help. The Germans, it was thought, would overrun them 'in less than a week'. On 21 March the Cabinet decided that Britain would not intervene militarily to preserve the Czech state, and would put pressure on the Czechs to make concessions to Germany on the minority issue. It was by no means uncertain at this early stage that a reasonable solution to the Sudeten issue could be found. Yet the real issue was not Czechoslovakia at all, but France. Britain had no agreement with the Czechs; the French did. If Germany invaded Czechoslovakia and France went to her aid, Britain would be obliged to help France. This was an obligation not of morality, but of necessity. German defeat of France would tilt the European balance so overwhelmingly against Britain that it could not be contemplated. The outcome could well be the fragmentation and defeat of the British Empire. There would be no point in fighting Germany, Chamberlain argued, 'unless we had a reasonable prospect of being able to beat her to her knees in a reasonable time and of that I see no sign'.[51] It was the central purpose of British strategy during the months of crisis in 1938 to avoid a European war before British rearmament was completed. The object was not so much to appease Hitler as to restrain France.

British strategy, based on a resonable balance of risks up to 1938, lost the initiative to Berlin and Paris in the summer of that year. Chamberlain's difficulty was to grasp clearly what either power would do. German demands of the Czechs were never clearly formulated, and shifted with each twist of the crisis: 'a perfect barrage of reports', complained Chamberlain.[52] It was never unambiguously clear whether or not France would fight if Czech independence were threatened, partly because the French premier, Daladier, and his Foreign Minister, Bonnet, had views diametrically opposed. At all costs Britain had to avoid an aimless drift into war. As the summer drew on this outcome seemed more likely. The Czech government would make no substantive concession to the German position; German attacks on the Czech state in the press became more frenzied. In August Chamberlain determined to try to seize back the initiative. With Czech agreement a mission was sent to Czechoslovakia headed by the British Minister Lord Runciman to find the basis of a settlement between the Sudeten Germans and the Czechs. The British were not hostile to the idea of autonomy for the Sudetenland; faced with this view and uncertain of either French or Soviet support, the Czechs finally submitted. But even while negotiations with the Sudeten minority on the British proposals were in session, Hitler announced his rejection. Chamberlain found himself in the worst possible position. From a situation of watchful detachment in March, Britain had become entangled in a situation from which she could not be extricated and which carried more surely the threat of war than any other course Britain might have pursued.

On 8 September Chamberlain revealed to his colleagues one more coup, Plan Z. 'I keep racking my brains to try and devise some means of averting a catastrophe,' he wrote some days before. 'I thought of one so unconventional and daring that it rather took Halifax's breath away.'[53] Plan Z was a simple one: to fly to Germany to meet Hitler face to face and ask him what his demands really were. It is not entirely clear why Hitler accepted, though it must have been hard to resist the flattering and direct attention of the leader of the British Empire, for which Hitler still had a lingering respect. On 15 September Chamberlain entered an aircraft for the first time in his life and flew to meet Hitler at his summer retreat at Berchtesgaden. He arrived feeling 'quite fresh' and 'delighted with the enthusiastic welcome of the crowds who were waiting in the rain'. On his three-hour train journey to Berchtesgaden every station and crossing was thronged with Germans shouting good wishes. Hitler and Chamberlain met together for three uninterrupted hours. At the end a rough agreement was reached. Discussions on self-determination for the Sudeten Germans would be initiated; in return Hitler would stop short of invasion. As he left, Hitler became almost amiable: 'when all this is over, you must come back. . . .'[54]

Reluctantly the British Cabinet accepted; the French agreed, and after a difficult negotiation, the Czechs were compelled to accept the loss of the Sudetenland as the lesser of two evils. On 22 September Chamberlain flew back to Germany to meet Hitler at Bad

Godesberg on the Rhine. The two parties were installed, symbolically, on either side of the river. Chamberlain was ferried across to meet a different Hitler; the areas for cession would be occupied in two days. After a bitter exchange Hitler altered the date to 28 September, then 1 October. Chamberlain returned to London. He had considered Hitler 'half-mad' all along. There were no further grounds for conciliation. The Cabinet rejected the Godesberg proposals as they stood; the French followed suit and promised to stand by the Czechs; mobilisation began in both countries. There had always been limits to British appeasement policy; Chamberlain's aim was to force Hitler to work within a framework acceptable to British interests. Though he did not believe the issue to be one of 'the great issues that are at stake', and though Britain's military preparations were meagre, the situation on 28 September was an unavoidable commitment to fight if German forces occupied Czech territory without agreement and by force. At the end it was Hitler, not Chamberlain, who climbed down.

On the 28th, while Chamberlain was telling the Commons of the gloomy outcome of his efforts, news was passed to him that Hitler had backed down. He had agreed to an international conference at which the Sudeten question would be worked out by agreement. The benches of the House erupted; Members crossed the floor in tears to shake Chamberlain's hand. What they did not know was that Chamberlain had made it plain through his envoy Horace Wilson in Berlin that if Hitler attacked it would 'bring us in'; and that on the 27th, at the prompting of the Italian Ambassador, he had written to Mussolini asking him to intercede and make Hitler see sense.[55] On 29 September the four leaders, without the Czechs, met at Munich. Hitler was ill-tempered, Chamberlain tired. Almost twelve hours of talks ended in the early hours of 30 September when the Munich Agreement was signed. The Sudeten Germans were given self-determination within the Reich, on boundaries agreed by the conference. At 1 a.m. Chamberlain asked to see Hitler privately. They met in Hitler's Munich flat with a German interpreter. Chamberlain asked Hitler to sign a joint declaration renouncing war between their two states, and accepting consultation and negotiation as the basis for solving problems in the future. Face to face with Hitler Chamberlain extracted in five minutes what fifteen months of diplomacy had failed to achieve; the framework for the Grand Settlement.

It is easy to see why Chamberlain saw Munich as a victory, and Hitler saw it as a defeat. From a position of military weakness and inferiority, with no firm allies, and an array of diplomatic imponderables, Chamberlain had almost single-handedly averted war and compelled Hitler, for the last time, to work within the Western framework. That frame was never committed to the survival of Czech integrity and the denial of self-determination to the Sudeten Germans, but it was committed to opposing the use of violence to achieve ends that could be achieved by discussion. To this extent the Czech problem was resolved on lines acceptable to the bulk of British and French opinion. It was a victory for diplomacy over force, though a hollow one for the Czechs. The British and French did what they had done for decades: drew and redrew the frontiers of lesser powers. That they were dealing with a powerful and predatory Germany made the achievement in the end all the more remarkable.

Chamberlain was the hero of Munich; history has judged him to be the villain. Nevile Henderson, writing congratulations from Berlin, guessed this outcome: 'Millions of mothers will be blessing your name tonight for having saved their sons from the horrors of war. Oceans of ink will flow hereafter in criticism of your action.'[56] But at the time there was an overwhelming sense of relief. Chamberlain received 40,000 letters of approval. In the Commons the Labour Member James Maxton thanked the Prime Minister for doing 'something that the mass of the common people of the country wanted done'. Even Chamberlain's critics saw the sense of preserving peace in 1938; Eden acknowledged that 'Munich has given us time at least.' Roosevelt telegraphed the simple words 'Good man'. Chamberlain's most vivid memory of the crisis was the sight of the thousands of Germans cheering almost hysterically as he returned from Munich. He was not just Britain's hero.[57]

The villain is a different Chamberlain: one of the 'Guilty Men' who failed to stand up to fascism in 1938 and fight; who put the self-interest of Britain's ruling classes before good sense and morality. A 'British Tory', as Roosevelt privately sneered, 'who wants peace at a great price'.[58] Yet it is difficult to see what room for manoeuvre Chamberlain really had in 1938. The list of factors cautioning peace was a formidable one. Chamberlain was protecting not just Britain but the British Empire. The simultaneous threat from Italy and Japan loomed larger rather than smaller as the Czech crisis worsened. Chamberlain had been premier for only a year; he was understandably not prepared to crown that period by deliberately courting a war that all his military advisers warned him would destroy the Empire. In 1938 the rearmament programme was only halfway to its goal and was facing major problems. Until it was complete Britain had almost nothing with which to threaten Hitler, except what General Pownall called 'our poor little army'.[59] The

RAF plans to bomb Germany proved on closer inspection in 1938 to be completely worthless. Though military intelligence rightly observed that Germany was far less formidable than the public image suggested, the element of risk was enormous. Most fearsome of all was the threat of the 'knock-out blow' from Germany's bomber force. Britain's elite were absorbed with this fear from the moment German bombers flew over London in the summer of 1917. The situation in 1938 was unpredictable. It is now clear that Germany almost entirely lacked the means to launch a bombing campaign against London; for that matter, the German armed forces had scarcely thought of war with Britain. But Chamberlain on his own admission was appalled by the thought that Londoners should be exposed to the full horrors of aerial bombardment for an issue so close to resolution. What was more important was the knowledge Chamberlain had that within twelve months Britain's military position would be quite different. 'From the military point of view,' General Ismay told him, 'time is in our favour. . . . if war with Germany has to come, it would be better to fight her in say 6–12 months' time than to accept the present challenge.' But the situation in September 1938 was so bad that General Ironside thought 'no foreign nation would believe it.'[60]

Armed with such intelligence Chamberlain was hardly in the position to issue military threats. Nor did he have confidence that he would be bringing a united nation into war. The critics of British policy in the summer of 1938 were to be found only on the extreme right and left. Communists called for a united front against fascism, but Chamberlain distrusted them so much he could not even countenance bringing the Soviet Union into the discussions of the Czech problem. The nationalist critics around Churchill and Leo Amery were unable to win more than a handful of supporters in Parliament, and were widely distrusted in the country and the Conservative Party. Churchill was an isolated and embittered critic of Chamberlain. But his solutions to the Czech issue were hardly realistic in the context of European politics in 1938 – an international guarantee of Czech independence and the submission of the Sudeten issue to the League of Nations. In the 'Munich Debate' in the Commons on 5 October he accused the government of accepting an 'unmitigated defeat', and urged that the Czechs would have achieved a better deal left to themselves with Nazi Germany, while knowing full well that left to themselves the whole of Czechoslovakia would have been overrun by German troops.[61] Churchill's enthusiasm for collective security and the League united him incongruously with much of the Labour opposition, which persisted in arguing that a common democratic front with the Soviet Union would have averted Munich and ended the arms race. The Labour Party itself remained divided; a minority favoured more military spending and an active struggle against fascism, but were hostile to the idea of uniting with Chamberlain Conservatives to promote it. The young Hugh Gaitskell writing in 1938 faced this conscientious dilemma: 'while prepared to fight for the democratic ideal . . . there is little to attract us to fighting merely to preserve the territorial integrity of the British Empire.'[62]

The overwhelming bulk of the population was still repelled by the prospect of war, particularly 'continental entanglements'; many were hostile even to increased levels of rearmament, so that the government was compelled to soften the blow of increased taxes and defence spending through an orchestrated propaganda campaign in the press and the cinema. The popular attitude to the Czech issue was fragmented. In the Empire as a whole the issue was much clearer. All the Dominions except New Zealand were hostile to the idea of fighting for Czechoslovakia. On 1 September the Prime Ministers of both Australia and South Africa confirmed that they would not become involved on Britain's side. On the 24th the four High Commissioners in London of New Zealand, South Africa, Canada and Australia announced that 'the German proposals *can't* be allowed to be a *casus belli*,'* and they continued to press this view up to the 28th, the day that Hertzog, the South African premier, got unanimous parliamentary approval for a declaration of neutrality. The fear of Empire disunity was an important one to Chamberlain, as it would have been for any British Prime Minister. 'There would be no point in fighting a war that would break the British Empire,' explained Britain's Chargé d'Affaires in Washington, 'while trying to secure the safety of the United Kingdom.'[63] Chamberlain was too alive to opinion not to be oppressed by the difficulty of taking a divided country and a divided empire into war. When he stood on the tarmac on his return from Munich at Heston airport he waved Hitler's signature and promised 'Peace for our time'. The peace was almost universally acclaimed.

What the cheering crowds did not see was Chamberlain's almost immediate regret at uttering the promise of peace. As his car made its way through the throng he turned to Halifax: 'All this will be over in three months!' Later that night the enthusiasm of the crowd outside No. 10 carried him away again. Not only 'Peace for our time'

* Italics in original.

but 'peace with honour'. He regretted this too. He was too much of a realist not to see that what he had bought was a breathing space until such time as 'the issue of peace and war might be contemplated with less anxiety than at present'.[64] Munich had been a time of great danger, almost a disaster for the British Empire. The breathing space was not to be wasted. There existed still the possibility of peace on the basis of the declaration. But it was only a possibility; if Hitler went back on his word, home and foreign opinion, the moral argument, would all be on Britain's side. There also existed the much greater probability of war with Germany in the near future, something that British planning had anticipated for two years. Chamberlain saw the British options plainly: 'Hoping for the best, but preparing for the worst'.

More than ever was he convinced that he alone could steer the Empire through the difficult months ahead. 'I know I can save the country,' he wrote in March, 'and I do not believe anyone else can.'[65] The effect of Munich convinced him that his dual strategy was the right one, to search for a settlement if one existed but to continue every effort to prepare Britain for war. The pace of rearmament did not slacken after Munich, but quickened. The lesson that Hitler took from the crisis was that he could take his next steps in Eastern Europe without war; the British lesson was the exact reverse, that Hitler's next violent step would bring conflict. In October Chamberlain explained that 'it would be madness for the country to stop rearming. . . . We should relax no particle of effort.'[66] Chamberlain had been a rearmer before Munich; he remained one thereafter. On 27 October Inskip was installed at the head of a new Committee on Defence Preparations and Accelerations. Every aspect of mobilisation was now put under scrutiny. Sir John Anderson was placed in charge of civil defence preparations. Gas masks were distributed to every man, woman and child; air-raid shelters were dug; Air Raid Precautions officials recruited and drilled an army of volunteers. Purchasing missions were sent to the United States to procure stocks of metals and chemicals and to buy aircraft. The brakes on rearmament finance were lifted with all the economic dangers that that entailed. Chamberlain clung to the belief that military preparations would deter Hitler once he realised the extent and thoroughness of British defences. But the preparation had to include the possibility of fighting. In November 1938 the army Chief of Staff was 'confident we can win a long war'. By the end of the year he was confident that within twelve months Britain could win a short war too.[67]

The breathing space called for political initiatives as well. Chamberlain sought to capitalise on the temporary advantage won at Munich, but he had few illusions left about Hitler. According to one official, whenever Hitler's name was mentioned, Chamberlain 'made a face like a child being forced to swallow castor oil'.[68] He revived the idea of detaching Mussolini from the fascist bloc, and reopened discussions. In January 1939 he visited Mussolini together with Halifax. He was pleased with the reception from the crowds in Rome, but the talks were inconclusive, for Chamberlain had little he wanted to offer. Mussolini was unimpressed, as he told Ciano: 'These, after all, are the tired sons of a long line of rich men, and they will lose their empire.'[69] The visit encouraged Mussolini to be more, not less, ambitious in the Mediterranean. The visit also alarmed France and infuriated Chamberlain's anti-appeasement critics at home. Approaches to Germany had the same effect. There is no doubt that Chamberlain's strategy was widely misunderstood. He was anxious not to lose the momentum set up at Munich to pursue a general settlement, but only on terms acceptable to British interests. This meant an acceptance of German domination in Central Europe, but British leaders had long expected that, as Germany recovered her economic power and military strength. 'This predominance was inevitable,' Halifax believed, 'for obvious geographic and economic reasons.'[70] British capitalism had begun to pull out of Central Europe before Munich; after September economic hegemony in the region passed to Germany. At the same time a stream of intelligence information was arriving in London suggesting that the Nazi regime was in deep crisis. One informant revealed that the German workers' feelings had been 'roused to the point where, if they were in possession of arms, they would physically revolt . . .'.[71] Other sources, predominantly conservative opponents of Hitler, suggested imminent economic and financial chaos. The intelligence picture encouraged Chamberlain to pursue economic approaches to Germany confident that Hitler was in too vulnerable a position to refuse. Contacts were established with the so-called German 'moderates' in the hope that they might pressure the German government to be more conciliatory, or, if Hitler fell, bring Germany back into the international fold on peaceful terms.

There was much wishful thinking in this, but Chamberlain was wedded to the simple view that all leaders, dictators included, were politically sensitive to the dangers of economic collapse. Halifax was much less sanguine. He thought economic problems would push 'the mad dictator to insane adventures'.[72] While Chamberlain vainly explored avenues for settlement, Halifax began to emerge as a political force in his own right. He reflected a growing mood in the country and in Parliament that definite and clear limits should now be placed on German ambitions. He did not want to repeat the experience of September: 'No more Munich for me.'[73] The alternative to appeasement was to isolate Germany diplomatically, to strengthen international support for Britain, and to take the fateful step of making, for the first time since the Great War, a real Continental commitment. Though the Prime Minister clung to the hope of settlement, he did not need much persuading that the cause was a forlorn one. Between October and February almost nothing was achieved of substance. By then Chamberlain was more confident that rearmament made British firmness a possibility, and that Germany's political and economic position was deteriorating swiftly. These changes, he wrote to his sister, 'enable me to take that "firmer line" in public'.[74] From February conciliation of Germany was replaced by deterrence and encirclement, then war.

On 6 February Chamberlain signalled the change when he announced in the Commons a British commitment to support France in Europe militarily. Rumours of a German attack on Holland, and fears that the French in exasperation at the lack of British firmness would join forces with Hitler, accelerated the decision, but it was in effect unavoidable if Hitler were to be confronted with a serious deterrent. Later in the month it was agreed to hold joint staff talks; Chamberlain authorised at last the building of an expeditionary force. The same month the Committee of Imperial Defence sat to draw up Britain's plan for war. The plan was a realistic one, based on British strengths and weaknesses. It was based on the assumption that British forces would be fighting with French against Germany, and possibly, though not certainly, Italy. The Soviet Union and the United States would remain neutral; Japan would not strike for fear of America. The lesser powers in Eastern Europe would stand aside, including Poland, in whom 'it would be unwise to place any substantial reliance on assistance, active or passive'. Using their financial superiority and naval power, the Western allies would stand on the defensive behind the Maginot Line and blockade Germany, while they built up material resources for a massive offensive. 'Once we had been able', concluded the plan, 'to develop the full fighting strength of the British and French Empires, we should regard the outcome of the war with confidence.'[75]

The military planning and strategic initiatives preceded the next act of the drama, the German occupation of the remainder of Czechoslovakia on 15 March. So too did the change in public mood towards Germany. The seizure of the Czech state accelerated the change but did not cause it directly. Public opinion, prompted to some extent by official propaganda, swung in a violently anti-German

SHAVALLO 1/-

News Chronicle

POPPY DAY

PLEASE GIVE GENEROUSLY

No. 28,870 ONE PENNY FRIDAY, NOVEMBER 11, 1938

Pogrom Rages Through Germany

INCENDIARY MOBS WRECK SHOPS, SYNAGOGUES

Officers Try Vainly To Protect Jews

Hitler Turns Down Mercy Call

From Our Own Correspondent

BERLIN, THURSDAY.

WHILE BERLIN LOOKED THIS EVENING AS IF IT HAD BEEN BOMBED, OFFICIAL GERMANY STOOD WITH ONE EYE ON THE FOREIGN PRESS AND ONE HAND ON THE THUMBSCREW OF ANTI-JEWISH TERROR.

In plain language, inspired comments threaten that if the foreign Press pays too much attention to Germany's revenge on her Jews for the murder in Paris of the diplomat, Herr Vom Rath by a 17-year-old Polish-Jewish boy, then official reprisals will be carried out against the German Jews.

In some streets in the capital every second shop is wrecked. Hundreds of shops, offices and institutions run by Jews have been raided by Nazi hooligans, who smashed, burned, looted and then ran.

At least seven synagogues in Berlin were burned. The same occurred all over the Reich.

The riots swept the finest streets of Berlin. A shambles was created by shouting, jeering squads of young men. In some cases they clashed with army officers, who seemed to be the only persons left in the Reich who dared to stand up for decency and restraint.

POWERLESS OFFICERS

What They Did

Smashed Windows of Shops in Berlin

Tom Mooney, In Prison, Says—

"SONG IN MY HEART"

From Our Own Correspondent

NEW YORK, Thursday.

TOM MOONEY, the Labour leader who has been in gaol for 22 years for a "crime" which most of the world believes he never committed, gave an interview today in San Quentin Prison, California.

His voice reflected new hope for freedom, which comes from the election as Governor of California of the Democrat, Mr. Olson, who has announced his intention of granting a pardon.

Asked, however, if he had had a definite promise, Mooney said: "Mr. Olson has made me no promise, and I have asked none from him."

Mooney was obviously intent on saying nothing that might hinder Mr. Olson's efforts to free him.

TO KEEP HIM IS

Tom Mooney before his life sentence—

—and when he was photographed in March, this year

LATE NEWS

The *News Chronicle* reported Kristallnacht on Armistice Day, 1938. The pogrom's effect on British public opinion was dramatic – both left and right demanded that Hitler be stopped.

German direction after Munich. Relief at the rescue of peace was turned to anger at Hitler's continued threat to the security of Europe. When pollsters asked in October 1938 whether the public would fight rather than hand back German colonies, 78 per cent favoured war.[76] Opposition to high levels of rearmament evaporated, except on the pacifist left. Appeasement was becoming a dirty word, though support for Chamberlain in the opinion polls remained as high by the late summer of 1939 as it had been a year before. The Nazi pogrom on Kristallnacht on 9 November 1938 contributed to the revulsion against Hitlerism. Two different responses began to blur together in the months that followed: on the one hand a popular anti-Hitler movement fuelled by hostility to fascism in general and fears for democracy; and on the other a growing nationalism among the British social elite directed at Germany as a threat to empire. There was no widespread enthusiasm for war among either group, but a public belief that the only way to solve the European crisis was to stand up to dictators, to call their bluff, to deter from real strength. Though Chamberlain shared this belief in deterrence and negotiation from strength, he had the misfortune to be identified increasingly by his critics with the view that accommodation must be made with the fascist leaders at all costs. This was not Chamberlain's view. Much less separated him from the anti-appeasers in 1939 than is usually assumed. If he had a fault it was to place for too long confidence in the possibility that all leaders were susceptible to reason and good intentions, even Hitler.

The Prague crisis had a real impact on Chamberlain for it ended once and for all any further reliance on German good faith. At dinner on the following day with Halifax he solemnly declared: 'I have decided that I cannot trust the Nazi leaders again.'[77] The following day he travelled to Birmingham to address the Unionist Association. He rewrote his speech. He knew he spoke not just to the crowded hall but to the whole country. In a powerful and emotional speech, he outlined the reasons for Munich, the narrow options of British policy, the deep disappointment that Hitler had betrayed an opportunity for permanent peace. Appeasement, he confessed, was not a 'very happy term' nor one that accurately described his wider purpose, which was to ensure 'that no Power should seek to obtain a general domination of Europe'. But now Germany was a threat to British liberty. This, Chamberlain announced, 'we will never surrender'. If the threat of domination should come Britain would resist it 'to the utmost of its power'.[78]

In March the British government were forced to confront directly the dilemma from which Chamberlain had tried unsuccessfully to rescue the country for two years. Rightly or wrongly, the occupation of the rump Czech state was seen as the point at which the interests of the Empire were challenged directly. The choice was a stark one, either to accept the German domination of Europe and the collapse of British prestige and political influence, or to face the very real prospect of war. 'In these circumstances,' Halifax told his colleagues, 'if we had to choose between two great evils he favoured our going to war.'[79] That the British government and people made that choice in the summer of 1939 is not difficult to understand. Even though he faced an agonising time in doing so, Chamberlain recognised the necessity of confronting Hitler with force next time. He hoped to the end that Hitler would back down and accept the Anglo-French preponderance of strength, but he, too, prepared for the worst.

It is only on these terms that the unilateral British guarantee to Poland, announced in Parliament on 31 March, can really be understood. Immediately after Prague, the British searched, with some desperation, for a way of making clear to Hitler what the limits of the Western position were. It was only chance that the guarantee was made to the Poles, for it was in this direction that German policy now clearly turned. The British government would have preferred a general bloc of Eastern European countries encircling Germany, but relations between the Soviet Union and her western neighbours, to say nothing of relations with Britain, were so poor that the chances of giving Berlin a rapid warning were slight. Instead Chamberlain seized on the Polish issue as the opportunity publicly to place limits on German expansion and to still the growing chorus of demands at home for action.

The Poles were, of all the Eastern states, the one the British liked least. The issues of Danzig and the Corridor were, like the Sudetenland, not issues on which Britain would have fought if a peaceful settlement could have been reached. The British never pretended to make any serious attempt to give Poland military assistance, or to provide material or financial help during the summer that followed. They placed intermittent pressure on Warsaw to be reasonable over the fate of Danzig. The Polish guarantee was not intrinsically concerned with Poland. It was a gauntlet flung down at Hitler; a challenge that if he violently overturned the independence of any other European state he would tip the scales of the balance of power and find himself at war. The connection was not immediately obvious, but British opinion made it seem so. Lord Dawson of Penn explained the connection to a friend in July 1939:

> It is not so much a question of Danzig itself, but Danzig means the Corridor and after the loss of Danzig and the Corridor Poland would lose her access to the sea, wither away and suffocate. . . . After that it is only a step to Romania and her oil-fields, the Black Sea, the Dardanelles, the Mediterranean and the Suez Canal, one of the principal arteries of our Empire. So that if Danzig falls, the British Empire will be at stake.[80]

The Polish guarantee was only part of a wider and muddled effort to construct an international political net in which Hitler would be trapped. Two weeks after the guarantee similar pledges were made to Roumania and Greece. Turkey was wooed with promises of trade and cash. The government privately added Switzerland, Holland, Belgium, Tunis and the Scandinavian countries to the list of those whose territorial integrity they would defend by war. The United States would not be drawn, but Chamberlain found Roosevelt 'wary, but helpful', willing to add economic weight to the great effort to rearm. This suited him, since he preferred American neutrality to participation: 'we should have to pay too dearly for that,' he later argued.[81] The real key was the Soviet Union. With great reluctance Chamberlain bowed to the pressure of his Cabinet and accepted exploratory talks. The Chiefs of Staff thought that Soviet assistance would bring certain German defeat; they hoped a revival of the wartime triple entente might make war unnecessary. Chamberlain remained opposed to the idea, but was outvoted in Cabinet. On 24 May he agreed to begin direct talks. He assumed that the Russians were all too eager for an agreement which he continued to regard as worth little more than mere words. Molotov received the British proposal of a collective pact with hostility; it was 'calculated to ensure the maximum of talks and the minimum of results'.[82] From the Soviet side a military pact was also demanded, and guarantees of all the Baltic states. The British Ambassador reported that 'it is my fate to deal with a man totally ignorant of foreign affairs and to whom the idea of negotiation is utterly alien.'[83] British leaders despaired of getting any agreement on terms acceptable to them, and deplored the long weeks of haggling over small points. They continued the talks partly for fear of driving the Soviet Union towards Germany, with whom it was known through intelligence that secret contacts had been made, and partly to avoid taking any blame from public and international opinion for the failure of the talks. In July the British agreed to discuss the military pact proposed by Molotov; but they sent only a junior representative who had no power to make an agreement, and who could find no way of persuading the Poles to accept military help from their powerful neighbour. Chamberlain was unconvinced that Stalin and Hitler could reach any kind of agreement, but he was prepared for anything from the Soviet side. The failure of the talks, and the signature of the German–Soviet pact in August, confirmed for Chamberlain his initial mistrust. The army Chief of Staff thought the Soviet leaders 'the utter limit in double crossers'.[84] But by August the international situation was much more favourable and the loss of a Soviet alliance easier to bear.

By August Britain's military preparations were also greatly improved on March. During 1939 the government spent half its revenue, swollen by further tax increases, on defence, double the level of 1938. In the summer months British aircraft production began to overtake German without the addition of French output. In April conscription was introduced in peacetime for the first time. Over the summer months the army scrambled to organise an expeditionary force for immediate despatch to France. The RAF drew up detailed plans for the bombing of German industry in the Ruhr. The Royal Navy prepared its mobilisation in stages, reaching a state of operational readiness by early August. The flesh was hastily being put on the skeleton of full-scale mobilisation; the plans of 1935–6 were now producing mature fruit. There were plenty of gaps still to be made good, but the structure was altogether sounder than a year before.

The same could not be said for the British economy. Chamberlain's repeated fear that 'the burden of armaments might break our backs' was realising itself under the pressure of emergency.[85] The balance of payments crisis grew deeper as Britain sucked in the extra imports for defence. British gold reserves fell to half the level of 1938 as capital flooded away from London in search of safer havens. The first signs of inflation were evident. The Chancellor of the Exchequer became more insistent as the year went on that Britain faced imminent financial collapse. 'We shall find ourselves in a position', he told the Cabinet in May, 'when we should be unable to wage any war other than a brief one.'[86] The 'fourth arm of defence' on which Chamberlain, for one, had laid such stress threatened instead to become a formidable liability. It was clear in the summer of 1939 that Britain could not continue to rearm indefinitely; economic advice suggested that such levels of preparation could not be sustained in peacetime much beyond the end of the year. Oliver Stanley at the Board of Trade drew the obvious conclusion: 'There would, therefore, come a moment which, on a balance of our financial strength and strength in armaments, was the best time for war to break out.'[87]

HOW TO GAS-PROOF A ROOM

Civilian war preparations, 1938. Gas bombs were the main fear.

The truth was that the financial effort and the military preparations unwittingly created a timetable which was very difficult to alter. From the start British rearmament was planned with the idea of a potential conflict in 1939. The decision to make a great armaments effort in 1938 and 1939, and the decisions after Munich on mobilisation planning locked British leaders into a structure of expectations which were increasingly difficult to transcend. War could not be fought with any confidence in 1938; but neither could war easily be postponed much beyond 1940. Here again was the imperial dilemma; high and expensive levels of rearmament threatened to undermine the very stability and security they were designed to defend. Of course there was a way out: Hitler might, as Chamberlain hoped, back down in the face of British military might, and the defence effort could perhaps be relaxed. If he did not, British choices about the timing of war were severely circumscribed. The same problem could be found on the political front. During 1939 the British public adjusted itself to a war mentality. 'It's in the air you breathe,' wrote Orwell.[88] The population throughout the country braced itself for the crisis that had been postponed at Munich. German officials who visited London in July expressed a genuine astonishment at the talk everywhere of imminent war. The British saw their choices in much starker terms than did their enemies. 'We must finish the Nazi regime this time,' confided the army Chief of Staff in his diary; 'To compromise and discuss is useless, it will all happen again. If the Nazi regime can be so discredited that it disappears . . . without war, so much the better. If that doesn't happen we must have a war. We can't lose it.'[89]

The outcome of the final crisis over Poland was not in doubt. Either Hitler conformed to Western standards of international behaviour or there would be war. The situation was made clear to Hitler on numerous occasions. On 22 August Chamberlain, on his own initiative, wrote personally to Hitler to spell out the determination to fight if Germany invaded Poland, but the willingness to accept the reasonable resolution of all problems without force. Lines of contact were kept open with Berlin in case Hitler should have a sudden change of heart. More should not be made of these contacts than they merit. It was unsurprising that the avenue to a peaceful settlement should be kept open to the last, since that could now be achieved only on British terms and would amount to a major diplomatic victory. The British might well have given Danzig away on their own terms. But the determination to resist any use of force, and to interpret such violence as a threat to the Empire, was maintained consistently throughout the final crisis, by Chamberlain no less than by Parliament and the country. Chamberlain was fully aware that to refuse this obligation would just as surely destroy British influence and prestige as the failure to make it in the first place. The political cost of abandoning Poland in 1939 would certainly have been Britain's status as a major power.

As the Polish crisis reached its climax, the wider international picture became clearer and more favourable. Though the Soviet Union was now a confirmed neutral, the strategic assumptions in British war planning had already anticipated that. In the last week of August, there was evidence that Italy would not after all fight alongside Germany; neither would Japan, nor Franco's Spain. 'Germany', Inskip told Hankey, 'is rather isolated.'[90] For Chamberlain the most important news came from the Empire, not Europe. By late August the Dominions had moved from strong support for appeasement to staunch support for war. Commonwealth unity was, according to Chamberlain, 'all important'. The Dominions, like Britain, began after Prague to see the real dangers posed by the Axis powers. In April 1939 the new Australian Prime Minister, Robert Menzies, let it be known that 'If Britain was at war, Australia was too.' New Zealand was drawn closely into British defence planning during 1939 and gave Chamberlain unqualified support during August. In Canada the premier, McKenzie King, had preached appeasement since the Imperial Conference of 1937. But gradually in the late summer of 1939 the nationalist revival in Britain and France began to affect both Canada's populations and an evident enthusiasm to defend democracy against fascism and aggression replaced a widespread isolationism. The exception was South Africa. Even here Britain's old Boer enemy, Jan Smuts, was able to blunt the isolationism of the Afrikaner nationalists sufficiently to bring South Africa into war by a narrow parliamentary majority on 4 September.[91] Fortuitously, Britain was faced in late August with just the kind of conflict British planning had postulated all along, against one enemy rather than three, side by side with a powerful ally and a united Empire.

When Germany invaded Poland on 1 September, in defiance of the British challenge, the Cabinet authorised a whole range of necessary war measures. Halifax sent a warning to Berlin that failure to withdraw German troops would lead Britain to fulfil the obligation to Poland. The final ultimatum and declaration of war had to be co-ordinated with France, which wanted a forty-eight-hour delay to permit evacuation and initial mobilisation to take place. On 2 September Ciano proposed a conference of all the major powers; Chamberlain and Halifax could only accept it on the complete withdrawal of all German troops from Poland, something which both they, and Ciano, knew to be impossible. But the problems with both France and Italy led to an unfortunate delay in sending the final ultimatum, and aroused suspicion in Parliament that Chamberlain was seeking to avoid war. By the evening of 2 September the French would still not agree to co-ordinate an early ultimatum. Chamberlain's statement to the House was poorly delivered and evasive. 'We were anxious to bring things to a head,' he wrote to his sister a week later, 'but there [was] the French anxiety to postpone the actual declaration of war as long as possible. . . . There was very little of this that we could say in public.'[92] His speech brought a storm of protest; he retreated to Downing Street where he complained to Halifax that people were 'misinterpreting the inability to give a time limit to be the result of half-heartedness and hesitation on our part. . .'.[93] Angry telephone calls to Paris failed to produce a co-ordinated ultimatum. Chamberlain met the Cabinet at 11.30 that same night and agreed a British ultimatum to be handed to Ribbentrop at nine o'clock the following morning. The parliamentary revolt was averted; Chamberlain suffered in the last hours of peace the revenge of the Commons for trying to be for too long what 'Chips'

Channon called 'a very personal government – very one man!'[94] The following morning in Berlin Sir Nevile Henderson arrived at a deserted German Foreign Office. There was no one to meet him except Hitler's interpreter. They stood solemnly opposite each other while the ultimatum was slowly read out. Two hours later Chamberlain broadcast to the nation that Germany and Britain were at war: 'what a bitter blow it is for me that all my long struggle to win peace has failed.'[95]

The British Empire fought Germany in September 1939 not to save Poland, but to preserve the international system of which she was a major architect and a prime beneficiary. It was a system difficult to defend, and by the late 1930s difficult to justify. The Empire that Britain fought to preserve was in the final stages of disintegration, surrounded by powers hostile to the status quo, and enfeebled by internal disunity and crisis. The great depression of 1929 gave the old imperial structure a final lease of life as Britain fell back more and more on the economic support of the Empire, but the strategic problem could not be solved. Britain lacked the means and the willingness to play the imperial role she had played at so little cost and with such profit before 1900. Only Chamberlain believed it was possible to square the circle, to achieve military revival, financial security and social unity without war. It is not clear that this was ever a realistic possibility. Britain's relative decline and her retreat from global power were evident already in the 1930s, though accumulated prestige and residual strength still made her a desirable friend and a substantial foe. Like the Habsburg Empire in 1914, Britain fought in 1939 to preserve an empire that could no longer be preserved.

The generation that took Britain into war in 1939 was brought up in the great heyday of the Empire, when Britain was the centre of the world economy, and a force for a liberal, moral world order. They never seriously questioned either proposition: that the Empire was a necessity and that it was a source of good in the world. 'I cannot imagine anything', Chamberlain said, 'which would do more injury to the general welfare of the world than to allow the British Empire to decay. . . . '[96] Britain's ruling classes were brought up on the idea that British imperialism was a moralising force, a force in the world worth defending whatever the risk. This was, Churchill believed, the great heritage of the 'English-speaking peoples': 'to think imperially, which means to think always of something higher and more vast than one's own national interests'.[97] In 1939 it was not fascism that they were fighting, but the challenge to that moral, English order which they thought sustained British power and wealth for everyone's good. Within two years the whole fabric of that empire faced bankruptcy; at war on every imperial front, without a major ally save a Russia close to defeat herself, Britain depended entirely for her continued war effort on the financial goodwill of the United States. In this sense Chamberlain, like his nineteenth-century ancestors, was right to see 'Peace the first British interest'. What made war a certainty was not simply the logic of Chamberlain's own policy of rearmament and large-scale deterrence – which Hitler failed to grasp at any point in 1939 – but the seismic shift in popular opinion in 1939. 'I can see that war's coming,' wrote Orwell in 1939. 'There are millions of others like me. Ordinary chaps that I meet everywhere, chaps I run across in pubs, bus drivers, and travelling salesmen for hardware firms, have got a feeling that the world's gone wrong. They can feel things cracked and collapsing under their feet.'[98] In 1939 the old ruling class, the guardians of Empire and world responsibilities, joined forces with a democratic population which sensed a danger much more immediate and directly menacing and fought not to defend the Empire, about which many of them cared little, but to defend Britain.

CHAPTER THREE
FRANCE

> The Englishman is not intelligent, he does not grasp things quickly. He realises his danger only in the moment of extreme peril. History eternally repeats itself. We have not finished with Germany. . . . Any understanding with her is impossible, and England, whether she likes it or not, will be compelled to march with us at the moment of danger in order to defend herself. Despite the misunderstandings and the dissensions that may separate us now, England will be forced to come to France's side exactly as in 1914. . . .
>
> (Georges Clemenceau, c. 1928)

In 1919 French soldiers returned to the villages and towns of France, victors of a war of revenge. They were greeted by grandfathers who had fought the Germans in the Franco-Prussian war of 1870 and lost. Defeated, they had been forced to accept an army of occupation, pay a very great war indemnity and agree to a humiliating peace treaty which severed Alsace and Lorraine from the French state. Now it was the turn of France to repay Germany in her own coin. Frenchmen were united on this point; for all the rhetoric of peaceful reconstruction and international co-operation, the Peace Treaty of 1919 was built around the occupation and dismemberment of Germany and the payment of reparations for the devastation Germany had caused. Lloyd George regretted the outcome: 'France is a poor winner.' But the central issue for Frenchmen was the opportunity, against all expectations, that victory had given them to reverse the long-term decline of French international power and to find a permanent security against the revival of the German threat. For the next twenty years France was obsessed with the fear that the opportunity had been lost. The struggle for domination over the continent of Europe between Germany and France, a struggle almost lost in 1914, was the central issue facing every French statesman and general from the Armistice of 1918 to the late afternoon of 3 September 1939, when France found herself once again at war with her historic rival.

Even while the victorious peace was being drafted, French leaders knew that the problem of Germany would never disappear, though its potential for damage could be limited. 'Mark well what I'm telling you,' said Georges Clemenceau, France's great war leader, and her representative at the Peace Conference in Paris, 'in six months, in a year, five years, ten years, when they like, as they like, the Boches will again invade us.'[1] With a prophetic accuracy France's other great war leader, the supreme Allied commander, Marshal Foch, warned his countrymen: 'This is not a peace: it is an Armistice for twenty years.' Throughout those twenty years French politicians and soldiers tried to come to terms with this stark reality: the peace could not be permanently enforced, and Germany, slowly, but apparently inexorably, regained her former vigour. No other victor power shared this French dilemma; foreign statesmen failed all too often to understand that the anxieties, vacillation, uncertainty, the loss of will displayed in France was a product of this deep but comprehensible fear that history would repeat itself.

To the other victor powers the French position at the Peace Conference of 1919 seemed very different. Where they sought a peace of magnanimity, the French seemed bent on a peace of revenge. The negotiations between the Allies were punctuated by bickering and argument over French claims against Germany and French plans for Europe every bit as bitter as the arguments between the Allies and their defeated enemies. The British and Americans were convinced that France, now apparently at the zenith of her power, with no rival left in Continental Europe, was planning to subvert the internationalism of the conference, and its offspring, the League of Nations, by a new imperialism of her own. 'At the back of all this,' wrote a British official in April 1919, 'is the French scheme to suck Germany and everybody else dry and to establish French military and political control of the League of Nations, conceived as an organization for the restoration of France to a supreme position in Europe and her maintenance in that position.'[2] The experiences of 1919 fuelled the view of British politicians that French leaders were provincial and devious: 'underhand, grasping, dishonourable'.[3] By the end of the Peace Conference the entente between Britain and France was strained almost to breaking point.

Yet on most major points the French got what they wanted. Germany was disarmed; her colonies divided between Britain and France; her western territories put under military occupation; a network of new states in Eastern Europe established; reparations demanded from Germany for the damage caused to Belgian and French territory which Germany would pay into the 1980s. Most important of all Alsace and Lorraine, the territories seized by Bismarck's victorious armies in 1870, were returned to France.

A pacifist demonstration in London in 1935. The dominant feeling in the democracies was 'never again'. Politicians had to take account of popular protests against war when confronting aggression.

Neville Chamberlain in front of the camera for a national broadcast. He proved to be a master of the new media in the 1930s, the first British politician to recognise its potential in winning support for unpopular policies, in this case for increased defence spending.

'Shadow factories replace marshlands: silent allies of Britain's air force.' In 1936 the government paid motor manufacturers to set up new factories to help with air rearmament, 'shadowing' the work of the aircraft factories. This factory, set up by the Standard Motor Company in Coventry, was among the most modern production lines in Britain.

Air power was at the core of the British rearmament effort. The Wellington bombers and the first Supermarine Spitfire illustrated here were the backbone of the new generation of aircraft for the RAF in the early years of the war.

The first children's gas-masks are demonstrated to the press, October 1937. The government was determined to provide protection for all civilians against gas and bomb attack; by 1939 all Britons had a gas-mask.

In the heart of London, September 1938, trench shelters are being dug in Lincoln's Inn Fields in case of war over Czechoslovakia.

French Communists demonstrate in the streets of Paris, 9 February 1934, in protest against the anti-parliamentary right and its 'capitalist' allies. Three days before right-wing riots had led to fifteen deaths and hundreds of injuries.

In the mid-1930s French politics became sharply polarised between right and left; politics took to the streets. Here two young Communists (*above*) carry a wreath to the funeral of a miner, killed by a royalist. The right-wing League of Solidarity (*below*) parade their banners for a service at Notre-Dame, February 1935.

The French Prime Minister, Edouard Daladier, returning from the Munich Conference, September 1938. Like Chamberlain, he returned to scenes of relief and elation: 'the blind fools' was his comment on the crowds at the airport.

Aerial terror was the nightmare of the 1930s: it was widely believed that 'the bomber will always get through'. Here the threat is an illusion: French bomber and transport aircraft on a training exercise over Paris in 1938.

France's armoured forces were more than equal to those of Germany. The heavy tanks seen here in the 1938 Bastille Day Parade down the Champs-Élysées outclassed their German equivalents. The following year Winston Churchill, watching the tanks roll by, 'thanked God for the French army'.

Two views of the French Maginot Line. French military leaders believed that their only chance of security was to fortify the whole frontier against German attack. The northern defences (*left*) were too light to keep the Germans out; the main defensive wall of underground tunnels (*right*) and massive artillery in Lorraine was never put to the test.

Clemenceau's hope that an independent republic of the Rhineland could be set up, as a buffer between France and Germany, dominated by France, was refused by the other Allies, who would only accept its permanent demilitarisation; but France was given control of the industrial wealth of the Saar basin, and *de facto* control of the whole Saar region for fifteen years. Here was security of a sort to prove Foch wrong, and it was the most that her allies would permit. As it was, the peace seemed to usher in what H. G. Wells called 'the French millennium' with 'nothing left upon the continent of Europe but a victorious France and her smashed and broken antagonists'.[4]

But the French position was based on an illusion. France had not won the war alone, but only with the help of her major allies. Faced by Germany on her own, she would almost certainly have lost the war. The power she enjoyed in the Europe of the 1920s was a result of the weakness of others as much as her own strengths. Revolutionary Russia was isolated, the great powers of Central Europe enfeebled beyond recognition. France possessed for the moment the world's largest land army, almost the largest navy and an air force that worried even the British, though the economic cost of sustaining such forces was evidently beyond her. The isolationism of the United States in the 1920s and the gradual withdrawal of Britain from any active role on the Continent left France with a temporary ascendancy greater than at any time since Napoleon. The extension of French influence in Africa and the Middle East as a result of the peace settlement – Syria and Lebanon from the defeated Turks, Togoland and Cameroon from the Germans – brought France to the height of her global power as well.

The reality was very different. The war had weakened rather than strengthened France. During the slaughter of the Great War, France lost one-quarter of all her men aged between eighteen and twenty-seven, a higher proportion than any other nation. Four million Frenchmen carried the wounds of that conflict.[5] The war destroyed the enduring value of the French franc, unchanged since Napoleon's time. By 1920 it was worth only a fifth of its pre-war value, while France was saddled with enormous debts from the war and a bill for war-pensions, which twenty years later still consumed over half of all government expenditure.[6] To make matters worse France had lost most of her overseas investments during the war, including the investments in tsarist Russia which had provided an income of sorts for over two million Frenchmen. Finally there was the devastation wrought by the warring armies along France's eastern territories, which in the end the French themselves paid more to repair than the Germans. By 1924 the French economy was deep in crisis, rescued in the end only by a timely devaluation of the franc and a brief export revival, before being plunged once again into crisis in the 1930s.

It is against such a background that sense can be made of the almost frantic efforts by French statesmen to uphold the letter of the Versailles Treaty against Germany. The schedule of reparation demands ran from an annual monetary sum, through deliveries of coal and machinery, to the demand for 1000 rams, 2000 bulls and 500 stallions.[7] The enforcement of these demands, in the face of German reluctance and British mistrust, became the centre-point of French diplomacy throughout the next decade. But it was doomed to failure. Germany certainly paid something, but much less than France wanted, or believed Germany could pay. Britain and the United States preached moderation and flexibility to her. In frustration France resorted at last to force. In 1923 French soldiers were sent into Germany to occupy and secure the Ruhr, Germany's industrial heartland, from where supplies of German coal could be sent back to France. The occupation aroused the fury of her erstwhile allies, while the Germans pursued a policy of passive resistance. To make matters worse many of the occupying troops were from French Africa, arousing a storm of protest from friend and foe alike against the black threat, which was, according to Bernard Shaw, 'holding down Europe, and holding up civilisation'.[8] Then, on Easter Saturday, 31 March, French troops again fired on Germans. A handful of French soldiers, led by Lieutenant Durieux, entered the Krupp works in Essen to make an inventory of the Krupp garage. The soldiers were faced by a silent and hostile crowd of Krupp workers. Stones were thrown; the French soldiers, anxious for their safety, fired into the air. Then they turned a machine gun on to the advancing crowd. Thirteen Krupp workers were killed at close range; fifty-two more were injured. On any scale of international conflict the incident was small enough, but it symbolised an enduring hatred. Gustav Krupp ordered that every year the works would organise a pageant to the memory of the fallen workers. It was held every year down to 1939.[9]

By 1926 the last French troops left the Ruhr. But the damage was done. The effort to make Germany pay harmed France's reputation internationally and alienated Britain and the United States, the very powers that had helped to draw up the settlement in 1919. The British reserved their most energetic attacks for the French premier, Raymond Poincaré, who seemed to them to personify all the worst traits of provincial, petty-bourgeois France. He does things, complained Lord Curzon, 'no gentleman would attempt'. 'He just was not', recalled Lord Vansittart, 'our idea of a Frog.'[10] The whole

German propaganda capitalised on the use of French colonial troops in Germany. France's allies were also appalled.

point was that Poincaré was just that. Preoccupied with fulfilment and security, the loyalty of France's leaders was, understandably enough, to the ordinary Frenchman, not to the ordinary German. The failure of the British and Americans to understand or accept this placed a gulf of incomprehension and mistrust between the wartime partners. Even Winston Churchill, later so stern a critic of British appeasement, thought the French should be forced to make 'sweeping' concessions to the Germans, including, of all things, 'a recasting of . . . the oriental frontiers of Germany'.[11]

This was, of course, exactly what France was not prepared to do. Deprived of the goodwill or practical support of both Britain and America, the weakness of her post-war position was starkly revealed. Before the Great War French isolation had been ended by a firm alliance with the crumbling tsarist state, which presented Germany with the perennial insecurity of a two-front war. The Russia that emerged after 1918 was a different prospect altogether. The bolshevik revolution put a permanent barrier in the way of reviving the hammer and anvil of the two-front alliance. Instead the hammer and sickle posed a threat not just to the international order, but to the social stability and political survival of France herself. Communism posed a glaring threat to the ageing, liberal parliamentary state; the Third Republic was torn by labour disputes after 1918. No consensus could be found in France in the 1920s for inviting the enemy beyond the gate to join hands with the enemy within. So instead France turned to the new states of Eastern Europe, Poland, Czechoslovakia, Yugoslavia, Roumania, in the hope that another second front could be constructed there, a *cordon sanitaire* keeping bolshevism out of Europe and keeping Germany hemmed in within the frontiers of Versailles.

The result was a patchwork of agreements, some military, some not, worked out during the 1920s: with Poland in 1921 and 1925, with the Czechs in 1925, with Roumania in 1926, Yugoslavia in 1927. The French had no illusions about the strength of these ties. They were supplemented by the League of Nations, with its commitment to 'collective security', a commitment on the part of France's League colleagues that was never to be put to the test in Eastern Europe. But since the small Eastern states shared the same fears of German and Russian ambitions that the French held, there was something to be said for the strategy. And in the context of the 1920s and early 1930s, when France was still manning the pump of the European power vacuum, there was a great deal for France to gain, in trade and goodwill, by playing the role of Europe's policeman in the East. But the whole strategy, a product of circumstance and realism, contained all the seeds of the crisis that was to engulf France in the face of Hitler. Unable to reach an alliance with communist Russia, France opted for a network of alliances with the weaker states of Eastern Europe which she could not defend effectively, and which would, almost inevitably, involve France in conflict with a revisionist Germany, the one thing the French were trying to avoid.

In fairness the French themselves were well aware of the paradox they confronted. Spurned by the democracies, repelled by Russia, feebly embraced by the new national states of Eastern Europe, France began to turn to the course that had seemed impossible in 1919 or even 1923 – reconciliation with Germany. At Locarno in Switzerland on 16 October 1925 a formal accord was signed between the major European states which guaranteed the frontiers of Western Europe. The initiative had come from Germany, but was warmly welcomed by France, for Germany was now willing to agree voluntarily that the settlement on France's eastern border was a permanent one. This suited a growing mood in France of pacifism and internationalist idealism; Aristide Briand, the Frenchman who brought home the agreements from Locarno, hailed them as a turning point: 'we are Europeans only.'[12] Much was made of the 'Locarno' years; after 1925 the French economy began to prosper; war receded into the background; Briand crowned his career by drawing up a pact in 1928 to outlaw war altogether as an instrument of national policy, signed by sixty-five states, including Germany. Yet the French position remained as brittle as ever. There was no firm entente with Britain – in 1928 the RAF drew up contingency plans for a 'Locarno' *war* against France should she ever violate German territory[13] – the Eastern alliances were a poor substitute, and Germany, revived economically, secretly rearming, the hydra of Europe, had said nothing about her eastern frontier at Locarno. Revisionism in Germany was not an invention of Hitler; all political circles in Germany shared this desire in the 1920s. The French well knew that when Germany was strong enough French security would once again be in the melting-pot.

In the absence of real guarantees for her security, France turned to the only solution that seemed to make sense: a strong, fortified, defensive wall stretching the whole length of the French eastern frontier. The idea of the 'Great Wall of France' had first been raised in the 1870s but was rejected. After another conflict with Germany the idea made insistent sense. France would build a great rampart against which future German armies would hurl themselves and be repelled. For many French generals this was a strategy that denied their generalship. The French army was brought up on the virtues of the offensive. But the lessons of the First World War were clear: the initiative now lay with the defence. Marshal Pétain, hero of the defence of Verdun, argued for the 'continuous front', for 'battlefields prepared in peacetime', for a long defensive corridor stretching from the North Sea to the Mediterranean. This view won the acceptance of the politicians, many of whom had served, or whose sons had served, in the trenches. André Maginot, who became Minister of War in 1922, was just such a man.[14]

Maginot was one of that remarkable breed of French ministers who in 1914, and again in 1939, left their offices to join the army on the outbreak of war. Starting as a private, he was promoted rapidly to sergeant, and was seriously wounded in 1915. After the war he became a widely popular Minister of Pensions before becoming War Minister. He was obsessed after his experiences with the future safety of France. He was a native of Lorraine whose ancestral home had been destroyed by shelling in the early stages of the war. He became, understandably, a champion of Pétain's continuous front, and was conspicuous in the arguments about the merits of fixed

DEFENDING FRANCE, 1925-40

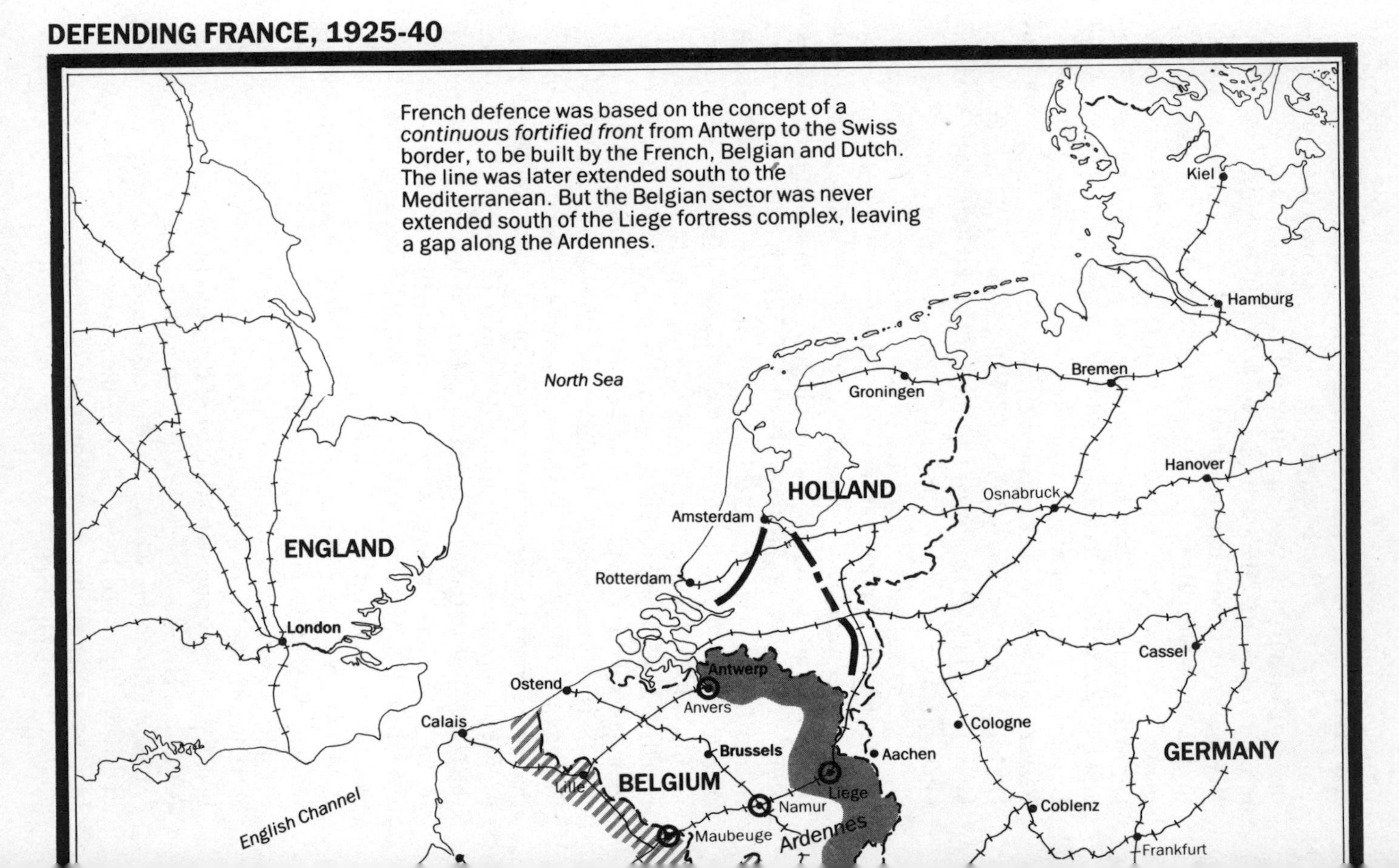

French defence was based on the concept of a *continuous fortified front* from Antwerp to the Swiss border, to be built by the French, Belgian and Dutch. The line was later extended south to the Mediterranean. But the Belgian sector was never extended south of the Liege fortress complex, leaving a gap along the Ardennes.

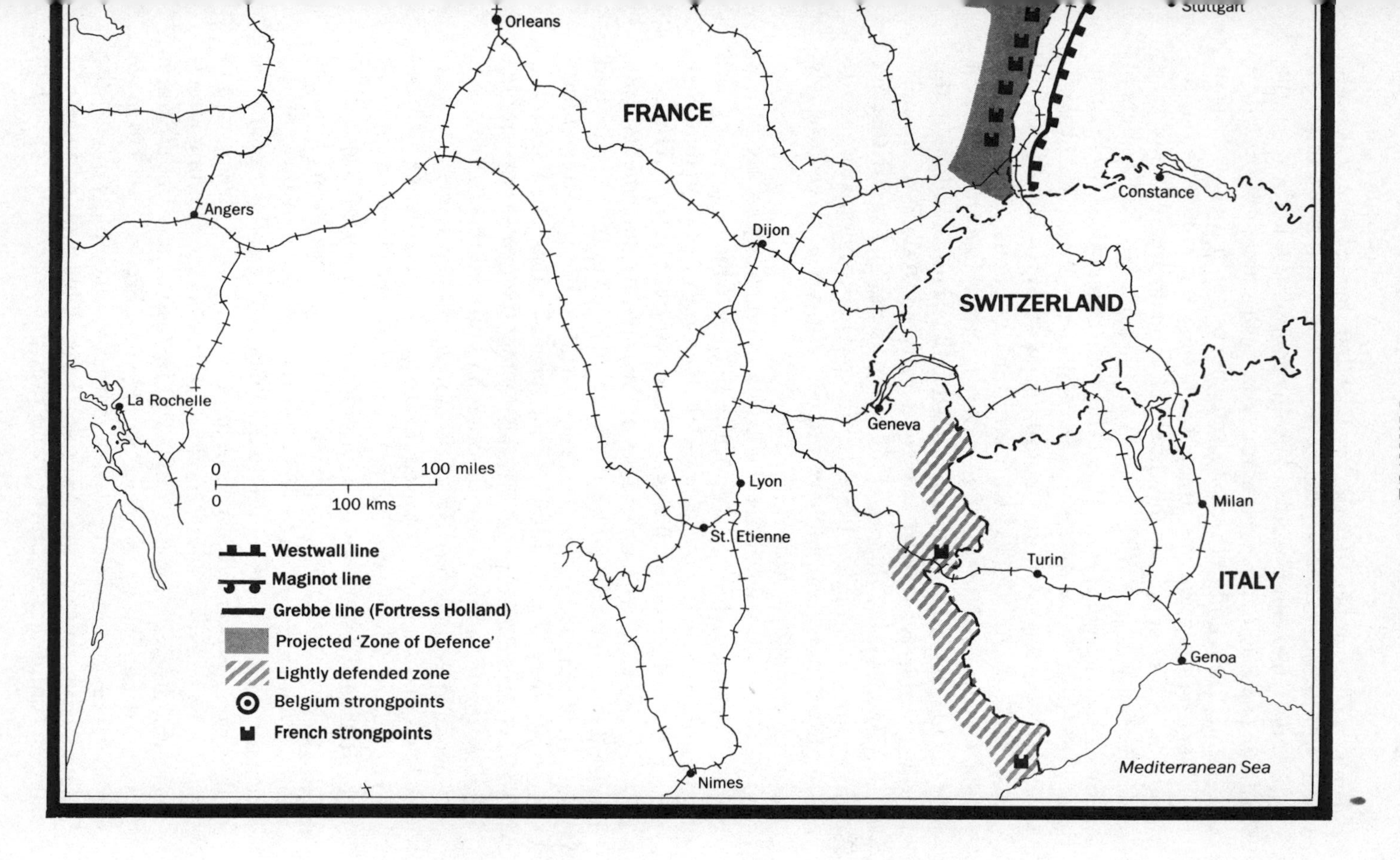
Stuttgart
Orleans
FRANCE
Angers
Dijon
Constance
SWITZERLAND
La Rochelle
Geneva
0
100 miles
0
100 kms
Lyon
Milan
St. Etienne
Turin
ITALY
Genoa
Mediterranean Sea
Nimes
Westwall line
Maginot line
Grebbe line (Fortress Holland)
Projected 'Zone of Defence'
Lightly defended zone
Belgium strongpoints
French strongpoints

defences. In December 1929 the French Chamber of Deputies finally voted almost three billion francs for a four-year programme of construction for what would become popularly known as the Maginot Line. The money was nowhere near enough to provide a continuous front, and in the end almost six billion francs were spent on French fortifications by 1939. Even then the front was hardly 'continuous'. Despite the myths that soon arose of the Line's impregnability, it in fact covered in any depth only the frontiers of the recaptured provinces of Alsace-Lorraine. Here there were three defensive layers facing the enemy – a small advance garrison of *gardes mobiles* to provide an initial holding operation, a second line of stouter defensive positions, with anti-tank weapons, machine-gun emplacements and barbed wire, and then a third line on the nearest hills based around large forts and fixed artillery units, hidden in the hillsides and served by a vast underground system of tunnels, barracks and supply depots. This line was designed to withstand artillery fire even from the largest guns, and aerial bombardment. It was manned by regular soldiers and conscripts who served a whole year underground at a time.

Over the rest of the frontier the Line was much less secure. It was decided that the whole length of the frontier which ran along the Rhine from Strasbourg to Basle should have only a limited defensive system, since the river itself was seen as a sufficient barrier. The Line here consisted of a double row of infantry emplacements with machine-guns and anti-tank weapons concealed in the hillsides and ridges facing the Rhine. On the French–Italian border stronger forts were built opposing the only narrow lines of attack. The area that presented the greatest problem was the low-lying area opposite the Belgian frontier where German forces had pushed through in 1914. The wooded section further to the south, the Ardennes, through which German soldiers poured in 1940, was considered almost impassable by any great number of troops and equipment, and was to be defended by a plan of demolition to supplement what difficulties nature had already supplied. But the low northern plain was another matter. The whole object of the Line was to prevent the Germans from outflanking the French defences, but the topography of the region prevented any system of underground defences, and denied hills or ridges where forts could dominate oncoming forces. There was also a diplomatic difficulty. In 1920 France and Belgium had signed a military pact which would allow French forces to move into Belgium on the outbreak of hostilities to take up position at the Belgian equivalent of the Maginot Line. This would make the rampart complete, yet it meant that French defence was dependent on the goodwill of her Belgian allies. French leaders realised that to build their own defensive wall on the Franco-Belgian frontier would be tantamount to abandoning the Belgians to their fate, and would anyway be a poor military substitute for the solid Belgian defences. By way of a compromise Pétain provided a limited defensive battlefield for the region and gambled on Belgian good faith.[15]

If André Maginot personified that powerful French sentiment of 'never again', the Line that bore his name has come to symbolise the defensiveness, the conservatism, the *faiblesse* of France in the face of the German revival. 'Maginot-mindedness' now stands not only for lack of will and initiative, but for wilful self-delusion as well. Despite the deficiencies of the Line, Frenchmen wanted to believe that their fears of invasion, of history repeating itself, could be set to rest. It is all too easy to blame the French after the débâcle of 1940 for trading on illusion, to insist that a strategy of defence is intrinsically demoralising. Yet the Maginot Line was not mere military fantasy; it was the product of a very realistic assessment of French strengths and weaknesses in the face of increasing isolation abroad. France in 1919 was a satiated power, in the sense that she had no desire to extend her territory in Europe, and no more opportunities to extend her territory overseas. The French position was by its nature defensive; an offensive strategy ran directly counter to the pacifism, the revulsion against war that the experience of the trenches produced. If some sort of consensus could be reached on the need to defend French soil against attack, there was little support for an active foreign or military policy. The Line acknowledged how difficult it was going to be to rouse the French people again for another bloodletting. It also acknowledged the growing weakness of France. By 1938–9 the number of conscripts would reach an all-time low because of the low wartime birthrate. The Line was a more efficient way of using French manpower, faced by a much larger German population. French industry was no longer the equal of German; the Line not only gave protection to the vulnerable heart of French industry in the north-east and Lorraine, but would make it less necessary to match Germany gun for gun. Finally, the Line was designed to break German forces in a long war of attrition. It was a central aspect of Pétain's strategy that the Line would act as part of a wider strategy of blockade and attrition, and that when the enemy had been worn down by fruitless attacks against it, the French army would storm out from behind its rampart and destroy the enemy with massive offensive blows.[16] Under such circumstances it would have been surprising if the French had not built their 'Great Wall'. The fault lay not with the conception of a defensive line, but in its execution.

The Line was not finally completed and manned until 1938. In the meantime France continued to rely on the temporary ascendancy won in 1919, still clearly visible a decade later. In the late 1920s France furiously pursued the fruits of peace, not war. The French economy enjoyed its only real boom between 1913 and the 1950s. French culture enjoyed a dazzling revival; tourism blossomed on a scale hitherto unknown. André Citroën and Louis Renault battled in Paris to supply the second-largest car market outside America. Frenchmen began to embrace the future again; thoughts of revenge subsided; the concrete was setting on the Maginot Line.

Two things conspired to bring this interlude to an end: the Great Crash and the rise of Hitler. The effect of the economic collapse was not felt immediately in France, for her economy was less dependent on trade and industry, while a healthy balance of payments had stored up large quantities of gold in the Bank of France, producing the financial equivalent of the Line. But if France was sheltered from the worst of the economic blizzard, her allies in Eastern Europe were enfeebled by it, and Germany brought close to bankruptcy. French bankers bore much of the responsibility for this; so too did French politicians who refused to budge on the question of reparations until 1932, when it was clear even to them that Germany simply could not pay. French financial strength protected the small French producer and *rentier*, but internationally it backfired. By helping to fuel the economic crisis in Germany, the French produced what they feared most, a political crisis that brought to power at last a radical, revisionist government in Berlin.

French self-interest during the depression alienated Britain and the United States as well. Few tears were shed abroad when the French economy in turn began to go into steep decline in 1932, at just the point that the shattered economies of the other powers were beginning to revive. The paradox of French decline and international recovery can partly be explained by just this lack of goodwill. The pound and the dollar were both devalued to save British and American exports. The French government hesitated to follow suit for fear of destroying confidence in the future of the French economy, and from fear of alienating the thousands of small French investors through renewed inflation. Instead French exports remained in the doldrums for most of the 1930s. By 1934 France found her overseas trade cut by almost half from the level of 1928. Tariffs kept out cheaper foreign goods, but contributed to the prevailing spirit of protection and self-interest. But the decline of the French economy owed as much to conditions within France. The government remained committed to the ideals of Adam Smith or even Malthus: not only did the state reject the recovery strategies of the American New Deal or the German 'New Plan', with their strong dirigiste elements and proto-Keynesianism, but it deliberately restricted output and cut government expenditure, to match supply to demand. The result was financial suicide: as demand fell, tax receipts from the inefficient French revenue system fell sharply, much faster than government expenditure. As a result governments that were wedded to monetary orthodoxy found themselves facing a wider and wider budget deficit. Each deficit produced a further frantic round of cuts in wages and services. By 1935 French industrial production was one-third lower than in 1928 and barely recovered for the rest of the decade. The situation in the French countryside was even worse. Agricultural prices fell by 50 per cent, until the price of wheat reached its lowest point since the French Revolution.[17] The sharp fall in peasant income, in a country with a backward agrarian system, spelt serious crisis. France relied on rural demand to keep afloat the millions of small businesses, the cafés, craft workshops and stores scattered throughout provincial France. When the peasant pulled in his belt so did the artisan and shopkeeper. Much of France was potentially self-sufficient. Economic crisis produced the same effect as international crisis. The French peasant and producer pulled into their shells; conservative and defensive, they retreated into prepared positions and sat there.

The political consequences of economic crisis were profound. The Third Republic had experienced slow but almost continuous economic growth since its inception in 1870. When that growth was at last reversed in the 1930s the crisis exposed deep social and political divisions in France. Some of the rifts were old ones revived by economic failure, the division between town and countryside, between labourer and *patron*, between secular, liberal urban bourgeois and nationalist, clerical elite. In the past these conflicts had been resolved within the framework of the conservative republican state. In the 1930s the old conflicts were expressed in a different language altogether. The economic crisis brought new forces into French political life, anti-parliamentary, radical, dangerous: on the left the Communist Party, on the right a whole spectrum of fascist and quasi-fascist movements. Willy-nilly French domestic politics came to reflect the wider international conflict between right and left.

The Communist Party was the direct beneficiary of the crisis of French industry. Unemployment increased threefold between 1931 and 1935; so too did Communist Party membership. In 1936 its numbers trebled again and it made huge gains in the 1936 elections, recruiting not just from the working class but from poor peasants and rural workers as well.[18] For the French ruling classes who feared communism as much as, if not more than, they feared the Germans the growth of rural radicalism was an alarming development. There were signs of growing violence and discontent in the 1920s as the peasantry at last woke up to the reality of mass democracy. Under the impact of the depression farmers began to organise themselves to protest their lot. Most prominent of the new peasant politicians was the populist demagogue, Henri Dorgères, a butcher's son from Burgundy who by 1935 had 35,000 followers; they marched in distinctive green shirts beneath the motto 'Believe, obey, fight' and the emblem of crossed pitchfork and sickle. The farmer, thundered Dorgères, was 'the only sound force in the nation, undefiled by orgies, cocktails or night clubs'. If this was not quite the stuff of peasant *jacquerie*, it frightened the old republicans; peasant votes had brought Hitler to power in Germany.[19]

On the right there were plenty like Dorgères only too willing to blame the bankrupt, corrupt republican regime for French ills. The late 1920s had already seen the growth of what became known as the 'leagues', loosely organised extra-parliamentary movements demanding firm government, moral renewal and an end to bolshevism. Though very few could be classified as genuinely fascist, the echoes from Rome and Berlin were unmistakable. Some were unashamedly fascist, Marcel Bucard's *Francistes*, or Jean Renaud's *Solidarité française*. Here were to be found Frenchmen who were pro-German and anti-Semitic, seeking the revival of a decadent Europe through a Franco-German rapprochement. The *Action Française* of Charles Maurras shared the anti-Semitism but was hostile to Germany and communism too. Its watchword was 'Neither Berlin nor Moscow'. But the most famous of the leagues, the *Croix de Feu*, was an authoritarian, nationalist movement committed to restoring the French values of family, social order and nation. It was far from pro-German. The movement got its name from the medal awarded to men for bravery under fire in the Great War, but it quickly spread beyond the veterans who first joined it. Under the leadership of Colonel de la Rocque the movement grew to the point where it had two million adherents in 1936. Taken together the leagues became much more than a mere political nuisance. They drew their strength from the petty bourgeoisie, squeezed between organised labour and large-scale industry, frustrated at the effects of economic decline, but frustrated too by the long years in which the Republic had been dominated by the parliamentary centre and centre-left. The effect of their radicalisation was to polarise French politics more clearly between extremes. The right-wing parties flirted with the leagues; the moderate left parties warily drew closer to the communists. The scene was set for a confrontation that would paralyse not just France's domestic politics, but her foreign policy as well.[20]

These new forces in French political life gave notice to the embattled parliamentary regime in a great outburst of political rage in February 1934. In February a traditional liberal coalition government was trying to cope with the aftermath of a messy corruption case, the 'Stavisky Affair'. Stavisky was a small-time swindler who grossed 200 million francs in eight years of corrupt dealing. Deputies, judges and policemen were implicated. When Stavisky was found in a room in Chamonix with a bullet in his head, it was rumoured that the police had arranged the 'suicide'. The government was accused by the right-wing press of complicity in Stavisky's crimes and in the attempted cover-up. The Prime Minister, Chautemps, resigned and his place was taken by Edouard Daladier, an energetic Radical-Socialist from Provence who inflamed opinion even more by immediately sacking the Paris Prefect of Police, who was popular with the right, and promoting a judicial official to high office who was one of those suspected of shielding Stavisky.

In protest at Daladier's inept handling of the Stavisky Affair, the leagues agreed to meet in central Paris for a major demonstration. The issue itself was not that important; but it became the excuse for focusing all the disillusionment, anti-parliamentary sentiment and anti-left feeling of the extreme right. The plan was to assemble from all over Paris at the Place de la Concorde and from there to march on the Chamber of Deputies. On 6 February the leagues gathered one after the other at special assembly points all over Paris, some outside the Opéra, some at the Hôtel de Ville. By five o'clock the Place de la Concorde was filled with protesters. Gendarmes and infantry surrounded the Chamber and blocked the bridge which led from the square. To cries of '*à bas Daladier!*', '*à bas les voleurs!*' the crowd rioted. Armed with broken chairs, railings and asphalt torn up from the Tuileries gardens they repeatedly stormed the bridge. Barricades were set up and vehicles set on fire. After almost three hours the police lost patience. Under fire themselves they fired repeatedly into the rioters. It took a further five hours to clear the square. Bitter fighting continued for most of that time. In all fourteen rioters and one soldier were killed, and 1326 injured, many seriously. What had begun as a protest meeting almost became a coup; the following day Daladier resigned and a new government of National Solidarity was formed under the right-wing premier Gaston Doumergue. The leagues were satisfied; the street had triumphed over the ballot-box.

The riots of 6 February shook the Republican regime to its foundations. Though it proved to be only a brief explosion of anger, there were widespread fears of fascist revolution, of communist counter-coup. After the riots the language of French politics became harder and more strident. And the polarisation between extreme left and extreme right profoundly inhibited the choices that could be made in foreign policy. Reparations and the League of Nations had satisfied both sides in the 1920s. In the 1930s the choice was more starkly presented as a choice between communism and fascism. Of course the choice was not as stark as this, but the middle ground of French politics, the common-sense nationalism of the old republican parties, was submerged beneath fears of disorder, revolution and collapse. No doubt such fears were exaggerated, but the example of Italy, then Germany and in a short time Spain as well made it clear that democracy was a fragile plant in the Europe of the 1930s. Fear of social crisis gave French appeasement in the 1930s its realism and necessity.

Yet the social crisis could not have come at a worse moment for France. Weakened internally, France became a spectator of the great changes that followed Hitler's assumption of power in Germany. Within the space of three years the whole brittle system, the many straws at which France had clutched, slipped from her grasp. It took some time for the fact to sink in. The French reaction to Hitler initially failed to take him all that seriously. 'Hitler will not last long. His fate is sealed,' André Tardieu told the French Ambassador in Berlin.[21] Only slowly did it dawn on French statesmen that Hitler was there to stay. Before Hitler conflict with Germany was a possibility; but then so was reconciliation as equals. With Hitler that prospect evaporated, and conflict became unavoidable. In 1933 Germany stormed out of the League and the Disarmament Conference. In 1935 Germany openly declared her rearmament in defiance of Versailles. That same year Anglo-French relations deteriorated still further when Britain signed a bilateral naval pact with Hitler, condoning German military expansion. In turn French attempts to endorse Mussolini's invasion of Ethiopia in 1935 alienated Britain and, in the end, Italy too. Pierre Laval, the unfortunate statesman who had negotiated agreement with Mussolini, found himself politically isolated at home and abroad, a symbol to foreign opinion of the decline of French patriotism and the rise of the politics of *facilité*, of cheap appeasement.[22] In 1936 the final blows were struck: in March German troops reoccupied the demilitarised zone of the Rhineland, tearing up the Locarno and Versailles treaties at one stroke; and in the autumn King Leopold III withdrew from the Franco-Belgian pact, declaring Belgian neutrality: 'we should pursue a policy which is exclusively Belgian. . . .'[23] The generals had always assumed that Germany would eventually push her military frontier into the Rhineland again, and the Maginot Line was constructed on that assumption; but the loss of the fortified Belgian frontier was a disaster from which French strategy failed to recover before the war.

Nor were France's Eastern alliances in much better shape. The building of the Line profoundly disturbed the smaller states with which France was allied. If France lay secure behind her rampart, why should she risk fighting for Czechoslovakia or Poland? It was a view shared increasingly by many Frenchmen. Moreover French leaders had come to recognise that real security against Germany had always rested on the Russian factor. Though communist Russia was still deeply distrusted she appeared less threatening than in 1917 and a pact of non-aggression was signed in November 1932, followed two years later by a pact of mutual assistance. But almost as soon as the ink was dry the French right, now deeply worried about the rapid and sudden rise of French communism, had second thoughts about the alliance. Pierre Laval, who signed the Pact after its chief architect, Louis Barthou, was assassinated in Marseilles, was a convinced anti-bolshevik: 'I don't trust the Russians; I don't want them to drag France into war,' he told General Gamelin in November 1935. He refused staff talks, which might have given the Pact real teeth. It was ratified by the French Chamber in 1936 after a severe mauling from right-wing deputies. Phillipe Henriot called on his fellow Deputies to reject a treaty which would 'place French money and soldiers at the service of revolution'. And a new but significant note was sounded in the debate: France should stand aside from 'this new struggle between Teutonism and Slavism'. The battle-lines of French foreign policy were the battle-lines of French politics as well.[24]

The German reoccupation of the Rhineland, Hitler's response to the Franco-Soviet Pact, was a dramatic challenge to France, a gauntlet flung in the face of Versailles. When the news broke on the streets of Paris in the late morning of 7 March there was consternation, talk of mobilisation, even talk of war. In the Chamber Georges Mandel, the radical disciple of Georges Clemenceau, echoed his one-time mentor in calling for France to mobilise and drive the Germans from the Rhineland. But in the end France did very little: and history has judged her harshly for it. Yet the circumstances could hardly have been less propitious. France was deep in political crisis, ruled by a caretaker government in the run-up to the parliamentary elections. The French generals, victims of government cutbacks, advised caution. The French public mood was against war and for peace. Abroad, France feared isolation. Britain refused to act over the Rhineland, relations with Italy were rapidly deteriorating over the Ethiopian affair. The last thing French leaders wanted was a repetition of the débâcle in the Ruhr in 1923, when they were cast in the role of aggressor for trying to uphold the letter of the Treaty. Nor did Frenchmen in 1936 know what we now know of the unyielding appetites of the new Germany. France needed a sterner cause to rally the nation in 1936, one that would heal the growing rifts in French society.

That cause was the Popular Front. The Front was born on Bastille Day, 14 July 1935, when a procession of 400,000 marched through Paris singing the Marseillaise and the Internationale. The crowds that day represented a historic compromise between communists, socialists and the Radicals, between the French working classes and the French petty-bourgeoisie. From the speakers' platform that afternoon came appeal after appeal to the great spirit of 1789, to the uniting of the Third Estate in defence of Liberty. Fascism at home and fascism abroad prompted the traditional cry: 'The Republic in danger!' The Popular Front was born of this powerful desire to save democracy. Much else divided communists from Radicals, but on this issue, on the need to rally the nation in defence of political freedom and social justice, all were agreed. In the elections of 1936 the Popular Front parties campaigned on the promise of economic revival and social reform; on a firm line against the fascist leagues; on a promise not to destroy capitalism, but to manage it. On foreign policy there were deep divisions between pacifists, who were mainly socialists, and the other two alliance parties which favoured rearmament against foreign fascism. The divide was glossed over by appeals to collective security and international goodwill. Everywhere the language was of justice triumphing over injustice, of co-operation over self-interest, of peace over strife. In May 1936 the Front won a clear victory at the polls: 330 seats against the 222 of the right. The left celebrated a new direction in French political life, an end to the politics of shoddy compromise and drift. Léon Blum, the socialist leader, became Prime Minister, promising '*Une France, libre, forte et heureuse*'.[25]*

* 'One France, free, strong and happy'.

Some, at least, of this promise was redeemed. A policy of modest reflation was introduced to halt the crisis of government cuts. A wheat office was set up to control the output of France's major crop and help peasant incomes. New social expenditure was planned for housing and welfare. Most important of all Edouard Daladier, leader of the Radicals in the Front, was appointed War Minister with a brief to increase French arms spending in the face of the mounting threat from the right abroad. In September 1936 a vast programme of 14 billion francs was announced, divided evenly between the three major services.[26] Blum, who had always been an ardent disarmer and pacifist, came to accept the arguments of his alliance partners that France could produce peace abroad only from a position of strength at home: 'It is necessary to accept the eventuality of war to save the peace.'[27] It was a curious argument for the leader of a party whose rank and file had demonstrated a month before at St Cloud in favour of disarmament. At the great 'Rally for Peace' Blum himself had spoken. The 'Mothers of France against war' had marched past him; an aeroplane, symbol of that terrible threat that lay beyond the Rhine, traced out the word '*Paix*' in the sky above the crowds. Yet in his office in the Air Ministry, Blum's Cabinet colleague Pierre Cot, the enthusiastic and air-minded young Minister, planned the creation of a French independent air force that could carry bombs to German homes.

This contrast was symptomatic of a deeper contradiction in the strategy of the Popular Front. For the movement elected to restore a sense of unity and social peace, to heal the wounds of post-depression France, produced an almost entirely contrary effect. The difficulties faced by the front were manifested almost before it took office. In Paris the working classes, frustrated by persistent wage-cuts, short-time working and managerial arrogance, embarked on a city-wide strike movement to remind the new government of its obligations. The strikes began in late May in the automobile industry. On 28 May the Billancourt works of Louis Renault, a notoriously authoritarian *patron*, were occupied by a largely good-natured section of the workforce, calling for holidays with pay and the downfall of Renault. The strike was contagious; by 6 June over a million workers were on strike in and around the capital, department stores closed, newspapers disappeared from the streets, food perished at the railway stations for want of deliverymen.[28] Street rumours circulated about revolution and overthrow; for the right it confirmed the Jacobin nature of the new regime. Frightened by the determination and extent of the strike movement the business leaders capitulated. The strikes ended when on 7 June a comprehensive

The left attacked the arms trade – and the prime role of French capitalism in its spread – as the international network of merchants of death.

agreement was reached at the Prime Minister's official residence, the Hôtel Matignon, between French capitalism and French labour. The package of reforms included the eight-hour day, a five-day week, paid holidays and a 12 per cent increase in wages. The Matignon Agreement was accepted by businessmen with great reluctance and ushered in an era of mistrust and hostility between labour and manager that undermined all the efforts to revive France's ailing industrial economy.

For the right in France the strikes confirmed what they already feared, that the Popular Front was a front for the triumph of communism. Their fears were greatly exaggerated, for the Front made every effort to avoid provoking any counter-revolution by appearing too radical. But the mere existence of an alliance with Maurice Thorez's Communist Party was evidence enough to the right that Blum and Daladier had made a Faustian pact. If the Popular Front recalled for them the triumph of liberty over despotism, the spirit of the storming of the Bastille, the Communist Party was Robespierre and the Terror. They reserved their bitterest reproaches for Blum himself: 'a man to shoot, but in the back'.[29] The right feared an imminent communist coup. Communist activity was evident throughout the Empire, in Indo-China, Algeria, the Middle East. One opposition Deputy summed up the mood when the Front came to power: 'Many foreigners have left Paris in a hurry. They believe in an imminent revolution. . . . There is talk of the collapse of the franc, and even the taking over and looting of private dwellings. . . .'[30] In retrospect the alarms of 1936 were as unreal as the fears of fascist takeover in 1934, but at the time the panic was real enough. The result was a collapse in confidence at home and abroad in the French economy. The socialists knew that they would confront the so-called 'wall of money', the financial establishment that was thought to control the destiny of French business and much else besides, but the effect of the Front victory was worse than they expected or deserved. Throughout 1936 a flight of capital out of France gave material form to the fears of the right. So severe did the loss become that in September Blum was compelled to devalue the franc, and over the next two years the franc lost almost 60 per cent of its value, while the government grappled with a persistent budget deficit, and industry remained starved of funds to invest. A financial strike was revenge for the occupation of the factories.

The survival of bitter class conflict destroyed what chance the Popular Front had of strengthening France either at home or abroad. It was always going to be difficult to offer social reform, economic revival and large-scale rearmament all at the same time.

Blum himself acknowledged the tension between a policy of guns and butter; 'it is difficult to carry out simultaneously a bold policy of social reforms and an intensive policy of rearmament.'[31] Reluctantly the government cut back on its social programmes, to the disillusionment of its supporters. The reflation inaugurated in 1936 instead produced inflation and industrial stagnation, 'stagflation'. Industrialists were unwilling to invest, trade failed to revive even after devaluation, and prices climbed rapidly, eroding the gains made in working-class wages in 1936. By 1938 industrial production was lower than it had been in 1936, and unemployment an endemic problem. This produced yet a further round of labour unrest and protest, and frightened the bourgeoisie into sending its savings in ever greater quantities to safer financial harbours abroad. The Popular Front ended up by satisfying nobody, friends or enemies. And the effect on its international position, far from rallying the nation, was to produce the view expressed by the American Treasury Secretary, Henry Morgenthau, that 'the French were a bankrupt, fourth-rate power.'[32]

This was the cruellest contradiction of all. Committed to the fight against international fascism, and for international peace, the Popular Front produced a fundamental shift in French attitudes to foreign policy that left French strategy in a complete confusion, from which it only emerged months before the outbreak of war in 1939. Up to 1936 the right had maintained the traditional nationalist position in favour of rearmament and a policy of strength towards Germany; the left was predominantly pacifist, wedded to the League and co-operation. The rise of the Communist Party in particular and the Popular Front in general threw the nationalist right into disarray. If the left now talked of the fight against international fascism, of rearmament and firmness it could only be doing so to further the cause of communism: 'Behind the Popular Front', announced a right-wing manifesto in 1936, 'lurks the shadow of Moscow.'[33] It was widely believed that communist enthusiasm for national defence was a ruse to further the cause of Comintern, to get France to fight Russia's battles. The right swung towards pacifism of a different kind, opposed to left-wing warmongering and in favour of appeasement towards fascism. The right had always had fellow travellers of fascism. Now their voice was heard more insistently: 'Rather Hitler than Blum'. Not everyone on the right accepted that this really was the choice, but as long as the strategy of war was identified with the left, the right withdrew from further confrontation with Hitler and Mussolini. The irony was that the left itself was far from uniformly 'nationalist' in this new sense. A great part of the Popular Front was pacifist by conviction, and was deeply disturbed by the plans for rearmament. Disillusioned by Blum, many socialists came to accept the view of the right, that communism in France did represent a real threat to peace.

The shift in the position of the left and right, and the deep fissures revealed in French politics by issues of foreign policy, came to a head over the question of intervention in the Spanish Civil War, which broke out in July 1936. This war was seen as a replica of what might happen in France if the reactionary elements of the army resorted to force against the Front. Arguments in France reflected the divisions between fascism and communism that had been violently revealed in Spain. The right demanded a policy of non-intervention and hoped for a Franco victory; the communists demanded intervention in a crusade against fascism; the socialists demanded peace. Blum compromised by declaring non-intervention while turning a blind eye to the flow of arms and volunteers across the border. Fearful of a right-wing backlash in France, and lacking any assurance from Britain of help in intervening in Spain, Blum opted for the only course that seemed politically acceptable, while knowing that a nationalist victory would leave France exposed to the threat of the extreme right on three frontiers. But the failure to intervene also disappointed the Soviet Union and made it difficult to rely on her support if it were needed in confronting Hitler. The Franco-Soviet Pact of 1935 remained largely a dead letter; the right were firmly opposed to any military links with Russia, and doubtful of Russian military capability, while Blum and Daladier were equally wary of any foreign ties which strengthened the hand of the communists in the parliamentary alliance. French diplomacy was trapped in a situation of permanent stalemate. The only success of the Popular Front was to revive in a limited way the flagging entente with Britain, though at the price of a growing dependence on British economic assistance when the franc collapsed in 1937. Blum saw the democratic entente as a 'primordial condition' of French foreign policy. Predictably even this aroused the growing anglophobia of the right, where the talk was now of Franco-German rapprochement, or even a Latin bloc of France, Italy and Spain against the British Empire.

The results of the Popular Front, which had aroused such optimism and élan in the summer of 1936, were deeply disillusioning. Social conflict did not go away but intensified. The French economy did not revive, but became plagued by inflation, a mounting deficit and a massive flight of capital. The social programmes could no longer be funded. Even rearmament had to be cut back again in 1937 to try to save the franc.[34] When Blum attempted to push new decree laws through the Senate in June 1937 to curb the outflow of capital, the Bill was rejected. Blum resigned, dispirited and humbled, and the Popular Front alliance, strained in every direction, limped on into the early months of 1938. Against such a background, French foreign policy failed to develop the coherence and sense of purpose the left had wanted; instead it merely served to heighten tensions at home, while doing almost nothing to secure the safety of France. It was a fitting climax that Hitler's next challenge, the union with Austria in March 1938, should have coincided with a ministerial crisis which left France temporarily without a government. French nationalism was still too frightened of French communism to respond.

It is against such a backcloth that the drama of Czechoslovakia was played out. French appeasement in 1938 was warmly embraced by only a few Frenchmen, those who from ideological conviction believed in what Alphonse de Châteaubriant called a 'European salvation through the Teutonic renaissance'.[35] For the rest appeasement was accepted with mixed feelings, a realistic assessment of possibilities in the face of economic stagnation, military unpreparedness, social division. When France came face to face with the prospect of war with Germany again in 1938 all these factors grew in stature. France was not as weak as she believed in the face of the dictators, but the risks of testing her resolve seemed enormous, and we should not ignore them. France was living in an age dominated, according to the writer Simone Weil, by '*le desarroi, l'anxiété*': a disarray that 'touches and corrupts every aspect of life, every source of activity, of hope, of happiness'.[36]

It was this France that Edouard Daladier inherited from the Popular Front when he once again assumed the premiership a few weeks after the *Anschluss* with Austria. His new government was based on a parliamentary alliance that included sections of the right, a loose alliance that forced him to tread with extra political care in the months before Munich. He was a man of great ministerial experience, slow, sombre, almost sullen, with a reputation for energy tempered by an almost pathological indecisiveness. On a speaker's platform he could look almost 'Napoleonic', but his nickname betrayed his weaknesses: 'the bull with snail's horns'. He was the personification of the middle ground of French society, a republican patriot from the petty-bourgeoisie, instinctively on the side of the peasant and small-townsman, a man of strong prejudices, but shrewd judgement. He was a champion of French rearmament, deeply distrustful of communism, but equally hostile to fascism. If he lacked the stature of a Clemenceau or a de Gaulle, he nonetheless brought France back from the crisis of '*desarroi*' to a position in 1939 where Germany could once again be confronted with honour.

Not even Daladier could do this in 1938. When Hitler turned to Czechoslovakia in the spring of 1938, the French were at last called to account for that network of alliances made in the 1920s with the Versailles states. Though the French Ambassador in Prague could assure the Czech President Beneš in April that France 'would always be faithful to her word',[37] the mood in Paris was much more pessimistic about saving her ally. It was by no means clear that France would be in a position to be both willing and capable of helping Czechoslovakia. Daladier was prepared to fight Germany if the Czech state were actually invaded, but in practice made every effort to secure a settlement that would prevent German invasion. The Chief of Staff, General Gamelin, had already declared in April that it was impossible to give effective military assistance to Czechoslovakia.[38] When Daladier visited London on 27 April, it was already clear that neither Britain nor France was prepared to take the lead in the Czech problem for fear of being drawn into war by the other. By a process of elimination it was agreed that pressure should be put on the Czechs to make concessions. Though Beneš could never quite bring himself to believe that the French would abandon their allies, France had been gradually withdrawing from an active role in Eastern Europe for some time. French capital was in flight not only from Popular Front France but from the insecure economies of the East which were gravitating inexorably towards Berlin. As the crisis deepened French leaders were mainly united in the view that, given France's domestic situation and the determination of the British to abandon the Czechs, the retreat from Eastern Europe should continue. On 17 July the French Foreign Minister cast the Czechs adrift. 'France', he told the Czech Ambassador, 'would not go to war for the Sudeten affair.'[39] Two months later the French government co-operated with the British in forcing Beneš to accept an ultimatum agreeing to the cession of the Sudeten territories to Germany.

This was not an honourable course, though it was an understandable one. Daladier faced throughout the crisis from April to September serious limitations on his freedom of action. Some of these were military in character. Gamelin spelt out early in 1938, in a memorandum reminiscent of British justifications for appeasement, the sheer range of strategic difficulties faced by France. The army was not yet trained for an offensive against Germany, neither was the Maginot Line complete or manned. French interests around the world were threatened, not merely in Eastern Europe. Nothing should be done to alienate Italy lest Mussolini should tear apart what Daladier called 'the seam between the two zones' of France's Empire. In the Far East the French Empire was threatened by Japan without, and communist agitation within. These views were echoed by military leaders throughout the year. General Requin, appointed to lead French forces against the Reich if war should come, mournfully contemplated 'the death of a race'; and General Vuillemin, head of the French air force, never veered from his assertion that his air force would be 'wiped out in a few days'.[40] Though the threat of German air power was exaggerated, it had a powerful effect on French opinion at the time. Daladier was warned again and again that war with Germany in 1938 would mean the destruction of Paris through a cruel bombardment. The French intelligence service told Daladier on the very day of Munich that the Germans had 6500 aircraft of the very latest type ready to fly (almost four times the true number). Guy La Chambre, Daladier's Air Minister, told the American Ambassador that 'the safest place for the next two years in France would be a trench.'[41]

The other limitations were domestic. French rearmament was renewed again in April 1938, with a big increase in the allocation to the air force, but slow progress was made because of shortages of skilled labour (exacerbated by the forty-hour week and *le semaine de deux dimanches*) and shortages of raw materials and modern factory space. 'Stagflation' had taken its toll of French industrial efficiency and French trade. Rearmament with modern weapons had a high price. In 1938 France was already spending more than two and a half times what she had spent on the military in 1913. Daladier was as well aware as Chamberlain that appeasement would buy time to complete rearmament. But the other issue was public opinion. It was the view of the British Ambassador in Paris that 'All that is best in France is against war, almost at any cost.'[42] The unfortunate thing was that the only party *for* war, the communists, was the party Daladier deeply distrusted, and the right hated. In June 1938 Maurice Thorez, the communist leader, publicly explained communist support for the Czechs: 'The Czechs are dear to us . . . because they are also the associates of the great Soviet people.'[43] It was widely agreed that only bolshevism would profit from another war in Europe; the contradiction in French nationalism born in response to the Popular Front lived on until Munich.

The desire to avoid war was identified most closely with Georges Bonnet, the man Daladier chose as his Foreign Minister in April 1938. Bonnet was very different from Daladier; a highly educated,

Exploiting the popular fear of the bomber: a poster demanding improved defences from the Daladier government.

experienced politician, he was necessary to Daladier to maintain his centrist coalition in the Chamber. He was a realist whose views of foreign policy were pragmatic and insular. He it was who urged appeasement on Daladier at every opportunity, and who worked closely with the Chamberlain group in London, for whom he proved a fortunate ally in the French camp. He was trusted by no one, neither his own officials, nor Daladier, nor the British. His desire for accommodation with Germany, his 'realistic' view of European unity might have made him a hero in the 1960s, and almost made him one in 1938 when all those afraid of war, pacifists and internationalists, peasants with memories of the slaughter, bourgeois frightened of the prospect of communism, rallied behind the Bonnet view of the Czechs. Had Daladier wanted war in 1938, such sentiments were a compelling constraint; they are echoed in the words of Sartre's hero, Mathieu: 'These fellows are right. . . . Their fathers were responsible for a fantastic massacre, and for the last twenty years they have been told that war doesn't pay. Well, can they be expected to shout: "To Berlin!"?'[44]

Daladier allowed himself one moment of hesitation. On 25 September he finally refused to accept the timetable for German occupation demanded by Hitler at his meeting with Chamberlain at Bad Godesberg. If Germany attacked Czechoslovakia to extract its demands Daladier said that France 'intended to go to war'.[45] What had seemed at one time a sensible policy of concession by the Czechs now appeared as an international humiliation for France. The French Cabinet was divided, but Daladier was not prepared to allow 'the immediate entry of thirty German divisions . . . for this will mean war'.[46] French military preparations began: the blackout was ordered, railway stations removed their nameplates, reservists were called up. On 26 September General Gamelin flew to London to discuss Franco-British plans for immediate action against Germany. Whether Daladier would in the end have carried his Cabinet colleagues, the Chamber and the country into a war with Germany remains uncertain. For the necessity of doing so was removed when Chamberlain secured Hitler's agreement to a four-power conference at Munich. Daladier had no choice but to follow suit, since France could not contemplate confronting Hitler alone. His journey to Munich, with Bonnet pointedly left behind in Paris, was a humiliating journey to Canossa. The British had failed to give France firm support for fear of encouraging French bellicosity; but France needed that support to confront Hitler convincingly. Daladier had no stick with which to beat the British, and found himself, hostile, taciturn, unsmiling, sitting with Chamberlain to sign away the only genuinely democratic state in Eastern Europe.

The episode profoundly affected Daladier; the overwhelming desire to avoid its repetition recurred throughout the year that led to route,war. In France Munich brought a great outburst of relief. Léon Blum admitted that he was 'divided between a feeling of shame and cowardly relief'. André Gide confided to his journal the view that Munich was 'reason winning a victory over force'.[47] Bonnet returned to his constituency at Périgueux to be plied with flowers and cries of '*vive Bonnet*', '*merci Bonnet*'. The dignitaries of the town hoped to name a street '*Septembre 30*' in memory of Munich.[48] But there were voices of dissent. The communists called Munich 'a triumph of class selfishness'; on the right of his own party Daladier was faced with growing hostility. Even as the enthusiastic crowds cheered their returning leaders French nationalists awoke to the damage Munich had done to French prestige and reputation abroad. When Daladier himself arrived back at Le Bourget airport he was astounded to find his way lined with ecstatic men and women rejoicing at peace. 'The blind fools,' was his bitter reaction.

Daladier's options throughout the Czech crisis had been impossibly narrow. Munich was an outcome he would have done much to avoid if he could. The result was to leave France and French security in a worse position than ever. In two years French ascendancy had been utterly overturned. Her Eastern alliances were exposed as worthless; the Soviet Union was alienated by the sacrifice of Czechoslovakia; Italy assumed a growing arrogance in her relations with France; and France herself was forced, much against Daladier's will, to follow the British 'governess' without any real promise of reciprocal help if French security were threatened. France was now faced with an unenviable choice: either to accept German domination and to reach close ties with Hitler, or to put Munich behind her and accept the prospect of war. France, said Daladier, had to choose 'between a slow decline or a renaissance through effort'.[49]

In the weeks following Munich French politics was plunged once again into confusion as the stark choice was contemplated. Daladier well knew that 'effort' meant confronting not just Hitler, but the continuing economic and social crisis. Without solving that the effort would crumble. Bonnet, supported by others on the right, was all for accommodation with Germany, capitalising on the soothing words Hitler and Ribbentrop now used towards France. Daladier had run away from confrontation now twice in his career: once in 1934 faced with riots outside the Chamber; again in 1938 faced with an unruly Hitler. The path of accommodation, of *facilité* must have seemed overwhelmingly inviting in October 1938. It is still not altogether clear why Daladier did not take it; but in a mass rally in Marseilles he chose the moment to announce that he was going by another route, the way of *fermeté*, of firmness, the way he had wanted to go instinctively since April 1938: '*J'ai choisi mon chemin; la France, en avant!*'[50]*

His was not the easy route; the conflict between *Munichois* and *bellicistes*, between appeasers and advocates of firmness, did not disappear. Daladier himself was no warmonger, but he would not accommodate Hitler and he would no longer tolerate the politics of stalemate. He recognised clearly that to be strong abroad it was necessary to be strong at home. This meant facing the solutions of the Popular Front head on. The political alliance had already broken apart before Munich, but communist support for war in September made their isolation complete. Daladier attacked the communists, winning increasing support from the right as he did so and permitting the reformation of the traditional nationalist bloc. The attack on communism was completed by a frontal assault on the social achievements of the Popular Front. The forty-hour week was already weakened before Munich; from October Daladier insisted that the forty-hour week would have to go. In November he took on the unions and the Communist Party. By a series of special decree laws, passed without reference to Parliament, public works were abandoned in favour of rearmament, taxation was sharply raised, civil servants were sacked to help balance the budget, and the forty-hour week was overturned and Saturday working resumed. The changes were announced by Daladier's new Finance Minister, Paul Reynaud. His appointment had a significance of its own, for Reynaud was a leading *belliciste*, who had tried to resign over Munich. He was a staunch anti-communist and a French nationalist of the centre. His was the stance Daladier now wished to promote.

Reynaud's task was not only to destroy the legacy of the Popular Front; it was his responsibility to get the stagnant French economy going as well. In a broadcast on 12 November Reynaud told his fellow countrymen the truth about their economy: 'We are going blindfold towards an abyss.' He ordered a vast increase in rearmament spending, four times the level of 1938, 93 billion francs against 29 billion. The country's finances and industrial effort were directed entirely to putting France on to a war footing. The effect, far from frightening France's capitalists, was the exact reverse. The franc stabilised; money began to pour back into France from abroad; trade

* 'I have chosen my path; forward with France!'

revived; a stream of modern machine tools flowed across the Atlantic. After ten years of slow decline French industry began to answer Daladier's call for 'effort'.[51] Not everything could be done at once; and nothing could be achieved if the government failed to convince labour to co-operate. Yet the reaction to the Reynaud reforms was immediate confrontation. On 30 November the unions and the Communist Party called a general strike. But this time the outcome was very different from 1936. Public employees were placed under emergency powers and ordered to stay at their posts. Police and troops were drafted into Paris. The unions hesitated and split. When the strike came on the 30th it was a dismal failure. Only 2 per cent of the railway workers came out. Elsewhere strikers were sacked. The Renault works were occupied as they had been in June 1936, but this time there was no dancing and pageantry. Daladier ordered the *gardes mobiles* to disperse the strikers with tear gas.[52]

The Popular Front era ended in violence as it had begun. Firm government won Daladier the enthusiastic support of the centre and the right, divided his own party and alienated much of the left. Daladier was not entirely at home with his new political allies, nor they with him, but he knew that the rallying of patriotic forces, including the nationalists of the left as well as the right, would require the temporary sacrifice of social justice or even civil rights. And after the general strike public opinion did begin to move in Daladier's direction. Despite the noisy greeting for Munich, an opinion poll taken shortly afterwards showed that 70 per cent favoured the view that France and Britain should stand up to Hitler next time. Thirty-seven per cent of those polled opposed Munich. By June 1939 76 per cent favoured going to war if Germany tried to seize Danzig by force from Poland.[53] Somehow Daladier had succeeded in producing a consensus of sorts between the *bellicistes* of the left and the nationalists of the right, without which firmness in foreign policy would have been impossible. Simone Weil detected a quite different mood among Frenchmen in 1939: 'Today there is almost nothing else in their minds but the Nation.'[54]

That there was a nationalist revival in France in 1939 is not in doubt. But Frenchmen were still divided over their view of what the nation was. Daladier's nationalism was the traditional republican brand: 'I am the son of a worker, and I am a patriot.'[55] For the left the nation was for liberty and against fascism; for the nationalists of the right France was still historic France, the France of Joan of Arc and Napoleon, and most, though not all, were anti-German and anti-Italian. These different versions of nation were linked by the fact that both Italy and Germany were fascist powers: to oppose

Hitler and Mussolini was to defend the working class and to defend *la belle France* at the same time. But the nationalist revival owed as much to the government's willingness to combat the French Communist Party, whose role under the Popular Front had so alarmed the French right. Daladier placed every restriction on the communists, closed their newspapers, harassed communist politicians. The retreat of domestic communism coincided with its final defeat in Spain in May 1939. Victory for the nationalists there was hailed by the French right as a triumph in the international conflict with communism. Freed from this anxiety it was now possible to turn to the pressing question of French survival as a great power. Government propaganda stressed the revival of French military strength, the unity of the Empire, the evil nature of the German regime. Italian calls for the return of Tunisia, Corsica and Nice stirred up a fierce anti-Italian feeling across all sections of the population in 1939. Fear of Germany and hatred of Italy produced a patriotic response that united Frenchmen who on other issues remained divided.[56]

The revival should not be exaggerated; there was still a great deal of confusion and demoralisation in France in 1939 as well. Weil's 'anxiety' continued to coexist with the nationalism. Peasants continued to cheer the defenders of Munich, so anxious were they to avoid the killing fields again. The prominent pro-German appeasers of the right argued their case right up to the outbreak of war and beyond. The conflict between collaborators and resisters was born long before Vichy. But for the moment French patriotism had replaced political decadence. The ordinary Frenchman did not welcome war, but he welcomed Hitler less.

Even patriots realised that France could not make her 'effort' alone. Yet in the aftermath of Munich France found herself as isolated as ever. Though reasonably confident of British collaboration the French could never be sure that Britain would not leave France in the lurch to face Germany on her own. The myth of *la perfide Albion* died hard in French political circles. Daladier himself had the lowest opinion of the British ruling classes. He told the American Ambassador that he 'fully expected to be betrayed by the British. . . . he considered Chamberlain a dessicated [*sic*] stick; the King a moron; and the Queen an excessively ambitious woman. . . . he felt that England had become so feeble and senile that the British would give away every possession of their friends rather than stand up to Germany and Italy.'[57] No doubt Daladier was letting off steam; but French leaders were deeply worried that Britain would reach a settlement with the dictators at her expense. The British in their turn were deeply hostile towards the French, whose country, Chamberlain thought, 'never can keep a secret for more than half an hour, nor a government for more than nine months'.[58] British hostility had been fuelled in the 1920s by French intransigence over Versailles; in the 1930s it was fuelled by fear of communism and disorder in France. What kept alive the anaemic entente was the common commitment to democracy and common fears for empire. On the French side there was another factor; they knew that without the economic and financial and military assistance of Britain there was no hope whatsoever of facing up to Hitler. 'We could only defeat Germany in a war', wrote the War Ministry in April 1939, 'if we were assured, in every possible respect, of total British assistance.'[59]

The greatest achievement of Daladier in 1939 was to win from the British a firm commitment. In November 1938 Chamberlain had refused Daladier's request for joint staff talks. But in January the French intelligence services fed to London rumours that Hitler was about to launch a pre-emptive strike against Britain. There were hints that France might leave her to face the Germans unassisted; Bonnet's policy of pursuing German friendship, though not endorsed by Daladier, gave the British the impression that secret diplomacy was leaving them vulnerable and isolated. The air of uncertainty surrounding French intentions forced Chamberlain's hand. On 6 February he made the commitment Daladier was waiting for: 'The solidarity that unites France and Britain is such that any threat to the vital interests of France must bring about the co-operation of Great Britain.'[60] Staff talks were initiated on 13 February, though they did not begin serious military planning until April. The French wanted more than this however. If Hitler were to be denied a free hand in the east, which would swing the balance of power entirely in his favour, Britain would have to give guarantees not only to France but to her allies in Eastern Europe. This the British had never done. The German occupation of rump Czechoslovakia came at just the time that Daladier was forcing the British hand on Eastern Europe. If there were any lingering doubts about German intentions and the necessity for Anglo-French collaboration, they were laid to rest at Prague. In the next month Chamberlain gave the guarantee to Poland, a similar guarantee to Roumania, and committed Britain to conscription. Daladier was far from happy with the Polish guarantee, for he had not forgiven the Poles for helping themselves to Czech territory during the Munich crisis. Though there existed a Franco-Polish alliance from the 1920s, France had distanced herself from Poland after the Poles signed the pact with Germany in 1934. But for Daladier Poland was important not for herself – the military knew that France could give the Poles little serious military assistance – but because she had helped to cement the entente with Britain.[61]

Daladier was unhappy about the Polish guarantee for another reason: it would make more difficult the second strand of his diplomacy, an alliance with the Soviet Union. As it became clear in April 1939 that Germany was now preparing to do to Poland what had been done all too recently to the Czechs, French leaders made every effort to find some way of getting a Soviet commitment to help them against Germany, to revive, at the last hour, the old entente of 1914. There were difficulties to be overcome, for the right still disliked talking with communism, and the French generals were doubtful of the value of Soviet military assistance. But Daladier and Bonnet both shared the view that if the Soviet Union could be brought in, Hitler would not risk a fight over Poland. At the centre of French firmness was the desire to deter Hitler if they could, rather than fight him. Faced with a determined coalition of the other great powers of Europe, it seemed inconceivable that Hitler would risk conflict. Intelligence from Berlin suggested that the German economy was in deep crisis, and that Hitler was facing mounting political opposition. Much of this turned out to be wishful thinking, but it is easy to see why French leaders, with a reviving economy, a massive increase in military spending, a firm commitment from Britain and hope of one from Russia saw themselves back in the position of the 1920s, able to dictate to Germany from a position of strength.

Much was indeed illusion. The strong fears the French had had about the Polish guarantee proved to be a real stumbling block with the Soviet Union. When military talks began with Soviet leaders in August 1939 the key issue rapidly became whether or not Poland would allow the passage of Soviet troops through Polish territory in her defence. The Poles were adamant: not a single Soviet soldier would be allowed on to Polish soil. Bonnet and Daladier made frantic efforts to force the Poles' hand, efforts which had everything in common with the efforts made with Beneš in 1938. The French could not understand the stubbornness of the Poles, for whom Soviet help seemed a lifeline. But at the height of the delicate negotiations with the Soviet Union, on 19 August Beck, the Polish Foreign Minister, rejected Soviet help: 'We have not got a military agreement with the USSR. We do not want to have one.'[62] Daladier telegraphed frantically to the head of the visiting mission in Moscow, General Doumenc, asking him to sign anything he could with the Russians. It was all to no avail; the Soviet Union had been secretly negotiating with Hitler's Germany and had kept the talks with France going only to pressure the Germans into making concessions. On 23 August the Nazi–Soviet Pact was agreed, and the idea of the Franco-British–Soviet bloc collapsed.

Daladier found himself facing in August 1939 the same dilemma he had faced a year earlier. Bonnet urged him to force the Poles to give Danzig to the Germans. Daladier hoped that at the last a reasonable settlement could be reached that would satisfy Germany but would not humble France. But of one thing he was determined: if Germany invaded Poland France would fight, Russian help or not. He did not relish the conflict but France was in a much stronger position than a year before. The Empire, long neglected by Paris, had been rallied to the cause of the motherland by the energetic and *belliciste* Minister of Colonies, Georges Mandel. He doubled the colonial army in twelve months, set up armaments works in Indo-China, organised the resources of the Empire for the war effort, and launched a propaganda campaign at home under the slogan '110 million strong, France can stand up to Germany.'[63] France had carefully cultivated the United States as well, and now a stream of aircraft and supplies bought with French gold was reinforcing the French war effort, and would restore the balance with Germany by early 1940.[64]

By September 1939 British and French aircraft output and tank output exceeded that of Germany. By May 1940 French monthly production alone was as great as German, rather over 600 aircraft per month. In addition France was being supplied with 170 aircraft a month by the United States. In terms of quality the new generation of French combat aircraft, the Dewoitine 520, the Morane-Saulnier 406 and the Bloch 152, were the equal of their German or British counterparts. By May 1940 4360 modern aircraft had been produced. German strength before the battle of France was 3270 aircraft of all types. In tank construction the French enjoyed both a qualitative and a quantitative advantage. By May 1940 the French had built 4188 modern tanks with a gross weight of over 60,000 tons. The Germans had built 3862 with a gross weight of 36,000 tons, though this figure included 1400 of the light Mark I tank which was little more than an armoured car. The French army had concentrated its tanks in northern and eastern France, 3254 against the German 2574. Among the French tanks were over 300 of the formidable *Char B 1 bis*, the best heavy tank in Europe.[65] The French General Staff had the added advantage that they were fighting behind the Maginot Line, which was now fully manned. The confidence in military circles in the autumn of 1939 was based on the solid evidence that France's rearmament effort and defensive strategy would make it very difficult to lose the coming war; with the addition of British forces and American equipment prospects of winning were brighter than at any time in the 1930s. 'We can face the struggle,' Gamelin told Daladier in August, 'we have a respectable parity in equipment.'[66] What French military leaders failed to anticipate was the point of German attack, where the line was most vulnerable, and the tactic of force concentration, pitting the whole of German air and armoured strength in three great columns of attack which splintered the long French line, as Nelson had done at Trafalgar.

On 23 August the National Defence Committee was called together. Bonnet argued that the Poles deserved to be abandoned. Daladier asked the military chiefs for their views. The Air Minister reported that great progress had been made. The navy was on a war footing. The army had a million men under arms already. General Gamelin stated clearly that for France to abandon Poland would be disastrous for French strategy. The French position would then only deteriorate. Gamelin was for war. So too, with great reluctance and heart-searching, was Daladier. He had to face the logic of the '*l'effort du sang*' he had set in motion the year before. He would not give way to Hitler again. On 27 August he told the American Ambassador: 'there was no further question of policy to be settled. His sister had put in two bags all the personal keepsakes and belongings he really cared about, and was prepared to leave for a secure spot at any moment. France intended to stand by the Poles, and if Hitler should refuse to negotiate with the Poles over Danzig, and should make war on Poland, France would fight at once.'[67] The issue was not Poland – for Gamelin had already informed Daladier that France could do little to save the Poles, who would be defeated 'in three months' – but the issue was France and French honour. If France stood aside while Germany gobbled up Poland, France would be reduced, willy-nilly, to the rank of a second-rate power. In the end the terms of the conflict were the same terms they had been in 1914: France or Germany.

There was one final twist to the story. Georges Bonnet, whose presence at the Foreign Office Daladier more and more regretted, made every effort to settle the crisis by diplomacy rather than war, even if it meant accepting German hegemony. The Polish Ambassador in Paris became alarmed that Bonnet was 'preparing a new Munich behind our backs'. There was every sign of this when, apparently at French instigation, Italy proposed a conference on 31 August to settle all outstanding European issues, including Poland. Bonnet grasped at the proposal with both hands. But Daladier and Gamelin suspected a trap. The General was firmly against 'a crushing new Munich'. So, too, was Daladier, though he realised that the *Munichois* would use his refusal to blame him for war. The following day Germany invaded Poland.[68] Daladier explored the prospect of a conference, not because he sought an appeaser's way out, but because the issue of taking his people into war again was an issue so weighty that he did not dare to take it if there remained any prospect of making Hitler see sense. The conference was a chimera. Its collapse signalled the collapse of the politics of *facilité*. On 2 September firmness was in the saddle. General mobilisation was ordered; parliament was recalled and a vote on the ultimatum to Germany and for war credits passed unanimously by both houses. 'Poland', announced Daladier to the Chamber,

> is our ally. These pledges have been confirmed. At the price of our honour we would only buy a precarious peace, which would be revocable, and, when we have to fight tomorrow, after having lost through it the esteem of our allies and other nations, we would only be a wretched nation, sold to defeat and to slavery.[69]

The Chamber stood and cheered his declaration.

Much has been made of the failure of Britain and France to synchronise their declarations of war against Germany. There is no mystery here, no final grasp at the lifeline of appeasement. The French constitution required a formal vote of parliament before any ultimatum could be sent. The Chamber could not be recalled until 2 September at the earliest. Gamelin then insisted that the declaration of war should be postponed if possible for up to forty-eight hours to allow the crucial early stages of mobilisation to take place without the threat of German bombing. Evacuation procedures could be carried out before a formal state of war existed. As the French Ambassador in London, Charles Corbin, reminded the angry British callers at the Embassy that night, France had six million men to call to the colours. Mobilisation meant a real upheaval in France, much more than in Britain. France had its ultimatum, which was sent at 10.20 on the morning of 3 September. War was declared at 5.00 p.m., six hours after Britain, whose ultimatum had been sent earlier to avoid a parliamentary revolt. In the evening Daladier announced the conflict to the nation: Germany 'desires the destruction of Poland, so as to be able to dominate Europe and to enslave France. In rising against the most frightful of tyrannies, in honouring our word, we fight to defend our soil, our homes, our liberties.'[70]

Throughout the last weeks of crisis French leaders, appeasers and non-appeasers alike, hoped for an agreement that would satisfy both

Germany and Poland and would leave France with her security and prestige still intact. There was no such solution, for Hitler had decided that France was too feeble to resist. His version of France was the version of Bonnet, of social conflict, of demoralisation, of decadence; the France of strikes, pacifism and luxury; the France of Jean Cocteau, whose only comment when he heard of the declaration of war was 'How will I get my opium?'[71] What Hitler failed to see was the other France that struggled to the surface slowly and with difficulty during 1939, and which, at the last moment, prevailed enough to carry France to war.

There was something grandly tragic about the French predicament between the wars. In 1939 the French faced Germany fully in the knowledge that war might well mean the defeat and destruction of France. A final surge of rearmament and a Maginot war might avoid defeat, but France could not avoid what seemed to many a bitter destiny, to stand in the very front line against revived Germany. Simone Weil found Frenchmen awaiting the conflict 'passively, like waiting for a tidal wave or an earthquake'.[72] Some Frenchmen refused to accept that this was France's destiny; 'who will die for Danzig?' was heard in Paris in August 1939 competing with Mandel's '110 million strong'. France entered the war divided and anxious, if determined. The American Ambassador watched the soldiers go: 'The men left in silence. There were no bands, no songs. . . . There was no hysterical weeping of mothers, sisters and children. The self-control and quiet courage has been so far beyond the usual standard of the human race that it has had a dream quality.'[73]

There was nothing sentimental about France's road to war. France had been one of the greatest powers in Europe for three centuries; she wished to hold that power a moment longer. For seventy years France had been a republic and a democracy; Frenchmen, most Frenchmen, did not want to lose that either. There was another road, to accept the reality of declining power and German domination. In the 1930s France became a deeply conservative, defensive society, split by social conflict, undermined by a failing and unmodernised economy and an empire in crisis. All these things explain the loss of will and direction in the 1930s. The difficult thing to explain is why France revived, not her decline. For decadent France appeasement was a policy of realism. For France revived, the war with Germany had something of the unreal about it. History was repeating itself. The posters on the walls of Paris in September 1939 echoed the battlecry of the Great War: '*on les aura!*' The armistice was over.

CHAPTER FOUR

ITALY

> the tendency towards imperialism is one of the elementary trends of human nature, an expression of the will to power. Naturally every imperialism has its zenith. Since it is always the creation of exceptional men, it carries within it the seeds of its own decay. Like everything exceptional, it contains ephemeral elements. It may last one or two centuries, or no more than ten years.
>
> (Benito Mussolini, 1932)

On 16 May 1940, Winston Churchill had been British Prime Minister for less than a week. The German armies were pushing deep into France, and the Allies could not halt the advance. He had written candidly to Roosevelt that 'the scene has darkened swiftly . . . the small countries are simply smashed up one by one, like matchwood.' He continued: 'We must assume, though it is not yet certain, that Mussolini will hurry in to share the loot of civilisation.'[1] Italy's position was ambiguous. She was bound to Germany by a Pact of Steel; the two fascist leaders were photographed at ease in each other's company, and Britain was aware of the many discussions which had taken place to engineer Italy's entry into the war on the German side. Yet messages suggesting that Italy should act as a mediator, telegrams hinting that Italy could be 'bought off' by judicious concessions, and would remain neutral, continued to reach the British and French governments from Rome. There had even been tentative negotiations for Italy to supply Britain with arms, which could only have been used against Italy's ally.

The letter which Churchill sent to Rome on 16 May was a final appeal to Mussolini to draw back from commitment to Germany. His sweeping rhetoric appealed to *il duce*'s taste for the grandiloquent. Churchill recalled, 'I look back to our meetings in Rome and feel a desire to speak words of goodwill to you as Chief of the Italian Nation. . . . Is it too late to stop a river of blood flowing between the British and Italian peoples?' He for one 'had never been an enemy of Italian greatness nor ever at heart a foe of the Italian lawgiver'. Churchill concluded, 'Down the ages . . . comes the cry that the joint heirs of Latin and Christian civilisation must not be ranged against one another in mortal strife. Hearken to it, I beseech you.'[2]

In the spring of 1940 Italy faced just the dilemma she had faced in the First World War. Before that conflict too Italy had been formally bound by treaty to Germany, but had joined the war in 1915 on the side of Britain and France because they offered more, and stood a better chance of winning. Once again, in 1940, Italy enjoyed the flattering attentions of both sides. Most Italians favoured peace; Mussolini wanted to profit from the war by joining the winning side at the right time. It was political realism, not ideology, that brought Mussolini to fight with Hitler against Western powers on the point of capitulation. Churchill was repudiated in 1940, as the Germans in 1915, because Britain did not offer enough. Under the broad wings of German expansion, Mussolini hoped to turn Italy at last into a major power.

This was an ambition harboured by Italians long before the coming of war in 1939, long even before 1914. For Italy arrived late on the European scene, in a Europe already dominated by established great powers. Only in October 1870 had Rome become the new capital of the modern Italian state. The city was a uniquely potent symbol of national unity; it provided a visible and physical link between the new Italy and the past glories of the Roman Empire, whose history Italian children learned from their first days at school. For nationalists, like Mazzini and Garibaldi, Imperial Rome was a source of political inspiration. Mazzini talked of creating a new 'Rome of the People', the lineal descendant of the 'Rome of the Emperors' and the 'Rome of the Popes'. Late in his life, Garibaldi adopted the Roman eagle, the most potent image of the former empire as a 'symbol [no longer] of conquest but of work, progress, and civilisation'.[3]

The civilising mission of the new Rome was carried wherever Italians settled or migrated. By the 1880s they had scattered throughout Europe, North Africa and the Levant. Each year more than 300,000 left Italy, but many retained their national identity and their links with the mother country. Port cities like Tunis, Beirut or Tripoli became quasi-colonies, with Italians far outnumbering all other Europeans. They spread farther into Africa, down the shores of the Red Sea. Italy had colonists but lacked an empire. This lack was felt acutely; without imperial possessions Italy could never hope to join the exalted club of great powers. Italy needed colonies, it was argued, for sound practical reasons. Her population was increasing rapidly; over six million Italians emigrated between 1870 and 1910, lost to the motherland. Colonies would soak up Italy's surplus population, and strengthen Italy's international position and her economy. The natural, historic area for empire was that of the first Rome, the Mediterranean and Africa.

Italy's first faltering steps to imperial status followed the tracks of Italian migrants and traders down the Red Sea to the Horn of Africa. This was one of the few remaining areas of the world not yet claimed for the old European empires. Promoters of Italian empire held out the prospect of 'Vast zones of colonisable land', which 'offer themselves . . . to the exuberant fecundity of Italy'. In 1890 the colony of Eritrea was established. Beyond in the African hinterland lay the independent empire of Abysinnia, present-day Ethiopia. It was on this that Italian eyes turned. The Prime Minister, Francesco Crispi, urged on his countrymen to pursue empire for 'the dignity of our country and the interests of civilisation. . . . now we are in Rome we must create a new world. . . .'[4]

Yet Italian imperialism led not to glory but to national humiliation. The highland people of Ethiopia had already protested against Italian incursions in Eritrea and in 1887 massacred five hundred Italians. When Italian forces pressed further into Ethiopian territory, war ensued. In 1896 Menelik, Emperor of Ethiopia, attacked the advancing Italians at the town of Adowa. In a matter of hours he destroyed the colonial army in Africa of 25,000, of whom 6000 were Italian and the remainder *askaris*, native soldiers. Those Italians unlucky enough to be captured by the Ethiopians were castrated, while the *askaris*, whom the Ethiopians considered traitors, had their right hands and left feet hacked off. This 'barbarism' fed back into Italy's political mythology; a generation later, in 1935, Mussolini remarked that British statesmen had plainly been 'got at by the Ethiopians'. After 1896, Italians looked on the Ethiopians as savages, who should be taught a lesson.

The humiliation of Adowa stopped Italian expansion in its tracks. Not until 1911 did Italy return to the scramble for empire, when a war broke out between the crumbling Ottoman Empire and Italy over control of the one remaining part of the North African coast, Tripolitania, not under the British or French flag. This was a war Italian nationalists were confident Italy could win. But the outcome was almost a disaster again. Turkish resistance was fierce. By 1912 there were 100,000 Italian troops in North Africa; 3000 Italians died. When the Turks abandoned the conflict Italy controlled only a small coastal strip. But the outcome was, unlike Adowa, indisputably a victory. Fifty years after the founding of Italy, an empire was at last created on the Mediterranean shore. The triumph in Libya, as the new colony was called, created a sense of national confidence. Italy had been obsessed since the founding of the new state with a sense of national inferiority, as 'the least of the great powers'; victory in Libya permitted Italians to pursue the elusive status forfeited at Adowa.[5]

But in practice the war in Libya had exposed the limitations of Italian power. The victory almost paralysed the Italian army. Some units were down to half their effective strength, and by the end of the short campaign Italy had thrown almost all her most modern equipment – including machine-gun units and aircraft – into a colonial war. By November 1912 the Chief of Staff, General Alberto Pollio, was forced to admit to his country's German ally that Italy could no longer fulfil her military alliance obligations in Europe. When war broke out in 1914 Italy's military weakness gave her the opportunity to abstain from the conflict. Italy became neutral, but quietly solicited offers for her intervention. Italian foreign policy displayed a crude opportunism. The pressures of war put Italy in a strong bargaining position and flattered her pretensions to be taken seriously by the warring states. In 1915 in the Treaty of London the Western Allies succeeded in offering Italy enough to make intervention tempting: a strip of territory on the eastern coast of the Adriatic, a string of Mediterranean islands and the promise of large tracts of the Ottoman Empire. These concessions echoed the demands of Italy's more ambitious imperialists and nationalists that Italy should become the major power in the Mediterranean basin, securing an empire for Italians at the expense of Arabs, Greeks and Slavs.

The Italian Prime Minister, Salandra, described Italy's policy as *sacro egoismo*, a sacred egoism. Yet there was nothing unique about Italian ambitions. Italy shared with all the states of Europe the belief in the necessity of empire, of racial conquest, of a system dominated by the interests of the great powers. It was the manifest benefits that such a status bestowed that made Italians so anxious to achieve it. When the war ended with the Western powers victorious Italy was determined to claim her birthright, all the concessions promised in the Treaty of London, without compromise. Italy sat at the Conference of Versailles as one of the big four, side by side with Britain, France and the United States. She used her position to obstruct at every turn attempts to deny her what had been promised by Britain at a moment of great peril four years before. While Versailles preached self-determination and international justice, Italian leaders still worked in the idiom of spoils and spheres of influence, the language of diplomacy when the war broke out. Now Italian help was no longer needed, her erstwhile allies treated Italian claims with disdain and outright hostility. The Permanent Under-Secretary at the British Foreign Office, Sir Charles Hardinge, voiced a wide-spread prejudice when he described the Italians as 'the most odious colleagues and Allies to have at a Conference . . . the "beggars of Europe" are well known for their whining alternated by truculence.'[6] When it became plain to the Italian Prime Minister, Emanuele Orlando, that Italy was not to be given what she had been promised he stormed out of the Conference. The Italian delegation only returned to sign the Treaty later in the year.

The issue that most incensed Italian opinion was the port of Fiume at the head of the Adriatic Sea, widely regarded as an Italian city though ruled by the Austrian Empire until 1918. The Conference hoped to give it to the new Yugoslav state. When Orlando protested, Woodrow Wilson retorted: 'I know the Italian people better than you do!'[7] He was wrong: the issue united Italians where intervention in the war had divided them. The failure to give Italy what was promised created what Italian nationalists called 'the mutilated peace'. Italy's humiliating treatment at the Conference evoked a powerful nationalist reaction in Italy. In September 1919 the poet, Gabriele D'Annunzio, led a thousand war-veterans from Italy's crack troops, the *arditi*, to occupy Fiume and seize it for Italy by force. The adventure stirred Italian memories of Garibaldi and the Thousand who had fought to unite Italy sixty years before. Despite widespread condemnation D'Annunzio stayed put; in 1924 the powers agreed to allow Italy to keep Fiume. Force triumphed over discussion. Italian nationalism provoked the first violent revision of Versailles.[8]

Italian nationalism grew with the crisis over the First World War. It was a potent ingredient in the political instability that confronted the Italian state when the war was over. The experience of modern war was a harsh one. Italy lost 460,000 dead and many more wounded and disabled. Large numbers of Italians had been moved from the villages and small towns to work in the arms factories of the north, or to fight, poorly trained and with inadequate weaponry, to keep Austria out of Italy. It was difficult for them to return to traditional civilian life; many veterans experienced a bitter sense of rejection, of not belonging to the older Italy. This disillusionment fed into Italian politics. At the end of the war Italy faced economic chaos and political crisis. Heavily in debt, the Italian economy was debilitated by budget deficits, a chronic balance of payments crisis and rising inflation. The resulting social tensions threatened to make Italy ungovernable. The socialist movement, strengthened by the demand for labour during the war, became for the first time a major parliamentary force, while the unions encouraged direct action and the occupation of the factories. The countryside was the arena for a different kind of class war, between landless and landed. The returning soldiers had not fought for Italy only to abandon her to the international revolution. Bands of veterans, sporting uniforms, organised themselves to resist the socialists. By 1920 Italian politics was carried violently on to the streets.

One man personified this nationalist revolt: Benito Mussolini, leader of one of the largest of the veterans' organisations, the *fasci di combattimento*, the Fascists. Once a socialist himself, the son of a radical peasant from the Romagna, Mussolini was turned by the war into an ardent nationalist. He fought at the front, where he was wounded on a training exercise in 1917. Invalided out of the army, he plunged himself into the forefront of radical right-wing politics. He was a far cry from the traditional conservative political circles that still dominated Italian politics. His socialism made him a natural rebel; his nationalism was a popular people's nationalism, dedicated to overthrowing what he viewed as the spineless and corrupt parliamentary regime and creating a new vigorous, authoritarian Italy, run not by the old political ruling class of aristocrats and political hacks, but by a movement of the masses. Fascism found its support among the peasants, shopkeepers and petty-bourgeois frightened of socialism but disillusioned with Italy's conservative heritage. The movement was led by veterans and political romantics; it thrived on its image as a violent, exciting force, pledged to save Italy from communism and revive the nation.

In the crisis years of the post-war period Fascism took root. Its radical temper matched the mood of a population increasingly uncertain about what direction Italy was taking. But Fascism had to compete with other claims on mass support, the socialists and communists, and a new christian democratic *Popolari* party, and at first it did so poorly. In the 1921 elections the socialists and *Popolari* were the two largest parties: Fascism, now organised as the Fascist Party (PNF), secured only thirty-five seats in parliament, 7 per cent of the total. Although its reputation as a violent, street-based movement might win it local support from worried businessmen and farmers, it made it less attractive as a national political party. It was also a movement divided against itself. Mussolini succeeded through a combination of political cunning and force of personality to emerge as the undisputed head of the movement in 1921, but he was always aware of powerful rivals within its ranks. By 1922 the movement gathered pace; the threat from communism receded, and Fascism took the credit; Fascist power-brokers were entrenched in local government; Mussolini became the focus for the continuing discontent with the economic crisis and the feebleness of parliamentary rule.

There were the ingredients here for an obvious compromise. Mussolini wanted a national platform for the movement and for himself; the old ruling class, its grip on Italian politics rapidly loosening, looked for social alliances which would give them a foothold in the new age of mass politics. In the May 1921 elections the first signs of an alliance between old conservatism and new nationalism were evident. During 1922 the links became closer. In the endless arguments over parliamentary coalitions, a constant merry-go-round of governments, the prospect of an alliance with Fascism, an unknown force with a strong nationalist character and a mass following, grew more inviting. In October 1922 the King agreed, at the prompting of conservative statesmen, to ask Mussolini to form a government. Against even his own expectations, the peasant's son became the new ruler of Italy.

A typical British cartoon of Mussolini from 1938.

Benito Mussolini later claimed that an old Italy of sloth and incompetence had been swept away in a tide of Fascist dynamism after his 'seizure of power' in October 1922. Fascism was popular because it sought to fulfil the long-standing national aspirations of

Italy – for a new empire and a place of honour in the world. Mussolini promised direct action not negotiation. In 1922 he wrote: 'today in Italy is not the time for history. Nothing is yet concluded. It is the time for myths. Everything is to be done. Only the myth can give the strength and energy to a people about to hammer out its own destiny.'[9] It was what many Italians, except those on the left, wanted to hear. The first myth was that the Fascists had marched like an invading army on Rome, and 'seized power' from the nerveless hands of the old politicians. Mussolini wrote the first lines of this melodrama when he met the King to be appointed Prime Minister. Still wearing his Fascist black shirt (rather than the frock coat normal for royal audiences), he announced to Victor Emmanuel III, 'Majesty, I come from the battlefield – fortunately bloodless.'[10] He had in fact arrived on the overnight train.

Although the external elements of Italian Fascism – uniforms, mass parades, grandiloquent architecture – were replicated in Hitler's Germany, there were marked differences between the two totalitarian states. The Fascist Party entered power with only four seats in the Cabinet, although these ministries controlled the key levers of power. But the armed forces remained loyal to the monarchy, and Mussolini never attained the complete grasp of Italian society that Hitler later exercised in Germany. Nor did he have the same undisputed control over the PNF that Hitler achieved over the Nazi Party; rivals were pushed to the margins, or sent to the colonies; there was no mass-bloodletting like the Night of the Long Knives in Germany. Rather than 'seizing power' the Fascists eased themselves into control of the state, and their rule was never wholly secure.

The second and more complex myth concerned the impact of Fascism on Italian society. The official version was that Fascism *transformed* Italy. In the celebrations of the tenth anniversary of the March on Rome and the seizure of power, Mussolini declared to a huge crowd in Milan: 'the twentieth century will be the century of Fascism. It will be the century of Italian power; it will be the century in which Italy will return for the third time to be the leader of human civilization.'[11] In 1932 Italy was declared 'fascistised'. The process had been a slow one. Mussolini had initially shared power with his conservative sponsors. A multi-party system existed in name, although Fascist deputies crowded the benches of parliament after a new electoral law gave them the bulk of the seats. But as the Fascist movement gathered further support, attacked its enemies and repressed all serious opposition, the regime assumed a more dictatorial character. After 1926, the 'Napoleonic Year of Fascism' as Mussolini put it, all associations, political parties and public bodies were brought under the control of the state. Socialist, communist and liberal opponents were imprisoned or exiled. Newspapers and journalists were gagged, while anti-Fascists who had fled abroad were deprived of their citizenship. Local government was placed under the authority of Fascist prefects, and in July all local elections were abolished. On 3 April the trade union movement was, euphemistically, 'brought into alignment with the doctrines of Fascism'. In its place the Fascist movement embarked on the experiment of the 'corporative state', integrating labour and management into Fascist corporations, organisations designed to impose social order and replace the political conflicts of the age of classes.

Fascism succeeded in attracting more support as it became more authoritarian, partly through careful alliance with other powerful groups in Italian society, the Catholic Church, big business, the monarchy and court, and partly through its manifest success in bringing political stability of a kind, and an economic revival. Mussolini won the confidence of Italian businessmen by placing men they could trust in charge of economic policy. Economic revival was essential to Fascism's political survival. Mussolini did not gamble with the economy, but used the power of the state to create a secure environment in which orthodox policies could work effectively. Between 1922 and 1929 the budgets were balanced, agriculture expanded, industry more than doubled its output, and the balance of payments deficit was halved. Fascism promised modernisation without social crisis. It brought a different style to Italian politics, strident and populist. The successes of the regime were trumpeted through a propaganda machine that helped ordinary Italians to identify with the goals of the movement, and with Mussolini in particular. He became *il duce*, the leader. Loudspeakers in the streets relayed his speeches to his people. Fascism became a way of life for a great many Italians. At the cost of civil rights and political freedom, Mussolini succeeded in creating a 'Fascist' consensus in Italian politics.

Mussolini depended on the projection of a strong propaganda image, as the saviour and defender of the new Italy. He preached a politics of 'dynamism', in which the regime gave an impression of constant movement, initiative and drive, even if the reality was sometimes rather different. He was what the Futurist artist Marinetti called 'a mystic of action'.[12] The propaganda of 'dynamism' was an end in itself in securing political support, and creating the image of a radical movement prepared to confront issues rather

THE NEW ROMAN EMPIRE, 1912-40

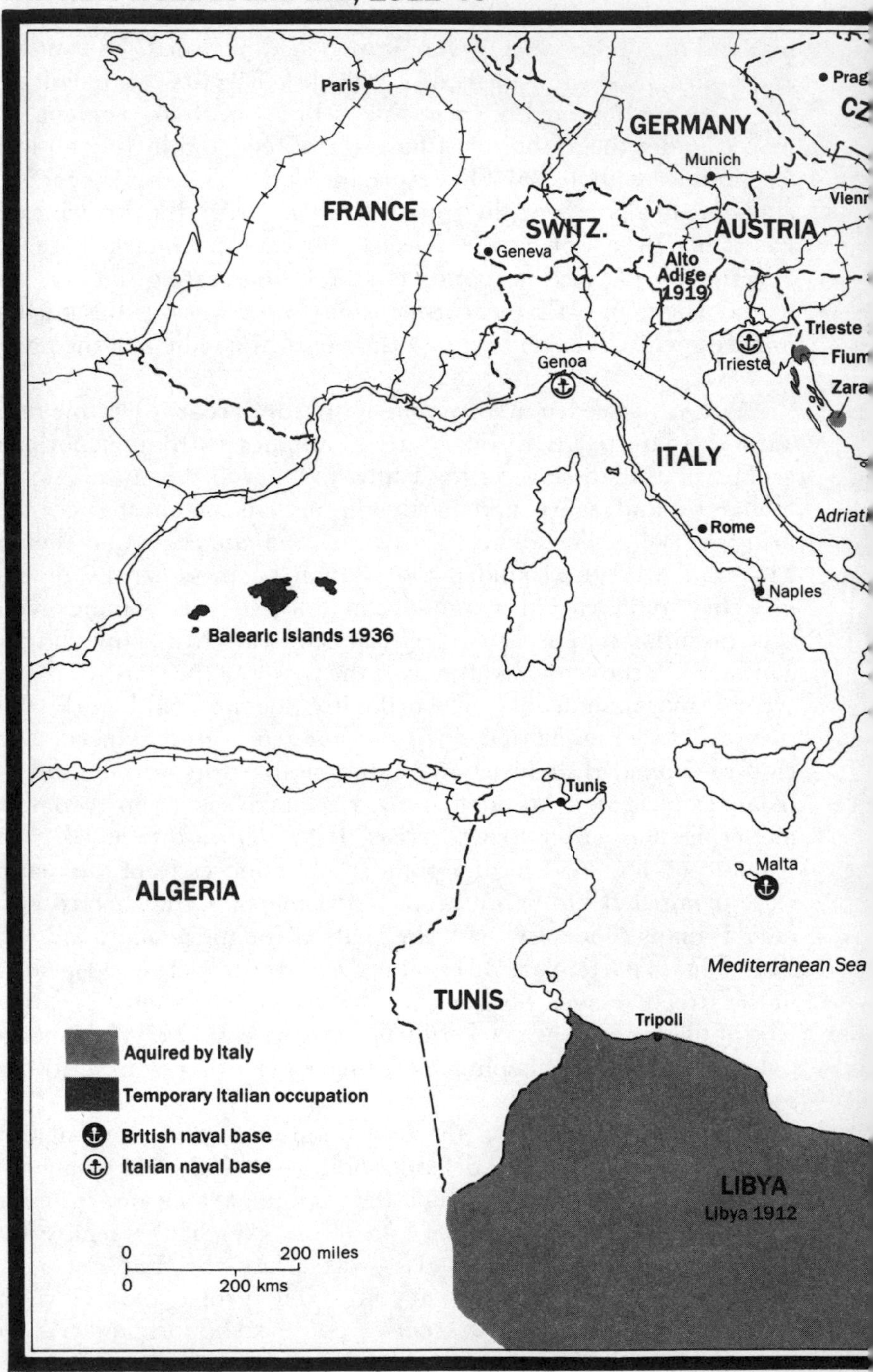

POLAND
KIA
USSR
pest
Odessa
RUMANIA
Buchurest
Black Sea
LAVIA
BULGARIA
Constantinople
IA
GREECE
TURKEY
Dodacanese
Islands
1912
SYRIA
Alexandria
Cairo

than shirk them. Italy's problems were deliberately dramatised. Mussolini launched a series of Fascist 'battles'. There was a Battle of the Lira to support the national currency's value in world markets; a Battle of Grain to increase Italy's agricultural production and reduce the dependence on foreign imports. Mussolini used the campaign to remind Italians of his own humble roots in the peasant mass of Italy; he was photographed famously, bare-chested, helping to gather in the harvest. There was a Battle for Births, to arrest Italy's sinking birthrate. This included taxes on bachelors, prizes for the most prolific mothers; the most fecund of all (ninety-three women who had produced between them 1300 children) were presented to Mussolini in December 1933. He had specified twelve as the ideal family size; one loyal prefect telegraphed that he would personally seek to implement the Duce's wishes.[13]

The most successful and dramatic consequence of his doctrine of action was a Concordat with the papacy. Relations between the Italian state and the Vatican had been bitterly hostile since the 1870s. The Vatican attacked the 'godless' Italian state, which had removed all Catholic instruction (and even the crucifixes) from the schools; every previous attempt to resolve the many issues in dispute had foundered. Mussolini was without any religious belief, but he recognised the power of the Church to undermine the political and social objectives of Fascism in Italy. He pressed hard for a settlement of all outstanding issues, showing his good intentions with a series of unilateral gestures. The crucifixes were replaced in all schools, the priests were allowed back into elementary schools, and chaplains were appointed to the armed forces.

Agreement was finally signed in February 1929. There was no real amity between the Church and the state; Fascism and Catholicism were still competing for the same ground – the minds and souls of Italians – but the truce proved of great value for Fascism. Mussolini had healed Italy's running sore. His reward came when the Church campaigned for a pro-Mussolini vote in the national elections of 1929, in which 89.63 per cent of the electorate voted, more than ever before in the history of the nation; 8.5 million voted for the Fascists, 135,000 against. The 'no' vote was largest in the cities where anti-clericalism was strong; in the country the parish priests delivered their flocks to the voting booths to vote 'yes' for the Lateran treaties and *il duce*. The Concordat bridged the great divide in Italian politics, and helped to create a growing sense of stability in Italian society. It was the chief symbol of Fascist consensus.

During all the years of Fascist consolidation, Italian foreign policy remained much more subdued. It was the least adventurous or revolutionary aspect of the new Italy. Although Mussolini could make his foreign policy sound more bellicose and strident than the old negotiating style of the patrician Foreign Ministry at the Palazzo della Consulta, in reality he followed, if recklessly and energetically, the well-established lines of Italian foreign policy. There were sensible grounds for diffidence; until Fascism was domestically secure there was little to be gained by running excessive risks abroad. Mussolini lacked any real experience of foreign affairs. Though he named himself Foreign Minister, a position which he held except for a short break until 1936, he left the day-to-day conduct of Italian external policy to the experts. There was no sudden infusion of eager Fascists into the diplomatic service; the Duce was served by the same staff at the Foreign Office as his predecessors; just one senior official refused to work under him. Mussolini insisted only on moving the Foreign Office from the quiet of the Palazzo della Consulta to the Palazzo Chigi, in the very heart of Rome, close to his own offices.[14]

The priorities of Fascist foreign policy were almost indistinguishable from the aims of pre-war diplomacy: to consolidate the hard-won empire in Africa, and to play the part of a great power in Europe. Mussolini was determined to be taken seriously, to be treated as an equal of the other victor powers, to reverse the humiliating treatment at Versailles. This meant the pursuit of a European policy. Mussolini adopted the trappings of post-war liberal League diplomacy to win the respect and co-operation of the other League powers. He happily signed the Locarno Treaty in 1925 since it not only restricted Germany's room for manoeuvre, a key aim of Italian policy, but also gave the clear impression that Italy was now a responsible, weighty power, together with Britain and France one of the arbiters of Europe. In reality the two Western states still regarded Italy as very much a junior partner, to be patronised and appeased. They found it difficult to take seriously a man who arrived flamboyantly at Locarno by speed boat across the lake surrounded by black-shirted, posturing aides; or who whipped up popular xenophobia with ranting, radical rhetoric. Austen Chamberlain, the British Foreign Secretary, was condescendingly surprised to find Mussolini was a 'man with whom one could do business'. But when he stepped out of line, as he did when Italian forces occupied the Greek island of Corfu in 1923 in protest at the murder of an Italian officer, Britain took the lead in compelling Italian withdrawal.[15]

Mussolini got very little from his co-operation with Britain and

France: neither real international parity, nor practical concessions. While Mussolini guaranteed France's eastern frontier against German attack in the Locarno Agreement, no guarantee was given to Italy protecting her from a revival of the German threat. The prospect of a union between Germany and Austria terrified Italians, who wanted to keep a powerful Teutonic state away from the Brenner Pass. On the border with Austria Italy had her own nationality problem, with 200,000 ethnic Germans in the province of South Tyrol, renamed Alto Adige in 1919, who were subjected to a vigorous, sometimes vicious, campaign of 'Italianisation'. Italy played protector to the new Austrian state, a reversal of fortune relished by Italians. Italian influence was pushed into Central Europe and the Balkans to replace the Habsburgs. Italy was every bit as anxious as France about what would happen if Germany once again became a major power in Central Europe. Yet the fear was never quite strong enough to persuade Italy to come to a firm alliance with France and Britain; that smacked too much of the idea that Italian foreign policy depended upon the goodwill of the two leading states. Mussolini was never willing to put himself in the position of Orlando at Versailles, begging for recognition.

Ten years of active politics in Europe did not really advance Italy's status. In March 1933 Mussolini made one final, theatrical attempt to secure parity with the great powers. Mussolini proposed a pact between Britain, France, Italy and Germany to create a Directorate which would arbitrate in all European problems. Other countries argued fiercely against the proposal, Poland in particular claiming that it would put the small states at the mercy of the great. That was precisely Mussolini's intention; he wanted to fix Italy as one of the 'big four', rather than among the bevy of smaller states.[16] But the group never functioned as Mussolini had intended. Although the Pact was formally signed in July 1933, it gradually became clear that the new German Chancellor, Hitler, had no intention of subordinating his interests to the Pact or to the League system. Nor were Britain and France happy with the rather vague alternative to the collective security of the League; the Directorate withered on the vine. The Pact marked the high-water mark of Mussolini's efforts to be respected as a power of the status quo.

By the early 1930s Fascism at home and abroad had reached something of an impasse. The period of domestic consolidation was over; the 'dynamic' face of Fascism was giving way to an altogether more static and conventional aspect. The success of the Concordat and the emergence of consensus marked, indirectly, a shift within the

Fascist movement. The true revolutionaries, the radical wild men of the Party, were pushed away from the centre of government; where possible, Mussolini kept power out of the hands of potential rivals. He followed D'Annunzio's advice: 'Don't beplume your subordinates too much.' Any 'old Fascist' who became too powerful or too independent was replaced. Dino Grandi, who was given the Foreign Ministry in 1929, was suddenly removed from office in 1932 and posted as Ambassador to London. Mussolini resumed the post himself. Italo Balbo, who became a national hero after a spectacular flight across the Atlantic, was sacked from his position as Air Minister and posted to govern Libya, far away from Rome. His vacant post fell to Mussolini also. The Party now provided the structure and hierarchy for the new corporate state. The revolution was institutionalised: PNF officials became cosseted and well-paid servants of the state. Radical Fascists complained that Mussolini had 'imposed a hierarchy on Fascism' and 'changed its content'. By 1932 the party of violent action which had once dosed its enemies with castor oil, kidnapped and murdered its opponents and waged war in the streets had 'changed its political outlook'. Now, grumbled one nationalist, 'Fascism is all for hierarchy, tradition and respect for the law.'[17]

Fascism passed through 'dynamism', and moved on to the creation of new myths. Great efforts were made to dramatise the achievements of the regime. A great Fascist exhibition was mounted in Rome to mark the tenth anniversary of the Fascist rise to power, and to provide a permanent monument to the Fascist age. The official handbook described it as embodying 'the will of *il duce* in whom all the mysterious forces of the race converge'.[18] Mussolini became the greatest myth of all, the saviour of Italy. *Mussolini ha sempre ragione*, Mussolini is always right, was daubed on walls and placards. As the Fascist revolution aged it came to depend more on Mussolini himself as the rallying point. Nor did the dictator remain immune from the image he projected. Increasingly he played the role assigned to him. In 1932 he told the German historian and biographer, Emil Ludwig, that he planned 'a complete renovation of my country'. When Ludwig asked him if it was his purpose to impose his own vision on Italy, he 'answered decisively' that it was.[19]

Mussolini was all too aware that Fascist political enthusiasm was slackening. By 1932 his mind was turning to new initiatives: 'It has become ever more plain to me that action is of primary importance. This even when it is a blunder. Negativism, quietism, motionlessness, is a curse. I advocate movement. I am a wanderer.' He made the point openly to Ludwig: 'I am burning my boats, I make a fresh start.'[20] His answer was to move from promoting Fascism at home to promoting Italy abroad. In the 1920s his foreign policy was cautious and conventional, his domestic policies radical; in the 1930s the order was reversed. His aim was to pick up the threads of Italian pre-war expansion and to build an empire. His model was Julius Caesar – 'The greatest man that ever lived'; his aim was to extend Italian influence in the historic areas of Roman expansion, 'Asia and Africa'.

This desire was not a sudden inspiration. Mussolini had always argued that Italy must win its place in the sun and become a great imperial power. Before 1922 he had argued that the older, established states deliberately excluded Italy: 'In the west there are the "haves". They are our rivals, our competitors, our enemies; and when they sometimes help us it is . . . something between alms-giving and blackmail.' He attacked 'the bourgeois and plutocratic "haves"' of the Western world; Italy would find her destiny in the Middle East and Africa, where the 'have-not' powers could build fresh empires.[21] In the mid-1920s, in power, he had already made up his mind that at some point Fascism must 'found an empire', that this was the only way to redeem the nationalist pledges to make this 'the century of Italian power'.[22] These were aims that were widely approved in nationalist and colonial circles in Italy. The *mal d'Africa*, the 'ache for Africa', was a traditional component of Italian diplomacy. Mussolini wanted to give Italians a new empire: 'the tendency towards imperialism is one of the elementary trends of human nature, an expression of the will to power. . . .' The success of the enterprise rested, he thought, 'upon the authority of the leader'.[23]

Mussolini did not begin with any very clear idea about how the new empire would be secured, or where, though Ethiopia was high on the list. In March 1934 he announced the new direction in Italian policy to the national assembly of the Party:[24]

> The historical objectives of Italy have two names: Asia and Africa. South and east are the compass points towards which the interest and will of Italians are directed. To the north, there is nothing to do, to the west nothing either, either in Europe or beyond the sea. Of all the great powers, the closest to Africa and Asia is Italy. . . . Italy's position in the Mediterranean . . . gives it the right and duty to accomplish this task.

The new direction was a public repudiation of the 'European' policy that he had pursued through the first decade of Fascism. For Mussolini recognised the real limitations to playing the European great power. The failure of the Four Power Pact had shown him that Italy was still not treated as an equal. His role, as a go-between, was dispensable by the other states. Far more problematical was the rise of a new Germany. If Hitler was bent on aggrandisement in Central Europe, in Austria in particular, then Italy could prevent him only by dependence on Britain and France, the very position Mussolini wanted to avoid.

An alternative was to face up to Germany alone, which he did when Austrian Nazis murdered the Austrian Chancellor Engelbert Dollfuss in 1934. The Duce mobilised the Italian army and fortified the northern frontier. His energy and determination impressed foreign governments. The United States Ambassador to Austria wrote to the State Department: 'This action by Mussolini undoubtedly did [most] to have Hitler take energetic action to stop any invasion by the Austrian [Nazi] Legion. I hold no brief for Mussolini, but I am confident that had he not taken the decisive action he did . . . the fat would have been in the fire.'[25]

The experience of 1934 showed Mussolini that with two active militarist powers in Central Europe, the competition was too hot: a clash was eventually inevitable and Italy would be the loser to German military strength. The revival of German power forced Italy to turn southwards, just as Mussolini's new imperialism pulled in the same direction. He kept up the pretence of a European role, signing declarations, expressing a willingness to disarm, mouthing the slogans of collective security, while awaiting the opportunity to begin the 'dynamic' phase of Fascist foreign policy.

The long regime of caution was over; yet the new direction carried all kinds of dangers. Mussolini hoped to be able to fulfil his ambitions by adopting a traditional, Machiavellian approach to empire-building, seizing local, regional opportunities when and where they arose. His role models were the great nineteenth-century diplomatists, Cavour and Bismarck. He had great confidence in his ability to manipulate the system in his favour now he had served his diplomatic apprenticeship: 'I do not hesitate to learn from my earlier experiences.'[26] These might well have shown him that the move south and east would bring him into conflict with imperial Britain and France. An African policy trespassed directly on their vital interests. It led ultimately to Italy's international isolation, and to a close bond with the one state, Germany, that Italians distrusted most.

This was almost certainly not the outcome that Mussolini expected from the new drive for empire. For many Italians, as for their leader, it was merely a case of picking up the imperial reins dropped by the feeble regimes before Fascism: invigorated by Fascist spirit, by what Mussolini called 'the moral unity of the nation' and by a new militarism, the Italian people would achieve what all new, young nations deserved. Mussolini was very conscious of this historic link, of the continuity of Italian empire. Later, at the height of the Ethiopian crisis, in 1935, he told the French Ambassador to Rome: 'Cost what it may, I will avenge Adowa.'[27] Fascist policy in Africa was presented to the Italian people as a belated revenge for what D'Annunzio called 'the shameful scar'. 'With Ethiopia we have been patient for forty years,' Mussolini told 'a huge and enthusiastic crowd' gathered before the Palazzo Venezia in October 1935: 'Now, enough. . . .'[28]

Ethiopia was regarded as a 'natural' area of Italian expansion. There were strong economic arguments put forward for conquest. Mussolini talked of exporting ten million Italians to the colonies; one colonial governor reckoned that East Africa alone could absorb fifteen million white settlers. The suggestion of limitless mineral riches, even oil, under Ethiopia's barren soil was a further spur (though much oil remained undiscovered, beneath the sand of Italy's other colony, Libya). Yet the most compelling arguments were for glory rather than treasure. The King was won over to the strategy by promises of new titles and subjects. Revenge on Ethiopia was a propaganda prize of great value to Mussolini; and it had the advantage that the area was already one that the rest of the world had come to regard as a sphere of Italian influence. The *politica periferica* promised real gains at much less risk than a policy in Europe. Italy had sponsored Ethiopian membership of the League in 1923 against Western opposition; in 1928 Ethiopia was bound closely with a treaty of friendship and trade. In 1932 Mussolini ordered work to begin on plans to turn friendship into formal control. In December of that year, three years before the actual invasion, the Minister for Colonies, Emilio de Bono, a close political ally of Mussolini, drew up the invasion programme: 'I have submitted the project for eventual action against Abyssinia to Mussolini. It pleases him. . . . We must be ready by 1935.'[29] A year later Mussolini instructed him to produce detailed operational plans for a campaign in October 1935; at a Cabinet meeting on 8 February 1934 this date was confirmed and the timetable of military and economic preparations set in motion.[30]

The exact timing of the planned assault on Ethiopia owed much to circumstances. Italian leaders could see that Ethiopia was rapidly building up armed forces of her own, and might well prove a more difficult conquest only a few years hence; Adowa had to be avenged, not repeated. Ethiopia was already slipping away from dependence on Italian trade; by 1934 80 per cent of her imports came from Japan; much of the investment in the region came from Britain and the United States, undermining the Italian position throughout East Africa.[31] Italy's historic influence was strongly challenged by Japan, which saw Ethiopia as an independent empire like herself, resisting European encroachment. A wedding arranged between a Japanese princess and the nephew of the Ethiopian Emperor, Haile Selassie, was called off only after strong Italian protests in Addis Ababa. There were also problems nearer home. Mussolini was all too aware of the revival of Germany and of German rearmament. He was anxious not to let the Ethiopian affair weaken his position in Europe at the Brenner frontier; an attack in 1935 would give him time to rearm and complete the operation before German military strength had revived too much. An early attack would also answer the strong objections of his generals that the campaign was far too risky, the distances too great, Ethiopian resistance likely to be considerable, and the attitude of Germany, Britain and France unpredictable. Ethiopia was a risk which Mussolini took in the end because of his desire to 'act', to keep Fascism on the boil, to satisfy the nationalist chorus for Italian glory.

Yet he was too astute a politician not to recognise that any advance in Africa could be achieved only with the agreement, willing or unwilling, of Britain and France. He judged that he could gain most if he could negotiate from strength. Britain, which depended so heavily on communication with her distant eastern Empire, was exceptionally vulnerable in the area of the Red Sea. In British eyes, Italy already posed a threat. With her Arab friends and allies she controlled the Arabian coast as far as Aden and much of the southern section of the African shore as well. By the early 1930s the Italians were using the Arab gambit against the British throughout the Middle East. Italy was quick to capitalise on Muslim fears and hatreds. In coffee houses and tea rooms throughout the Middle East, popular music played from cheap Italian-supplied radio sets, tuned to Radio Bari, the Arab station of the Italian government. Interspersed with the entertainment was effective propaganda against Britain and Zionism.[32]

Italy, who had for ten years treated the Senussi of Libya with ferocious brutality, now posed as the supporter of Muslim liberty. In March 1934, Mussolini had told the Fascist Assembly in Rome: 'A few hours by sea, fewer still by air suffice to join Italy to Africa and to Asia. . . . It is not a matter of territorial conquests . . . but of a natural expansion which should lead to a collaboration between

Italy and the nations of the Near and Middle East.'[33] Three years later, the Duce visited Tripoli and in an elaborate ceremony was presented with the Sword of Islam by local Muslim dignitaries. He accepted the Sword, a replica of the symbolic weapon once borne by the Ottoman Caliph in defence of all Muslims, and spoke of Italy's intention to 'show her sympathy towards Islam and towards Muslims throughout the world'.

The Arab campaign was an irritation which Mussolini hoped would encourage the British to allow him a free hand in Ethiopia. But in the end it was France rather than Britain that gave the adventure informal blessing. Worried by German moves and anxious to secure France's position in Eastern Europe, the French Foreign Minister, Pierre Laval, began to explore the possibility of a rapprochement with Italy. In January 1935 Laval visited Mussolini in Rome where a series of 'accords' were drawn up between the two states. The most important from the French point of view were those dealing with Europe: Italian support for the French position in Eastern Europe, the promise of support for Italy over German moves against Austria. But for Mussolini the most important promise was over Ethiopia. French fears for her European security outweighed all other political issues and Laval happily promised to forgo French economic interests in East Africa; later, in a moment of informal discussion with Mussolini, he pledged French *'désintéressement politique'*, a free hand for Italy in Ethiopia.[34]

This was a diplomatic coup of great significance. Mussolini now saw that fear of Germany could be used to extract Western acquiescence in his new imperialism. When Germany declared her rearmament in March 1935 the situation continued to move in Italy's favour. Mussolini met with the British and French Prime Ministers at Stresa in northern Italy to work out their common reaction to the deliberate German violation of Versailles. German repudiation was publicly condemned, but the communiqué issued at the end of the conference referred only to the necessity of keeping the peace of Europe. Mussolini took this to mean that both Western powers would turn a blind eye to his African plans. During contacts at a lower level, Italian officials at Stresa had made it clear what Italy's intentions in Africa were: there was no protest from the other powers. Silence, Mussolini assumed, implied consent. During the summer months mobilisation preparations continued. The only problem now faced was Germany, which had reacted strongly against the Stresa declaration, and was sending arms and technical assistance to the Ethiopians. Italian diplomats became genuinely concerned that Hitler's Reich had earmarked

Ethiopia for the site of a new German colonial empire in Africa.

Britain and France were very willing to accommodate Italy up to a point, if it kept her away from Hitler. What they were not sure of was the full extent of Mussolini's plan. In April Mussolini ordered his Ambassador in London, Dino Grandi, to spell out in no uncertain terms his intention to conquer Ethiopia. The British reaction surprised and then angered him. Instead of a reasonable acquiescence the British government warned him of the dangers of flouting collective security and attacking a fellow member of the League. The two Western states were prepared to make some minor adjustments in territory and to grant Italy economic privileges, but they assumed, wrongly, that Italy needed Western co-operation too much to risk an open breach. Mussolini found this attitude 'absolutely unacceptable . . . the equivalent of trying to humiliate Italy in the worst possible fashion'. By July he was resolved to attack Ethiopia come what may: 'Put in military terms, the problem admits of only one solution . . . with Geneva [the League], without Geneva, against Geneva.'[35] His ambitions were now too public to back down without a disastrous loss of face. He was convinced that the Western powers were bluffing, and ignored the frightened warnings of his ministers. Not for the first time Mussolini acted on his own instinct. At the last moment, with British naval vessels clustered in the Mediterranean, Mussolini got news from London that Britain would not impose military sanctions. He replied with a triumphant declaration on 2 October, the day before the invasion, in which he blamed the Western powers 'who at the peace table' in 1919 'withheld from Italy all but a few crumbs of the rich colonial loot. We have waited thirteen years, during which time the egoism of these Allies has only increased and suffocated our vitality.'[36]

A final appeal to hold back came from an altogether unexpected quarter. Hitler was worried that Mussolini was impetuously risking a general war with the other powers over Ethiopia which would lead to Italian defeat and Western revival. The time was not yet ripe, Hitler informed Mussolini, for a showdown between the 'dynamic' and 'static' states.[37] Mussolini was deaf to all appeals. On 3 October 1935 Italy invaded Ethiopia; almost the first act of the war was a bomber raid on the town of Adowa. The advance by the huge Italian army – totalling three army corps – was full of symbolic meaning. One elderly general raised the same flag over the town of Adigrat which he had last hauled down as a junior subaltern after the disaster of 1896. When Adowa was captured, the Duce telegraphed: 'ANNOUNCEMENT RECONQUEST ADOWA FILLS THE SOUL OF THE ITALIANS WITH PRIDE.'[38]

In fact the war with Ethiopia had disastrous consequences. The campaign itself quickly became bogged down. In December an Ethiopian counter-offensive fuelled with German and Japanese armaments, drove Italian forces back. British and German military opinion was agreed that Italy was unlikely to win the war. The British and French Foreign Ministers now drew up a further variation of the schemes proposed in the summer, giving Italy territorial concessions and guaranteed influence but maintaining an independent Ethiopian state. Mussolini was under strong pressure from his own Party to accept the terms of the so-called Hoare–Laval Pact. Italy had been immediately isolated diplomatically through her invasion of Ethiopia, with the League of Nations applying economic sanctions. Since 70 per cent of Italian trade was with League members it was assumed that the pressure would bring Italy to a negotiated settlement. The assumption was nearly correct; in December Mussolini seriously considered accepting the proposed Pact rather than risk military humiliation. He was prevented from doing so only by the public outcry in Britain when the Pact was discovered and rejected by Parliament. Instead of a negotiated agreement, Mussolini found himself facing a hostile Britain and France and a hostile League, the very outcome he had sought to avoid. The final blow came with the British vote in March 1936 for oil sanctions against Italy, cutting her off from the one import that was vital for her war effort.

Italy adapted quickly to the threat of sanctions. The United States was not a member of the League and was unhappy about sanctions that might 'bring on a European war in the near future' or might, as one State Department official feared, end in Italian defeat in Africa which would 'bring in its train not only revolution in Italy', but 'communism or near-communism thrust into the heart of Europe'.[39] The United States continued to supply oil to Italy, reducing her direct supplies to the mainland, but tripling supplies to Italy's colonies. Most of the additional oil Italy needed came from Roumania, which supplied 31 per cent in 1934 and 59 per cent after the invasion. In the end the British backed down from imposing a full naval blockade on Italy – owing to lack of resources and French hesitancy – and the oil continued to flow. But conflict with the Western states was averted by a narrow margin.

The threat of sanctions united public opinion behind Mussolini. The war was popular at home. Women exchanged their gold wedding rings for iron substitutes to swell the national bullion reserves. The Queen was the first of 250,000 Roman women to offer her ring in a ceremony held at the War Memorial in Rome. When the war began to go Italy's way in February 1936 under a new commander, Marshal Badoglio, he became a national hero. But the victory was won only with a massive war effort, using all the modern weapons of war against Ethiopian tribesmen armed with rifles and spears. The campaign was completed by bombing and gassing. In May the whole of Ethiopia was annexed and on the 9th Victor Emmanuel was declared Emperor. The King received the news, Mussolini recorded, with 'tears in his eyes'. The Pope presented the new Empress of Ethiopia with a Golden Rose.

Mussolini now enjoyed a new role as conqueror and imperialist; his reputation in Italy reached its highest point. Italians were happy to accept the fruits of victory in an area of historic Italian interest, if they could be got without the risk of war with the great powers. But the acclamation fed Mussolini's belief that he could lead Italy herself to greatness. When in July 1936 civil war broke out in Spain Mussolini decided, spontaneously, to support the nationalist rebels against the republican regime. The decision was not entirely surprising; contacts between Italian fascism and the Spanish right went back to the founding of the Spanish Republic in 1931. Mussolini was anxious that communism should not gain a foothold at the mouth of the Mediterranean, the 'Italian Sea'; the conflict was presented to Italians as an extension of the domestic conflict against Marxism carried on since 1922. But to a great extent the decision was Mussolini's alone. There was no detailed planning as there had been in Ethiopia. And, unlike the African adventure, intervention in Spain produced no patriotic resonance in Italian society. The two senior military commanders, Balbo and Badoglio, were firmly against direct intervention; the Spanish nationalists asked for weapons not men, especially not the Fascist militia which made up much of the contingent in Spain and proved ineffective on the battlefield. The strategic advantages – a base in the Balearics ('our formidable new pawn on the Mediterranean chess board')[40] and a friendly 'fascist' Spain – were also nebulous. The propaganda benefits of 'victories' in Spain were slight, while the catastrophic Italian defeat at Guadalajara could not be fully covered up by the propagandists. Mussolini confessed his impatience with the Italian people to his son-in-law, Count Galeazzo Ciano, recently promoted to Foreign Minister: 'As long as he was alive he would keep them on the move "to the tune of kicks on the shin. When Spain is finished, I will think of something else. The character of the Italian people must be moulded by fighting."'[41]

War had become an addiction for Mussolini. His conversation had

ITALY IN AFRICA, 1912-40

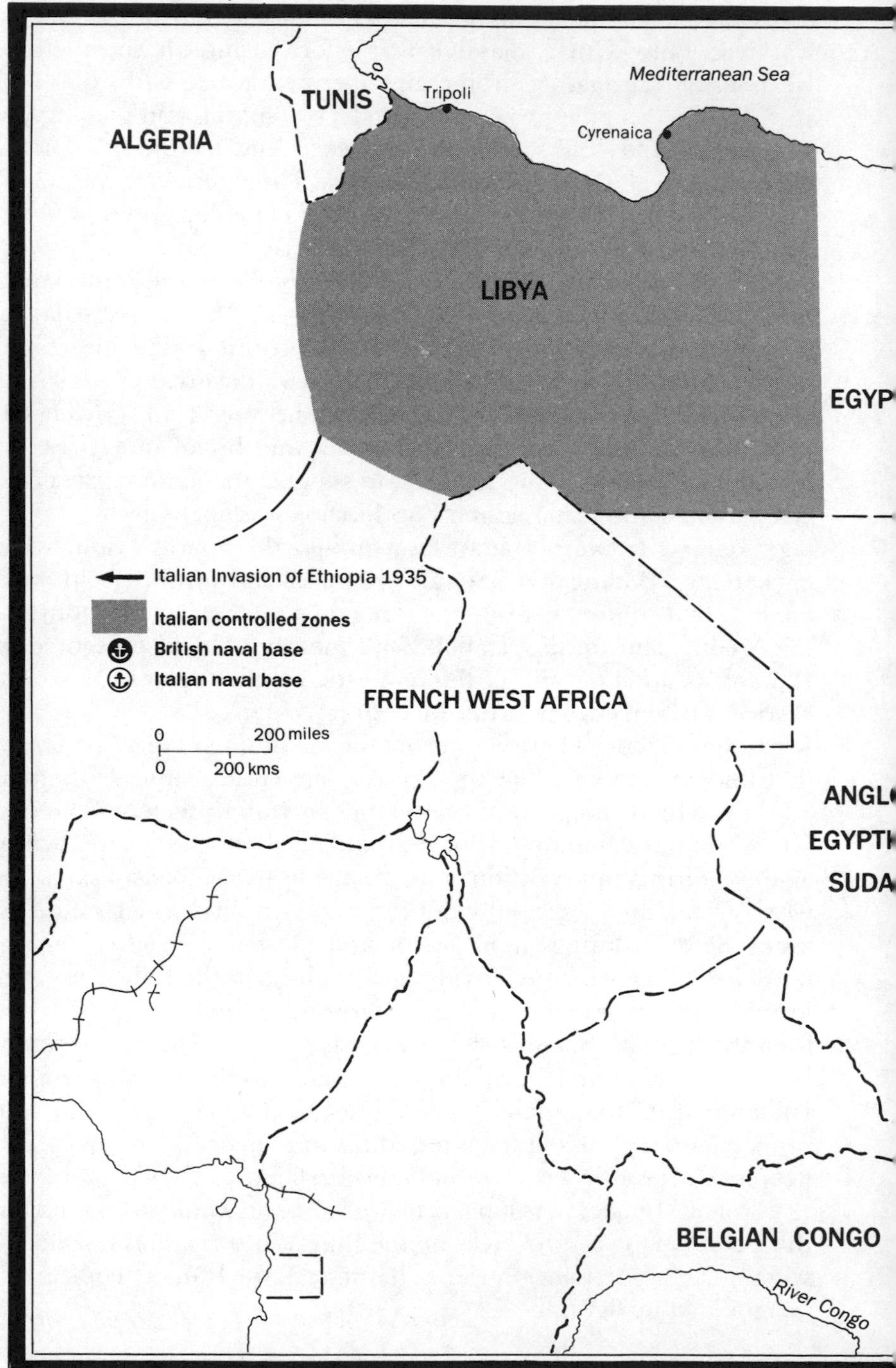

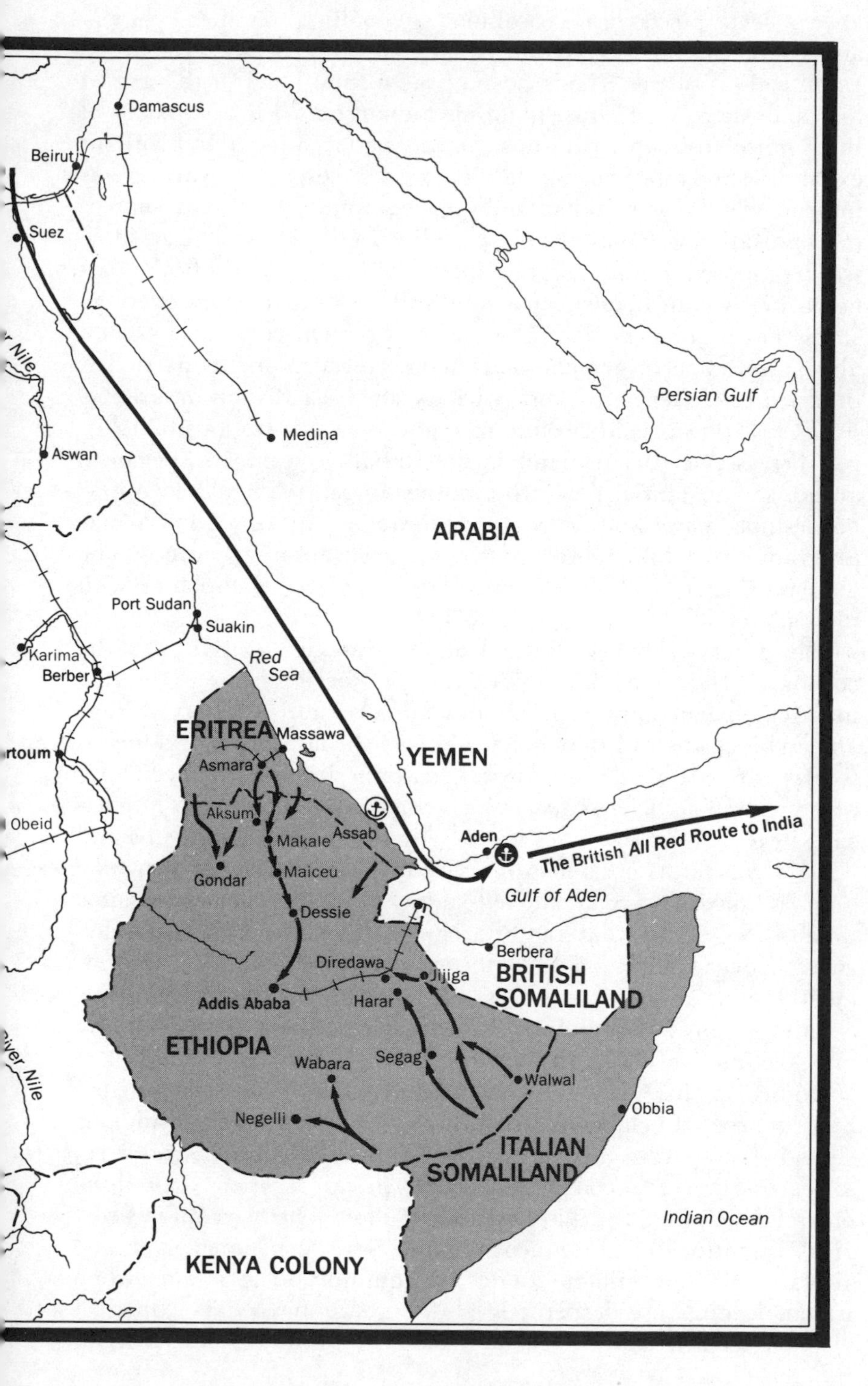
Damascus
Beirut
Suez
Nile
Aswan
Medina
Persian Gulf
ARABIA
Port Sudan
Suakin
Karima
Berber
Red Sea
ERITREA
Massawa
Asmara
rtoum
YEMEN
Aksum
Assab
Obeid
Makale
Aden
The British All Red Route to India
Gondar
Maiceu
Gulf of Aden
Dessie
Berbera
Diredawa
Jijiga
BRITISH SOMALILAND
Addis Ababa
Harar
ETHIOPIA
Segag
Wabara
River Nile
Walwal
Obbia
Negelli
ITALIAN SOMALILAND
Indian Ocean
KENYA COLONY

always been spiced with a vocabulary of conflict, but after Ethiopia and Spain, he came to see himself as a great war leader. In March 1938, jealous of the King's position as formal head of the armed forces, he appointed himself and his monarch as 'First Marshals of the Empire' to create a spurious equality between them. Yet without expanding and modernising Italy's armed forces, future warfare was in jeopardy. Much Italian military equipment was antiquated; mechanisation was only slowly spreading in the army. The air force was composed mainly of biplanes; the navy, Mussolini's own favourite, was in better shape, but still contained many over-age ships. The limited effort in Ethiopia and Spain forced Italy to spend almost as much of her national income on armaments as richer, industrialised Germany, and twice as much as Britain or France. From 1937 onwards Mussolini, who now bore sole responsibility for the three service departments in the Italian government, began to authorise substantial new programmes of rearmament. Two new battleships, *Roma* and *Impero*, were ordered. In July 1938 a new programme of 5 billion lire for army modernisation was agreed. The air force began a major programme to replace its biplanes with monoplanes.

The great weakness of the Italian strategic position was the economy. Italy was heavily reliant on foreign sources of raw materials, particularly coal, oil and iron ore, and was very vulnerable to blockade, as Ethiopia had shown. She lacked the real means to play the part of a great power. Mussolini declared the need for a policy of self-sufficiency, *autarchia*, which would build up import-substitutes, divert resources from civilian to war requirements and free Italy as far as possible from economic dependency. In 1936 he ordered 'maximum economic self-sufficiency in the shortest possible time'.[42] To ensure that the strategy worked, the state extended controls over the economy like those in Germany, on trade, investment, labour utilisation. By 1939 the state owned 80 per cent of the country's arms capacity. Italy was transformed into a war economy in peacetime.

Ironically, this effort weakened Italy as much as it strengthened her. The cost of belligerency in Ethiopia and Spain was prodigious enough. There were 300,000 troops stationed in Ethiopia from 1935 to 1940, and over 50,000 in Spain. The African campaign raised the budget deficit from 2½ billion lire to 16 billion. The two conflicts cost great quantities of equipment; Spain alone consumed over 700 aircraft and nine million rounds of ammunition at a time when Italian forces were desperately short of supplies.[43] The 'Spanish ulcer' weakened Italy as it had weakened Napoleon; intervention,

Mussolini later confessed, 'bled Italy white'. Economic revival in the 1920s was replaced by economic stagnation and crisis. Real wages fell, the balance of payments gap yawned wider, government finances were out of control; businessmen and workers resented the growing regimentation by the state. The immediate effect was to strain the consensus established in the 1920s. Opposition was never strong enough to challenge Mussolini directly; state repression saw to that. But from 1937 onwards Mussolini lost the wholehearted support of many Italians for warmongering.

The wars also transformed Italy's international position. During 1936, as a direct result of Ethiopia and Spain, Italy moved out of the Western camp and closer to Hitler's Germany. This was a product of necessity rather than intention, a consequence of Mussolini's flouting of the League. As one German diplomat put it: 'the new German–Italian friendship was created not by the spontaneous inner urge of two countries which are similar in nature . . . but ad hoc, on rational grounds as the result of necessities confronting both of them.' What they both had in common was the fact that 'they were have-nots in contrast to the powers which were satiated by the peace treaties.'[44] Mussolini still regarded his powerful northern neighbour with mistrust, though he envied Hitler's willingness to take great risks. When the two leaders first met at Venice in 1934 Mussolini disliked the insignificant 'degenerate' who greeted him; Hitler was repelled by Mussolini's pomposity. Mussolini could never reconcile himself fully to the fact that although he was demonstrably the senior fascist in Europe, Hitler had greater national power behind him. They were drawn together in 1936 only because they were both rejected and isolated by the Western states and the League. The fact that they were both fascist powers gave the relationship a gloss of ideological brotherhood and dictatorial solidarity, but co-operation between them was always more cautious and formal. Italy was useful to Hitler as a fascist outpost in the Mediterranean keeping Britain and France away from Central Europe. Germany was useful to Mussolini as a source of economic assistance for rearmament, and as a power to divert the attention of Britain and France from Italian adventures in the Mediterranean. Each saw the other as an instrument in his own power game; manipulation rather than friendship bound them together.

In October the informal contacts established in Spain by German and Italian forces fighting side by side for Franco were enlarged into an agreement reached between Ciano and Hitler which became dubbed the 'Rome–Berlin Axis'. The Germans had a low opinion of the Italian agreement and of Italians generally; Göring rated them lower than Slavs.[45] But the one thing Ciano offered was formal confirmation that Italy would keep out of Central Europe. This did not quite give Hitler a free hand in Austria but almost so. Mussolini abandoned his role as protector of the post-war settlement in Austria and endorsed closer relations between the two German states. In return Hitler was happy to acknowledge that Africa and the Mediterranean formed Italy's *spazio vitale*, her living-space. In October 1936 Germany recognised the Italian conquest of Ethiopia. A year later Italy joined with Japan and Germany in the Anti-Comintern Pact, a public commitment to the joint fight against world communism. When in March 1938 Hitler finally occupied Austria, Italy made no move. 'Italy is following events with absolute calm,' Mussolini told Hitler's special emissary. 'Tell Mussolini that I will never forget this . . . never, never, never, whatever happens . . .' replied Hitler.[46] Mussolini had once been Hitler's exemplar; now he crudely aped his co-dictator. The Italian army was ordered to introduce a new Fascist marching style, the *passo romano*, which turned out to be nothing more than a Latin goose-step. In 1938 Mussolini finally introduced anti-Semitic legislation into Italy; it proved a widely unpopular move.

Mussolini never ruled out the possibility that he might get a better deal from Western appeasement, but the public alignment with Hitler made such an outcome more unlikely. Whether he liked it or not he was regarded in the West as a radical power, bent now on overturning the existing system, brought together with Germany, so Vansittart thought, 'by the similarity of their systems and the similarity of their appetites'.[47] Italy was part of a fascist 'bloc' and was counted as a potential enemy. The West now showed interest in Italy only to the extent that some kind of wedge could be driven between the two Axis states. Mussolini saw himself as the potential 'arbiter' of Europe; the other powers saw him as a catspaw.

This ambiguity was fully evident at Munich in 1938. The conference was hailed as a triumph for Mussolini in his role as one of the 'big four' solving European crises. It was certainly a triumph for Grandi in London in persuading Chamberlain to ask for the conference. Mussolini relayed this decision to Hitler and presented as his own terms for settlement a memorandum drafted in Berlin but there was little part for Mussolini in the conference itself. His son-in-law noticed that he was 'brief, cold' with Chamberlain and Daladier, and stood awkwardly in the corner of the room, or moved around 'with his hands in his pockets and a rather distracted air'. Ciano put this down charitably to the fact that 'his great spirit, always ahead of events and men, had already absorbed the idea of agreement'.[48]

The real discussion was between Britain and Germany. Munich was a hollow triumph; Italy's role was no greater than it had been at Versailles twenty years before.

After Munich Mussolini's options became starker still. The German success fed his desire to share with Hitler the opportunity presented by Western weakness to 'change the map of the world',[49] to make Italian policy genuinely independent of the approval of the West. But at the same time he knew that Italy was not yet strong enough to risk war with a major state. Tied down militarily in Africa and Spain, with a weakened economy, Italy did not pose the same threat as Germany. Chamberlain confessed that if he could get a German settlement he would not 'give a rap for Musso'. On the other hand Mussolini was aware that Britain and France were not the powers they had been in the 1920s. His analysis of the old empires as decadent and spineless, first formulated in 1935, seemed truer after Munich. When Chamberlain and Halifax visited Rome in January 1939 to see if there existed the prospect of detaching Italy from Germany, Mussolini was unimpressed: 'These men are not made of the same stuff as the Francis Drakes and the other magnificent adventurers who created the empire.'[50] Nevertheless, Mussolini wanted Britain to take him seriously and resented how little the British had to offer. He blamed poor relations on 'ignorance' and 'lack of understanding', on the persistent view of Italy in Britain as 'a country badly depicted by second-rate picturesque literature'.[51] British leaders failed to realise how important Italian pride was. If Chamberlain had played on Mussolini's vanity he might well have achieved more.

Mussolini's view of France was even more jaundiced. After Munich the Party radicals orchestrated a campaign of anti-French activities, culminating in a demonstration in parliament where Deputies chanted the names of territories they were sworn to return to Italy – Corsica, Nice, Tunisia. Mussolini did nothing to tone down the attacks, joining in himself with a newspaper editorial entitled 'Spitting on France'. Relations with France reached their lowest ebb during late 1938 and early 1939. Yet Mussolini could not risk an open breach; during 1939 Italy had to appear to be a threat, while not actually courting reprisal. In more sober moments Mussolini, advised by his generals, knew that Britain and France were, decadent or not, stronger than Italy.

Nevertheless Mussolini made during the early months of 1939 the fateful decision to complete the programme begun with Ethiopia four years before, to turn Italy into the new Roman Empire. On 4 February he addressed the Fascist Grand Council to announce his

Ciano, seen unkindly in this 1938 British view as empty-headed.

long-term programme. Italy, he declared, was 'a prisoner of the Mediterranean'. The time had come to free Italy from the prison, whose bars were Malta, Cyprus, Corsica and Tunis and whose jailers were Gibraltar and Suez. Italy must 'march to the ocean'; the outcome was inevitable: 'we will find ourselves faced by Anglo-French opposition.'[52] Though Mussolini never liked to admit it to himself, the only way in which this revision could be achieved was with German assistance. Germany, he told the audience, had the role of 'covering Italy's shoulders' in Europe while the Mediterranean was won. For Italy this was by 1939 a fact of life. She was too weak to pursue imperialism on her own. It was evident that only Germany would permit Mussolini to embark on a major programme of territorial revision and expansion, and be strong enough to prevent interference with his plans. Neither Britain nor France could offer Mussolini what he wanted without denying their own interests. There were domestic considerations too. Mussolini had nailed his colours firmly to the mast of imperial glory; his political survival was bound up with the energetic prosecution of Italian interests. 'The prestige of a leader victorious in war is never questioned,' he told Ciano in January.[53] He shared the caution of public opinion only to a limited extent; he exploited opportunities but he wanted triumphs as well. He was Caesar as well as Machiavelli; in 1939 he crossed the Rubicon.

By 1939 the initiative lay firmly with Germany. Hitler's occupation of Prague in March 1939 caught him entirely unawares; at first he was so dismayed by German secretiveness and the 'establishment of Prussian hegemony in Europe' that he toyed again with the idea of joining in an anti-German coalition with Britain and France, a revived 'Stresa Front'. But he quickly saw where the reality of the situation lay: if Germany had now established hegemony, it only made sense to side with the stronger. The day after the Prague coup Mussolini told Ciano that he was 'decidedly in favour of an alliance with Hitler'.[54] But he also accepted his son-in-law's suggestion that the Prague coup should be matched by one for Mussolini too, the military occupation of Albania. This was a 'natural' step like Ethiopia, so much so that one Italian diplomat thought it made as much sense as 'raping one's own wife'. For Albania was under effective Italian protection and had been since a client king, Ahmed Zogu (King Zog) was put on the throne in 1934. Mussolini had already hinted in characteristic style in November 1938 that a formal annexation was on the agenda: 'I announce to you the immediate goals of Fascist dynamism. As we have avenged Adowa, so we will avenge Valona [a skirmish in 1920]. Albania will become Italian.'[55] On 6 April Italian forces mounted an invasion after less than a week of preparation; after a brief and inglorious engagement the country was taken over. The balance within the Axis was in Mussolini's eyes restored. He began to plan the invasion of Greece and Yugoslavia.

A few weeks later the Spanish Civil War came to an end with the nationalist victory. The Italian legions marched at the head of the victory parade through Madrid. Mussolini personally welcomed them back to Italy. His stock domestically was rising again: peace was restored and peace was popular. Yet for Mussolini the future held not peace, but war. He was only halfway to his goal of Mediterranean warlord: a fresh initiative was needed. For some time the German and Japanese governments had been trying to reach a more formal military pact with Italy. Talks broke down on Japanese fears of provoking the Western powers. Now that Mussolini had restored his prestige by matching German with Italian 'dynamism', he began to contemplate a unilateral approach to Germany with the offer of an alliance which he was inclined to call the 'Pact of Blood'. There was strong resistance to such an idea inside Italy. The generals were hostile to further dangerous commitments; public opinion was violently anti-German. Secret police reports showed a growing wave of opposition to war, economic crisis and the link with Nazism. 'Bitter and violent criticism' was reported from Milan; so too was 'disgust and hostility for all things Germanic'.[56] Mussolini knew that he was increasingly on his own and resented the humiliating evidence of anti-German sentiment. No doubt honour had something to do with his decision: 'We cannot change our policy. We are not whores,' he told Ciano in March.[57] In May he sent Ciano to Berlin with authority to sign an immediate agreement with Hitler pledging full military assistance in the event of German involvement in war.

On 22 May the agreement was signed; Mussolini changed its name to the more teutonic 'Pact of Steel'. The Germans were surprised and suspicious at Mussolini's move, though pleased enough that Italian promises might neutralise the threat from the West over Poland. But Hitler said nothing to Ciano about his plans in the East, and the German armed forces were instructed to give away no details of strength, operational plans or modern equipment in staff talks with their Italian opposite numbers. Mussolini's own motives are not easy to judge, for the Pact not only tied him more closely to Germany and gave even less chance of a way out to accommodation with the West – 'Italy', thought Daladier, 'was firmly in the opposite camp' – but it also alienated a great many Italians and marked the onset of the decline of Mussolini's personal appeal. Yet there were solid grounds of *realpolitik* in the Pact. Germany was pledged to support her ally to the hilt if Italy found herself at war with Britain and France. The Pact, Mussolini argued, 'secured our backs to the Continent'. He judged Germany to be the stronger power, but the Pact was a pact of equals, an important point for Mussolini's *amour propre*.[58]

Most important of all Mussolini thought he now had some kind of control over German ambitions. The last thing he wanted was a general war before Italy was ready. He came away from the negotiations convinced that Germany would avoid any major war for at least three years. He fixed the time when Italy could face the Western powers with her rearmament completed as late 1941, early 1942. Ribbentrop gave the same date to Ciano and to Mussolini as the point when Germany, too, would be ready. Mussolini did not trust the Germans, but he could not believe that they would fail to tell him at all of their military plans for 1939. A few days after the Pact was signed he sent a further memorandum by personal courier to Hitler outlining his view of future Axis strategy and laying great stress on the need to avoid war for three years as an effective condition of the alliance. 'Only after 1943,' he told Hitler, 'can a war have the greatest prospect of success.' Until then Italy had to complete her programme of six capital ships, the renovation of her heavy artillery, the transfer of strategic industries southwards away from French bombers, and so on.[59] There was no German reply. Once again Mussolini made the mistake of confusing silence for consent. The memorandum was then circulated to all Italy's senior officials and military leaders, who were given to understand that Italy had three clear years to prepare for what Mussolini called 'a war of exhaustion'. This action helped to calm domestic fears of war and reduce hostility to the German agreement, and reflected a more sober and realistic assessment of Italian capabilities on Mussolini's part.

The German intention to confront Poland took Mussolini completely by surprise; on 4 July 1939, Ciano wrote in his diary: 'From Berlin, no communication, which confirms that nothing dramatic is in the offing.' Two weeks later, hints from Bernardo Attolico, the Italian Ambassador in Berlin, warned of a 'new and perhaps fatal crisis'. Mussolini dismissed the rumours: the Ambassador was frightened by his own shadow. Ciano began to question Hitler's real intentions: by 20 July, intelligence reports indicated 'troop movements on a vast scale. Is it possible that all this should take place without our knowledge after so many protestations of peace made by our Axis colleagues? We shall see.' A week later, Ribbentrop 'has affirmed the German intention to avoid war for a long time'.[60]

By the first week in August, even the Duce sensed that war was in the air, and took fright. Wrote Ciano:

> The outbreak of war at this time would be folly. Our preparations are not such as to allow us to believe that victory will be certain. Now there are no more than even chances. On the other hand, within three years, the chances will be four to one. Mussolini has constantly in mind the idea of an international peace conference.

Ciano was sent to Salzburg to elicit the truth from Hitler; the day before he left, Ciano noted, 'The Duce is more than ever convinced of the need of delaying the conflict. . . . I should frankly inform the Germans that we must avoid conflict with Poland, since it will be impossible to localise it, and a general war would be disastrous for everybody. Never has the Duce spoken of the need for peace so unreservedly and with so much warmth.'[61]

At the Salzburg conference relations between the Italian and German delegates were cool and hostile. At dinner not a single word was exchanged between the two parties. On 12 August Hitler assured Ciano that his decision to attack Poland was 'implacable'.

Ciano found that Hitler listened with only half an ear to his complaints that Italy could not risk general war and that the Italian public was hostile to war. Ribbentrop assured him that conflict would be localised. German leaders were confident that the West would back down; Italian support was necessary as a diplomatic gambit. 'I return to Rome', wrote Ciano in his diary, 'completely disgusted with the Germans, with their leader, and their way of doing things. They have betrayed us and lied to us.'[62] The discovery of German plans threw Mussolini into total confusion. Since the signature of the Pact of Steel, he had been sending belligerent messages to Berlin, reassuring Hitler that the two fascist states would 'march together'. After he discovered the full extent of German duplicity, he veered erratically from saying that 'honour compels him to march with Germany' on one day, to declaring that he 'is convinced that we must not march blindly with Germany' on the next. The attractions of Britain and France grew much greater, and 'extreme cordiality on both sides' replaced the frozen relationships that had persisted for the whole of 1939. Meanwhile, the Italians temporised with Hitler, saying that they lacked the resources to enter the war, and asking Germany to make up the deficiencies. The shopping list was deliberately inflated (18 million tons of coal, oil, steel and other resources for immediate delivery) 'to discourage the Germans from meeting our requests'. By 28 August, it was accepted in Berlin that Italy could not help Germany directly in what was still regarded as a local war; Hitler asked only that her neutrality should be kept from Britain and France. Ciano immediately summoned the British Ambassador, and 'acting as if I could no longer contain my feelings, I say . . . "we shall never start a war against you and the French."'[63]

Unlike the German leaders, Mussolini was convinced that if Britain and France said they would fight, then they would. Italy was simply not prepared for such a conflict. Anxious police reports continued to come in: 'The entire population has very little feeling for the war; they don't want it and they disapprove of it.' Badoglio warned that the armed forces were barely operating at '40 per cent capacity'. When Mussolini investigated the exact strength of Italian forces he found not the 'eight million bayonets' he had flamboyantly promised, but only ten equipped divisions out of sixty-seven, and only 600 operational aircraft instead of the 2000–3000 he expected. He privately gave vent to 'bitter words', but the truth could not have come as a surprise.[64] Italy had not recovered from the losses and expense of years of warfare. Unlike the German armed forces, Italy's troops had been fighting for almost four years, and her economy had been severely dislocated by the cost. Mussolini had made it abundantly clear to Hitler that the Pact of Steel was aimed at a war in three years' time. Though he disliked having to back down he had no support among his own ministers and generals for war with the Western powers. He later ruefully reflected: 'Had we been 100% ready we should have entered the war in September 1939 instead of June 1940.'[65]

As the intelligence on Mussolini's decision became evident in the last week of August 1939 it did little to deflect the other powers from their course. Hitler recovered from the shock and argued that Germany would be better off with Italian neutrality, which would still force Britain and France to keep forces in the Mediterranean. On the other hand, Italian neutrality was seen by the Western powers to strengthen their position and encouraged them in the view that Hitler, shorn of his ally, would back down. The French wanted to use the knowledge to get Mussolini to intercede once again with Hitler as he had done before Munich. On 31 August Ciano, at Bonnet's prompting, did float the idea of a four-power conference, but with little hope of success. British leaders suspected a diplomatic manoeuvre to shield Hitler's next aggression, while Hitler simply ignored it. When war broke out on 3 September it confirmed the Italian judgement of Western firmness, a fact that Mussolini took pleasure in reminding Hitler of a few months later. Still, Mussolini could not bring himself to declare neutrality; he called his stance non-belligerency, as befitted a fascist leader.

On the day that Britain declared war, Mussolini recovered some of his optimism. He believed 'that after a short struggle peace will be restored'. Ciano thought differently: 'I am not a military man. I do not know how the war will develop, but I know one thing – it will develop and it will be long, uncertain, and relentless. The participation of England makes this certain. England has made this declaration to Hitler. The war can end only with Hitler's elimination or the defeat of Britain.'[66]

In the long run Ciano was right. But in the period of the phoney war Mussolini's diagnosis seemed more likely. Like the early stages of Italian neutrality in the First World War, non-belligerence gave Italy's leaders the chance to exploit any opportunities which the course of the war might bring to strengthen Italy's own interests. This did not exclude the possibility of belligerence itself. The idea of not fighting at some point Mussolini found difficult to accept: 'Italy cannot remain neutral for the entire duration of the war without resigning her role, without reducing herself to the level of a

Switzerland multiplied by ten.'[67] It was Italy's failure to intervene in 1914 that had turned Mussolini in the first place from a socialist to a nationalist; without Mussolini it is improbable that Italy would have intervened this time. He fixed the point of Italian intervention at the spring of 1941, when the rearmament drive would be nearer completion. In the meantime he explored all the options open to him now that the other powers were at war. Whichever side Italy supported with her seventy divisions, her 'aerial legions' and her sleek, fast new navy, would be the winning side. It was highly probable, though not inevitable, that this would be Germany.

This outcome was not a foregone conclusion. There was strong pressure for neutrality from Mussolini's colleagues and Party bosses. During the last weeks of 1939 a Cabinet reshuffle brought to the fore a circle of leaders around Ciano who all favoured abstaining from any German war. Police reports showed that the public continued to hold 'a blind faith in the Duce's ability to keep . . . out of the war'.[68] Italy's neutrality, while welcomed at first by Hitler, placed a real strain on Italian–German relations. In October Hitler warned Mussolini that his position could lead 'to the end of her imperial ambitions in the Mediterranean'.[69] In turn Mussolini lectured Hitler on his miscalculation in September over Western firmness, and on the Pact with Russia: 'I feel you cannot abandon the anti-semitic and anti-Bolshevist banner which you have been flying for twenty years. . . . Germany's task is this: to defend Europe from Asia.'[70] A German Embassy official informed Berlin that 'the broad mass of the Italian people never liked us. . . . They disapprove of German policy, which in their opinion is responsible for the war.'[71]

As if to confirm these tensions, Mussolini acted to strengthen his northern frontier with Germany. He issued instructions that the work on fortifications opposite Germany should be speeded up during the winter of 1939–40 'to the extreme limits of our capabilities'. By May he wanted a guarantee from the generals that his north-eastern frontier was impregnable 'in the most absolute sense of the term'. In February parliament approved 1 billion lire for the work, but only 600 million for the French border, and half as much for the Yugoslav. Italian soldiers admired the Maginot Line and the French army; they believed that, secure behind fortified, static defences, Germany could be withstood.[72] At the same time Mussolini kept open lines of communication with the Allies, flattered by the unaccustomed position of having something important to give to both sides. But while the Western powers toyed with the idea of using Mussolini to produce a compromise with Germany, they did not want to make the kind of concessions that Mussolini expected, and feared the effect on domestic and world opinion of talking with fascism. Nor, in the end, was Mussolini prepared to accept anything short of Mediterranean hegemony as the price for holding back, and this the Allies were fighting to defend.[73]

Mussolini's options were narrow from the moment that he found himself bracketed in the eyes of the Western powers with the revisionist, fascist bloc. For all the domestic arguments against the alliance, and Mussolini's instinctive opportunism, it was difficult to avoid the German embrace. With Germany or against her, Italy was bound to feel the effects of German conquest. Mussolini was determined that Italian intervention must come, as he told Hitler in January 1940, 'at the most profitable and decisive moment'. His military chief, Badoglio, convinced of Italy's continued military weakness, advised intervention 'only if the enemy was so prostrated to justify such audacity'.[74] Intervention depended on the certainty of German victory; otherwise Italy would be served better by a compromise peace, in which Germany did not achieve complete continental hegemony and the Allies lost their ability to dictate to him in southern Europe. As Mussolini candidly confessed to Ribbentrop in March, 'the question of timing was extremely delicate.'[75]

By March the situation had changed in one important respect. The Franco-British blockade was beginning to bite. Italy was more dependent than Germany on the world market and the distortions produced by the war hit harder. But until March supplies of coal by sea from Germany had been allowed through the net. On 1 March Britain blockaded Rotterdam and cut Italy off from vital supplies of German coal. Coal could now only come by train through Italy's northern frontier with what had once been Austria and was now 'Greater Germany'. Britain promised to supply coal to Italy in return for Italian arms supplies, but Mussolini did not dare risk alienating his powerful German ally by accepting; nor did he want a return to powerless dependence on the West.[76] Prudence and economic reality dictated a growing commitment to Hitler. On 18 March the two leaders met for a brief face-to-face discussion on the Brenner Pass. The Duce arrived early in the morning, and waited 'with anxious elation' in heavy snow; Hitler's train was delayed. When he arrived, the group posed for photographs in Mussolini's state railway coach. There was a short meeting which ended by 12.45 p.m., and fifteen minutes later Hitler was hurrying on his way back to Innsbruck. In conference with the German leader all Mussolini's reservations disappeared; he did not dare to act the neutral or the peacemaker. Mussolini feared Hitler, but was fascinated by him. Co-operation with the West, he agreed, was out of the question: 'We

hate them.' 'Italy's entry into the war was', Mussolini told him, 'inevitable'. Her honour and her interests demanded it.[77]
Though Mussolini still talked of postponing intervention to the spring of 1941, he ordered the army to prepare for a possible mobilisation in May 1940. Intervention was now 'only a question of knowing when and how'. The immediate success of German arms when France was invaded in May answered the question. All Mussolini's doubts were swept away. There are times, he later recalled, 'when history catches you by the throat and forces you to take decisions'.[78] By the time that Churchill was appealing to him in the middle of May he was certain that the Pact of Steel again 'guides Italian policy today and tomorrow in the face of any event whatsoever'. Now at last he was presented with the opportunity to establish the new order in the Mediterranean. Britain and France 'no longer had any "élan vital"' he assured Ribbentrop. Their time had come; now it was the turn of 'the young nations'.[79] Italy was in the position to break the bars of her prison. When Roosevelt sent an appeal to Mussolini to remain neutral he replied that 'Italy cannot remain absent at a moment in which the fate of Europe is at stake.'[80]

On 29 May he fixed the date of intervention for 10 June. He did not want to intervene too soon, since the military were so wary of fighting; neither did he want to wait until France was utterly prostrate, in case Germany repudiated his help. Nor did Mussolini want to be seen simply kicking an enemy when he was down. German victory was almost assured; Mussolini did not believe that Britain would, or could, fight on alone. He did not want to be a spectator at the peace conference as Italy had been so often before. He made the best of Italy's military situation. The army was 'not ideal but satisfactory'. There were now twenty-four divisions fully prepared, and 1032 combat-ready aircraft.[81] He privately believed that Italy might get its own phoney war on the French border, a belligerent at Hitler's side but without the risk of a disastrous offensive. He kept his views more to himself to avoid conflicts with the 'neutralists'. On 10 June he declared Italy's belligerence. Hitler, unknown to his ally, considered Mussolini's commitment merely a 'foray for booty'. The German generals were dismissive of Italian assistance. For Mussolini it was the fulfilment of a long-cherished ambition. Italy, he told an audience on the evening of 10 June, below his balcony in the Palazzo Venezia, was 'entering the lists against the plutocratic and reactionary democracies'.[82]

At the last moment Mussolini, 'utterly calm' in the face of the final critical decision, decided to launch an active offensive against a fatally weakened France.[83] The campaign turned into an *opera buffo*.

Thirty-two Italian divisions were repulsed by five demoralised French divisions, while Italian casualties far outnumbered those of her enemy; Italian airmen came off badly in combat with French aircraft, and thereafter filled their action reports with accounts of successful attacks on undefended towns, roads and bridges in the Loire valley.[84] But by now Mussolini was already preparing for the peace, speculating on Italian empire, reflecting on the prospects of alliances with defeated France and cautious Russia to hold Germany in check, bathing, for a brief spell, in the prospect that Italy would become the great power Fascism had always promised.

In 1939, and again in 1940, Italy was faced with the problem of matching ambitions to resources. The success of Fascism had been, since 1922, to conceal the growing strains in the equation. Italy was not a great power, the Roman Empire could not be recreated, the Mediterranean was not *Mare Nostro*. Mussolini certainly raised Italy's international status and provided hard-won achievements in Africa and Spain. But in the process he succeeded in persuading much stronger powers, France and Britain, that Fascist Italy was a dangerous, revisionist state. In challenging their power, Mussolini over-stretched Italian resources and ran much greater risks, which finally exposed Italian weakness. Mussolini's misfortune was to tie himself to the one state in Europe which saw through Italian ambitions. Hitler had no illusions about his ally; by December 1940, he remarked cheerfully that failure had the 'healthy effect of once more compressing Italian claims to within the natural boundaries of Italian capabilities'.[85] German armies were needed to save Italy from disaster in Greece and North Africa. This had always been the paradox of Italy's position: only German help could bring about the revision Italy wanted, but German help would cost Italy the international independence of action revision was supposed to achieve. As the French Ambassador, André François Poncet, said to Ciano when he left to close his Embassy on the day Italy finally declared war: 'The Germans are hard masters. You too will learn this.'[86]

When the Lateran Treaties were signed in 1929, the Pope described Benito Mussolini as 'the man of providence'. The Duce led his country into war in the belief that he was indeed Italy's providential saviour, alone able to determine her future. It was at his insistence, against the advice of his generals and his ministers; Fascist Italy was organised to fulfil the Duce's whim. He believed that he was a great war leader, and that his nation needed to be tempered in 'the fire of battle'. He expressed his war aims in 1940 in terms of imperial advantage, of booty, political destiny and economic power. But there was a compelling personal reason: he could not bear the humiliation of neutrality – 'nobody likes a neutral'.[87] Benito Mussolini had been, in his own words, 'sufficiently dishonoured'.

CHAPTER FIVE
THE SOVIET UNION

> The Soviet Union is indifferent to the question which imperialist brigand falls upon this or that country, this or that independent state.
>
> (*Pravda*, September 1938)

> It is our duty to think of the interests of the Soviet people, of the Union of Soviet Socialist Republics. . . . The countries which suffered most in the war of 1914–18 were Russia and Germany. Therefore the interests of the peoples of the Soviet Union and Germany do not lie in mutual enmity. . . . The fact that our outlooks and political systems differ must not and cannot be an obstacle to the establishment of good political relations between both states.
>
> (Molotov, August 1939)

Between 16 and 20 August 1920 the Polish legionnaires of Marshal Pilsudski attacked and almost annihilated six Soviet armies commanded by the young general, Mikhail Tukhachevsky. The Red Army suffered a humiliating defeat in the battle for Warsaw; its remnants straggled back into the Soviet Union while Poland pushed its frontiers a hundred miles further east into Russia. The defeat marked the end of Lenin's hopes of turning the communist revolution he had led in Russia in October 1917 into a revolutionary struggle across Europe. It was a bitter blow and Soviet leaders did not forget it. Almost twenty years later, on the morning of 17 September 1939, the Red Army swept in force across the Polish border and occupied the whole of eastern Poland until it met the German forces coming the opposite way. The Soviet Union, like Germany, had never been party to the post-war settlement of Versailles. Soviet revisionism and German revisionism met half-way on the rivers of central Poland.

Between the two invasions by the Red Army much had changed. But for Soviet leaders one thing remained constant: the fear that at some point the capitalist powers would unite to destroy the world's first and only communist state. 'Between our proletarian state and all the remaining bourgeois world', wrote the bolshevik general, Michael Frunze, 'there can only be one condition of long, persistent, desperate war to the death.'[1] That threat did not become hard reality until the summer of 1941. Yet in the interval there was much to fuel those fears; deeply distrusted by every other state, loathed by many shades of political opinion abroad, the Soviet Union had no illusions about her isolation and the profound hostility of the outside world. Even Lenin, at a dark moment in 1918, agreed that 'without a world revolution we will not pull through'.[2] The central plank of Soviet foreign policy was the survival of the revolution; in the 1920s and 1930s that meant avoiding war at all costs until the Soviet state was strong enough and stable enough to defend itself. For Soviet leaders the survival of the Soviet Union was the precondition for the survival of the revolution, even at the expense of ideological consistency or, on occasion, of communism abroad. During the inter-war years Soviet foreign policy was dominated by the desire to stand aside from the conflicts of the capitalist world, to become, in Lenin's memorably mixed metaphor, an 'oasis of Soviet power in the middle of the raging imperialist sea'.[3]

The revolution of October 1917, Lenin's revolution, did not destroy the crumbling tsarist state. That had already been done in February when an unholy alliance of disgruntled generals, frustrated liberal politicians and hungry workers forced the Tsar to abdicate. Unable to revive the dilapidated economy or repair the wreckage of Russia's war effort, the new regime was itself thrust aside by the radical wing of the Russian socialist movement, its ranks swollen in 1917 by all kinds of popular forces determined to make something of the revolution. The Bolshevik Party, a handful of far from disciplined revolutionaries in February, grew into a mass movement capable of seizing political power and promising social transformation in October. The impact of this second revolution went far beyond the borders of the old Russian empire. The most radical section of the labour movement had won control of a state whose potentially vast economic and military strength had already been recognised before the First World War. The Bolshevik Party, which changed its name to the Communist Party of the Soviet Union, saw itself as the vanguard of a worldwide revolutionary movement, with allies among all the labour movements and socialist parties of the other states. Its victory was a symbolic challenge to the old liberal world order as surely as the French revolution had once challenged the *ancien régime*.

The bolsheviks were confident that the imperialist war that brought them to power in Russia would release the forces of social revolution all over Europe, even in the colonial empires beyond. In March 1919 the Communist International was established, drawing together socialist parties committed to fighting for the world revolution which would necessarily follow the first blow struck in Russia. It called on workers everywhere to 'wipe out boundaries between states, transform the whole world into one co-operative commonwealth'. 'It will not be long,' Lenin told the assembled delegates, 'and we shall see the victory of communism in the entire world. . . .'[4] Lenin, for one, did not believe that communism could survive in Russia unaided by the rest of the world proletariat. Even less did he believe it when, against his expectations, revolution petered out in the other states of Europe or was crushed by a powerful reaction. Inside the Soviet Union a bitter and protracted civil war was fought between the newly formed Red Army and a motley array of separatist and counter-revolutionary movements. The anti-communist cause was fuelled by Western money and equipment and, finally, by direct armed intervention by all those states which feared the implications for their own safety of communist victory in Russia. Intervention ushered in what Churchill called 'the campaign of fourteen states'. The Soviet Union was attacked from the south, north and east, by forces from Britain, France, the United States, Japan, Canada and a host of lesser powers. The armed intervention finally ended in 1920 with Soviet communism still intact. The states involved were faced with too many difficulties recovering from the impact of war and demobilisation to mount an offensive of any real strength against the Red armies. But the defeat of Red forces before Warsaw showed what a close-run thing survival had been. From being the epicentre of world revolution, the Soviet Union had become the oasis.

Lenin himself had a realistic view of the Soviet situation: 'We must remember that we are at all times but a hair's breadth from every manner of invasion.'[5] By 1920 the Soviet Union found itself permanently on the defensive, where in 1917 it had thought only of advancing. This posed a fresh dilemma for the Soviet leadership. The reality was not world revolution but isolation. Under these circumstances it was difficult to see how the revolution could survive. After the destruction of the civil war, which brought the Russian economy almost to the point of complete collapse, the government was compelled to make concessions to the peasantry and the small-businessmen in order to keep the towns fed and supplied. The 'New Economic Policy' permitted the development of small-scale capitalism and the private cultivation of the land. Serious doubts were now expressed by Soviet leaders and intellectuals about whether socialism could be built at all in a country composed largely of peasants and handicraftsmen rather than factory workers. The argument sharpened antagonisms already existing among the Communist Party elite. Trotsky urged temporary accommodation with the

RUSSIA'S LOSSES, 1917-25

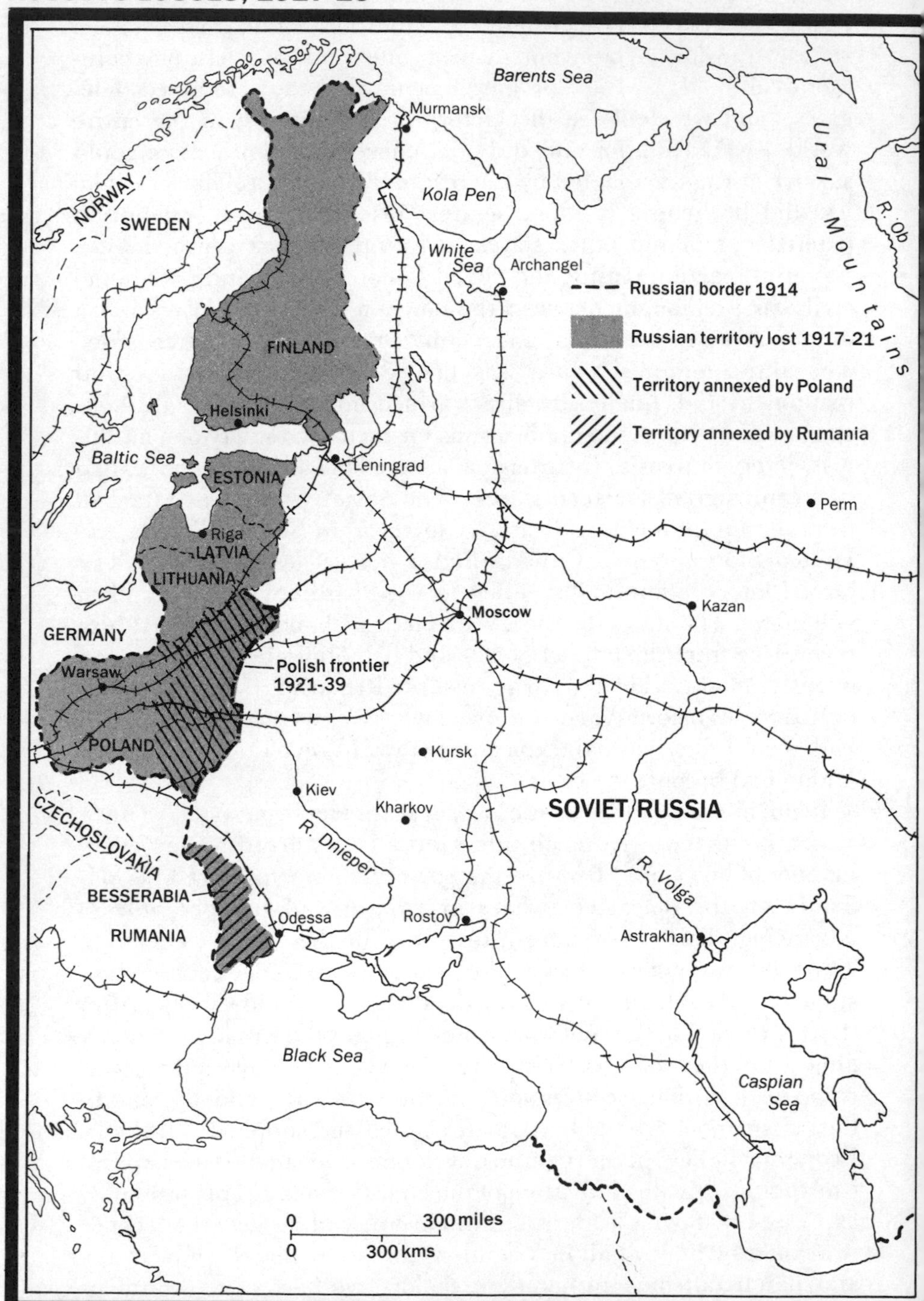

Autarky, the concept of Italy as a productive, self-sustaining nation, became the keynote of Fascist ideology in the 1930s, celebrated by this exhibition in Rome. The slogan 'Mussolini is always right' identified the Duce as the embodiment of the whole Italian people.

Mussolini and Pope Pius XI sign the Lateran Accords in February 1929. By the alliance of church and state Mussolini resolved the central problem of Italian politics; the Pope declared him to be the 'Man of Providence'.

Italy's 'destiny' in Africa: the Italian army which invaded Ethiopia brought bundles of posters in its baggage. Images of Mussolini and the King of Italy were pasted on walls in towns and villages of the new Italian empire.

'Victorious Italian soldiers salute the flag', a carefully posed propaganda display in Ethiopia. The drummer boy in the front rank symbolises the dedication of Italian youth to the goals of the Fascist state.

Mussolini, depicted on a vast wall poster in Tokyo, 1937. In November 1937 Mussolini signed the Anti-Comintern Pact with Germany and Japan, drawing Italy closer to the other powers committed to overturning the status quo.

Modernity – electrification, the grandiose Moscow subway, aviation – were all used as symbols of Soviet advance. At a 1935 rally in Red Square models of the latest Antonev airliners *Lenin* and *Maxim Gorki* were carried aloft by members of the Youth Aviation League. By 1939 the Soviet Union had the world's largest air force.

United States business played a vital role in the development of the Soviet economy: the control panel of this power station was designed and installed by the American General Electric Company. Then as now, the Soviet Union sought good diplomatic relations with nations that supplied technical assistance.

The industrial Five Year Plans transformed the face of the Soviet Union and laid the basis for its future military might. This new steel plant at Novokuznetzk in Siberia was one of many new centres of heavy industry located on virgin lands, far from existing centres of population.

Stalin jokes with Ribbentrop as Molotov signs the Nazi-Soviet Pact on 24 August 1939. The secret protocols of the pact envisaged 'a territorial and political rearrangement' of Eastern Europe: Poland and Lithuania were to be divided between them, while the Soviet Union would be free to recover Bessarabia from Roumania.

'Territorial rearrangements': Soviet armoured cars thrust into eastern Poland on 17 September 1939 while the Germans advanced from the west.

capitalist powers as a prelude to continuing the revolutionary struggle, the 'permanent revolution'; Bukharin favoured gradual social development, at the pace of the peasant; Stalin, the Party Secretary, was committed to a third course, the development of 'socialism in one country'. Stalin, like Lenin, was convinced that in the plain absence of revolution outside Russia, and in the face of the hostility and intolerance of the 'alliance of all the world's capitalist powers', the only sensible course was to take the resources to hand inside the Soviet Union and, somehow or other, use them to build a socialist society. Stalin did not abandon the ultimate goal of world revolution; rather, he sought to secure its citadel first, the hostile hinterland later. 'We can build Socialism', he told Party comrades in 1925, 'by our own efforts.'[6]

The success of these efforts depended not only on Soviet conditions but on the willingness of the outside world to tolerate the growth of a genuinely socialist state in their midst. At the end of the civil war Lenin detected a 'breathing-space' for Russia, but there was no guarantee that it would last. Lenin advocated an extreme form of revolutionary pragmatism. Outwardly the Soviet Union declared herself to stand for peaceful coexistence and economic co-operation with the capitalist world; in practice the Soviet state was forced to take what it could, when it could. Where possible Lenin hoped the Soviet Union could play off one imperialist power against another; when necessary the Soviet Union would even co-operate with imperialist powers if there was something she needed badly enough. Anything, Stalin later wrote, 'which is a necessity from the standpoint of Soviet Russia, is also a necessity from the standpoint of the world revolution'.[7] Tactical flexibility was possible because Russia had everything to gain and little to lose.

Such flexibility even made it possible to employ as the Soviet Union's first Commissar for Foreign Affairs George Chicherin, an aristocratic official from the tsarist Foreign Office who had subsequently become a menshevik, a social democrat in the group opposed to Lenin's bolsheviks. He was appointed Foreign Affairs Commissar because of Lenin's respect for his skills and industry, and because of his command of foreign languages. He was a skilful diplomatist, but never belonged to the Party's inner circles. He was typical of the generation of 'bourgeois' experts recruited to the cause, and he was a supreme practitioner of the pragmatic diplomacy advocated by the revolution's leaders. His survival owed something to the fact that his preferences, to the extent that he expressed them, coincided with those of his bolshevik colleagues. He was a committed revisionist, hostile to the Versailles settlement, and dismissive of the League of Nations, the 'robbers' league'.[8] Ever mindful of the dire necessity for peace, he saw the League as a mere front for the violent ambitions of the capitalist states, orchestrated by the most reactionary and vicious of them all, Great Britain. Here he echoed a widespread feeling in Soviet political circles that not only was Britain the main inspiration behind the intervention in 1919–20, but British imperialism was the most intractable and unscrupulous enemy of socialism in the 1920s.

It was fear of what Britain might do that forced Chicherin to seek what friends he could. In the early 1920s this extended even to Germany, the enemy of a few years before. Like the Soviet Union, Germany was an outcast from the international system, a victim of the greed of the imperial powers. Like Germany too, the Soviet Union was no defender of the post-war settlement. More important, each had something the other wanted: the Russians needed advanced industrial equipment and technical aid; the Germans needed markets desperately, and a place to rearm in secret. In 1922, at Rapallo in Italy, the two states signed an agreement to expand economic ties and mutually renounce all claims for reparation arising from the war. In 1926 the Treaty of Berlin extended this agreement to a firm political commitment; in the event of either power being attacked the other would maintain a benevolent neutrality. The economic agreements were important for Soviet industry, but the real significance of the agreement with Germany was the flattering fact of recognition by one of the other major powers. It set a pattern in Soviet diplomacy for dividing her potential enemies by bilateral agreements with at least one of them. The other real beneficiaries were the German armed forces. The Soviet Union offered facilities for training and weapons-testing forbidden under the terms of the Treaty of Versailles. At the Kama river, in Kazan, a special tank unit was set up where German firms could experiment with the most up-to-date equipment; at Saratov a school for studying poison gas; at Lipetsk an airfield was provided where the new generation of German fighters and heavy bombers were tested out, and hundreds of young Germans given technical and flying experience. By 1928 800 officers of the German armed forces were working in close co-operation with the Red Army, discussing tactics, training methods and technology. In 1933, when the bases were finally shut down after the rise of Hitler, the Soviet Chief of Staff, Tukhachevsky, admitted that 'The Reichswehr has been the teacher of the Red Army, and that will never be forgotten.'[9]

Another unlikely friend was the United States. Though the

American government refused to recognise the Soviet state, economic relations were established very early in the regime's history. Industrial practice in the United States was imitated by Soviet technicians and engineers. A regular flow of American machines and industrial equipment fuelled Soviet industrial development. Lenin himself was greatly attracted to the new ideas of Fordism, of industrial rationalisation as a key instrument in the Soviet fight against the ways of old Russia. Lenin had a film of the Ford factory at work in his private film collection; Ford engineers helped set up the Soviet Union's first tractor and motor-car factories. Between 1920 and 1926 over 25,000 Fordson tractors were acquired to revolutionise Soviet agriculture; Soviet apprentices were trained in the United States at the Henry Ford Trade School; and Soviet technical schools and factories hung banners on the walls proclaiming 'Do it the Ford Way because it is the best way.'[10] Of course the Soviet leaders never lost sight of the fact that the United States was a leading capitalist power. Soviet industry needed the collaboration and technical equipment of the industrialised West, but only in order to strengthen communism. The same was true of Germany, where Soviet officials collaborated not with the large and powerful German labour movement, but with the most reactionary sections of the German armed forces and big business. They fully recognised the political limits of co-operation. The survival of communism and the safety of Russia produced strange bedfellows, but hostility was never far beneath the surface.

The Soviet Union lived in constant fear of war. Chicherin's period in office was punctuated by regular war scares – in 1923, triggered off by a visit of Marshal Foch to Poland, in 1925 in response to the Locarno Treaty, another British step, according to *Pravda*, in 'preparation for war against the USSR',[11] in 1926 in response to nothing in particular. Some of the war scares were mere shadowboxing; some were produced deliberately by Party leaders anxious to test the patriotic and revolutionary credentials of their Party opponents. But underlying the pattern of regular false alarms was a consciousness of the overt hostility excited abroad by communism. Anti-communism was sustained outside Russia with an almost messianic zeal. So powerful did the fear of communism become that it helped to fuel the rise of fascist movements whose whole rationale rested on removing the threat of 1917. Among the great powers it was not so much fear of Russia herself, clearly weakened by years of civil war and internal upheaval, as fear of what they saw as an insidious internal subversion, master-minded by a fifth column loyal to Moscow, and led by the working-class shock troops of the communist parties that sprang up in every state outside the Soviet Union. These parties were linked by the Communist International. Despite Soviet protests that the organisation was a private, independent body which happened to be based inside the Soviet Union, no one had any illusions, communist or non-communist, about the relationship between the Soviet Union and Comintern. Soviet leaders in the age of 'socialism in one country' saw the Comintern as a way not only of spreading revolution, but of supporting the Soviet Union. With the rise of Stalin's power in Russia the strategy of Comintern moved demonstrably away from Trotsky's 'permanent revolution' to a position where it actively promoted the interests and instructions of Soviet communism alone. Communist parties became, in Léon Blum's words, 'Russian nationalist parties'.[12]

On these terms Comintern proved something of a mixed blessing in Moscow. The very existence of foreign communism so closely linked with Moscow fuelled the hostility and anxieties of the capitalist world, making war more rather than less likely. The close links with Moscow also made it difficult for communist parties to co-operate with other socialist parties, permanently weakening the labour movement and alienating many workers from communism altogether. The real paradox was that the Soviet Union counted on the growing economic and social stability of the capitalist world to provide the 'breathing-space' she needed, while simultaneously supporting those very movements committed to rocking the capitalist boat. The paradox was cruelly exposed when the growth of communist activity in Italy and Germany actually resulted in the triumph of a radical nationalism virulently hostile to everything Marxist. Yet for much of the 1920s the Soviet Union failed stubbornly to grasp the nature of the fascist threat. Fascism was seen as a symptom of the breakdown of the bourgeois world system; the real enemy was still the powerful imperialist bourgeoisie operating from London, centre of world capitalism.

If proof of this assertion were needed, it was provided by the British themselves in the great war scare of 1927. *Pravda* in June 1927 carried an article by Stalin alerting his countrymen to the 'real and actual *threat* of a new war'.* Litvinov, Deputy Commissar for Foreign Affairs, pointed the finger directly at Britain, whose ruling class wanted nothing more than to turn Russia into a 'colony for British bankers'.[13] The cause of the mounting war hysteria in the summer of

* Italics in original.

1927 was modest enough. Against a background of rising Conservative anger at Soviet interference in British labour disputes, the more vocal anti-communists pushed the Home Secretary into authorising a raid on the building of the Soviet Trade Delegation. The leader of the anti-Soviet lobby was the MP, Locker-Lampson, who the year before had set up the Clear Out the Reds Campaign, launched with a rally at the Albert Hall attended by at least eighty other MPs. A halfhearted police search of the Trade building revealed nothing more than three innocuous military documents; but armed with the evidence the delegation was accused of spying and sent back to Russia. Diplomatic relations were severed.[14]

The Soviet Union was used to this kind of communist-baiting. But this time it coincided with other disturbing bits of evidence. In April the Soviet mission in China was also raided, and Chiang Kai-shek began a violent assault on the Chinese Communist Party. In June the Soviet representative in Warsaw was assassinated. In Moscow there were alarming echoes of 1914, of Sarajevo, of encirclement. By July Soviet leaders had developed a full-fledged conspiracy theory. No war came and it is easy to dismiss Soviet fears as a flimsy piece of propaganda. Yet in the context of the 1920s and the recent experience of intervention, many Soviet officials and the Soviet public saw reason enough to be apprehensive. Of all the war scares it carried the most plausibility.

The real impact of the war scare of 1927 was not on Soviet foreign policy but on politics inside Russia. Good Jacobin that he was, Stalin seized on the threat of war to isolate the few remaining internationalists among the Party leaders and to rally the Soviet people to the revolution. The year 1927 marked a watershed in the development of the young Soviet state. After the war scare Stalin and his supporters in the state apparatus finally succeeded in defeating rival cliques in the Party. By raising the cry 'the revolution in danger', Stalin was at last able to get general acceptance that socialism in one country could be secured only by transforming the Soviet Union rapidly, and profoundly, from a weakly defended, primarily agrarian state into a militarily powerful, industrialised state.

The drive for the modernisation of the Soviet Union, which was launched with a Five Year Plan for industry a few months after the war scare had died down, is unavoidably linked with the name of one man, Josef Stalin. This view exaggerates the extent to which Stalin was involved in either the planning or the execution of the 'Great Leap Forward'; but it does highlight the central fact that it was unquestionably Stalin's political will that pushed Russia forward through the tumultuous years of economic revolution. Stalin, the son of a leather-worker from Georgia in southern Russia, was one of the few bolshevik leaders in the 1920s to come from a genuinely working-class background. A prominent bolshevik activist before the war, he came to Lenin's notice because of his role in a famous bank robbery in Tiflis in 1907 carried out to boost bolshevik funds. Unlike the intellectual exiles of Russian socialism, Stalin served his time in tsarist jails. He brought to the revolution a very literal, proletarian ambition. Though not uneducated, he despised intellectual socialism and deliberately adopted a political style that was coarser and more calculatingly brutal than that of his diffident middle-class colleagues. For Stalin the revolution was genuinely a workers' revolution; through capitalist oppression the worker was a remorseless, even violent enemy of all things bourgeois. Stalin was on the left of the revolutionary movement, eager for social transformation, impatient at the slow pace of change in the 1920s, but utterly convinced that socialism could triumph in the backward, peasant-dominated society he confronted.

His rise to personal power in the Soviet Union can partly be explained by this revolutionary commitment; but it owed as much to Stalin's own political intelligence. He was above all a survivor. His political methods were unscupulous and secretive. Stalin himself was not a particularly charismatic figure. Short, with greying hair and pockmarked cheeks, he was a reserved, almost timid figure in public, polite and subdued with foreign visitors, but given to bouts of ill-temper and vindictiveness in private. He was consumed by a conviction that someone was needed to safeguard the revolution, that Marxism permitted 'heroes'. He was the appointed guardian, the revolution was all: 'I shall ruthlessly sacrifice forty nine per cent, if by so doing I can save the fifty one per cent, that is save the Revolution.'[15] During the 1920s, as the Party Secretary-General, he out-manoeuvred all his potential rivals in the Party to build himself a powerful base of support throughout the local party cadres. By the late 1920s his political position was unassailable. He used the 1927 war scare to isolate and enfeeble his remaining opponents for failing to respond to the 'external danger' by closing Party ranks. By 1928 he was in a position to pursue the transformation of Russia, the 'revolution from above', on his own terms.

Stalin was all too aware of the central problem confronting the Soviet state. If the war scare was more fiction that fact, it nonetheless highlighted the fact that ten years of communism had failed to make the revolution secure. Soviet society was still backward militarily and industrially weak, almost swamped by its vast rural base. A weak Soviet state would always be a tempting prize to the outside world, as Stalin himself explained in one of his few memorable public speeches:

> One feature of the Old Russia was the continual beatings she suffered for falling behind, for her backwardness. She was beaten by the Mongol khans. She was beaten by the Turkish beys. She was beaten by the Swedish feudal lords. She was beaten by the Polish and Lithuanian gentry. She was beaten by the British and French capitalists. She was beaten by the Japanese barons. All beat her – for her backwardness; for military backwardness, for cultural backwardness, for political backwardness, for industrial backwardness, for agricultural backwardness. . . . We are fifty or a hundred years behind the advanced countries. We must make good this distance in ten years. Either we do it, or they crush us.[16]

Stalin could see evidence of backwardness throughout Soviet Russia. Instead of modern state-run farms, the Soviet countryside was studded with tiny villages grimly hanging on to an archaic agriculture and pre-revolutionary peasant values. Instead of an extensive, progressive industry, most commercial and industrial life was still in the hands of petty tradesmen and old-fashioned craftsmen. In large areas of Soviet society the Party writ hardly ran at all. The proletariat, the social heart of the revolution, was small, poor and hostage to the villagers whose grain they needed to survive. For ten years the communist revolution relied on the co-operation of bourgeois 'experts' who had served two masters, Tsar and Soviet. Stalin gave himself ten years to wake the sleeping giant.

The revolution from above struck Soviet society from two different directions: first of all a massive state-orchestrated industrialisation, then a revolution in the countryside to drive the peasants into the factories. Under two successive Five Year Plans Soviet industry was transformed. Industrial output in 1928 had only just regained the levels of 1913. By 1932 it had doubled, according to Soviet figures, and more than doubled again over the next five years. Even the most conservative Western estimates agree that at least two-thirds of the Soviet claim was clearly true.[17] Top priority went to those industries that would directly strengthen Soviet military potential. Soviet planners had learned the lessons of total war, armament in depth, from the German strategists they read and talked with in the 1920s. Military security depended on raw materials and skilled workers as much as it did on planes and tanks. Under the Five Year Plans the Soviet Union got both. Steel output increased from 4 million tons to 18 million; oil production from 11 million tons to 28 million. From producing fewer than 1000 aircraft in 1930, Soviet factories were turning out over 10,000 a year ten years later; in 1930, 170 old-fashioned tanks, six years later almost 5000 modern machines. Soviet rearmament was on a scale unmatched by any other power. The Five Year Plans did very little for Soviet living-standards but they laid the foundations in the 1930s of the Soviet superpower.[18]

The second line of attack was on the countryside. In January 1930 Stalin launched the major campaign to collectivise Soviet agriculture, to end the centuries-old system of strip and patch farming with horses and handpower, and to substitute large, rationalised, state-owned farms, with tractor and mechanical reaper. The enterprise was a vast one. Collectivisation confronted the great bulk of the Soviet population with a bleak choice: to abandon the land so hardly won in 1917, and the habits formed from centuries of depredation and hardship, or to stand, bewildered and vulnerable, against the revolutionary storm that broke over them. For some of the peasantry there was no choice. Stalin had already identified a specific enemy of the revolution in the countryside, the *kulak*, the rich farmer who threatened to bring in capitalism by the rural back door. The *kulak* (in Russian meaning 'fist' – someone who holds on to what he wants) was neither rich by Western standards, nor very politically conscious, nor very numerous. But he was made to stand for the forces of reaction, responsible for backwardness, for wrecking revolutionary prospects. Between 1930 and 1933 an army of Soviet officials and policemen, urged on by the ascendant radicals in the cities, descended on the villages, arresting and deporting anyone who was deemed to be a *kulak*. In effect this meant anyone who resisted the collective farm. Millions of peasants did do so. They fled to the towns, slaughtered their livestock, burned their stocks. A new civil war raged over the Soviet plains as communists exacted a bitter revenge on those who were holding up progress and socialism. It was a messy, almost planless, confrontation, trading on denunciation and envy, investing in ambition and violence. Peasants already forced into collectives turned against those still outside; each new wave of *apparatchiks*, officials from outside, cut their teeth on a further round of deportations and executions. In three years the Soviet landscape was transformed. Almost all the land area was collectivised; millions of peasants died of starvation or in the labour camps set up for deportees. The industrial proletariat grew from three million to ten million in seven years as dispossessed young farmers were sent to build the industries of the new industrial cities, Magnitogorsk, Stalingrad, Lugansk.[19]

This was an upheaval greater than anything that had happened in 1917. There was no guarantee of the outcome. The revolution from above was far from a totalitarian master-plan. Its successes depended on individual initiative and revolutionary enthusiasm; the organisation of the revolution was fractured and arbitrary. The centre had little control over what many of the little Stalins in the provinces were doing. The programme Stalin launched in 1928 was a great gamble. Though its long-term aim was to strengthen the Soviet Union, an aim that was without doubt achieved, in the short term the Soviet state teetered on the edge of anarchy, weakening it yet further in the eyes of the outside world. Fortunately for Stalin the capitalist world itself was plunged in crisis in 1929 at just the time that the great Soviet experiment was under way. The Great Crash, which Soviet leaders gleefully hailed as evidence that the capitalist system was in its final death throes, brought a number of advantages. Western powers were keen to provide the Soviet Union with some of the vital resources for her own industrialisation as their markets melted away in the West. By 1932 almost half of all Soviet imports came from Germany. Britain once again became a major supplier, as economic expediency triumphed over ideological distaste. The Great Crash and the depression that followed also strengthened communism abroad and threatened the social stability of imperialist regimes. Soviet weakness was unlikely to go punished at the height of this crisis.[20]

But there was also a price to pay. Soviet leaders were all too aware that the recession would sharpen antagonisms between the capitalist powers which might, in the end, be turned against the Soviet Union. In 1931 Japan occupied Manchuria, and assumed a long common frontier with the Soviet Union. In Europe the security and co-operation of the 1920s was giving way to renewed talk of rearmament and a profound lack of confidence in collective security. In 1933 Hitler, the most vocal and uncompromising of the new generation of anti-bolsheviks, assumed power in Berlin. For some months the Soviet Union made desperate attempts to maintain the connection with Germany which had been at the centre of her strategy since 1922. German machine tools were vital for Soviet industrial expansion; in 1931 there were 5000 German engineers working in Soviet industry. Soviet officials and commissars went out of their way to assure the Nazi regime that the change of government made no difference to Soviet friendship. The Soviet Union stood back while the largest communist party in Europe was broken up and terrorised by the Nazi SA. Only by the end of 1933 did relations perceptibly cool with the German refusal to tone down press attacks on the Soviet Union. Co-operation with German armed forces came to an end in October 1933. But even in 1934 Molotov, Chairman of the Council of Commissars, could publicly announce that the Soviet

A 1930 poster denouncing Fascism, the long arm of the international capitalist conspiracy.

Union had no other wish 'than to continue further good relations with Germany . . . one of the great nations of the modern epoch'.[21] Only the Nazi–Polish pact, signed in 1934, brought the relationship to an end. Not even the Soviet Union could swallow German concessions to the state in Europe it hated most.

Clearly the writing was on the wall. In January 1934, at the 17th Congress of the Soviet Communist Party, Stalin chose the occasion to warn Party comrades of new dangers: 'Again, as in 1914, the parties of bellicose imperialism, the parties of war and revenge, are coming into the foreground. Quite clearly things are heading for a new war.'[22] Yet the revolution from above was still in motion. The Soviet Union needed peace abroad; or, failing that, had to find a way of keeping out of conflict. The rise of Japanese militarism and the break with Germany forced the Soviet Union to rethink its foreign policy entirely.

The option chosen by Soviet leaders, qualified support for the Western strategy of collective security, was a curious choice. The one thing that the growing international crisis had already made evident was how feeble a reed collective action was likely to be. Certainly the support of the Soviet Union might have done something to reverse this trend, but Soviet motives for the *volte face* in her foreign policy were always suspect in the West. As far as the Soviet Union was concerned there was not much alternative. 'What other guarantee of security is there?' asked the new Foreign Affairs Commissar, Maxim Litvinov. 'Military alliance and the policy of the balance of power? Pre-war history has shown that this policy not only does not get rid of war, but on the contrary unleashes it. . . .'[23] There was nevertheless something understandably incongruous about Soviet enthusiasm for the League that Stalin himself dismissed as the 'organisational centre of imperialist pacifism' run by a France that he regarded as 'the most aggressive and militarist' of all powers.[24]

Yet the appointment of Litvinov in 1930 to succeed Chicherin was a sign of sorts that such a change in Soviet strategy was possible. Litvinov, son of a Jewish merchant from Russian Poland, was an old bolshevik, close to Stalin, though very different in personality. He was an outgoing, almost urbane diplomat, popular abroad to the extent that any communist was popular, more naturally drawn to the democratic West than other Soviet leaders. Though he never openly trusted British and French statesmen, he was, of all Soviet leaders, the one most likely to be able to mend the broken bridges between the two sides. Already within his first three years of office

Litvinov had signed a whole rash of non-aggression pacts with European states – Finland, Estonia, Latvia, Poland, even France. In 1933 formal diplomatic ties were established with the United States for the first time. Roosevelt found the Soviet experiment 'interesting'. Litvinov saw the American recognition of the Soviet Union as a way 'to avert the Japanese danger'.[25] He saw more clearly than other Soviet leaders the dangers posed by fascism. He calculated that the only chance of isolating or containing the fascist powers lay in working more closely with Britain and France. This was the cornerstone of Soviet strategy for the next five years.

The critical test of goodwill on both sides was the issue of Soviet entry to the League of Nations. Since by 1934 both Japan and Germany had already left the League, Soviet admission was a rather hollow gesture. But French ministers were insistent that any closer ties between their two countries could be secured only if the Soviet Union agreed to join the League. On 18 September 1934 the Soviet delegates finally took their seats on the League Council, publicly endorsing the post-war peace settlement, which in private they continued to condemn. The Soviet Union hoped to complete the task of reintegration into the international system with a multilateral pact including both Germany and France, but this was a forlorn hope. As relations with Germany worsened, Litvinov had to be content with a pact of mutual assistance signed in May 1935 with France. There was little chance of a similar political agreement with Britain, but firmer economic ties meant that by the mid-1930s Britain had supplanted Germany as the Soviet Union's chief source of supply. In a whole host of minor ways Soviet leaders sought to capitalise on the thaw in relations with the West, while losing no opportunity to remind their new partners in the League of the responsibilities of good-neighbour diplomacy.

It was evident to Stalin that the Comintern, still mouthing slogans of world revolution and remorseless conflict with bourgeois democracy, was something of a barrier to good neighbourliness. In 1934 Comintern was forced to fall into line, and pose as a good defender of democracy and collective action. After the mauling the German Communist Party had experienced during the first year of Nazi rule even the most hardened anti-bourgeois could see that hostility to democracy had its negative side. In 1933 Comintern members were still being sent on revolutionary 'manoeuvres', like the ones organised in France in August in the Aisne–Oise river system, where members were taught how to build a barricade of boats, use explosives and organise a general strike of rivermen.[26] In 1934 the terrorist image was abandoned altogether, and communist parties everywhere adopted the strategy of the Popular Front, of active co-operation with all democratic and republican parties in hostility to the 'open terroristic dictatorship' practised by fascist regimes.[27] It is evident that the switch to the common fight against fascism was popular with ordinary communist members. It reduced the conflict to two common denominators and aligned communism clearly on the side of 'good' for the first time since 1917. The war against fascism was a just war.

To be convincing, Comintern had to be respectable. Its vocabulary changed; instead of words like 'dictatorship of the proletariat', 'revolution', 'social fascists' (this last directed at the non-communist labour movement), its publications were now sprinkled with 'anti-fascism', 'democracy', 'peace', 'independence'.[28] In 1936 the new Russian constitution, the Stalin Constitution, was promulgated, hailed by communists everywhere as a model for world democracy. In a widely publicised press interview, Stalin asserted that 'the export of revolution is nonsense'. Communism became the thinking man's politics; support for its professions of peace and brotherhood was to be found in intellectual circles throughout the world. Comintern did not hide the ultimate goal entirely. In 1938 it trumpeted that the Popular Front tactic 'in its further development will inevitably lead to the overthrow of rotting capitalism'.[29] But, where it could, Comintern dissimulated; for it was in the interests of Soviet survival that it should.

Concealment took all sorts of forms. In 1932 the German communist Willi Münzenberg organised in Amsterdam a World Congress against War which invited thousands of distinguished delegates from all over the world. The Congress launched the League against War and Fascism which set up branches worldwide. The American branch could claim 16 million supporters by 1939, led by distinguished scientists and men of letters.[30] Yet the whole organisation was a thinly veiled front for communist recruitment of intellectuals and fellow travellers, even spies. Spying was the primary function of an even more bizarre front organisation, the Foreign Excellent Raincoat Company. Founded in Belgium at the instigation of the communist spy Leiba Trepper, the company opened seventeen other outlets for retailing rainwear all over Europe, each of which was the base for establishing a network of communist agents. The most successful was the Foreign Excellent Raincoat business in Berlin; this set up the Red Orchestra spy-ring based on Göring's Air Ministry, which supplied confidential military material to Russia until 1942.[31]

Within a year the Soviet Union was tranformed from an unrelenting critic of the imperialist powers to an enthusiast for foreign democracy and the international status quo. It was a tactical switch that inevitably invited distrust. It was never clear in the West whether communist democracy was more than skin-deep. Differences were buried; Popular Front governments with communist support emerged first in Spain in February 1936, then in France in June. But the differences were buried only beneath a light covering of propaganda topsoil. Communists would not actually take ministerial responsibility, and the old enmities between moderate socialists and revolutionary communists in the workplace could not be so easily eroded. For her part, the Soviet Union was quickly disillusioned with the flirtation with collective security. The French did agree to sign a mutual assistance pact with the Soviet Union in May 1935, but no sooner was it signed than the new French Foreign Minister, Pierre Laval, made every effort to render it ineffective. French conservatives disliked having to deal with communists at all, and the agreement was left toothless in the absence of any military discussions between the two parties.[32] Then came the Italian war in Ethiopia and the German occupation of the Rhineland. The Soviet Union stood firmly by the letter of the law; her League partners tried to reach accommodation with Mussolini, and took no action against Germany. Neither France nor Britain liked being chided by the Soviet Union for their failure to stand by the League. The final test of the good intentions of both sides came with the outbreak of civil war in Spain in July 1936. Britain and France did nothing to rescue the Republic and its Popular Front government, leaving the Soviet Union, as Stalin saw it, in the front line in defence of democracy. Here was the perfect opportunity to construct an international Popular Front against European fascism.

The failure of co-operation over Spain was a painful lesson for Soviet strategy. It served to confirm what Soviet leaders had suspected all along, that Western statesmen were only halfhearted defenders of collective security, more hostile to communism than to fascism. The ideological divide was as great as ever, but it was self-interest as much as ideology that seemed to govern Western attitudes. Stalin had never shed his dislike of the British Empire, and he interpreted British inaction over Spain as a calculated attempt to drive the Soviet Union into a war with Germany from which the imperial powers alone would profit. This attitude was to colour Soviet attitudes to the West profoundly throughout the period leading to German invasion in 1941.

The Spanish Civil War bankrupted collective security. The Soviet Union sent supplies and technical experts to Spain, leavened with secret policemen detailed to hunt down Trotskyite opponents of the Stalin line. Sovet action served to widen the rift with the Western powers. Litvinov continued to mouth the slogans of League diplomacy until 1939, but it was more form than substance. Nothing could disguise the fact that the Soviet Union was once again in the position of vulnerability she had tried so hard to avoid. From 1937 the Soviet Union faced an involuntary isolation. The German alliance was lost in 1934; the rapprochement with the West had proved valueless. Japan in China and Germany in Europe were a growing menace to Soviet security, and no guarantees or pacts could be secured against either. Instead the three aggressor powers, Germany, Japan and Italy, produced a pact of their own, the Anti-Comintern, directed specifically at the Soviet state. Throughout 1936 and 1937 the Soviet Union continued to put out feelers to Germany, confident that some common ground could still be found despite the ideological confrontation. In December 1937 Litvinov told a French reporter that co-operation with Nazi Germany was 'perfectly possible'.[33]

It was just at this point of growing isolation and insecurity that a new storm broke inside the Soviet Union. The years of forced collectivisation and industrial expansion had been punctuated by periods of intense conflict and violence between peasants and officials, between rival cliques in the Party apparatus, between locality and centre. The party that struggled to bring about the Great Leap Forward unleashed a wave of popular revolutionism that it simply could not control. At the centre Stalin demanded constant communist vigilance against anyone who deviated from the Party plans and harsh punishments for anyone deemed to have done so. In the provinces a new generation of younger peasants and workers adopted slogans of 'popular criticism' and directed their attacks against bourgeois experts whose communist credentials were suspect, or against corrupt officials, provincial Party barons and 'wreckers and saboteurs' who held up the march of revolution. In 1937 the two movements, revolution from above and from below, converged in a terrifying crescendo of revolutionary lawlessness and violence.

The victims of the terror that gripped the Soviet Union in 1937 were drawn indiscriminately from all walks of Soviet life. The enemy of the revolution was anyone who was defined as such or denounced as such. In a great number of cases the victims were ill-educated, poorly trained officials, managers or officers who could not cope with the demands made on them by the industrialisation and modernisation drive. Their technical incompetence was defined as sabotage;

peasants who drove their new tractors too hard, foremen who could not read the instructions on their American machine tools, managers who could not meet their quotas were all tarred with the same counter-revolutionary brush. They were hunted out by the remorseless officials of the NKVD, the Soviet Interior Ministry, spurred on by the ascetic and forbidding figure of N. E. Ezhov, a revolutionary puritan who saw it as his mission to tear out the last lingering vestiges of reaction from the healthy Soviet body.[34]

The *Ezhovschina*, the great terror of 1937, had a momentum all its own. Even Stalin became anxious that the movement might imperil the great gains made since 1928, and tried to rein it back during the course of the year. Yet there was no way in which he could control the often spontaneous and contagious waves of local, popular violence. And in the end it was Stalin who bore much of the responsibility for the terror visited on the state apparatus itself, for it bore all the hallmarks of the strategies of Party purging and show trials that he had used to defeat his opponents since the 1920s. He had already authorised two major purges of the Party to eradicate criminals and careerists in 1933 and 1935. He arranged the first of the great show trials of his political opponents in 1936. Stalin, too, was the inspiration behind a great many war and spy scares in the past, and of a growing Soviet xenophobia. The grotesque accusations of fascist collaboration, espionage and counter-revolutionary plotting fitted all too well with the arbitrary practices of ten years of Stalinist justice. While the populist terror raged in the provinces, the revolution began to devour its own children. Large sections of the Party, the civil service and the armed forces were arrested, summarily tried and executed. Confessions extorted by torture implicated friends and associates. The Party became locked into a vicious spiral of suspicion, denunciation, betrayal and vengeance, from which none save Stalin and his inner circle was immune. The inspiration was Darwin, not Marx.

By early 1938 the bloodletting began to abate. But the damage had been done. The Soviet foreign service was in disarray. Litvinov survived for no very good reason, perhaps because Stalin was anxious to keep as many options open abroad as possible. But he lost both his deputies, his personal secretaries, the ambassadors to more than a dozen states and almost all the heads of the Foreign Commissariat departments. From the viewpoint of Soviet security the most damaging impact was on the armed forces; 35,000 officers, over half the entire officer corps, were purged, from Marshal Tukhachevsky, the Chief of Staff, to ordinary subalterns. The leading Soviet air strategists and the top Soviet aircraft designers were executed or imprisoned. Some 90 per cent of all generals and 80 per cent of all colonels fell victim.[35] In June 1937 almost the entire General Staff was put on trial accused of spying for Germany. Since many of them had been closely associated with the German forces during the pre-Hitler period and had kept up contacts even beyond 1933 there was an element of spurious plausibility. As one contemporary Soviet witness later wrote, 'I believed that what I read was true, that a military conspiracy really did exist, and the participants [in the trial] were connected with Germany and wanted to carry out a fascist coup in our country. At the time I had no other explanation for what was happening.'[36] Worse still from the Soviet view, the stories were at least half believed outside Russia too. The French government were all too ready to accept that Soviet opponents of Stalin had passed on secrets to the Germans and were more reluctant than ever to open any kind of military talks with the Soviet forces. The Germans were in turn indignant that they should be the butt of a conspiracy theory of which they were patently innocent.

Josef Stalin, in a 1938 cartoon, with a coffin for a body.

The impact of the purges on foreign opinion was entirely adverse. So much so that it is difficult to understand why, at such an awkward time in Soviet foreign relations, such a devastating and chaotic terror should have been unleashed. This fact alone suggests that the terror was a phenomenon very difficult to control, with a timescale and rationality that grew out of the great revolutionary upheaval of the early 1930s. Those who promoted the terror were more concerned with revolutionary purity than foreign opinion. Nor can we entirely dismiss the fears in Soviet political circles that there might exist some fascist international, black counterpart of the Comintern, recruiting forces hostile to Stalin in the Soviet Union.[37] The fear of the enemy within had deep roots in Soviet political culture running back to Lenin. Nonetheless, as the news of the terror filtered out of the Soviet Union it did nothing to reverse the path to isolation. 'At the moment,' complained Litvinov, 'no one wants anything to do with us.'[38] The rift that had already opened over Spain widened further. The only value either Britain or France had seen in co-operating with the Soviet Union was as an effective counter-force to Germany and Japan. The purges, it was generally agreed, had virtually eliminated the Soviet Union as a serious military force in the near future, and had turned the Soviet state in on itself, away from foreign affairs altogether. The British considered the Soviet Union to be 'stricken by sterility'; Coulondre, the French Ambassador, reported to Paris that Moscow was pursuing 'a policy of abstention'; Schulenberg, the German Ambassador, told Berlin that 'the purges reduced the specific weight of the Soviet Union in world affairs'.[39]

Since the Soviet Union was no longer a power to be reckoned with, the Western powers were able to adopt the attitudes they were more familiar with. The USSR was ignored and disliked as she had been in the past. The British Prime Minister, Neville Chamberlain, had a deep personal hostility towards the Soviet Union, 'half Asiatic', 'pulling the strings behind the scenes' to get Britain to fight Germany.[40] The animosity of French ruling circles was no less deeply felt. Soviet politicians were much more at home with this relationship too. In January 1938 Molotov publicly attacked France as 'refuge to all sorts of adventurers and criminal organisations, which are nothing but nests of vipers, nests of terrorists and diversionists, which openly pursue their hostile anti-Soviet activities . . .'.[41] In June Stalin told the American emissary Joseph Davies that 'England [was] determined upon a policy of making Germany strong . . . with the purpose of ultimately making Germany strong as against Russia.'[42] Both sides were deeply worried by the rise of German ambitions; neither side was now prepared to help the other keep the Germans in check.

While the Western powers discounted the Soviet Union, the fascist powers saw Soviet weakness as an opportunity to be exploited. The German Ambassador to Moscow sent back regular reports indicating the incapacity of the Soviet Union to interfere in Eastern Europe, and the evident unwillingness of the Soviet leadership 'to march in defence of a bourgeois state'.[43] Soviet isolation was one of the factors that permitted the onset of German expansion. The German occupation of Austria occurred on the last day of the last show trial, that of Bukharin. It was not even mentioned in the Soviet press until three days after it had taken place, and then only in the familiar terms of an attack on inert British imperialism.[44] The Czech crisis which followed was a different matter. For not only did the Soviet Union have a mutual assistance pact with France, but in the same year, 1935, she had signed a similar agreement with Czechoslovakia. The second of these pacts could only be activated on the all-important condition that France fulfilled her pledge to the Czechs at the same time. Under no circumstances was the Soviet Union going to put herself in the situation where she might face Germany alone. Here was another test, like Spain, of the West's commitment to collective security.

The Soviet Union insisted throughout the Czech crisis that she would stand by the letter of the agreement made in 1935. As early as February 1938 Potemkin, Litvinov's deputy, assured the Czech Ambassador in Moscow that his country would 'render assistance . . . in line with the pact of mutual assistance'.[45] This commitment was publicly repeated at intervals up to September. It may never be known with certainty whether the Soviet Union was in earnest. The Soviet leaders lost nothing by their honest commitment to the Pact, for they knew that it could be activated only if France made a firm commitment first. There was plenty of circumstantial evidence to suggest to them that France, tied, in their view, dishonourably to British apron-strings, would not fulfil her pledge to the Czechs in 1938. The real issue was whether France could persuade her allies in Eastern Europe, Poland and Roumania, to open the way to Soviet forces on their way to fight for Czechoslovakia. The French failure to secure agreement during the summer of 1938 was understandable, for neither of her Eastern allies relished Soviet troops on their soil. The Soviet Union had unsettled business with Poland and Roumania, both of which had seized Russian lands during the period of intervention and civil war eighteen years before. But there was certainly something in Soviet suspicions that the French had not tried very hard. By June 1938 Soviet leaders were resigned to Western appeasement. In a portentous speech on 26 June Litvinov announced to the West that 'The Soviet government . . . relieved itself of responsibilities for the future development of events.' More ominously Litvinov hinted openly that the Soviet Union now regarded herself as a revisionist power once again: 'it makes no difference to us, of course, which Power will exploit this or that colony, win this or that foreign market, subject to its rule this or that weak state'.[46]

There is also evidence that Soviet professions of support for the Czechs was merely designed to win goodwill abroad. The Soviet Union was a model member of the League during 1938, at just the point, as Litvinov privately admitted, that it 'had ceased to be reckoned with, ceased to be feared'.[47] By insisting in September 1938 that the Soviet Union would only help the Czechs with the authorisation of the League Council, as well as the commitment of France, Soviet leaders knew that they were asking for the impossible. Privately the Soviet leadership had agreed among themselves as early as April that military help was virtually impossible, and that the Czechs should adopt a 'conciliatory position' – a view not very different from that in Paris or London.[48] Throughout the period of crisis the Soviet Union was much more concerned with the threat from Japan in Manchuria where active fighting broke out on the border at Changkufeng in July 1938 and continued into mid-August. In September, when the anxious French at last asked Moscow whether military help would be forthcoming, the mood there had changed considerably. The Soviet answer was simply to turn the question back on the French – what would France do militarily against Germany? Of one thing Stalin was now determined, he was not going to be drawn into a war in which Germany and the USSR did the fighting while the West sat back. Litvinov was disappointed both by the feebleness of the West, who had, in his view, vastly overestimated the military strength of Nazi Germany, and his failure to persuade his government colleagues that collective action to deter Hitler was both desirable and practical. The days of collective security were numbered in Soviet foreign policy; talk of revision, hostility to the West, Soviet nationalism were in the ascendant. 'The Soviet Union', wrote Joseph Davies to Washington, 'is rapidly being driven into a complete isolation and even hostility to England and indifference to France.'[49]

Nevertheless there is evidence that the Soviet Union did make preliminary military preparations in September 1938. At the last moment Roumania agreed to the overflight of Soviet aircraft to bases in Czechoslovakia. Marshal Voroshilov, Commissar for Defence, later explained in detail that on 22 September a partial mobilisation of thirty infantry divisions and a number of armoured and cavalry units was ordered. The Czech leader, Beneš, assumed that, in the event of a German attack, Soviet help would be similar to the help sent to Spain two years before.[50] But foreign intelligence services could find no evidence at the time for this concentration of forces on the Soviet Union's western borders. The French secret service obtained information which confirmed that the troops in the area were not in any condition for combat. German intelligence, which was of all the services most anxious to find out Soviet intentions, searched in vain for the thirty divisions. A secret report from Bucharest to Berlin confirmed that at no time during September 'had the Soviet Union the intention of bringing into motion its war machine for the purpose of granting military assistance to Czechoslovakia'.[51] Even if military preparations were undertaken in September, it is much more likely that they were directed not at Germany but at Poland. The Poles hoped to profit from German moves by putting pressure on the Czechs to relinquish territory. Warsaw was warned by Soviet leaders that any move would lead to Soviet action against Poland. This was a contest the Soviet Union welcomed; Germany was another matter.

In the end the question is not so much whether the Soviet Union really did make military preparations to help the Czechs, but whether a firm offer of Soviet help would really have made any difference. For the reality was that through the whole crisis Chamberlain was determined to keep the Soviet Union at arm's length. The Soviet offers of pacts, military talks, common fronts were never taken seriously, and at the end Chamberlain was instrumental in rejecting any Soviet participation in the Munich conference in which the Czechs were formally abandoned. The whole drift of Western strategy was towards accommodation of German demands to prepare the way for more rearmament and a negotiated general settlement at a future date. There was never a point at which a genuine offer of substantial military help from the Soviet side would have altered this strategy, while such an offer held all sorts of dangers if Russian troops were once allowed to march westwards into Europe. Distrust of Soviet motives, particularly the loud revisionist noises being made in Moscow against Poland, mingled with severe doubts about the military capability of a state still in the process of killing off its generals and admirals. Nor could Britain bring any real military strength to bear in the autumn of 1938; military discussions barely took place between Britain and France. The prospect of hard military planning with the Soviet Union was virtually out of the question.

None of this reality was lost on Soviet leaders. Munich was a profound shock. The exclusion of the Soviet Union from the conference left her 'hurt' and 'humiliated'.[52] Isolation was complete and obvious. Everything pointed to what Stalin had most feared, co-operation between the states of capitalist Europe directed against the Soviet Union, either in concert or by giving Germany a free hand in the East directed against Soviet territory. 'The Soviet Union will stand alone,' complained the Soviet delegate at Comintern. 'Alone and unaided she will have to wage war against Hitler. . . . To save our country from this war, I would be prepared to treat with the devil.'[53] There was even talk of a Far Eastern Munich in which Britain would succeed in turning Japan, too, against the Soviet Union. This was a war scare of a different order. Everything that happened in the aftermath of Munich, the Anglo-German declaration, the Franco-German agreement in December, pointed from the Soviet view to an obvious conclusion. The capitalist powers were at last burying their differences against the common proletarian enemy. Appeasement could have no other logic; 'Chamberlain', observed the Soviet Ambassador in London, Ivan Maisky, 'is a hopeless case. He cannot mend his ways.'[54]

But mend his ways he did. In February the British began to make more encouraging noises to the Soviet Union. When Maisky visited the Foreign Office on 3 February he was received by the disarming news that Britain was not hostile to the Soviet Union but that 'engrossed in other grave problems it had somehow "forgotten" for a time to strengthen its relations with the Soviet Government'.[55] On 1 March Chamberlain himself visited the Soviet Embassy, the first time by any British Prime Minister. This was followed by exploratory talks on a possible Eastern European bloc to deter further German aggression, and finally, after the German occupation of Prague on 15 March, a unilateral guarantee by Britain of Polish and Roumanian territorial integrity. This did not entirely suit Soviet interests; the Poles were still 'Hitler's jackals', and Roumania still held Bessarabia, the stolen territories. But it at least showed a willingness to do something positive about the Nazi threat in the East, and gave Litvinov, whose personal star had waned after the débâcle of collective security at Munich, a last chance to see whether some co-operation with the West would give the Soviet Union the security it needed. The British guarantee transformed the Soviet position; even Chamberlain had to admit that to make the guarantees work Soviet co-operation might now be necessary. In Paris

French leaders were determined to try to reconstruct the alliance of 1914 to encircle Hitler; in Germany it suddenly became urgently necessary to neutralise the Soviet threat by driving a wedge between Moscow and the West. From being the outcast of Europe the Soviet Union was suddenly surrounded by suitors. The Soviet Union had become unwittingly the key to war or peace. *'L'arbitre de l'Europe'*, wrote General Gamelin in his memoirs, *'était donc le U.R.S.S.'*[56]

The Soviet factor is a vital one in explaining the immediate course of events that led to the outbreak of a general European war in September 1939. For six months the British and French sought to find a way to reconstruct on terms which they could accept the old entente that had circled Germany in 1914. For almost as long, the German leadership tried to prevent encirclement by reviving the spirit of Rapallo and buying Soviet neutrality. There were plenty of dangers here for the Soviet Union. War seemed a certainty; the question was which option would keep the Soviet Union out of it. For Stalin was no less determined in 1939 than in 1938 to keep the Soviet Union out of the fray. On 10 March, to the 18th Congress of the Communist Party, Stalin made the Soviet position clear to the whole world. Russia would 'continue the policy of peace'. It was the task of the Party 'to be cautious and not allow our country to be drawn into conflicts by warmongers who are accustomed to have others pull the chestnuts out of the fire for them'.[57] This was a signal to both sides: the West could not expect the Soviet Union to fight Germany for them; nor did Stalin exclude, by implication, accommodation with Germany.

Had Stalin already made up his mind in March to choose the German option? Though there can be no certainty, it seems highly unlikely. Stalin was looking not for any specific agreement, but for the one that would best secure Soviet interests. Until May most of the running was made by Britain and France. In April both Western powers expressed their willingness to reach some kind of agreement with the Soviet Union. On 17 April Litvinov gave them the Soviet terms: a Triple Alliance between them to guarantee the integrity of every state from the Baltic to the Mediterranean and to defend each other if attacked by Germany. Up to this point Stalin still believed that the West was stronger than the fascist bloc. In his March speech he suggested that appeasement had not been a product of Western weakness: 'Combined, the non-aggressive, democratic states are unquestionably stronger than the fascist states, both economically and in the military sense.'[58] A Triple Alliance honestly entered into might be sufficient to deter Hitler from further adventures.

From the Soviet side the problem was simply how honest Western intentions were. When the Triple Alliance was presented the British and French dithered. The British government had made the initial approaches only, according to the Foreign Office, 'to placate our left wing in England'.[59] This was hardly honest dealing. Nor could either of the Western powers accept an unconditional guarantee for the Baltic states on which the Soviet Union was adamant. Poland was fortunate to have its guarantee at all; Britain was not prepared to fight for Latvia and Lithuania. Nevertheless the British Chiefs of Staff made it clear that the only military hope for Poland was winning the support of the Red Army. Chamberlain was 'annoyed' at this view, but reluctantly bowed to the pressure of his Cabinet colleagues. On 25 May, almost six weeks after the Soviet offer, the British indicated their willingness to enter into treaty negotiations.[60]

In the long interval conditions had changed. Clearly at some point Stalin realised that Western foot-dragging and mistrust was not going to be easily overcome. The Triple Alliance was a long shot; the history of appeasement made it unlikely that the West would swallow it. In April German leaders began to explore the possibility of closer relations with the Soviet Union. Hitler left out the usual insults and attacks on bolshevism in his speeches; Goebbels ordered the press to end anti-Soviet attacks. Göring told Ciano that Berlin was going to try a '*petit jeu*' with the Soviet Union in mid-April.[61] Enough of this filtered back to Moscow to convince Stalin. On 4 May Litvinov was sacked; the Western ploy had failed to materialise. In his place Stalin appointed Vyacheslav Molotov, Chairman of the Council of Commissars, a noted Soviet nationalist, whose sympathies had long been with a pro-German rather than pro-Western foreign policy. Molotov – his name came from the Russian word for hammer, chosen for his habit of driving a point home in argument – was an intelligent, talented bolshevik who became Soviet premier at the young age of forty in 1929. One of Stalin's intimates, his appointment as Commissar for Foreign Affairs was a signal that the era of collective security was past. Berlin understood the implication. During May there were regular contacts between the two sides as they explored what each had to offer. On 30 May the German Foreign Office at last instructed their Ambassador in Moscow 'to undertake definite negotiations with the Soviet Union'.[62]

All of this was unknown to the West. Across the summer the British and French struggled with Soviet negotiators to find a form of words on which all could agree. Chamberlain deplored Molotov's 'stubborn inarticulateness'. The British had no doubt that the Soviet leaders were unprincipled, 'purely opportunist', and would do what suited the Soviet Union whatever agreement was signed.[63] On the Soviet side there were regular charges of insincerity and procrastination on the part of the British. Molotov found them unchanged from past confrontations: 'crooks and cheats', 'resorting to all kinds of trickery and dreadful subterfuge'.[64] By July the talks were deadlocked. They had the one advantage that public Western talks would spur on the Germans to make real concessions in the private negotiations. Stalin wanted to avoid any chance of the West reaching a separate agreement with Hitler. One final twist was needed. On 17 July the Soviet negotiators suddenly insisted that before a political agreement could be reached with the West, military talks would have to open. With growing reluctance the West agreed. On 11 August the British liner *City of Exeter* arrived at Leningrad. On board were two military missions from Britain and France. They were greeted by Soviet soldiers, and whisked away on the night train to Moscow.

On 12 August the two sides met for the first time. The French mission was headed by General Doumenc, the British by Admiral Drax, neither a very senior officer. The Soviet negotiators were led by Marshal Voroshilov, Commissar for Defence, and other high-ranking Soviet generals. It took just two questions from Voroshilov to expose the weakness of the Western position. On the 12th he asked both delegations whether they had the power to sign a military agreement there and then, as he did. Doumenc replied in the affirmative, but Drax could make no commitment. The Soviet delegation was visibly annoyed by the discovery. On the 14th Voroshilov asked the British and French delegations point-blank if they had secured the agreement of their allies Poland and Roumania for the passage of Soviet troops. Without such an agreement, argued Voroshilov, the military talks were useless. The answer was no. For six days the French made frantic efforts to get Polish agreement without success. On 21 August Voroshilov asked again about Polish co-operation. Daladier told Doumenc to speak on Poland's behalf regardless, in effect to lie about Polish intentions. The Soviet side were unimpressed. The talks petered out and were not revived. On 31 August Molotov addressed the Supreme Soviet on the outcome of the negotiations. He told the assembly that Britain and France had never really lost their deep distrust of the Soviet Union: 'they displayed extreme dilatoriness and anything but a serious attitude towards the negotiations, entrusting them to individuals of secondary importance who were not invested with adequate powers.'[65] It was the failure to take the Soviet Union sufficiently seriously that Soviet leaders found particularly galling.

Even while the Western missions struggled to maintain a semblance of dignity, the German and Soviet negotiators were in the final stages of reaching a comprehensive economic and political agreement. By August even the West had hints of an imminent agreement. Moscow kept the Germans dangling for as long as possible. Then on 12 August, as the British and French sat down to talk with Voroshilov, Germany was told that the Soviet Union would reach a political agreement. Anxious that Britain might yet secure her entente, Berlin agreed to all Molotov's demands on the 16th. On 19 August a comprehensive economic agreement was signed, giving the Soviet Union a credit of 200 million marks for machine tools and armaments. The following day, Hitler sent an urgent telegram to Stalin asking him to receive Ribbentrop on 23 August to sign a non-aggression pact whose terms had already been agreed by both sides on the 19th. On 21 August Stalin agreed. Forty-eight hours later Ribbentrop was in Moscow. He was given a warm welcome. He telegraphed back to Berlin that it was like being with 'old party comrades'. After a three- to four-hour meeting he telephoned to Hitler to get agreement to a Soviet sphere of influence over the Baltic. Hitler agreed, confident that any price was worth a Soviet agreement if it kept the West out of the Polish war. In the evening the Pact was agreed in detail and was formally signed the following morning among mutual expressions of goodwill and lasting friendship. In return for a promise of Soviet neutrality Hitler had made a whole range of concessions to Stalin. The secret protocol of the Nazi–Soviet Pact gave back to the Soviet Union the lands lost in Poland after 1917, and made the Baltic states and Finland into a Soviet sphere of influence. The trade agreement gave the Soviet Union access to the industrial and military equipment from Germany that she needed to complete her own rearmament.[66]

Expressed in these crude terms it is clear that Germany always had more to offer the Soviet Union in the summer of 1939. 'What could England offer Russia?', asked a German official of the Soviet Chargé d'Affaires in Berlin in July. 'At best participation in a European war and the hostility of Germany, but not a single desirable end for Russia. What could we offer, on the other hand? Neutrality and staying out of a possible European conflict, and, if Moscow wished, a German–Russian understanding. . . .'[67] When the Pact was finally announced it caused consternation abroad. The Western powers saw it as a betrayal, a U-turn of spectacular proportions. But it was not an altogether unexpected outcome. Germany and the Soviet Union had been allies in the 1920s. The Treaty of Berlin signed in 1926 was still technically in force. Even after 1933 the Soviet leadership tried to keep open the door to a possible rapprochement. There was a fund of understanding, even friendship, in Moscow towards Germany. Between 1922 and Rapallo and the German invasion in 1941 there were only five years when there was not active agreement and co-operation between the two states. The search for common ground between them even during the five years of Nazi hostility was an option that Soviet diplomats always kept open. Joseph Davies gained the clear impression in the spring of 1938 that the Soviet Union might seek a 'realistic union of forces with Germany in the not too distant future. . . . it is quite within the range of possibilities.'[68] His was far from being the only voice that raised this prospect. There was always a circle among Soviet Foreign Office officials which stressed the fundamentally revisionist character of Soviet strategy. The issue of Poland was bound to promote these sentiments. Molotov considered it 'the ugly offspring of Versailles'. Potemkin, Deputy Commissar for Foreign Affairs, warned the French Ambassador at Munich that appeasement had opened the way to a 'fourth partition of Poland'.[69] Germany could deliver the goods; the return of Russian Poland. The Western powers expected the Soviet Union to defend the one state whose territorial integrity the Soviets would never accept.

The Soviet decision in favour of Germany was not prompted simply by self-interest. The years of deep distrust and hostility between the communist East and capitalist West could not be swept aside in a matter of weeks by mutual expressions of goodwill. The West distrusted and disliked the Soviet Union even in the act of courting her in 1939. While smiling to her face, they grumbled endlessly behind her back, just as Molotov suspected. Chamberlain's view was clearly hostile: 'I must confess to the most profound distrust of Russia.' The French Foreign Minister thought 'the Soviet Union was to be counted on for nothing'.[70] A great ambiguity underlay the Western efforts for peace; anxious to deny Hitler a free hand in the East, they were no more willing to offer it to the Soviet Union. Hostile to fascist ambition, they were no friend to communism either. Nor, in practical terms, did they weigh the Soviet Union very greatly in the scales of power. The effect of the purges and the terror was to reduce the military status of the Soviet Union in Western eyes. It was widely believed that Polish forces would be just as useful as Soviet. The Soviet Union in turn rapidly reversed her view of the strength of the imperial powers when they laid their military cards on the table. When Stalin asked the British Ambassador how many troops Britain could offer to the 300 divisions of the

Red Army he was told, 'Two and two later'.[71] He repeated the figure to himself as if scarcely able to believe it.

The Soviet choice in August 1939 was a rational, even a predictable one. It was avowedly opportunistic but Stalin had never pretended that Soviet foreign policy was anything else: 'Politics is politics, as the old, case-hardened bourgeois diplomats say.'[72] What convinced him that a Western policy was doomed was the clear evidence of Western appeasement in 1939 and the obvious military weakness of Britain. 'British hegemony in the world', he later confided to Ribbentrop, 'only rested on the bluff of Britain and the stupidity of other countries.'[73] He could never be sure that Britain really would fight to save Poland. The closer it came to August the more likely it seemed that the British were hoping in the end to appease Hitler and turn him towards Russia. It was not a risk worth taking. It is not clear that Stalin knew what the outcome of the Pact would be; but it seems likely that he expected the British and French to back down, as Hitler did. When the Polish Ambassador to Moscow met Molotov on 3 September, the Soviet Minister asked him if the West would help Poland. The Ambassador gave a firm assurance; Molotov 'smiled sceptically and said "Well, we shall see"'.[74] In fact the Pact made war more likely. Hitler was convinced that he could now localise the conflict; Britain and France persuaded themselves that they would be just as well off fighting without Soviet help. But either way, Stalin had what he wanted: Soviet neutrality.

There followed three worrying weeks for Soviet leaders. If Russia had won neutrality, there was always the unpredictable. Just as the war in Europe was about to erupt, Soviet forces were engaged again by the Japanese in a large-scale battle for the heights of Nomanhan on the Manchurian–Siberian border. Soviet eyes were turned to the east when the German storm struck Poland. The Soviet Union refused to respond to Ribbentrop's call for her to invade Poland too on 3 September. Then German troops overran Poland in a fraction of the time everyone had expected, Stalin included. Now the danger arose that Germany might occupy all Poland, or end the war with the West with Stalin unrewarded. On 16 September a truce was signed with Japan. On the 17th Soviet forces completed the partition. To the astonished Poles the Soviet Union justified her action on the grounds that 'The Polish–German war has revealed the internal bankruptcy of the Polish state. . . . Left to her own devices and bereft of leadership, Poland has become a suitable field for all manner of hazards and surprises, which may constitute a threat to the USSR.'[75] On 28 September Ribbentrop returned to Moscow again to draw up a final and firm agreement between the two states. Warsaw, in the Soviet sphere, was swapped for Lithuania. Lasting friendship was pledged; a toast was drunk to peace.

The barrier to peace was, in Soviet eyes, no longer Germany but Britain. The partitioning powers called on Britain and France to give up the war, or accept responsibility for its continuation. 'It is not only senseless', preached Molotov, 'but *criminal* to wage such a war.'[76]* Now the crisis was past, the Soviet Union returned to the traditional refrain, suspended during the 1930s, that the ills of the world were largely down to British imperialism. After some initial hesitation and confusion following the Nazi–Soviet Pact, Comintern fell into line too. Communist parties everywhere hailed the Soviet victory over the Polish 'regime of reaction and terror'. Earl Browder, the American communist leader, branded the conflict 'a predatory war in the interest of British imperialism, using Poland, like Belgium, as an excuse'.[77] Attacks on fascism ceased; the enemy was once again the old class enemy. Now the threat was a war waged by France and Britain on the Soviet Union as they got the imperialist bit between their teeth. During the first months of 1940 news began to leak out that the Western Allies were planning to attack the Soviet Union in the Caucasus, to cut off oil supplies for her industry and her German ally. The plans were real enough: flights of light bombers were gathered at Syrian, Iraqi and Indian airbases, and detailed operational studies made for a sustained bombing attack on the oil production of Baku and Batum, attacks on Black Sea ports, and the minelaying of the mouth of the Volga. But the Western governments would agree to the attacks only if there was a hostile move from the Soviet Union first, and the German attack in the West ended any chance of conducting what would almost certainly have been an operational and political disaster for the Allies.[78]

The dangers to which the Soviet Union was now constantly exposed in Europe and Asia made the breathing-space won in August 1939 all the more important. The upheaval of the terror was almost two years behind. The policemen had fallen victim in the end to their own devouring terror. Ezhov was demoted to Commissar for Water Transport, and in January 1939 disappeared without trace. Secret police denounced each other and were denounced by their putative targets. By 1939 the Soviet system had stabilised. Stalin was in supreme control; the cult of personality was at its height. Whenever Stalin's name was spoken at the meetings of the central committees everybody applauded. Now the Soviet economy was ordered to use the breathing-space to build up the largest

* Italics in original.

defence forces in the world. The army expanded two and a half times in two years. Between June 1939 and June 1941 Soviet factories produced 7000 modern tanks and 81,000 artillery pieces.[79] The Soviet airforce was larger than the German, British and French together. The Five Year Plans, despite all the setbacks and conflicts, had turned the Soviet Union in ten years into the world's second-largest industrial state. New cadres were trained to replace the engineers and officers who had died in the terror. The Soviet Union was unquestionably one of the great powers again.

It was impossible to resist the temptation, with the European capitalist powers in conflict, to exploit the Soviet Union's growing strength and stability. In October Finland was told to hand over a vital strip of territory needed to safeguard Leningrad. The Finns refused and a fierce Winter War was fought which brought the Soviet Union what it wanted but at great cost. Fifty thousand Red soldiers died in the war, and the conflict alerted Hitler to the possible dangers of his powerful and unpredictable ally. German resources fuelled the Finnish war effort. On 14 December the Soviet Union was expelled from the League of Nations. In March 1940 the Winter War was ended. While the war raged in the West in May and June Stalin ordered Soviet industry to go on to a war footing, with a seven-day week and forced labour. On 14–15 June the Baltic states were occupied by Soviet troops; in August the three states were formally incorporated into the USSR. In the same month the Soviet Union demanded, and got, Bessarabia and the Bukovina from Roumania. The old equilibrium in Eastern Europe was torn up.

It was inevitable that Soviet expansion in Eastern Europe would run a great risk. Hitler had accepted concessions to bolshevism in August 1939 as a short-term expedient. Now he found that Stalin was playing him at his own game. A contest for the control of Eastern Europe had always been part of Hitler's dream. Now it was a necessity. In July 1940 Hitler resolved to act before Soviet strength became too great. The economy was ordered to build the resources for an army greater than 'all enemy armies together'.[80] Military planning was set in motion. In September a Tripartite Pact was signed with Italy and Japan dividing the world up into spheres of influence. Soviet objections brought Molotov to Berlin in November 1940. To Ribbentrop's halfhearted invitation to join the Pact Molotov produced a shopping list of fresh Soviet demands – virtual protectorate over Bulgaria and bases at the Turkish Straits. This time Germany had nothing she wanted in return; Hitler refused, more convinced than ever that war with the USSR was unavoidable. 'Molotov has let the cat out of the bag,' Hitler said when he had

RUSSIA'S EXPANSION AND ECONOMIC MODERNISATION, 1930-40

gone. 'This would remain not even a marriage of convenience. To let the Russians in would mean the end of Central Europe.'[81] Three weeks later he authorised Directive No. 21, 'Case Barbarossa', for the invasion of the Soviet Union. The greatest secrecy was called for.

The Soviet leaders knew that relations between themselves and German leaders had deteriorated during 1940. They were always aware of the transparent opportunism in the original pact between them. Soviet deliveries of food and raw materials were punctually made; German supplies were erratic and German forces tried to prevent the very latest technology from falling into the hands of the Red Army. Germany accepted the cession of Bessarabia only on condition that Roumania accept German domination of the rest of the country as compensation. Soviet foreign policy fluctuated uneasily between a fawning collaboration – Molotov congratulated the German Ambassador on the 'splendid success' in France – and a stolid imperviousness to the dangers excited by Soviet expansion. It may be that Soviet leaders genuinely failed to see that their actions might force Hitler's hand. On 1 August 1940 Molotov told the Supreme Soviet that 'no event will catch us unawares.'[82] It may be that Stalin genuinely believed that Soviet rearmament had rendered the country less exposed to the threat of invasion from just one power. Whatever the reason, the fact remains that in 1941 the Soviet Union was caught completely and devastatingly 'unawares'.

If the motives for the Nazi–Soviet Pact are clear enough, the explanation for the failure of Soviet forces to prepare for the German assault in the summer of 1941 remains obscure. It was certainly true that the diversion of German forces to the Balkans to defeat Yugoslavia and Greece in the spring and early summer of 1941 was seen by Stalin as evidence that Germany had opted to move south rather than east, and had left far too little time to defeat the Soviet Union in the remaining weeks of good fighting weather. Then there was the failure to defeat Britain, which still left Hitler exposed on the Western front. Litvinov insisted, reasonably enough, when he later arrived in July to take up the post of Ambassador to Washington, that Stalin thought 'it would have been madness on [Hitler's] part to undertake war in the east against such a powerful land as ours, before finishing off his war in the west'.[83] The Soviet strategic position was further strengthened by signing a non-aggression pact with Japan in April 1941, which freed Stalin to concentrate all his forces in European Russia to deter Hitler. All these strategic calculations made sense, even if the German armed forces had not pursued a very successful strategy of deception and misinformation to shield Hitler's real intentions. As it was German secretiveness was almost as successful as the Allied deception on D-Day three years later.

Almost, because information about an impending attack began to filter through to the Soviet Union as early as March 1941. The major source was a German communist spy, Richard Sorge, who worked in Japan. German military contacts in Tokyo fed Sorge unwittingly with vital secret information throughout the spring. On 5 March Sorge sent microfilm to Moscow of Foreign Office documents from Germany that indicated an attack in mid-June. On 15 May he radioed the exact date, 22 June. The German Military Attaché in Tokyo, Colonel Kretschmer, was indiscreet enough to tell Sorge that 'Germany had completed her preparation on a very large scale.'[84] All this information was available and much else besides. The British sent regular warnings that all their intelligence sources suggested the large-scale build-up of German forces on the Soviet frontier. So too did the State Department in Washington, the Vichy regime, the Swedish Foreign Office, and so on. The Soviet front-line forces themselves reported over 180 violations of Soviet air space by German reconnaissance aircraft up to 100 miles inside Soviet territory between April and June, which eventually prompted a formal protest to Berlin the day before the German invasion began.[85]

Stalin refused to be drawn. Everything was done to avoid provocation of Germany in the weeks before Barbarossa. Stalin was desperate to preserve the peace, as the many witnesses of these final weeks attest. He was hopeful of further 'satisfactory' negotiations with Hitler and expected political demands to precede any military threat.[86] On 14 June Tass published a special communiqué to allay the popular rumours that were now openly ciculating throughout western Russia. The rumours were spread, it said, 'by forces hostile to the Soviet Union and Germany, forces interested in the further expansion and spreading of war'.[87] Army leaders were much more anxious than Stalin. At a meeting in May they were so worried about the German threat that they forgot to clap when Stalin's name was mentioned.[88] Red Army intelligence produced 'Report No. 8', which showed conclusively that German forces were massed, battle-ready, along the Soviet border in early June. The Politburo, and Stalin, preferred the so-called 'Yugoslav Scheme', a detailed foreign intelligence report which showed German divisions scattered along the Atlantic coast facing Britain, and a formless group of divisions in the East 'resting'. The head of the Soviet Intelligence Administration, General Proskurov, argued in person with Stalin and other Politburo members that the Scheme was simply wrong. The following day he was arrested and shot. The new intelligence chief, and General Zhukov, Chief of Staff, both reluctantly endorsed the Yugoslav

Scheme. Stalin's word was final. Only on 21 June did an insubordinate intelligence officer distribute on his own account an intelligence warning of impending German attack to all Soviet army units in the west. Most of the telegrams did not reach their destination before German troops, at 3 a.m. on 22 June, attacked. By then Stalin had finally been persuaded by Zhukov to put the frontier forces on the alert, but these instructions, too, arrived only shortly before the German advance, far too late to permit serious preparation.[89] Molotov summoned the German Ambassador: 'Do you think that we deserve this?', he asked. Stalin could barely bring himself to face the reality; 'Hitler fooled us,' he is said to have muttered on hearing the news.[90]

The failure to prepare for the German attack has many possible explanations, though lack of information was not one of them. The real problem was that Stalin instinctively distrusted any effort to drive the Soviet Union into war with Germany. He could never be sure, had never been sure in the 1930s, that the capitalist world would not use the Soviet Union as a way out of their dilemma. The sceptical attitude to the wealth of intelligence information has to be set against this enduring cast of mind in the Soviet leadership. British attitudes in 1939, and again in 1940 with the Caucasus plan, were uppermost in Stalin's mind. The Soviet leadership did not preclude the possibility of a separate peace between Britain and Germany and a joint crusade against communism. The flight of Hitler's deputy, Rudolf Hess, to Scotland on 10 May was seriously reported in Moscow as evidence of an impending peace. The German campaign of misinformation made it difficult to sort reality from fiction. This made Stalin doubtful even of information fed to Moscow by anti-Nazis anxious to convince the Soviet Union of Hitler's new plans. Their evidence was so indiscreet and extensive that it was difficult for Soviet intelligence not to regard it as clumsy provocation and deliberate distortion. Nor should it be forgotten that the Nazi–Soviet Pact provoked a real enthusiasm in Moscow, and a strong belief that a lasting political agreement between the two new 'revolutionary' powers could be built. The Pact, as Mikoyan privately assured a young German diplomat, 'marked one of the most important moments in all history. . . . the alliance it brought into being was unbeatable.'[91] Stalin repeated often that he viewed Hitler as a man who could be trusted; honour among thieves.

Stalin had for so long inhabited a world of subterfuge, intrigue and dissimulation that it is easy to see that nothing in the summer of 1941 could be regarded as a certainty. Soviet finesse in the underworld of spies and spying was to an extent their undoing. Stalin's sceptical approach to the German threat was based on the conflicting character of much of the intelligence pouring into Moscow. British intelligence was itself divided over its interpretation of German moves. Some messages indicated an immediate military attack, others that Hitler was preparing to extort further economic and political concessions by a show of force across the border, a view that fitted much more closely with Soviet evaluations. Molotov later told Sir Stafford Cripps, the British Ambassador, that it had never occurred to the Russians that Germany might invade 'without any discussion or ultimatum',[92] the more so since the Soviet Union was supplying Germany with all that was agreed in the way of food and raw materials. *Lebensraum* was no longer regarded as necessary for Germany, if her needs could be met by peaceful Soviet co-operation. In the end it is hard not to escape the conclusion that Stalin simply could not bring himself to believe that Germany, leaving Britain still undefeated, would attack the Soviet Union in cold blood, with the Pact still intact, with the Soviet Union's vast military resources to overcome. Dividing up the spoils of Eastern Europe was one thing. A war to the death between two giant powers was the stuff of propaganda and fantasy. For once his revolutionary realism got the better of him.

The Soviet road to war was an involuntary one. The Soviet Union was the last in a long line of victims of German expansion. She had the misfortune to combine the supreme racial and ideological enemies of Germandom. The crusade Hitler launched in June 1941 was a crusade against bolshevism and against the Slav people. Lenin had foreseen this outcome long before: 'the existence of the Soviet Republic side by side with imperialist states for a long time is unthinkable.'[93] The fact of the 1917 revolution was enough to imperil Soviet survival at every turn. The failure of the Soviet Union to overcome her isolation and the mistrust and hostility of the other major powers owed a very great deal to what Goebbels called 'this struggle against the world danger'.

But it is not a complete explanation. The problem that the Soviet Union posed to the rest of the world was that sooner or later, like tsarist Russia before her, she would from her sheer size and economic potential become a power to dwarf those that surrounded her. This was a question not of ideology, but of power politics. The conflict over Eastern Europe was a conflict that predated 1917; the struggle for Asian influence went back a century. The Soviet Union gave Russian power a new dimension, but it was not just communism that mattered. The capitalist West traded with communism freely throughout the period; the imperialist powers even sought alliance with Moscow in the 1930s. Fascism and communism lived in uneasy embrace for two years. The real problem was that Soviet Russia, the incipient superpower, could not be accommodated in the crumbling international structure, any more than the tsarist empire in 1914. In 1942 Stalin told Sir Stafford Cripps that the Soviet Union had always been a force for change: 'The USSR had wanted to change the old equilibrium . . . but England and France had wanted to preserve it.'[94] By 1945 the old balance had disappeared for good.

CHAPTER SIX

JAPAN

> For over a century and a half the Asiatics have been pressed down by the Whites and subjected to Western tyranny. But Japan, after defeating Russia, has aroused the sleeping Asiatics to shake off the Western tyranny and torture.
>
> (Rin Kaito, c. 1935)

> England is already on the downgrade; Japan has started on the upgrade. The two come into collision because England is trying to hold on to what she has, while Japan must perforce expand. Territorial possessions and natural resources England has in abundance, she can afford to relinquish some. Japan has neither, and to her they are a matter of life and death.
>
> (Tota Ishimaru, 1936)

On the afternoon of Monday, 1 December 1941, Japan's leaders gathered at the Imperial Palace in Tokyo. An irrevocable decision was to be taken: either Japan would enter the war or she would yield to the economic sanctions applied by the United States. Throughout the summer of 1941, ministers had met to chart the deteriorating course of relations with the Americans; they had already agreed on war in principle. But only the Emperor could sanction war and his approval was far from a formality. Hirohito abhorred conflict and for more than ten years he had obstructed his governments' military adventures at every opportunity: he had even described the conduct of the imperial army as 'abominable'. After months of discussion, the issue of war or peace was now to be judged formally in a single afternoon.

The setting heightened this dramatic sense of judicial process. The Emperor sat on a dais, in front of an elaborate gold screen. Ranged to left and right in front of him, seated behind two long tables were his ministers, and the generals and admirals who now dominated the nation. Japan's new Prime Minister, Tojo Hideki, in office for less than two months, was a general and he was in power because he could control the army. He was not an impressive speaker, stumbling through his speech in a monotone, laboriously detailing the course of Japan's relations with the West since the end of the First World War. Tojo explained how the United States had consistently conspired against the interests of Japan. He concluded: 'Under the circumstances, our Empire has no alternative but to begin war with the United States, Great Britain and the Netherlands in order to resolve the present crisis and assure survival.' The director of the Cabinet Planning Board, Suzuki Teichi, spoke more briefly, and directly to the point; he too favoured war. Even the civilian ministers, although fearful of air raids on the capital, saw no alternative: 'If we give in, we surrender at one stroke what we won in the Sino-Japanese and the Russo-Japanese wars as well as the Manchurian Incident. We cannot do this.'[1] The Emperor listened, by tradition, silently while the arguments were presented; but afterwards, as the documents authorising war were sealed, he remarked quietly that the American demands were too humiliating: conflict was 'regrettable', but in this case the lesser evil. Few Japanese would have disagreed with his diagnosis. War was the logical, if undesirable consequence of almost half a century of Japanese history, a collision between two visions of the future for Asia.

The two contenders for the mastery of the Pacific were the United States and Japan.[2] For more than seventy years, Japanese leaders had been mesmerised by the United States: by its abundant wealth and huge size, by its capacity to change and grow. They saw Japan herself, like the USA, as a new nation. She had been reborn in the nineteenth century, but unlike America, a mish-mash of many peoples, the Yamato (Japanese) race was pure, growing from the most ancient of roots; the Emperor could trace his unbroken lineage back for 2600 years. In the 1920s Japanese scholars proudly attested that the Yamato race was 98 per cent 'pure'. This racial purity was, in Japanese eyes, a crucial distinction, giving her people a unique superiority. It would enable Japan to become the 'United States of Asia', outstripping all her neighbours in wealth and might, and, soon, to challenge America herself. In the equation of power, the other Western nations – France, the Netherlands – were negligible. Only Soviet Russia, and sometimes Britain, dominated the minds of Japanese politicians to the same extent as the United States.

The nation's potential lay in her national spirit rather than any material advantage. This preoccupation with spirit and race had disturbing consequences. The Japanese hatred of foreigners during her centuries of isolation was well known; less understood was the disgust the Yamato race displayed towards its own people of impure stock. The aboriginal people of northern Hokkeido, the pale-skinned and hairy Ainu, were persecuted, just as Europeans mistreated the native peoples of Australia and Southern Africa. Even those much closer racially to the Yamato race, the Koreans and the Okinawans, were treated contemptuously as colonial peoples, while the *eta* (the untouchables of Japanese society) were in effect enslaved.[3]

The United States had been midwife to a new Japan, born in the second half of the nineteenth century. Admiral Yamamoto Isoruku, whose battlefleet was steaming secretly towards Pearl Harbour as the decisive Imperial Conference was being held in Tokyo, used to remark that he had entered the Imperial Navy so that he 'could return Admiral Perry's visit'. Every Japanese understood his allusion. The first encounter between the industrialised West and the 'isolated' Japan had taken place on 8 July 1853 when American vessels arrived in Tokyo Bay. That moment of confrontation was constantly reproduced in Japanese prints and engravings; even decades after the momentous events of 1853, these highly coloured images were still being reprinted to supply the popular demand. The 'black ships' of Commander Perry and their lanky bewhiskered sailors were ludicrous in their ugliness but, at the same time, as menacing as any of the evil demons of Japan's mythology. The Americans had arrived uninvited, and in Japanese eyes their intrusion had fractured a stable, contented, self-contained society.

This forced encounter became an emblem of misunderstanding between the two nations; Admiral Yamamoto touched a raw nerve. He knew the United States well; he spent much of the early 1920s in the USA, as a Harvard alumnus, then as a naval attaché in Washington. He had toured the country and seen the industrial might of America at first hand, and knew that in a long fight the United States would overcome the slender resources of Japan: 'Anyone who has seen the auto factories in Detroit and the oil fields in Texas knows that Japan lacks the national power for a naval race with America.'[4] The only hope would be a 'moral shock' delivered to the heart of the United States. At the beginning of 1941, he had written: 'Should hostilities break out between Japan and the United States, it would not be enough that we take Guam and the Philippines, nor even Hawaii and San Francisco.' As Perry had sailed to the gates of Tokyo, so: 'To make victory certain, we would have to march into Washington and dictate terms of peace in the White House.' He added: 'I wonder if our politicians, among whom armchair arguments about war are being glibly bandied about in the name of state politics, have confidence as to the final outcome and are prepared to make the necessary sacrifices.'[5] None of Japan's leaders in December 1941 had Yamamoto's knowledge of their adversary; they were ill informed of the world beyond their own shores, and no one was more ignorant than the arch-exponent of war, the Prime Minister and War Minister, General Tojo.

The General's chauvinism was commonplace, for the Japanese found it hard to understand Westerners; but this incomprehension was not universal. The Social Education Association, founded in 1906, declared that the 'new' Japanese should be 'a great cosmopolitan people . . . who are not satisfied with the reputation of being a warlike nation but who try to be a model of a peaceful people . . . a cosmopolitan, humanitarian people'. As a state Japan should show 'an ability to engage in worldwide activities through harmonising internationalist and nationalist tendencies'. This redirection of the national characteristics – Japanese 'spirit' and 'flexibility' – would be for 'the good of the world'. These same visionaries went on to talk of how 'the whole of Asia is offering itself as a suitable field for Japanese action. . . .' The editor of the *Katsudo no Nihon*, one of a new crop of journals dedicated to making the Japanese good citizens of the world, declared, 'our expansive energy, now bursting out after a long period of polishing up and waiting, should not be channelled only in the direction of Asia, but should cover the whole of mankind.'[6] Other writers in the same journal suggested Korea and Manchuria as fields for expansion, with opportunities for Japanese investment in the Dutch East Indies; others favoured China and South America. These proposals were not merely flights of fancy; as the articles were published, large numbers of Japanese were emigrating to Hawaii (65,000 of them), to the Philippines, and even to Brazil. By 1907 more than 230,000 Japanese were living permanently overseas, while Japan also established factories in Java and Sumatra and invested heavily in the economy of the Indies. In this vision, the whole world was to benefit from the spirit and enterprise of Japan:

> From the ice-bound northern Siberian plains to the continental expanses of China, Korea and East Asia; farther south, to the Philippines, the Australian continent, and other South Sea islands; then eastward to the western shores of North and South America, washed by the shores of the Pacific Ocean – there is none of these regions which cannot be an object of our nation's expansion.

This was the language and ideology common to many nations around the turn of the century. It permeated the bullish imperialism of the United States of America, then busily fulfilling its 'manifest destiny' and absorbing the newly acquired Philippines captured from Spain in 1898; it expressed the aims of the British Empire, then seeking to build a new London as a worthy capital of a multinational

The Western view of Japan combined both racial contempt and apprehension. European states were too weak in the Far East to obstruct Japanese expansion, but were dismayed by and hostile to the rise of an Asian power.

New war, old weapons: young Japanese soldiers sharpen their swords for use during the Japanese advance into China. The Chinese fought with a desperation and resilience that amazed the Japanese, who had been taught to despise them. Japan's forces responded with ferocious brutality.

Crowds of refugees on the quays at Shanghai as Europeans and Chinese flee the advancing Japanese armies and the Japanese bombing of the city, December 1937.

With the collapse of the traditional friendship between Japan and Britain the Japanese Government sought new alliances, and found a ready response from Germany. This 'Hitler snowman' was used as propaganda to show that Japan's children had taken the *Führer* to their hearts, 1939.

The decision for war, Monday, 1 December 1941. The fateful Imperial council meeting at which war was officially sanctioned by the Emperor Hirohito, who described war between the United States and Japan as 'regrettable'. But it was the generals and admirals who made the decision, not the Emperor.

Franklin D. Roosevelt, President of the United States, speaking to his people over the radio networks. Roosevelt perfected the art of informal communication, reaching out to Americans in his 'fireside chats', his press conferences, and his set speeches on great occasions. He was an enigmatic and elusive politician, wary of commitment and always mindful of public opinion.

The symbol of recovery: Boulder Dam. The most dramatic monuments to Roosevelt's New Deal were the Tennessee Valley hydroelectric scheme in the east and the Boulder electrification project in Colorado. Government investment provided work on a huge scale at the height of the Depression; critics unkindly equated these huge structures with the vast public works of Fascist Italy, Nazi Germany and Communist Russia.

In the crisis years of the Depression, sinister movements appeared on the right of American politics. This American Nazi Party rally in Madison Square, 6 October 1935, provoked a monster anti-Nazi rally by American labour and Jewish groups. The movement turned American opinion against Hitler's Germany.

The sinews of war. American strength lay in her enormous productive capacity, which was mobilised to fuel the Allied war effort before 1941 and transformed the war when the United States was brought in by the attack on Pearl Harbor. (*Above*) A dockyard turns out mass-produced merchant shipping. (*Below*) The Army was to be fully recharged by America's huge automobile industry. American 'mechanised cavalry' on manoeuvres in the late 1930s.

The first shots of the world war: the attack on Pearl Harbor, 6 December 1941. Roosevelt called it 'a day of infamy'. Although war was expected, the determined Japanese assault exposed the complacency and technical inferiority of America's armed services. Yet Japanese leaders ignored the overwhelming US potential to create a huge army, navy and air-force, which would later result in Japanese defeat.

community of nations;[7] in France, still busy expanding into the last unoccupied recesses of Indo-China – Cochin China and Laos (1893–5) – it became *la mission civilisatrice.* But by 1906–7, when the Japanese discovered their destiny, there was no room for another expanding power. The Japanese might believe that 'apart from the white races the Japanese are the only ones with an aptitude for colonisation',[8] but none of the white nations was prepared to allow them the chance.

The Japanese were blocked off from their destiny, frustrated for reasons that were both racial and political. Many Westerners found the Japanese repellent. The American educator Henry Adams, touring the Pacific in the 1880s, wrote in a letter that he found the Japanese 'primitive' and that he could not 'conquer a feeling that Japs are monkeys and the women very badly made monkeys'.[9] That the 'monkeys' learned quickly and easily, embracing the products of Western technology (and particularly military technology) did not really alter their perceived status. The Japanese were mocked as slavish imitators of Western society, and their efforts to assume European ways ('monkeys in frock coats') despised. Yet the West could not ignore the growing strength of Japan. In 1900, when the Boxer rebels attacked foreigners in China, Japan contributed the largest contingent to the international relief force; foreign military observers noted, not without alarm, the Japanese officers' skill and efficiency.

The wariness which the Western nations felt towards the 'rising sun in the east' was transformed into real apprehension by the events of 1904–5. When Japan went to war with Russia in 1904, most Western officials believed it to be an unequal struggle: a major (if decrepit) European power against a small Asian state barely released from a mediaeval isolation.[10] Only after the Japanese armies had defeated the Russians at Port Arthur in 1904 and sunk an imperial fleet in the Tsushima straits did the Western nations begin to take full account of Japan, now described, with a mixture of fear and admiration, as 'the Prussians of Asia'.

The Western nations sought to channel her explosive growth. The British had learned the lesson of the Boxer expedition and recognised the potential of Japan; in 1902 they signed a treaty which would, they hoped, temper Japanese ambitions in Korea and Manchuria, while preserving British interests in China. For the Japanese, recognition by Britain was a diplomatic landmark. It marked their admission into the international system. It was a pact between equal sovereign states, not an 'unequal treaty' like so many that had been forced on the Chinese and other Asiatics in the past.

After the treaty of Portsmouth in 1905, which settled the Russo-Japanese war, the other Western nations followed Britain's example in reaching an understanding with the Japanese. In 1907, France negotiated a treaty which recognised Japan's new-found status in the Far East, while even Japan's arch-enemy Russia in 1910 agreed to divide Manchuria into Russian and Japanese 'spheres of influence'.

The United States responded immediately to the new power in the Pacific, and came to a rapid diplomatic understanding with Japan. President Theodore Roosevelt, the architect of the Portsmouth Treaty (for which he won the Nobel Peace Prize), had already come to a secret agreement with Tokyo before the signature of the Portsmouth accord; but fear lay behind the outward signs of friendship. The United States saw Japan as both an economic and political competitor. From 1907, the US accepted the possibility of a major war with Japan. 'Plan Orange' formed the basis for American thinking right up to Pearl Harbor; at almost the same time, independently, the Japanese navy began to consider a naval war with the United States. A few years later, the US Minister in Peking, William C. Calhoun, was writing 'Japan is ambitious, she is already a world power; she aspires to be master of the Pacific';[11] and a War College study of 1913 concluded that 'Japan is fully prepared to wage an aggressive war against a Trans Pacific Power, as far as her army is concerned.'

The white nations came to terms with Japan to ensure the security of their territorial interests in the East – the United States in the Philippines, France in Indo-China, Britain in India, China and Malaya. Russia shared a long border with China and wanted peace. These agreements with Japan were not attempts at friendship, as some Japanese imagined, but rather sprang from a desire to tame her potential disruptiveness.

The wild card in all these Asian considerations was the uncertain state of China. A war with Japan (1894–5) had hastened the slow decay of her central government. The Chinese armies had been outfought by the Japanese, and she lost Korea and Formosa. Her losses would have been still greater had not the European powers immediately intervened, and then snatched some of the gains away from the Japanese. Russia secured Port Arthur, Germany Kiaochow, while Britain gained a ninety-nine year lease on Kowloon from an enfeebled Manchu administration. Japan was left with a bitter sense of resentment from this first experience of the white nations working in concert.

Japan's leaders saw a pattern in the behaviour of all the Western nations. They perceived an inherent racialism: the West wanted to suppress the 'Asiatic hordes'. This aim extended to all Asian peoples, but found its clearest expression in their attempt to frustrate Japan's 'legitimate interests'. It was not difficult to find supporting evidence. The government in Tokyo noted how Japan had been robbed of the spoils of victory in 1894–5; how a victorious war with Russia had brought her much less than the Japanese people had legitimately expected. Japanese leaders watched the passage of legislation in the United States in 1902 against the immigration of the Chinese and, worse still, President Theodore Roosevelt's order in 1907 for the exclusion of Japanese migrants. Meanwhile in Australia, laws were being enacted to keep the country white for ever. Japanese administrations found prejudice and deceit in all their dealings with the Western powers.

The Japanese had a clear view of their recent history. They believed that they had only narrowly escaped colonial rule, or perhaps even worse, the fate of China, preyed upon by all the Western powers. They had lifted themselves from feudal stagnation by an effort of national will. From 1868, under the rule of the Meiji Emperor, enormous efforts had been made to modernise the country. The slogan of the new era was: 'Increase the nation's wealth, strengthen the army.' Economic and military advance went hand in hand, and much of the nation's new wealth was spent on the army and navy – rising to 24 per cent of Gross National Product in the second year of the Russo-Japanese war.[12] Although the proportion of national wealth spent on the armed forces declined, with a booming economy the overall budgets increased; by the outbreak of the First World War, Japan had created an efficient army of 306,000 and the fourth-largest fleet in the world (700,000 tons).[13] More significant was the growing proportion of the equipment made in Japan; where once warships were built abroad (mostly in Britain)[14] and small arms had been purchased from a variety of sources, by 1914 the great Japanese industrial empires (*zaibatsu*), in particular Mitsubishi and Mitsui, manufactured them at home.[15]

Japan's transformation had been achieved, so her leaders believed, by the efforts of the Japanese people alone: foreigners had played no part in this rebirth of a nation. Japan was the only Asian nation directly to benefit from the Great War between the European powers. On 23 August 1914 the Japanese declared war on Germany; her army and navy besieged the port of Tsingtao, the only German base on the China coast, while the navy occupied all the German Pacific possessions north of the Equator – the Marshall, Marianas, Palua and Caroline islands. They moved in complete secrecy and with such speed that the Australians discovered, to their horror, that they had acquired a new and unwelcome non-white neighbour.

The same policy of calculated aggression was applied to China, while the attention of the former 'interventionist states' was engaged in Europe. In January 1915, an ultimatum – 'The Twenty-one Demands' – was sent to the Chinese President. It was intended to secure the 'special position' in the affairs of China that had been a consistent Japanese objective for twenty years.

To Japan's planners, expansion on the mainland of Asia was essential. It was the only means of sustaining her growing population; only the mainland could provide the cheap raw materials lacking on the islands of Japan. The right to a 'special position' in mainland China was, in Japanese eyes, beyond question. Her diplomats and politicians drew the false analogy of the United States' Monroe Doctrine, under which the USA claimed a special influence over the states of Latin America, her 'backyard'. As Japanese confidence grew, nationalists shifted their emphasis from a 'special position' in China to a 'divine mission', nothing less than a Japanese hegemony throughout the Far East.

The economic value of the mainland – Korea and southern Manchuria – was real enough. The islands of Japan lacked oil and had scanty supplies of coal; and, with more than half of the land under forest rather than cultivation, Japan sometimes struggled to feed her people. The lure of the open plains of Manchuria was irresistible. In 1910, Korean independence was brushed aside and the protectorate established in 1896 was transformed into a crown colony; Japan also leased large tracts of southern Manchuria from China, with a view to incorporating these in a similar manner at a later date. In those new lands, 'the Yamato people' began to build their vision of a greater Japan. Industry and agriculture flourished on a scale unknown in the islands. The Southern Manchurian Railway Company, formed to run a line from Chanchun to the port of Dairen, became a general development corporation. It created a coal industry in the Fushan coalfield, explored for iron ore (and found huge reserves), and organised mass migration from the islands to the mainland to work the new farmlands and factories. For patriotic Japanese, Manchuria held the same promise that the virgin lands of the West had offered to the USA; the new lands, although separated by a tract of ocean from the heartland, were thought just as integral to the future of the nation as California was to America. A diplomat and minister, Shigemitsu Mamoru, wrote: 'the preservation of the rights which she held in Manchuria was to Japan . . . veritably a question of life and death.'[16]

This vision of the future did not square with the realities of sovereignty. Manchuria was not Japanese, but belonged to China. Under the terms of the lease, the Chinese government sanctioned any development which affected her sovereign rights. At every point, the Chinese delayed and obstructed Japanese proposals. They hoped to make Manchuria as inhospitable and unproductive as possible, and in particular they discouraged plans for long-term investment. Permission was refused for the mining of the vast and desperately needed iron-ore resources discovered at Anshan in 1909. This policy of obstruction enraged the Japanese; eventually, tired of endless and fruitless discussions, they brushed aside the treaty restrictions: an unfettered right to exploit mineral reserves featured strongly in the Twenty-one Demands of 1915.

Japan's pressure on China was brutal, unsubtle and direct. The Japanese were determined for economic and political motives to dominate northern China. The head of the Manchurian Railway explained: 'Manchuria and Mongolia are Japan's lifeline . . . an important point from which it is impossible to retreat if a nation expects to exist.'[17] But at the same time Japan wanted to participate in the international system, where the rules of conduct were set by the leading white nations. She could not afford to flout their standards of behaviour. The two objectives – hegemony in the East and participation in the concert of nations – were often at odds.

At the Paris Peace Conference, Japan played by the Western rules of international diplomacy. She took her place among the Allies, and behaved as a 'Western' nation. The results were disappointing. Japan achieved much less than she had hoped. Her delegation failed to obtain a declaration of racial equality in the Peace Settlement, mostly through the strenuous opposition of Australia, and was roundly attacked over the Twenty-one Demands. The grant of the former German territories in the Pacific as mandates failed to gratify her ambitions. Japanese aspirations were excessive, and they were not the only nation to be disappointed: another 'ally', the Chinese, was equally outraged at her treatment. But Japan's failure to gain her objectives at Versailles upset the balance of domestic politics. It reinforced the view of the growing number of radical nationalists that Japan could expect nothing from the international community: only her own strength and resources would guarantee the future.

The sense of exploitation reinforced nationalist memories of other slights at the hands of the West. In 1895 and in 1905, victories on the battlefield had been traded away at the negotiating table; Versailles merely continued the pattern. Throughout the 1920s, every negotiation with the West seemed to involve sacrifice of Japan's national interest. After the Washington Disarmament Conference, which opened in November 1921, Japan became a full partner with the Western powers in the 'Washington System'. This network of agreements sought to guarantee the stability of the Pacific and secure the future of China. In 1921, Britain, France, the United States and Japan signed a Four Power Treaty which recognised each other's rights in the Pacific; in February 1922, the stability of China was guaranteed by a Nine Power Pact, in which all the states with interests in China agreed to respect her sovereignty and independence. Any disputes were to be resolved in conference; the 'system' was the extension of the principles of Versailles into the Far East, and the Western nations felt that they had been fair, even 'generous', to Japan. In particular they had agreed to Japan maintaining a substantial navy in a period of overall disarmament.

Japan's fervent nationalists saw no gains, only betrayal and loss.[18] One delegate to the Conference was solemnly handed a dagger on his return: such an act of dishonour, agreeing to the treaties, should be redeemed by immediate suicide. This was no idle threat. Assassination was becoming increasingly common as a weapon in Japanese politics. In November 1921, the Prime Minister, Hara Takashi, was stabbed to death on Tokyo railway station; five weeks before, a banker was murdered in the same fashion. Between the death of the Meiji Emperor in 1912 and the outbreak of war in 1941, six Prime Ministers were murdered, and many other politicians killed or wounded.[19] Fanatical nationalists saw murder as the best means of breaking open the charmed circle of 'Western' university graduates and senior officials who managed both the economy and politics.

Traditional Japanese society was based on hierarchy and order; both were breaking down. The clearest evidence for this decay was the rise of factions, both civil and military. In government the spirit of the Meiji era was still dominant; 'Westernised' politicians and officials ran Japan. They were supported by the new Emperor, who came to the throne in 1926 and shared their ideals; his passion was marine biology, and his favourite pastimes were golf and ballroom dancing. Hirohito chose the name 'Showa' – Enlightened Peace – to be the emblem of his reign. The stronghold of the 'Westerners' was the Foreign Office, but the power of the extreme nationalists was growing strongly in every area of government. Extremists virtually monopolised power in Korea and Manchuria, and they were very active among the lesser officials in the provinces.

Social and economic change in the countryside and the small towns was barely visible. To Western eyes, the Japanese village still looked like a painting by Hokusai. But the countryside was in the throes of a violent transformation. The rapid growth of the towns and cities had been produced by a high birthrate and a flight from agriculture: between 1910 and 1920, more than 3 million peasants (probably about 5 per cent of the total population) had left the country for a life in the cities. It was becoming harder to make a living from the land, and when the silk industry – Japan's principal rural export – collapsed in the harsh world economic climate of the late 1920s, many families abandoned their holdings; there was famine and rice riots in the countryside during the early 1930s. A new style of landlord arrived in the countryside, urban investors who used cheap labour and more intensive methods of production to make a return on the farms. The resentments of those who saw themselves as dispossessed, especially those from the north-east (Tohoku), fed directly into the extreme nationalist movement.[20] The blood oath of the Ketsumeidan secret society called for the killing of all public figures in Japan who were thought to have betrayed their country internationally or 'to have enriched themselves at the expense of the farmers and peasants'; in the space of two months (February and March 1932) the group murdered a former Minister of Finance and a director of the Mitsui company. Regional and family ties bound local officials, army officers, peasants and landowners into a common hatred of the existing political and economic structure.

Political nationalism in Japan was disorganised, and entirely unlike that of Germany or Italy. It was dominated by old ties to family and region. Often an extremist party would be made up predominantly from a single clan; there was no dominant nationalist movement like the Nazi Party in Germany. Most of the groups, despite their grand titles and elaborate political programmes, were quite small and often violently at odds with each other. Here again ancient feuds and rivalries fed into the nationalist movement. Many of the murders and much of the general street violence were directed at other patriots who had split off from the main groups, rather than at true 'enemies'.

Even the use of the term 'fascism' to describe Japanese radical nationalism is misleading, since it describes only a single strand of the nationalist movement. The groups shared methods rather than ideologies. They all attacked dominance of society by the established political parties and the large industrial concerns (*zaibatsu*). As in Germany, the failure at the Paris Peace Conference was crucial for the development of extremism. The famous article by Prince Konoye Fujimaro (a future Prime Minister), 'Down with the Anglo-American Peace Proposals' published in 1918, provided a coherent argument for the anti-Western cause.[21] After the Versailles débâcle, the number of nationalist societies grew enormously – and continued to grow throughout the 1920s and early 1930s. By 1936 there were more than 750 active groups known to the police. The most dangerous were dominated by officers, like the Society of the Cherry, which supported the revolutionary nationalism of Kita Ikki; his book *An Outline for the Reconstruction of Japan* inspired Japan's 'fascists'.[22]

The shadow over civilian politics in Japan was the army and navy. The armed forces had been created on the German model, and under the Meiji constitution of 1889 were beyond civilian control. The Minister of War was always a serving officer, as was the Navy Minister; the armed forces operated as a state within the state. But this inner state was no more united than the political world outside. The army was controlled by cliques. For many years, this had been based on clan loyalties and regionalism, with officers of Choshu origins (a clan which had loyally supported the Meiji revolution in the 1860s) occupying all the important posts. But during the First World War this monopoly of power had been overturned. Other groups, formerly kept out of power, struggled for the senior commands.[23] The army had its own class-divisions, notably between the high-flyers, who attended the staff college, and the ordinary regimental officers, who had no hope of promotion to the highest ranks. The ideology of extreme nationalism began to create new groups,[24] uniting junior and senior officers in pursuit of a Japan purged of Western intrusions, a goal which superseded all earlier traditions of duty and obedience.

By the mid-1920s the army was out of control. Civilians who attempted to curb its power or cut its budgets were murdered, and the High Command stood back from the increasing turmoil. Officers who planned a *coup d'état* were given derisory punishments.

The navy had traditionally pursued a different course. By custom, it was an apolitical force. But this changed during the 1920s and early 1930s, as the admirals fought for the funds to sustain their grand strategy. While the army, with its crabbed petty nationalism, looked not much further than Korea and Manchuria, the navy took a world view. Its preoccupation was fuel reserves, once coal, and now oil. Barely 10 per cent of Japanese oil supplies were produced from internal sources, and the two principal external sources – the Americas and the Dutch East Indies – were vulnerable in time of war. The Japanese had beaten the Russians in 1905 with a fleet still partly fuelled by coal; after 1920, with a much larger fleet, a vastly increased merchant marine (up over 80 per cent from 1914), and an economy heavily dependent on exports, the navy planners believed that the nation's survival now depended on secure reserves of heavy fuel oil.

From 1926 to 1927, the navy searched everywhere for alternative fuel sources. It sponsored experiments in Manchuria into the liquefaction of fuel oil from coal shale, and the production of synthetic petroleum.[25] They underwrote oil exploration in Taiwan (a failure) and in the northern Sakhalin peninsula (more successful). Nothing resolved the basic supply problem. The navy began to store oil as a strategic reserve; by 1926, it had amassed 1.5 million tons. But Japanese naval officers knew that oil-storage tanks were vulnerable to attack; they had crippled the Russian fleet in 1905 by burning its fuel stocks.[26]

The differing strategic preoccupations of the army and navy fed back into foreign policy during the 1920s. The army assumed the probability of a war on the mainland; the great enemy would be Soviet Russia. The driving force behind army policy in the early 1930s was the nationalist preoccupation with Korea and Manchuria. By contrast, the navy's dominant thought was of lines of supply across the Pacific. Her potential enemies were the American and British fleets. From 1907 (coincidentally, the same year that the United States incorporated Japan into their war planning) the USA was the 'hypothetical enemy' used when the planners created their budgets. The American fleet was the benchmark for the Japanese. But the pressure placed on Japan to restrict the size of her fleet caused a profound split in the navy. The Ministry, which took a wider political view, accepted that the restrictions of the Washington Naval Treaty were reasonable; in exchange for limiting fleet sizes, the American and British had agreed not to extend their bases in the Pacific. But to the naval General Staff, under Admiral Kato Kanji, the restrictions were anathema. The Admiral later said that in his view war with the United States began on the day that the Naval Treaty was signed.[27] Certainly, from 1923, the Imperial National Defence Policy singled out the United States as being the power 'most likely to collide with Japan in the near future'.

From the early 1920s the army pressed for expansion on the mainland, while the navy argued for its Pacific-wide strategy. The disagreement between them was not wholly professional or ideological, but derived in part from the shrinking of the money available for military spending. Only in 1935 did the military budget reach the figure achieved in 1920; only after 1937 was the finance available to satisfy both the army and the navy. Many plans created by the armed services in the early 1930s were intended to win political rather than military battles: the enemy was a sister-service rather than some foreign foe.

The need to expand was never questioned. One of the few areas in which the army and navy were in agreement was that foreign policy could no longer be left in the hands of the politicians, who were holding up Japan's driving need to grow beyond her existing frontiers. Both the army and the navy had invested heavily in Manchuria, and looked upon it as virtually part of the homeland. There would be no naval opposition to any moves in Manchuria. The initiative rested with the army. From the winter of 1930, officers prominent in the Society of the Cherry began to plan a coup which would secure Manchuria for Japan, and would force the civilian politicians to adopt a more militant line in international relations. The navy also wished to put pressure on the civilians, after they had been (in their view) betrayed in the negotiations for the 1930 London Naval Treaty, which again restricted the size of the fleet. Military intervention against Chinese sovereignty in Manchuria was a decisive step, against all the treaty obligations accepted by successive Japanese governments. The Manchurian Incident of September 1931 was a strike against China, but it was also a military attack on the political system at home.

Although the planning of the Manchurian adventure was supposedly secret, the government in Tokyo was fully informed as the plot developed. Both Foreign Office intelligence and the police agreed that an 'incident' was being planned which would lead to the army in Manchuria, the Kwantung army, seizing power on the mainland. Military disaffection was unconcealed. An abortive coup by junior officers in Tokyo during March had failed only because senior officers refused to become involved. On 15 September, the Cabinet heard that a military coup might 'break out' in Manchuria on 18 September. For once, the anti-militarist politicians reacted decisively. Shidehara Kijuro, the Foreign Minister, was also caretaker Prime Minister. He had the power to act without Cabinet approval, although he was careful to enlist the active support of the Emperor. Shidehara ordered the War Minister to prevent the *coup d'état* in Manchuria. An order prohibiting any 'incident' was despatched by hand to the Commander-in-Chief in Manchuria. But the War Office sabotaged the mission. The message was entrusted to one of the founding members of the Society of the Cherry. To no one's surprise, he failed to deliver his message until after the rising was under way.

On the night of 18 September 1931 Chinese soldiers or 'bandits' supposedly blew up some three feet of the railway line at Mukden.

The Manchurian Incident was transparently a pretext for Japanese intervention; it subsequently transpired that most of the damage to the railway had been caused by Japanese artillery. The Kwantung army moved smoothly in accordance with a carefully preordained plan, and occupied key points throughout Manchuria, brushing aside Chinese troops where they met them. Within a few days much of Manchuria was in their hands.

For the army radicals the Incident was only the first move. Their aim was not just to capture Manchuria, but to begin the wholesale redirection of Japanese society. The leaders of the coup were reported as saying:

> When we return to the homeland this time we shall carry out a coup d'état and do away with the party political system of government. Then we shall establish a nation of National Socialism with the Emperor as the centre. We shall abolish capitalists like Mitsui and Mitsubishi and carry out an even distribution of wealth. We are determined to do so.[28]

The army plotters had judged the national mood correctly. The occupation of Manchuria was popular with all classes in Japan, and produced a wave of patriotic enthusiasm. It soon became impossible for the politicians to withdraw the *fait accompli*; in fact, few wished to do so. The only serious concern was with the possible international reaction to the move.

The Manchurian Incident caused a profound reappraisal of Japan's position within the international system. Until 1931, she had been regarded as a loyal but junior member of the concert of nations. From 1931 onwards two distinct interpretations of Japan's international status began to develop. For some Westerners, the issue was clear-cut: Japan had used force in Manchuria, so she became a pariah-state, the first government to defy the League of Nations; the only plausible Western response was ostracism or some form of punishment. The strongest advocates of a hard line were the Far East specialists in the State Department, although their policy proposals often fell on deaf ears in Washington. There were many more supporters for a soft line: the military and naval adventurism was, they whispered, only temporary. If Japan could be seen to 'benefit' from the international system, then the militarist cause would wither. The strongest Western advocates for a subtle approach were the outspoken US Ambassador in Tokyo, Joseph Grew, and his British counterpart Sir Francis Lindley.

For the British and United States governments, as well as for other states like France who had direct interests in the Far East, the issues were confused. Their first thoughts were economic and strategic. Britain and the United States had huge investments in both China and Japan; 300,000 jobs in the United States depended on the Japanese silk trade and by 1930 British exports to Japan were about equal to her commerce with China. Tariff legislation, which kept Japanese goods out of the British and US markets, had already embittered the Japanese, especially the Smoot Hawley Tariff Act which had passed into law in June 1930. The Western governments did not want to invite retaliation by precipitate action over Manchuria.

The ethical issues were also confused. Both governments recognised that Japan had brought her areas of Manchuria from economic backwardness to relative prosperity: the direct contrast with the bandit-ridden zones under the corrupt and ineffectual control of China demonstrated Japan's commitment in the region. Stanley Hornbeck in the State Department stressed the ambiguity of the situation:

> if China wins, China will be encouraged to persevere in the role of a trouble maker; if Japan wins, Japan will be encouraged to persevere in the role of self-appointed arbiter of international rights in the Far East. . . . if Japan wins, the principle of resolving international controversies without resort to force will have been given a terrific knock.[29]

A letter to the British Foreign Secretary Sir John Simon from an old friend, the Master of Peterhouse, Cambridge, accurately reflected private rather than public British attitudes:

> This I know sounds all wrong, perhaps immoral, when she [Japan] is flouting the League of Nations, but (1) she has had great provocation, (2) she *must* ere long expand *somewhere* – for goodness sake let (or rather, encourage) her to do so there instead of Australia's way and (3) her presence fully established in Manchuria means a real block against Bolshevik aggression.[30]

After the war was widened to include an attack in January 1932 on Chinese forces near Shanghai, under the horrified eyes of the Westerners living in the city, British and American attitudes began to harden; even so, there was little real prospect of joint action. The British Prime Minister remarked that 'You'll get nothing out of Washington but words. . . . Big words, but only words.' For his part, the Secretary of State Henry Stimson, was writing in his diary: 'I am afraid it is rather doubtful whether we shall be able to secure Great Britain to join us [in an appeal under the Nine Power Pact, of which Japan, Britain and the USA were all signatories].'[31] In practice,

British and American economic and political interests in the Far East diverged as often as they converged. The expansion of American business interests in the Far East, especially in China, had been made, as a Foreign Office report put it, 'largely at Great Britain's expense'.[32] By contrast, Japan was an increasingly significant market for Britain (£6.9 million annually compared with £7.8 million to China)[33] and the City of London had large financial investments in Japanese industry. The British were always suspicious (and often rightly so) that US policy was designed to spread the American business empire through the Far East.

However, they faced similar strategic problems. Japan, for all its small size relative to the Western powers, *was* the dominant force in the region. The British Chiefs of Staff, asked to appraise the situation, were blunt: 'The position is about as bad as it could be. . . . In a word we possess only light naval forces in the Far East; the fuel supplies required for the (thirty-eight day) passage of the Main Fleet to the Far East and for its mobility after arrival are in jeopardy; and the bases at Singapore and Hong Kong, essential to the maintenance of the fleet of capital ships on arrival, are not in a defensible condition.'[34] The United States, even with its Pacific base at Pearl Harbor, was still over 4000 miles from the scene of the action in China; even the Philippines, effectively the US forward base, was more than a thousand miles from Shanghai.[35] And, just as budgetary cuts had weakened the British fleet, so the effects of the economic depression were eroding US military spending. Even in numbers, the United States was barely superior. Japan had two aircraft-carriers to America's four, and she launched another during the Manchurian crisis. In heavy cruisers, a key vessel in Far Eastern conditions, the Japanese had both a numerical and a qualitative superiority.

In practical terms, the options available to the Western powers were limited: they could acquiesce in Japan's advance; they might impose economic sanctions (which could also cost them dearly); or they could offer China arms and money as their proxy in her war with Japan. Alternatively, they could take the minimum action and follow in the wake of the League of Nations. Over the next ten years they were to try virtually every possible permutation of these options. The one option not available in 1931 was military action.

The Manchurian Incident began what one Japanese scholar has called the Fifteen Year War.[36] In February 1933, the League of Nations censured Japan for her activities in Manchuria, although the League report by Lord Lytton in effect said that the Japanese had achieved the right ends by the wrong means. In his view the only solution was to 'follow lines similar to those followed by Japan'.[37] But the proposal of an autonomous Manchuria under Chinese sovereignty was unacceptable and the Japanese delegation withdrew from the League. However, the chief delegate, Matsuoka Yosuke, was careful to express his withdrawal only in terms of the quarrel with China: Japan would still 'endeavour to co-operate with the League in the preservation of world peace'.

In the aftermath of Japan's withdrawal from the League, a domestic propaganda campaign presented a picture of Japan pressured by outside forces.[38] In the decade after 1931, each new radical step, through the assault on China in 1937 and finally to the attack on Pearl Harbor in 1941, was presented as a response to Western attacks on Japan's vital interests. Ambassador Grew reported: 'The military themselves and the public through military propaganda are fully prepared to fight rather than to surrender to moral or other pressure from the West. The moral obloquy of the rest of the world at present serves only to strengthen not to modify their determination.'[39] Even the Foreign Ministry, hitherto the strongest bastion of 'Western' attitudes in the government, took up the extreme nationalist line, and a sharply aggressive tone entered Japanese contacts with the West. One Vice-Minister asked the British Ambassador: 'What is one to make of the contrast of people in the east working from morning to night to live on the borderline of starvation while any number of leisured ladies in London have nothing better to do than walk their dogs in Hyde Park? Isn't this simple fact enough to suggest a fundamental problem among nations?'[40]

In Japanese eyes, the solution to the 'fundamental problem' was a complete re-ordering of Asia under Japan's leadership. In March 1933, a new association, *Dai Ajia Kyokai* – Great Asia Association – was founded. Its founders assumed that the old international system under Western dominance was breaking up; Japan's withdrawal from the League would hasten the process. Three power groups would replace the old international order: the Anglo-American, the Soviet Union and the Asiatic. The Asiatic bloc would comprise Greater Japan, China, the Dutch East Indies and Siam, and under the leadership of Japan it would form a coherent trading bloc. The raw materials from the peripheral nations would supply the core industries in Japan, who would in turn export finished goods back to the suppliers of the raw materials. Prince Konoye, the most prominent member of the Great Asia Association, sketched out the new political philosophy in a long speech to Parliament in 1935:

Japan's action in Manchuria may be hard to justify from the Anglo-

> American point of view, or in the interest of maintaining the status quo. . . . we must be prepared to devise new principles of international peace based on our own standpoint, on our own wisdom. We must then boldly and candidly challenge the whole world with the righteousness of our principles.[41]

Konoye and others wanted to create what became officially known in the 1940s as the 'Co-Prosperity Sphere'. The idiom and ideology of the great Asian ideal was of Asiatic harmony and unity. A political scientist, Royama Masmachi, developed the concept of 'regionalism'. Japan's expansion, he said, 'should not be regarded as the construction of a colonial economy but rather the establishment of a regional structure for the co-operative destiny of the peoples of East Asia'. These ideas became widespread in university circles, growing out of antagonism to the Western colonial powers. To the advocates of Co-Prosperity, Japan should seek to benefit all Asians, instead of tyrannising them like the colonial Western nations. Each nation would find its 'proper place', as the Foreign Minister, Matsuoka Yosuke, expressed it when the government adopted the Great Asian programme in August 1940: 'the mission of Japan is to proclaim and demonstrate the *kodo* [Imperial Way] throughout the world. Viewed from the standpoint of international relations, this amounts, I think, to enabling all nations and races to find each its proper place in the world.' The concept of 'proper place' meant that, as in the Japanese family, the Yamato race would be the father, and the other nations subservient and dependent, fulfilling the role of children. A government pamphlet described the relationships between the nations of East Asia as being those of 'parent and child, elder and younger brother'.[42]

The advocates of Co-Prosperity argued that these relationships corresponded to the reality of Asian conditions. The colonial powers had, they said, done nothing for their subject peoples, a view shared by many educated Malayans, Indians, Burmese, Vietnamese and Indonesians. Western market capitalism, the Japanese claimed, had made the peoples of Asia bear the real costs of the economic depression. How much better would be an economic system run by Asians for the benefit of Asians, a structure based on Eastern concepts and ideals, rather than alien impositions from the West. This 'Great Asia' attitude was pervasive: the whole world was to be turned on its axis. The term 'Far East' disappeared from books and newspapers, because it was geography seen from a Western viewpoint; in Japanese school atlases, Asia became the new centre of the world. One enthusiast even renamed America as the 'Eastern Asia

Poster exhorting the people of Manchuria to discover and exploit the 'treasures of the soil'.

Continent' and Australia was to be 'Southern Asia Continent'. The same Professor of Geography at Kyoto Imperial University declared that in his professional opinion, since all the oceans of the globe were connected, they should all be known by the single name of the Great Sea of Japan.

The final definition of the Co-Prosperity Sphere was produced by the Research Section of the Ministry of War, working with the army and navy General Staffs and the Overseas Ministry. The work was completed just after war was declared in December 1941. Its proposals verged on fantasy. Not only was the whole of the Pacific to be brought under direct Japanese rule, including Australia, New Zealand and Ceylon, but also Alaska, the whole of Central America, Cuba, Haiti, Jamaica and the Bahamas; parts of Mexico and Peru were also marked for occupation. The East Indies, Burma (including part of India), Malaya, Siam and Indo-China were to become independent states within the Co-Prosperity Sphere.[43]

The intellectual origins of the Co-Prosperity Sphere lay not only in the theories of Royama Masmachi, but also in the 'world picture' of a political journalist, Togo Minoru, popularised some thirty years before. He observed that 'if our people succeed in constructing new Japans everywhere . . . and engage in vigorous activities throughout the Pacific, then our country's predominance over the Pacific will have been assured.'[44] But where the generation of 1906 had envisaged only a peaceful penetration, now the New Order was to be imposed by the imperial army and navy.

Throughout the 1920s and into the 1930s Japan spoke with contradictory voices because the military and political factions pursued conflicting policies. Foreign governments found it hard to accept that chaos and confusion rather than duplicity lay behind the turns of Japanese policy. Westerners in Tokyo could follow the struggles of the warring factions in the streets and in the courts. In the 1920s assassins had been lone fanatics; by the 1930s the army and political factions organised murder gangs, which systematically terrorised those who opposed them. Officers attacked fellow officers if they were not sufficiently radical and 'patriotic'. In May 1935, a young colonel murdered the head of the Military Affairs Bureau, General Nagata. He justified his crime on the ground that he had 'come to realise that the senior statesmen, those close to the throne, powerful financiers and bureaucrats, were attempting gradually to corrupt the government and the Army for their own selfish interests'.

There was almost open season on civilian politicians; assassination and military street violence became more frequent and indiscriminate. In February 1936, a group of young officers, modelling themselves on the heroic forty-five Ronin (dispossessed samurai warriors) of a Japanese legend, launched a full-scale attack on their military and civilian enemies. Bands of soldiers roamed the streets seeking their victims. At the house of the Finance Minister, whom they hated because he had imposed limits on the military budget, officers fired round after round from their pistols into his body and then slashed at him with their swords; as they left one of them apologised to the Minister's servants 'for the annoyance I have caused'.[45]

The February Incident was a full-scale putsch, not another act of random individual fanaticism; fearful of the consequences, the army began to purge its own house, retiring the hotheads or despatching them to distant commands on the mainland. But there would be no end to faction fighting until the politicians and the military could work in harmony; only with the appointment of Prince Konoye as Prime Minister in 1937 did the military find a pliant but able politician who shared many of their own ideals. By November 1937 the Emperor was telling his Keeper of the Privy Seal: 'Konoye is just watching the military do as they please.'[46] In practice Konoye was more than just a tool for the army; his strongly nationalist views were sincerely held. He resigned twice, but on each occasion returned to power after a few months, since no other figure seemed able to bridge the gulf between the armed forces and the civilians. So, from spring 1937 to October 1941, Japan possessed a leader whose objective, as he expressed it in 1937, was 'to reduce internal friction'. Konoye had an impeccable pedigree (the Fujiwara were among the most eminent families of Japan), and he also brought youth and energy into the business of government. He was trusted by all as an honest man without political ambition.[47]

In Konoye's eyes, foreign policy was the means to resolve Japan's inner tensions, which arose from overpopulation and a lack of resources. He could not resolve the issues between the factions, since the navy, the army and the 'Western' politicians were irreconcilable; but he succeeded, better than any other Prime Minister, in playing one faction off against another. The same sleight of hand extended to international relations. Since 1931, both the economic depression abroad and the further decay of the League system had worked to Japan's advantage. Japan, Italy and Germany all stood against the League system: Italy invaded Ethiopia in October 1935, while Germany denounced the Locarno Agreements of 1925 and reoccupied the Rhineland in March 1936. All three nations shared a contempt for the existing structure and aimed to dismantle it.

There was also some hope that, given the new fragility of international relations, Japan's misdemeanour over Manchuria would be conveniently forgotten. The conquest of Manchuria, soon extended to include those areas of China north of the Great Wall, had proved more difficult than the plotters had imagined in 1931. In 1932, a protectorate had been created in Manchuria; Manchukuo was to be 'independent' under Japanese guardianship, ruled by Pu Yi, who had been the last Manchu Emperor of China.

China was irrevocably divided between the nationalists and the communists. But they managed at times to make common cause against the Japanese enemy. The Chinese armies, both nationalist and communist, fought harder and more doggedly than the Japanese had thought possible, and both sides were willing to agree to a truce in May 1933. This gave Japan control north of the Great Wall, and to the south, a demilitarised zone, which would keep the Chinese and Japanese armies apart. The Japanese continued to push west into Mongolia, and down along the line of the Great Wall until Peking was an isolated salient in occupied territory. The Chinese nationalists under Chiang Kai-shek used the respite to attack the communist armies of Mao Tse-tung, driving them out of central China on a Long March to the far west.

By the mid-1930s neither the United States nor Britain had much enthusiasm for supporting the Chinese cause; but the war which broke out between China and Japan after a minor incident by the Marco Polo Bridge near Peking on 7 July 1937 destroyed any possibility of Japan's reintegration into the international community; after July 1937, Japan was set, as Ambassador Grew put it, 'on the war path'. Unlike the Manchurian Incident of 1931, the brief engagement between Chinese and Japanese troops was accidental, and the position was quickly stabilised. But factions on both the Chinese and the Japanese sides wanted to extend the conflict – Chiang Kai-shek because he believed that all-out war in China was the only way to involve the Western democracies on China's side, the expansionists at the War Ministry in Tokyo as a means to advance their Greater Asian schemes. Konoye was assured that the Chinese question would 'be solved inside three months', and on 27 July he announced to Parliament that Japan had taken the first steps towards the creation of a New Order in Asia.

At first the Japanese advanced quickly into China. Peiping and Tientsin fell almost immediately, but the Chinese fought desperately hard at Shanghai, and one Japanese division was trapped and annihilated by Chinese communist forces in the mountains of Shansi province. It was clearly not going to be over in three months. As the going became harder, the Japanese began to fight a more brutal war. When the nationalist capital of Nanking was captured in December, the Japanese commanders allowed an orgy of killing, which was widely reported by Western correspondents. In Japan, the news was censored and the capture of the enemy capital was celebrated as a national triumph. On 12 December, the day before the fall of Nanking, Japanese planes had attacked British and American gunboats anchored in the river close to the city. The American newspapers were full of stories and pictures of Japanese atrocities, and President Franklin Roosevelt demanded an immediate apology, which was eventually grudgingly forthcoming.

Japan acted in China as though the Western states had no rights in an Asian quarrel. The Tokyo government had always refused attempts by the League of Nations to mediate in the dispute between China and Japan, preferring direct discussions with the Chinese. But after 1937 it was impossible to pretend that the white nations were not involved. The Soviet Union provided aid to both the communist Chinese and the nationalists; by 1935, Nazi Germany was backing the nationalist regime with money, advisers and military equipment. The United States was more cautious. Roosevelt talked in terms of 'quarantines' and economic sanctions but did little. Even the Japanese attack on the American gunboat *Panay* in December 1937 aroused as much anti-war hysteria in the United States as any desire to punish Japan.

Within a year of their first confident advance into China, the Japanese were fighting an immensely costly and inconclusive war, quite literally bogged down after the Chinese burst the dykes on the Yellow River and flooded the countryside. By the end of 1937, the Japanese had more than 700,000 troops in China and the war was costing $5 million a day; almost half of all government expenditure was absorbed by defence.[48] By the second anniversary of the war, the Japanese had given up trying to fight a decisive battle with the elusive Chinese armies, and had begun a war of attrition. They aimed to cut off the Chinese from their sources of supply: all the main ports were occupied, and the navy blockaded the entire Chinese coastline. But the nationalist armies were still supplied by a narrow-gauge railway from Haiphong in French Indo-China, and over the tortuous Burma Road to Kunning.

China and Japan were the victims of their own fantasies. Chiang Kai-shek believed that the Western governments would rally to his cause; they did not. Indeed, Nazi Germany proved a more stable source of supply than either Britain or the United States. Chiang's preoccupation was not with the Japanese at all, but with the communists under Mao Tse-tung: Western support would enable him to construct 'a bulwark against bolshevism'. His miscalculation was dwarfed by that of the Japanese. From the time of the Sino-Japanese war (1894–5), Japan had had a low opinion of the Chinese, referring to them as 'chinks'.[49] Their dogged resistance, and in particular the opening of the dykes, amazed and infuriated the Japanese army, who turned to wholesale terrorisation of the civilian population. This, in turn, provided more willing supporters for the nationalist armies. By 1939, the stalemate was complete. The Chinese had lost most of their great cities, and their armies were constantly harried from the air. But the Japanese were working against the terrain; at each new assault the Chinese retreated a little further, while Japan's supply lines became a little longer and more vulnerable.

Japan's diplomats worked hard to preserve their country from the worst consequences of military adventurism. Roosevelt condemned the 'international gangsters'; the 'China Incident' pushed Japan further outside the international system. Ideologically, she felt at home with Germany and Italy, and there was strong pressure to construct a new alliance system among the 'have-not' nations. The immediate danger was not the remote threat of American displeasure, but a renewal of Russian empire-building. In July 1935, the 7th Congress of the Comintern called for an all-out assault on fascism; the Japanese watched as the Soviet armies on the eastern frontier were strengthened, and new airbases built within easy flying distance not only of the cities of Manchuria, but of the homeland itself. In March 1936, the Soviet Union signed a Mutual Assistance Pact with the government of Mongolia; one of the conditions was that Mongolia, with Soviet aid, should create an army of 90,000. The renewal of Soviet expansionism had long been foreseen by the army's strategists, and they supported the Foreign Office in their search for a new alliance. The Anti-Comintern Pact with Germany was signed in November 1936: it served the ends of two states pursuing parallel paths – Japan withdrew from the naval limitation talks in January, while Germany remilitarised the Rhineland in March. But there was no greater harmonisation of interests; Germany was still not sure whether to back Japan or China in the contest for Asia. In practice, she continued the profitable business of selling arms to the Chinese while simultaneously professing friendship for Japan.

The diplomatic revolution of August 1939, when Nazi Germany signed a Non-Aggression Pact with the Soviet Union, caught the Japanese entirely by surprise. The growing strength of the Soviet military presence in the East had resulted in numerous border incidents from the summer of 1938. The Japanese lost heavily to the superior Russian armour and artillery, but the Soviet Union realised that Japan would not concede her position in Manchuria without an all-out war. In late August, Japanese policy seemed in tatters. The war in China was unresolved, and the army was threatened with a major war on the northern front. The Anti-Comintern Pact had collapsed, and Japan's other potential adversaries seemed stronger and more threatening. Both Britain and the United States were rearming, and the American naval building programme first matched and then exceeded anything that Japan could undertake. But, by the end of September 1939, war had broken out in Europe, and Britain and France were engaged with Germany; as in the First World War, the Japanese believed that they could profit from the conflict in the West.

Within a year the prospects seemed better than ever before. France and the Netherlands had capitulated to Germany, and their possessions in the East, although still nominally under control from Europe, were ripe for takeover. In June 1940 the Japanese also concluded an agreement with the Soviet Union, which recognised the status quo in China and Manchuria. Neither side thought it would be a lasting peace, but neither wanted to engage in a major war with untold consequences. The China war dragged on, but the new situation even promised some improvement in that area. The French Vichy regime in Indo-China had no means to resist Japanese 'suggestions' that troops should be stationed in key towns in northern Indo-China, and that Japan should build eight airfields for use against the nationalists. The Haiphong–Kunning railway was closed. In the following month, July 1940, the Japanese persuaded the British (now resisting Germany on their own in Europe) to close the other access route to China, the Burma Road. Churchill conceded when his Chiefs of Staff told him that 'The overriding consideration was the need to avoid war with Japan.'[50]

In the summer of 1940 a unique opportunity apparently opened before the military and political leaders in Tokyo. The old interventionist powers were busily engaged elsewhere, while mutual deterrence controlled relations with the Soviet Union. The United States talked loudly but did little. Rich pickings lay before Japan: the mineral and agricultural resources of Indo-China and the oil wells of the Indies. The 'have-not' powers were now in the ascendant, and it was, they thought, the moment to divide up the world between them. In September 1940, Germany, Italy and Japan signed a Tripartite Pact, more commonly known as the Berlin–Rome–Tokyo Axis. This provided mutual support to any member who was attacked by another state not already engaged in the European conflict. It was not a blank cheque for aggression but it allowed Japan a sense of security: she could push the USA to all stages short of war secure in the belief that, if the Americans attacked, the Axis would support her.

For twenty years, the army had given direction to the nation: expansion into Manchuria and China – the northern strategy – had been the only policy agreed upon by all the military factions. The navy had played a subsidiary role, snatching the limelight when it could. But in the new conditions of 1940, the roles were reversed. The navy's strategy of the Southward Advance now seemed to promise security and stability, while the army floundered in the Chinese morass. This strategic transformation led directly to war with the USA.

In September 1940, Japanese troops landed in Indo-China, after an 'invitation' from the Vichy authorities. In July, the State Department had warned Tokyo against any move into Indo-China, even under the flimsy camouflage of an 'invitation'. The warning was backed by restrictions on the export of oil and scrap steel. It was an unambiguous threat: 78 per cent of all Japanese scrap steel – which produced 1.3 million tons of finished steel – came from the USA; 80 per cent of Japan's oil came from American-controlled sources. This was more than the 'loud talk' which had been the characteristic American response to Japan's provocation, from the *Panay* incident onwards. Roosevelt's plan was now to 'slip a noose around Japan's neck and give it a jerk now and then'.[51]

The Japanese reacted to the American embargo with a mixture of bravado, shock and despair. The war-planning section of the navy had long accepted that the Southward Advance would risk war with America. In April 1940, a conference of section chiefs agreed that 'now was the finest chance to occupy the Netherlands East Indies'; in June 1940, after the fall of France, Indo-China became 'a ripe persimmon' ready to be picked by Japan. Early in July 1940 the naval planners assured the Prime Minister, Prince Konoye, that 'the navy deemed it quite safe to move into Indo-China.' What they meant by 'safe' became clear in their policy paper entitled 'The Main Principles for Coping with the Changing World Situation'. This sketched out a detailed scheme for the incorporation of Indo-China, and the likely consequences. War with the USA was inevitable: the Americans' evil intentions had been made clear by the embargo. A blockade posed a mortal threat to Japan. So Japan needed to take over Indo-China to secure her strategic resources and crucial ports. The United States would respond to this initiative with a total trade embargo, so Japan should then seize the Netherlands East Indies and take the vital oil for herself. This would mean war with the USA, but Japan would then be in a position not to lose.

The expansionists pointed out that there was a strong likelihood that if Japan did not fill the vacuum in Indo-China and the Indies, either Britain or the United States would do so. Britain's attack on the French fleet at anchor in Oran harbour on 4 July was, they said, evidence of their enemies' utter ruthlessness in pursuit of their strategic goals.

The embargo began to bite in September and October, and it at first induced panic in the ranks of the planners. Although they had foreseen these sanctions in July 1940, it was as if they did not believe the logic of their own prediction. Yamamoto was scathing about the expansionists in a letter to Admiral Shimada in December 1940: 'To be stunned, enraged and discomforted by America's economic pressure at this belated hour is like a schoolboy who unthinkingly acts on the impulse of the moment.' The shock of the embargo did not bring Japan 'to her senses' as Roosevelt had hoped. The Chief of the navy General Staff, appointed in July 1940, was quickly

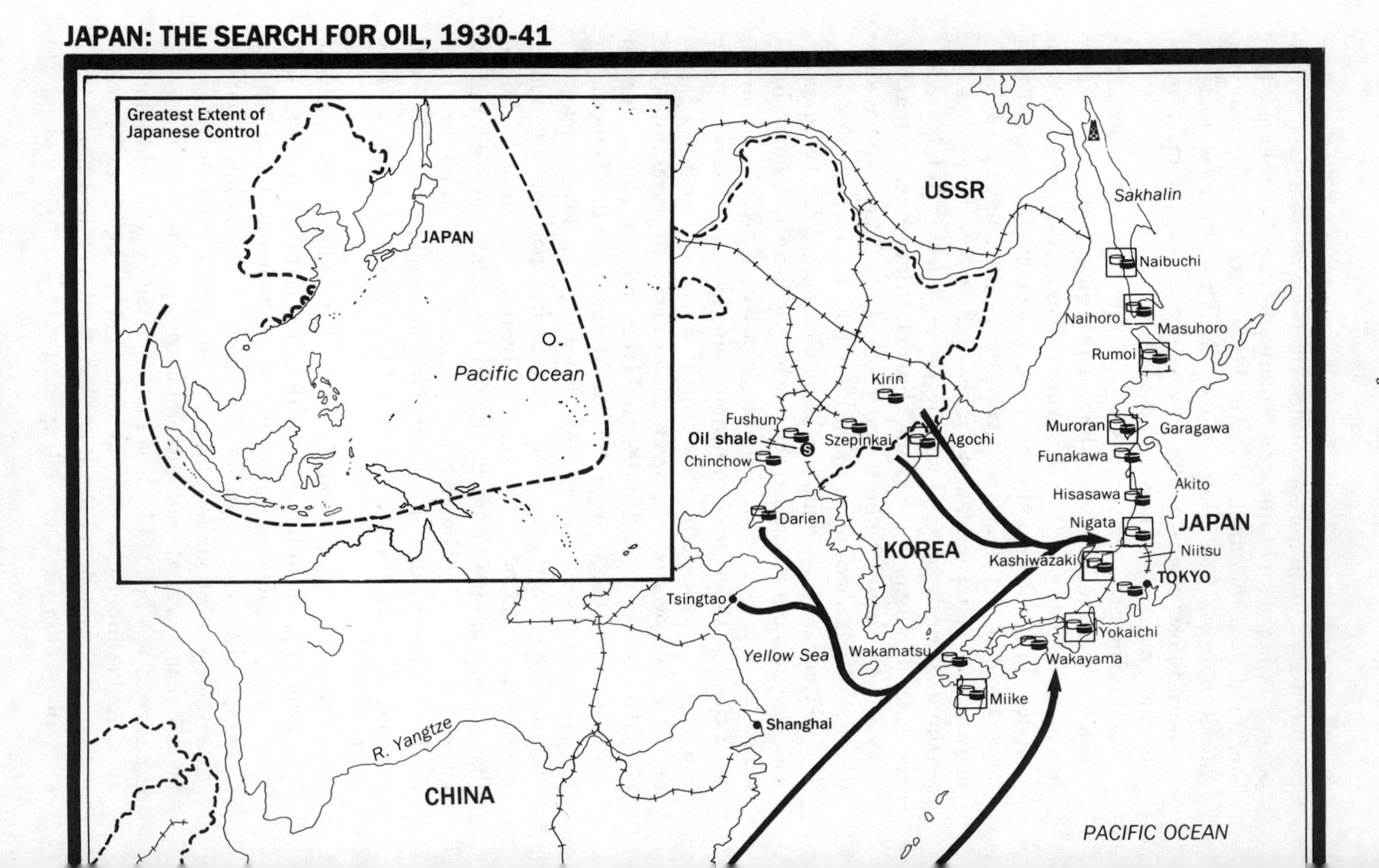
JAPAN: THE SEARCH FOR OIL, 1930-41
Greatest Extent of Japanese Control
JAPAN
Pacific Ocean
USSR
Sakhalin
Naibuchi
Naihoro
Masuhoro
Rumoi
Kirin
Fushun
Oil shale
Chinchow
Szepinkai
Agochi
Muroran
Garagawa
Funakawa
Akito
Hisasawa
Nigata
JAPAN
Darien
KOREA
Kashiwazaki
Niitsu
TOKYO
Tsingtao
Yokaichi
Yellow Sea
Wakamatsu
Wakayama
Miike
Shanghai
R. Yangtze
CHINA
PACIFIC OCEAN

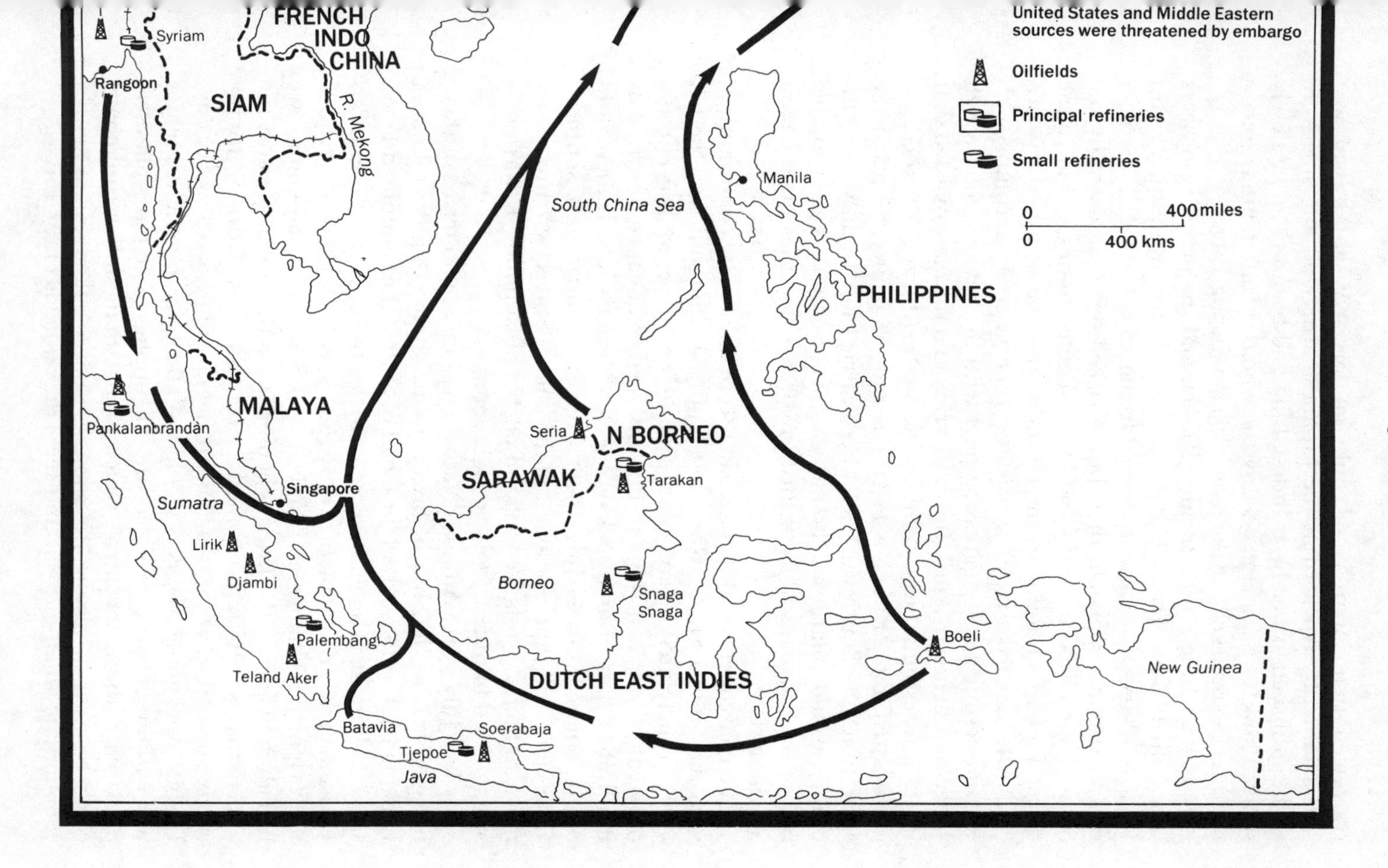
United States and Middle Eastern
sources were threatened by embargo
Oilfields
Principal refineries
Small refineries
0 400 miles
0 400 kms
FRENCH INDO CHINA
Syriam
Rangoon
SIAM
R. Mekong
South China Sea
Manila
PHILIPPINES
MALAYA
Pankalanbrandan
Seria
N BORNEO
SARAWAK
Tarakan
Singapore
Sumatra
Lirik
Djambi
Borneo
Snaga Snaga
Palembang
Boeli
Teland Aker
DUTCH EAST INDIES
New Guinea
Batavia
Soerabaja
Tjepoe
Java

convinced that Japan could only go forward: withdrawal was unthinkable. By April 1941, the Japanese army and air force were well established in northern Indo-China and began to move slowly south. Plans were made to occupy the whole of Indo-China; 40,000 men were earmarked for the new invasion during July.

But on 22 June Hitler invaded Russia, and the planning process was halted. The strategic balance had shifted dramatically: in Konoye's view, Russia had been 'driven to the Anglo-American camp'. If that happened, then Japan risked being attacked by the Soviet Union in Manchuria and by the United States at sea. In the discussions which followed the German invasion, it was the politicians who argued that now was the time to settle accounts with Russia, despite a non-aggression pact with the Soviet Union which Japan had signed in April. Both the army and the navy insisted that it was now essential to continue with the Southward Advance. No one wanted to fight the Soviet Union and the United States at the same time; the Southward Advance, carried out rapidly and efficiently, would enlarge the boundaries of the empire, gain valuable new resources, and still leave the army free to face the Soviet Union at a later date.

The consequences of this decision were immediate confrontation with the United States. Roosevelt had told Churchill that 'he felt very strongly that every effort should be made to prevent the outbreak of war with Japan', but any further advance southwards into Indo-China or an attack on the Netherlands East Indies could not be ignored. On 26 July 1941, after the occupation of southern Indo-China, all Japanese assets in the United States were frozen and much tighter controls were placed on US oil supplies. It was not a stranglehold but the noose was tightening.

By late July 1941, Admiral Nagano was talking in terms of there being 'no choice left but to break the iron fetters binding Japan'. Looking back at those days the Chief of Staff of the Combined Fleet, Ugaki Matome, who had served as the head of the Operations Division in the critical months of 1940–1 wrote: 'When we concluded the Tripartite Alliance and moved into Southern Indo-China, we had already burned the bridges behind us on the march towards the anticipated war with the United States and Great Britain.' By the end of July, oil was being used up at the rate of 12,000 tons per day. Despite stockpiling, reserves would not allow Japan to fight a major war without access to new, secure oil supplies. The navy planners prepared a draft document which stated that, unless diplomacy could be used to restore the supply situation, then Japan should contemplate an all-out war and seize the oil fields of the Indies.

On 4 September the navy plan came before the Cabinet, and after seven hours of heated discussion a policy was settled. This stated that:

> Our Empire will (1) for the purpose of self-defence and self-preservation complete preparations for war, (2) concurrently take all possible diplomatic measures vis à vis the USA and Great Britain and thereby endeavour to attain our objectives. (3) In the event that there is no prospect of our demands being met by the first ten days of October . . . we will immediately decide to commence hostilities against the United States, Britain and the Netherlands.

Every effort was to be made to prevent the USA and the Soviet Union 'forming a united front against Japan'. The United States, which could read the secret Japanese codes, was soon aware of the decision, although not of the angry disputes and dissensions over strategy which filled the hours of discussion between Japan's leaders.

Militarists' view of the war in Asia: Japan has snapped the chains of the ABCD powers (America–Britain–China–Netherlands).

When the plan was sent to the Emperor, he responded by demanding the presence of Admiral Nagano and the Chief of Staff, General Sugiyama. He asked the General how long he thought hostilities would last if the United States and Japan went to war. Sugiyama replied, 'About three months.' Eyewitnesses noted that the blood rose in Hirohito's face, and he asked Sugiyama in 'an unusually loud tone', 'As War Minister at the outbreak of the China Incident, you asked me to approve sending army troops there, saying that the Incident would be settled in a short time. But it has not been ended after more than four years. Are you trying to tell me the same thing again?' Sugiyama went to great lengths to explain that 'the extensive hinterland of China prevented the consummation of operations.' The Emperor was exasperated. 'Again he raised his voice: "if the Chinese hinterland is large, the Pacific was boundless."' 'With what confidence do you say three months?', he asked the Chief of Staff, who was 'utterly at a loss', and 'hung his head unable to answer'. Admiral Nagano stepped in to say that:

> Japan was like a patient suffering from a serious illness. . . . Should he be left alone without an operation, there was a danger of a gradual decline. An operation, while it might be dangerous, would still offer some hope of saving his life. . . . the Army General Staff was in favour of putting hope in diplomatic negotiations to the finish, but . . . in the case of failure, a decisive operation would have to be performed.[52]

The exchange between the Emperor and the military leaders ensured that serious attention was given to a diplomatic initiative, but it also revealed the sloppiness of Japan's strategic planning. General Sugiyama could not have answered truthfully, even if he had wished to do so. The structure of command in Japan, although it corresponded notionally to Western patterns, was unique. The Japanese had adapted the General Staff system from imperial Germany before the First World War. In both Germany and Japan quite junior staff officers created the detailed plans and submitted them to their superiors for approval; but in Japan, unlike the West, the senior officers performed a largely formal role, rubber-stamping the proposals laid before them.

The apogee of the system was the Imperial Council, which the Emperor attended but in which by tradition he took no active part. Hirohito's attempt to play a more active role was considered almost unconstitutional: his silence was an extension of the principle that a senior official should avoid criticising the work of his juniors, and humiliating them. There were many barriers to effective collaboration between the services. There was no central war planning staff, no group planning for the momentous encounter with the 'ABCD powers' – as the USA, Britain, China and the Netherlands were known. The army carried out its own planning, and secured its own resources and supplies; the navy did the same. No one in Japan knew precisely how much oil was available, because the navy and army refused to pool their reserves, or even to tell the Cabinet Planning Board roughly what they had in stock.[53] The navy ignored the difficulties in a trans-Pacific strategy; they consistently underestimated the power and resources of the United States and Britain, while overestimating the capacity of Germany to assist Japan. The navy began to plan the detail of a major war, knowing that their traditional plan – of luring an enemy into the home waters of Japan and fighting a decisive battle close to home – had been rendered obsolete by advances in ship (and particularly submarine) design.

All wars are governed by chance factors; but in Japan in 1941 there were no certainties at all. The success of the Southward Advance depended on an untried (and still undecided) experiment in naval warfare. Oil reserves were reducing daily, yet there was no way a fleet could be brought to battle efficiency before late November. By late December the weather in the northern Pacific would make naval warfare difficult and dangerous. Winter would also make a Russian attack in Manchuria unlikely, but the army planners wanted to be ready for an attack in the spring: they insisted that the Southern Advance be completed by March 1942, so that all resources could be turned north if necessary. Japan's timetable called for the southern conquests to be completed within 120 days of the outbreak of hostilities, which placed the probable outbreak of war in the first week of December 1941.

Although the Emperor had insisted on the primacy of negotiation, the time available was extremely limited, given the pressures of the war timetable. Already the October deadline set on 6 September seemed impossible, and on 24 October the new Prime Minister, General Tojo, agreed a new final deadline for negotiations with the agreement of the army, navy and the civilian ministers. It was to be midnight on 30 November 1941. A new negotiator was sent to Washington, but he was not told the reason for the deadline.

The American government followed the manoeuvres of the Japanese government through the deciphered telegrams; bad translations made it seem that the Tokyo Cabinet was set on war, engaging in negotiation only for the sake of gaining time. This was not true, but the scope for a peaceful settlement was small. Roosevelt was interested in the possibility of agreeing to the status quo, releasing some embargoed oil and food to Japan, and organising discussions between the Chinese and the Japanese governments. His mood of accommodation ended when he heard that the Japanese had reinforced their troops in Indo-China: he told Henry Stimson, Secretary of War, that it was 'evidence of bad faith on the part of the Japanese – that while they were negotiating for an entire truce . . . they should be sending this expedition down there'.

The proposal that the Secretary of State Cordell Hull presented to the negotiators on 26 November called for Japan to 'withdraw all military, naval, air, and police forces from China and Indochina'. In Tokyo, 'China' was read to include Manchuria. This was considered quite intolerable by every member of the Japanese government; it was this proposal that Hirohito considered 'too humiliating'. On 29 November a group of ministers met to consider the American note. The Foreign Minister Togo said there was 'no use going any further'; the Prime Minister added, 'there was no hope for diplomatic dealings'. On the following day the Cabinet met formally to prepare their resolution for the Imperial Conference; at a little after 2.00 p.m. on 1 December they assembled in the Imperial Palace to ask the Emperor for his rescript authorising war. Six days later at 7.49 a.m. Honolulu time, the first wave of Japanese aircraft launched their attack on the US Pacific fleet at anchor; at the same time the Japanese army attacked the British positions at Kowloon and bombed Hong Kong, while more bombers destroyed the airfields in Malaya; 100,000 Japanese troops swept down the peninsula towards Singapore. Two days later, on 10 December, two of the most powerful ships in the British fleet, the *Prince of Wales* and the *Repulse*, were sunk by Japanese bombs and torpedoes, a loss as dramatic for the British as Pearl Harbor had been for the Americans. On Christmas Day, Hong Kong surrendered and Singapore, once the British bastion in the East, submitted on 15 February 1942. The Southward Advance had succeeded at every point.

In July 1941, as preparations were being made for war, a despairing Prince Konoye discussed Japan's dilemma with his War Minister (and eventual successor) General Tojo. The General tried to stiffen his resolve: 'Sometimes it is necessary to jump with one's eyes closed from the veranda of the Kiyomizu temple [in Kyoto].'[54] Anyone jumping from the temple risked death, smashed on the rocks hundreds of feet below; there was the smallest chance of survival. Tojo was telling Konoye to trust to the samurai spirit of his ancestors, that it was better for the nation to die than to be dishonoured. Japan started on the war path in 1940 for twentieth-century motives of power and *Realpolitik*; she entered the war in December 1941 not so much in the hope of victory, but because the spirit of the nation demanded nothing less.

CHAPTER SEVEN
THE UNITED STATES

> Europe has a set of primary interests which to us have none or a very remote relation. . . . it must be unwise in us to implicate ourselves by artificial ties in the ordinary vicissitudes of her politics or the ordinary combinations and collisions of her friendships or enmities.
>
> (George Washington, 1796)

> We shun political commitments which might entangle us in foreign wars. . . . we are not isolationists except insofar as we seek to isolate ourselves from war. . . . if we face the choice of profits or peace, this Nation will answer – this Nation must answer – 'we choose peace'.
>
> (Franklin Delano Roosevelt, 1936)

When war broke out in Europe on 3 September 1939 most Americans were asleep. President Roosevelt on hearing the news hurriedly called his Cabinet and military advisers together. All were agreed that America should stay out of the conflict. The American Ambassador to London, Joseph Kennedy, dolefully telegraphed: 'It's the end of the world, the end of everything.' Roosevelt was determined that 'we are not going to get into war.' Even if he had thought otherwise he was bound by a formal Act of Congress to remain neutral. On 4 September, amid a throng of reporters and cameras Cordell Hull, Roosevelt's Secretary of State, solemnly applied the seal to the document invoking neutrality. That night Roosevelt broadcast to the nation in one of his familiar 'fireside chats'. It was a sombre performance, making clear the efforts the President had made for peace, and would make in the future: 'I hope the United States will keep out of this war. I believe that it will. And I give you assurance and reassurance that every effort of your government will be directed towards that end.' A Gallup Poll showed that 94 per cent of Americans agreed with him. Americans cared passionately about neutrality. This time they would not clear up the 'European mess'.[1]

The European powers knew this too. America featured little in their calculations as the crisis in the summer of 1939 ripened into war. It had been clear since the 1920s that America would not intervene in Europe. The withdrawal of the world's largest economy from an active role in world affairs contributed to the power vacuum of the 1930s which tempted the aggressor states to embark on their violent programmes of expansion. Yet in a little over two years the United States was at war with all the Axis powers, her forces in combat across two oceans. In five years the United States became a military superpower, fighting her greatest foreign war since the founding of the Republic in 1776. America's road to war was twisted by a great paradox: anxious to avoid war at all costs, American isolationists helped to create conditions abroad in which America's safety could only be secured by the largest war effort in her history.

The desire to avoid 'foreign entanglements' of all kinds had been a watchword of American foreign policy for more than a century. A sense of sturdy independence had prompted the creation of the Republic in the eighteenth century, free from the control and influence of the European powers. A very real geographical isolation permitted the United States to fill up the empty lands of North America free from the threat of foreign conflict. Great increases in territory and population, vast natural resources and a great burst of industrial growth transformed the country into the world's foremost and richest economy. American statesmen, sensing the dimensions of this new power, began to look beyond isolation, searching for a wider role in the world.

The arrival on the world scene in the late nineteenth century of a new vigorous democratic power directly challenged the monopoly long enjoyed by Europe. The United States claimed the moral high-ground in international politics. Providence had given to America a special destiny, a 'Manifest Destiny', to transform the world in her own image, to build a better world based on self-determination, democratic principles and liberal trade. She was refuge for the 'huddled masses' who had fled the oppression and penury of Europe. She championed the 'Open Door' to trade, guaranteeing open access to all the markets of the world. She helped to arbitrate with disinterest in the disputes of other powers. Faith in America as a force for good, an island of liberty in a sea of militarism and imperial greed, while it masked a good deal of American economic self-interest, was a real reflection of the way many Americans saw their country's role.

No one exemplified the high moral tone of American policy more precisely than President Woodrow Wilson, who took office in 1912, and led the United States into the First World War in 1917. The United States scorned 'the old corruption' of European politics, demonstrated by the secret diplomacy and rampant militarism which they thought had brought Europe to war in 1914. Wilson encouraged his compatriots to be 'neutral in fact as well as in name . . . impartial in thought as well as in action'.[2] But three years later, following unrestricted submarine warfare by Germany, America finally entered the war on the side of the Allies, committing troops to fight in Europe for the first time. Wilson, a Professor of Government at Princeton University before he became first Governor of New Jersey and then President, saw the chance to reshape the globe in the healthy image of the New World instead of restoring the bankrupt structures of the old. The war was a crusade for liberty. His programme for peace was embodied in Fourteen Points laid before Congress in January 1918. The document set an agenda for peace very different from the one battered and xenophobic Europe had in mind. Wilson claimed that all nations, great and small, should have the chance to live in harmony with one another. A League of Nations, formed from all the states of the world swearing a solemn covenant, would guarantee future peace. Under the benign hand of the United States, the Great War would truly be the war to end all wars.

The victor powers had little choice but to accept. American military help decisively turned the tide against Germany. American financial help, over $10 billion, helped to maintain the Allied war effort and kept Europe from financial chaos when the war had ended. America moved from the wings to the centre of the world stage. It was widely expected that the United States would dominate the post-war world. Europe was at its *fin de siècle*; American culture, absorbed with the remorseless pursuit of modernity, seemed poised to replace it. Yet, on the very brink of world leadership, America hesitated and stepped back. For all the attractions of Wilson's brand of liberal internationalism, it was a view of the world shared by only a small section of American society, predominantly among the East Coast elites where Wilson found his greatest support. There were plenty of Americans who had opposed entry into the war in the first place, and who were hostile to further entanglements once the war was over. The experience of war had been deeply alienating for many Americans; returning veterans were welcomed with less than open arms, and public opinion turned violently against war-profiteers and warmongering. There grew a deep suspicion that America had beeen duped into the war by an unholy alliance of American capitalists and European diplomats, by turn smooth-talking and devious. The people of the United States wanted to return to 'normalcy'.

The rejection of Europe was bluntly expressed by Congress when it refused to ratify the Versailles Treaty which Wilson had devoted his last year as President to achieving. He was broken by the struggle to get ratification. 'Dare we reject it and break the heart of the world?' he asked the Senate.[3] In increasingly poor health, and alternately prey to bouts of wishful thinking and petulant irritation, he travelled from platform to platform across America selling the Treaty. He was greeted with open hostility and indifference. To a great many Americans the issues were clear enough: Britain and France had taken American men and money to fight their war for them, and cynically used victory as an opportunity to expand their empires, and to establish a crude hegemony in Europe. Under the terms of the League Covenant, Europe might force America to send its young men abroad again. The most bitter pill, for a state with pretensions to world leadership, was the discovery that the British Empire – Great Britain and the Dominions – would have six votes in the new League Assembly against one for the United States. The solid evidence of French chauvinism and British hypocrisy convinced Senators that a treaty on these terms was not worth having. The Versailles Treaty, America's peace for Europe, became the sole property of Europeans.

As the 1920s passed, Americans were increasingly grateful that they had kept out of the League trap. The United States prospered while the nations of Europe struggled to rebuild their economies. America rejected foreign treaties but not foreign business. American investment in Europe expanded rapidly, American firms set up branches worldwide. American machinery and consumer goods flooded overseas. The new mass-production, mass-consumption culture found followers everywhere; Europeans drove Ford cars, danced to smart jazz, discovered the cinema. The spread of American economic influence seemed inexorable and irreversible. The only grounds on which America would interfere abroad were grounds of economic necessity. In 1924 and again in 1929 the United States interceded with her old Allies to adjust reparations and restore the economic health of Germany, angry at the impact of French policies of 'fulfilment'. Repeatedly throughout the 1920s American creditors tried to get Europe to honour the debts they owed to the US, with mixed results. The efforts made by the French and Italians in particular to avoid paying back what they had so greedily consumed in 1918 was a source of persistent friction. To the ordinary American investor the issue was straightforward: Europe borrowed the money and was honourably required to repay it. It is easy to find the roots of the growing conviction among America's isolationists in the 1920s that America had been asked to pay honest money for a war in which all the profit went to Europe.

There arose in the 1920s a powerful and enduring sentiment in American opinion that Europe was politically decadent and economically untrustworthy. For all the economic ties, an underlying distrust coloured relations between Europe and the United States for a generation. Many Americans found their thoughts echoed by the 'radio priest', Father Charles E. Coughlin, who broadcast each week from his shrine in Royal Oak, Michigan. He told them that 'the years identified with the Peace Treaty of Versailles, with the League of Nations . . . with repudiation of debts and with universal poverty – I honestly believe that in all history such destruction of ideals and such miscarriage of justice were never chronicled save during the years which witnessed the assassination of Christ.' He had no doubt where the blame lay: it lay with the Allies, Britain and France, who exploited the League to 'make the world safe for hypocrisy'. Britain, he believed, was the real villain: 'John Bull pulls the strings' to establish 'the supremacy of Great Britain'.[4] These were not the views of all Americans, but they were symptomatic of a general rejection of any relations with the European world stronger than a business contract.

Relations were soured still further when the American boom proved, in 1929, to be anything but irreversible. The ripples of the Wall Street Crash were felt all over the world; weaker economies dependent on American loans and American trade were sucked down into the whirlpool. Europe looked to the United States to take the lead in stemming the disaster which American speculation had triggered. But the US government did not accept that it was America's responsibility to solve the world's problems, for there were problems severe enough nearer home. By 1933 there were 13 million Americans unemployed, American trade was halved, American farmers ruined. During the world slump relations between Europe and America grew worse. The Crash virtually eliminated once and for all any chance of recovering war debts, and aggravated the economic nationalism of all the major states, making effective co-operation almost impossible. Europeans blamed America's aggressive capitalism for dislocating the world economy so savagely, and then withdrawing loans and setting up tariffs to keep out European goods. In 1930 the Hawley-Smoot Act increased the duty on almost 900 imported products, and stimulated a wave of protectionist reaction. The Act was viewed abroad as a deliberate move towards economic isolationism. The prospect for international economic co-operation faded as the slump deepened. In 1933 Britain hosted a World Economic Conference in London, in a final effort to get the major economies to agree on a package of international recovery measures. It was seen as the last chance for America to give a lead out of recession. But on 4 July, Independence Day in the United States, the newly elected President, Franklin Delano Roosevelt, sent the Conference his 'bombshell message', rejecting further international co-operation in favour of economic independence. 'Each nation', announced America's delegate to the Conference, 'must set its own house in order.'[5]

The growing estrangement from Europe was not mere selfishness. In the 1930s American leaders returned to some of the fundamental principles of American foreign policy, which had been compromised by intervention in Europe in 1917 and by the economic squabbles of the 1920s. They were the values expressed by Cordell Hull: 'a primary interest in peace with justice, in economic well-being with stability, and conditions of order under the law'.[6] There were principles here on which most Americans could agree; to promote them, the United States should avoid 'foreign entanglements', any kind of alliance or association outside the Western hemisphere. Instead the United States should act as a moral force in the world, stimulating an open and co-operative diplomacy, encouraging peaceful change where necessary, discouraging aggression. This was what Roosevelt called the 'good-neighbour policy'. It sprang from a very moral, democratic view of the world; America encouraged the weak against the strong, condemned tyranny and reproached the warmongers. In his Wilson Day address in December 1933 Roosevelt told his audience that 'from now on war by government shall be changed to peace by peoples.'[7] For all the sense of disillusionment from contact with the world of international politics, there was still a strong streak of idealism in American foreign policy.

But under Roosevelt there was a core of political realism as well. Peace would not be secured by fine words alone, but through the healing powers of economic expansion. At the core of American foreign policy lay a conviction that a return to the 'Open Door' trading system – an economic equivalent to honest diplomacy – would repair the damaged relations between the powers more surely than anything else. Not only would America's own prosperity be restored, but an expanding world economy would spread the benefits worldwide, and reduce political tensions. The greatest champion of this view was the man Roosevelt chose as his Secretary of State, the Tennessee Senator, Cordell Hull, who, like his President, was to remain a central figure in American politics for the rest of the decade. It was Hull's belief that 'trade between nations is the greatest peacemaker and civilizer within human experience'. Foreign policy really

USA: THE POLITICS OF ISOLATION, 1925-41

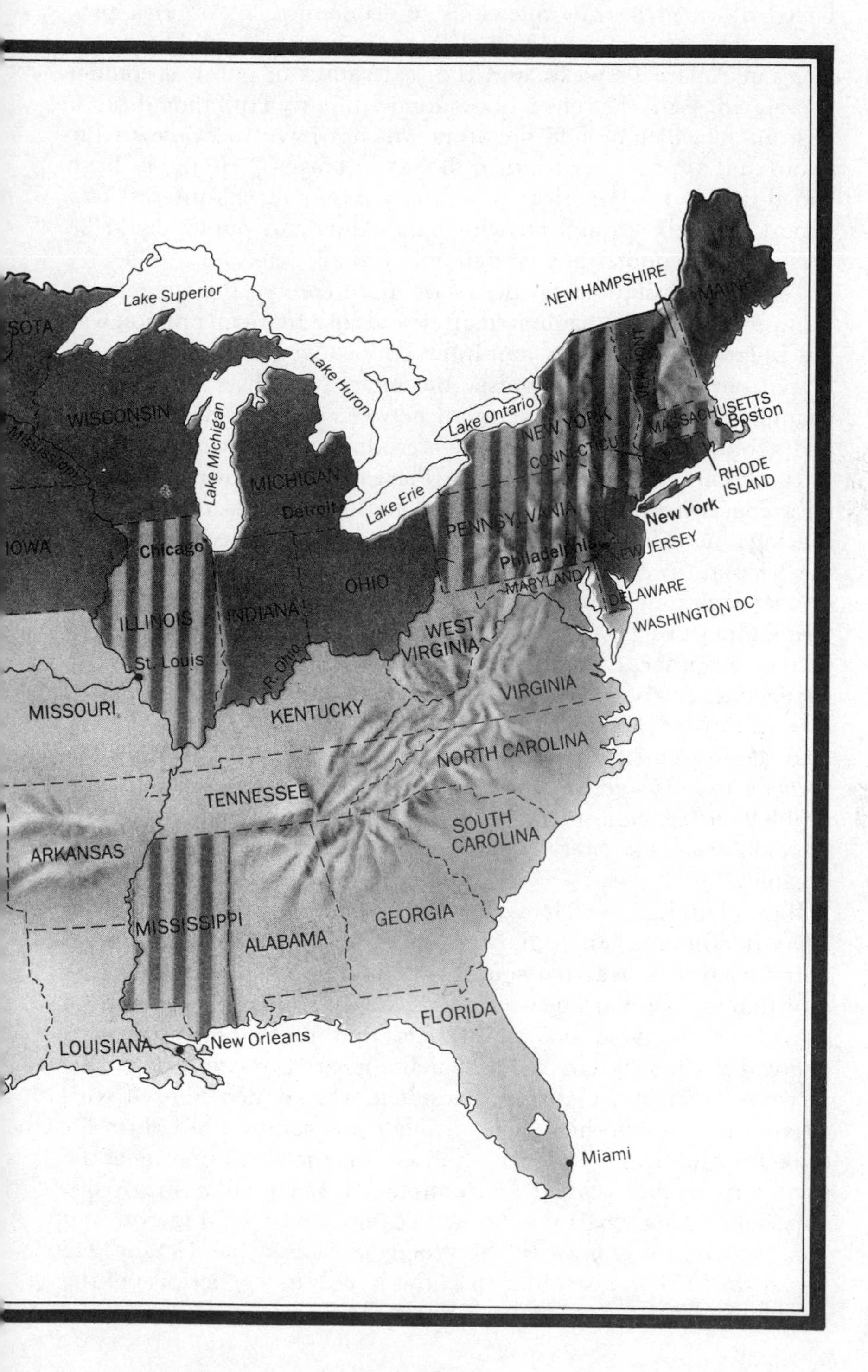
Lake Superior
SOTA
NEW HAMPSHIRE
MAINE
VERMONT
Lake Huron
WISCONSIN
Lake Michigan
Mississippi
MICHIGAN
Lake Ontario
NEW YORK
MASSACHUSETTS
Boston
CONNECTICUT
RHODE ISLAND
Detroit
Lake Erie
New York
PENNSYLVANIA
IOWA
Chicago
Philadelphia
NEW JERSEY
OHIO
MARYLAND
DELAWARE
ILLINOIS
INDIANA
WEST VIRGINIA
WASHINGTON DC
St. Louis
R. Ohio
VIRGINIA
MISSOURI
KENTUCKY
NORTH CAROLINA
TENNESSEE
SOUTH CAROLINA
ARKANSAS
MISSISSIPPI
GEORGIA
ALABAMA
FLORIDA
LOUISIANA
New Orleans
Miami

boiled down to narrow questions of economics: if America prospered, the world prospered too. Weaker economies would be pulled along in America's wake, and the real causes of political conflict eliminated. With the return of economic stability Hull thought that 'discontent will fade and dictators will not have to brandish the sword and appeal to patriotism to stay in power.'[8] He might have added that in the America of the 1930s economic self-interest was almost the only ground on which the American public could be persuaded to endorse any foreign policy at all.

The term 'isolationism' does not quite convey this search for traditional values. What united all strands of American opinion was not isolation so much as non-intervention. Non-intervention embraced not only the isolationists, but internationalists as well, who championed peaceful co-operation between peoples, disarmament and good-neighbourliness. Many were harsher critics of war and intervention than the isolationists. Their rejection of war was based on a conscientious revulsion, which had deep roots in American religious life. The peace movement in America existed long before the Vietnam protests of the 1960s. By the early 1930s it had an estimated 12 million members, and reached a radio audience of 45–60 million. In 1932 a procession of automobiles a mile long brought a petition for peace to President Herbert Hoover in Washington.[9] The pacifist movement was much larger and better organised in America than in Europe, and could not be ignored by American politicians. And the movement found common cause with the isolationists in their desire to avoid anything that would bring America closer to conflict abroad. Non-intervention bound them together, and greatly limited America's ability to act forcefully abroad for the rest of the decade.

If Franklin Roosevelt had a natural home it was among those who advocated internationalism, peace through co-operation and moral example. But he was too sound a politician not to recognise the direction the popular tide was taking, and he sought throughout his presidency to avoid doing anything that undermined his own political position too much, or which appeared to compromise his image as a caring, Christian President. He aligned himself with isolationism to help him carry through programmes of reform for ordinary Americans. Roosevelt himself was the very opposite of the small farmers and workers he championed. Born into a prosperous upper-class East Coast family, he became a successful lawyer and then moved into politics on the Woodrow Wilson bandwagon. He joined the Democrats rather than the Republicans, because of the attraction of Wilsonian idealism. But in the early part of his career he enjoyed the reputation of a political aristocrat, handsome, lively, socially adept, and not altogether serious. It was his undoubted talents as an organiser and leader that led to rapid promotion during the First World War, and by 1920 to the Vice-Presidential nomination. He was, a college friend later recalled, 'extremely ambitious to be popular and powerful'.[10] He was utterly absorbed by politics. Poised on the crest of political success he was struck down with polio in 1921, at the age of thirty-nine, and paralysed from the waist down. He withdrew from politics to recover. He failed to do so, and his fight against disablement made him into a more generous and broad-minded democrat and a tougher politician. In 1928 he re-entered politics as Governor of New York State. He lost none of his ambition or political shrewdness, but he was mellowed by adversity. In the 1932 Presidential election his success rested on his qualities of leadership and the projection of a humane commitment to the rebuilding of other lives shattered like his own.

He shared with ordinary Americans a deep dislike of militarism and war. This was not a product of mere political calculation, and he did not eschew the waging of war when it finally became unavoidable. Yet there is little reason to doubt his conviction, as a devout Christian, that war was abhorrent: 'I hate war. I have passed unnumbered hours . . . thinking and planning how war may be kept from this nation.'[11] He instinctively resented the bankers and arms-dealers who profited from war; though no hard-line isolationist, he shared with the isolationists a deep distrust of the great European empires. To him colonial peoples should be groomed for independence, not kept in servitude. European politics were dominated too much in Roosevelt's view by the 'money-changers in the temple', the shadowy men of the financial and imperial establishment who he thought ran European politics.[12] International peace could only be achieved when European states were like Democrat America: with progressive, popular governments committed to the rule of international law.

But Roosevelt knew all too well that he was elected as President not to promote democracy abroad, but to save it at home. His priority above all else was to preserve the American system which was rocked to its foundations by the worst economic recession in its history. The United States faced serious political and social crisis in 1932. There were 17 million Americans on public relief. There were fears of fascist conspiracy; people talked openly of the need for a dictator. In 1932 the American socialist movement polled 900,000 votes. America, wrote Hiram Johnson, veteran Republican from California, was 'closer to revolution than we have ever been in our lives'.[13] Poverty and hardship on a scale that America's loose federal system could barely cope with called for a strong leader willing to grasp the responsibility of mending America's shattered economy and restoring social peace. Roosevelt was no dictator, but he did promise to put 'America First'. 'Our international relations,' he stated in January 1933, 'though vastly important, are in point of time and necessity secondary to the establishment of a sound national economy. I favour as a practical policy the putting of first things first.'[14] His answer to the crisis was the 'New Deal', a comprehensive programme of state-backed recovery measures, with a strong progressive flavour. Roosevelt's central aim was to make America safe for democracy as the first, and vital, step to making democracy safe for the world.

It is easy to blame Roosevelt for not doing more abroad to stem the rise of fascism and the collapse of peace; but it is essential to understand how deep and disturbing the impact of the depression was in American society, after decades of rising prosperity. If in the 1920s American isolationism was a reaction to the ingratitude and duplicity of her erstwhile allies, in the 1930s it was a reaction to the shock of social crisis. To overcome that crisis Roosevelt had to mobilise all the forces of 'progressive' America, and this included a large part of the isolationist movement. Isolationists from both political parties were generally progressive in their domestic politics: that is, they accepted the pursuit of economic and social programmes to defend the small producer, consumer and wage-earner against the tide of economic hardship, and against the entrenched power of big business and the American establishment. In the early years of his Presidency, Roosevelt depended on the support of isolationists to push through the New Deal in the face of strong conservative opposition. Political expediency as well as economic necessity brought Roosevelt to depend on just those groups in American politics most opposed to American initiatives abroad. The result was a compromise: isolationists voted for New Deal legislation, while Roosevelt kept America out of world affairs.

The isolationists were not a formal political lobby, but they enjoyed widespread popular support. Some could trace their opposition to foreign entanglements back to the years before 1900, when the United States first began to flex its international muscles. They could be found in both main political parties and in all parts of America, but they were concentrated in the Republican heartlands of the Midwest and the Rockies. These were areas isolated even within America, entirely foreign to the events beyond America's shores. In these broad farmlands dotted with tiny townships, isolationists spoke up for the little man, the typical American small townsman and farmer, religious, often poor, hostile to or ignorant of Europe, with a profound distrust of the big city and the big corporation. They were far from being unpatriotic – 'America First' could have been their slogan. Some even supported rearmament later in the 1930s where it was clearly for self-defence. But small-town populism had a strongly radical flavour. In the South the populist Democrat Huey 'Kingfish' Long, a rival of Roosevelt until his death in 1935, campaigned for a 'share-our-wealth' society; Father Coughlin from his Michigan power-base set up the National Union for Social Justice, demanding a fair deal for the poor whites of small-town, small-farm America under the slogan 'We'll fight Communism; we'll fight Capitalism; Christianity must prevail'. Nationally, isolationists were led in the Lower House by Representative Hamilton Fish, the veteran Republican from Roosevelt's own state of New York; in the Senate by the influential progressives William Borah from Idaho, Hiram Johnson from California, Burton Wheeler from Montana, George Norris from Nebraska, Gerald Nye from North Dakota and Robert La Follette Jr from Wisconsin.[15] Most were Republicans, which made Roosevelt's balancing act all the more precarious. If he alienated them from support of the New Deal through an active foreign policy, he stood to lose millions of American voters.

Roosevelt certainly recognised the nature of this dependence. Republican isolationists voted more or less consistently for the major New Deal initiatives – public works, state aid for industry and agricultural reconstruction. After a brief internationalist foray in 1933, when Roosevelt secured American recognition of the Soviet Union on the ground that it was good for business, he held firmly aloof from international commitments including co-operation with the League. The initiative in foreign affairs passed over to Congress, whose mood was overwhelmingly isolationist. Increasingly America cut herself off from the European economy. The Johnson Act of 1934 prohibited any further loans to states that had not repaid war debts, cutting off credit to every European state save Finland. By the end of the decade America had 50 per cent more invested in Canada than in the whole of Europe.[16] This did not erode economic ties altogether, but it is significant that at the high point of American political isolation her economic relationship with Europe was at its most tenuous.

But far more important than any economic gesture was the gradual drift towards a formal declaration of neutrality. The immediate background to the move lay in the popular isolationist and pacifist backlash against armaments which had been gathering force since the late 1920s. In 1929 a major scandal broke when it was discovered that an agent of American shipbuilders, Captain William Shearer, had attended the Geneva Naval Disarmament Conference of 1926/7 disguised as a journalist, whose critical press reports had torpedoed the plans to disarm. Congress set up a special commission to investigate the traffic in arms in 1930. By 1934 there were widespread calls for controls over armaments. Arms producers were blamed for sabotaging disarmament and exploiting conflict. The climax arrived with the publication in March 1934 in *Fortune Magazine* of 'Arms and Man', a bitter attack on the armaments kings whose motto, the article suggested, was: 'when there are wars, prolong them; when there is peace, disturb it'. Gerald Nye, the populist farmer Senator from North Dakota, introduced a resolution for a full inquiry into the 'Merchants of Death', and Roosevelt did nothing to obstruct it.[17]

The Senate Munitions Inquiry sat from 1934 to 1936. Its brief was to expose the malpractices of the arms trade – the breaking of embargoes, industrial espionage, commercial corruption. It was staffed by radical young lawyers, including Alger Hiss, who was later to play a more prominent part as a victim of anticommunism. The inquiry led to the regulation of the arms producers, but it had the more important effect of keeping the popular, isolationist, anti-war momentum going. The discovery that arms merchants might actually promote and fuel conflicts abroad led to louder calls not just for the promise of non-intervention but for a formal declaration that America would remain neutral in any future conflict between other states anywhere in the world. Roosevelt, though anxious that his own presidential powers on questions of war and peace would be severely limited, was not opposed to neutrality legislation of some sort. He recognised that the isolationists were in the ascendant in Congress, and that they had found an issue on which internationalists could also agree. The provisional Neutrality Act passed the Senate by 79 votes to 2 in the summer of 1935. On 31 August Roosevelt signed it into law. In 1936 the law was renewed, and in 1937 a comprehensive and permanent Neutrality Act was passed. It included a mandatory arms embargo in the event of any foreign war, a ban on all financial loans to belligerents, a Control Board for American munitions-makers to prevent them selling arms, and the right for the President to embargo non-military goods destined for warring powers as well. The Act placed America outside any future conflict and made it clear at home and abroad that, whatever happened, America would not interfere. It removed at once a great weight from the scales of foreign peace.

To many Americans neutrality came just in time. As the world situation deteriorated in Europe and the Far East, Americans could look out from behind a high parapet of moral indignation and detachment. When Roosevelt suggested in January 1935 that the United States should join the World Court at The Hague he was bitterly attacked for trying to join the League system by the back door. Senator Homer T. Bone spoke for many Americans when he rejected any contact with 'the poisonous European mess'; Senator Thomas D. Schall put if more graphically: 'To Hell with Europe and with the rest of those nations.'[18] Roosevelt and Hull would both have preferred a more internationalist stance over Japanese agggression in China, or over Ethiopa or Spain. But Roosevelt was still too conscious of public opinion, which was solidly against intervention. If he hoped to complete the work of the New Deal, and win re-election in 1936, there was no question of challenging this mood. He was too shrewd and too ambitious a politician not to see this. Domestic recovery and stability was still ambition number one. In the run-up to the 1936 election he concentrated his efforts in the isolationist strongholds of the West and Midwest. At a historic speech at Chautauqua, New York, on 14 August 1936, Roosevelt declared his position publicly: 'We shun political commitments which might entangle us in foreign wars. . . . if we face the choice of profits or peace, this Nation will answer – this Nation must answer – "we choose peace".'[19] In November he won every state except Maine and Vermont.

For most of the second Roosevelt administration, from 1936 to 1939, American foreign policy was a mixture of dignified aloofness and deliberate inaction. There were strong overtones of appeasement, though unlike Britain and France America was not in a position to offer very much to the European dictators. She kept her foreign activity in Europe to a minimum. The situation in the Far East was rather different, for Japan's expansion into China was a more direct threat to American interests. But here too the American government was reluctant to confront the Japanese for fear of the domestic and foreign repercussions. The outcome was a policy towards Japan not very different from Britain's.

American foreign policy was moulded by isolationist opinion. Roosevelt was almost obsessive about public attitudes and the Presidential image. He arranged his own private access to opinion. In 1933 he set up a 'clipping' service which monitored 350 newspapers and 45 magazines daily for views on the Presidency. He read a great number of the letters which poured into the White House both for him and his wife. He had 8000 letters a day, four times the mailbag of his predecessor.[20] This permitted him to remain abreast of, even ahead of, public opinion, but the knowledge actually limited his room for manoeuvre. This was clear from the growing reaction against the New Deal, which ran into serious difficulties at just the time that Europe was plunging into crisis. It faced hostility not only from conservatives, who had never been reconciled to the deal, but increasingly from some of its erstwhile progressive supporters, who disliked the growth of state intervention and Presidential power that accompanied it. In 1937 the Supreme Court threw out two major pieces of New Deal legislation – the National Industrial Recovery Act and the Agricultural Adjustment Act – as unconstitutional. Roosevelt tried to save the rest of the programme by getting rid of the hostile judges and replacing them with Roosevelt supporters. The attempt at 'court-packing' made him more unpopular. In July 1937 he was forced to back down. During 1938 America was hit by a brief economic recession, and Roosevelt's own Democrat Party became deeply divided over the future of the New Deal strategy and lost ground in the mid-term Congressional elections. The effect of all these domestic problems was to inhibit Roosevelt even more from any kind of adventurism abroad.

This did not stop the President from continuing to pursue good-neighbour policies. Belief in the force of moral suasion and democratic example was a persistent theme in American foreign relations throughout the 1930s. Roosevelt harboured the view that all the world's problems could be resolved at some great conference of the powers, a proto-United Nations. 'Half the battle in talking with people', he later explained, 'is to look them in the eye, and let them look you in the eye.'[21] Sitting round a table, Roosevelt thought that good sense and goodwill would prevail; a moral world order could be restored and the danger of war would recede. In 1936 and 1937 he began to explore his idea seriously. He hoped Britain would take the initiative for him. In January 1938 a firm proposal was sent to Chamberlain for a great summit meeting. The British Prime Minister dismissed it as 'preposterous'; the Foreign Office found it 'mysterious and meaningless'.[22] Roosevelt's proposals for universal disarmament, limiting weapons to those needed for reasonable self-defence, met with the same incredulous response. European diplomatists regarded Roosevelt's moral endeavour with a sceptical eye, attributing much of it to the insularity of American statesmen. The view took root in Britain that Roosevelt's conception of foreign policy was 'dangerously jejune', that the innocent and fantastic schemes proposed were not serious suggestions but merely for domestic consumption.[23]

Inhibited by isolationists at home, distrusted by foreign statesmen, anxious about his political power-base, it is small wonder that Roosevelt adopted the line of least resistance. But, even if he had wanted to do more, there was a factor too often ignored by critics of American policy – American military weakness. Though the United States was soon to become the world's leading military power, in the 1930s a combination of anti-war politics, geographical immunity and fiscal stringency left no more than skeleton armed forces. The army could muster only 100,000 men in the mainland United States in the mid-1930s, when the French, Russian and Japanese armies were numbered in millions. Its morale was generally poor, long periods of bored inactivity punctuated by trips overseas and athletics matches. Its weapons mainly dated from the First World War or even earlier. The standard infantry rifle until 1941 was the 1903 Springfield. American soldiers were more at home with the horse than the tank. Major Eisenhower, who was later Supreme Commander of the Allied forces in the Second World War, complained in 1933 that America was left with 'only a shell of a military establishment'.[24]

The situation in the air force was just as bad. In September 1939 the Air Corps had only 800 combat aircraft, many obsolescent; the navy had 800 aircraft, mainly biplanes. Germany had 3600, Russia almost 10,000. American military aviation output in 1938 totalled only 1800, 3000 fewer than Germany, 1400 fewer than Japan. Only the navy was in better shape because it claimed the major role in defending the Western hemisphere and America's outlying possessions. But even here the effects of defence cuts had reduced it below the number of ships agreed with Britain and Japan in 1922 at the Washington Naval Conference, and its preparation for aerial and submarine warfare was still well behind that of its future enemy, Japan. The development of weapons and military basic research expenditure (a mere 2 per cent of the budget) were the victims of the rising tide of anti-militarism; but even without this the economic priority given to recovery programmes would have made it difficult to embark on large-scale rearming. If Roosevelt was unhappy about using the threat of military action in his foreign policy, he had very little to threaten with.[25]

So, from necessity as much as conviction, the Roosevelt administration faced the collapsing world order with words rather than deeds. Nowhere were the dilemmas of American policy more cruelly exposed than in the Far East. When Japan embarked on her expansion in Asia it was in the knowledge that the United States was unlikely to obstruct her. Though Americans instinctively sided with the Chinese against Japan, with the weak against the strong, the American government was reluctant to do anything that might provoke vigorous Japanese reaction. Roosevelt was particularly anxious to avoid taking any kind of unilateral action. Other states also had interests in China; America would only contemplate moral support or economic assistance for the Chinese if other states, particularly Britain, would do the same. British interests were always viewed as paramount. Britain had much more to lose with her Far Eastern empire, and she had ten times as much invested in the Far East as the United States. Since Britain did little to limit Japan, the United States saw no reason why she should be made to carry the can alone.

Japan was allowed to tear up the doctrine of the 'Open Door' to Chinese trade. American civilians were harassed and humiliated in Japanese occupied territory. In July 1937 Japan began open war with China. Since there was no formal declaration of war between them, the United States was not prevented by the Neutrality Laws from giving aid to China. Some Americans even volunteered to fight on China's behalf, as Americans had done in Spain on behalf of the Republic. But most agreed with their President that the United States would never be 'pushed out in front as the leader in, or suggester of, future action' against Japan. This was true even when American interests were directly threatened. On 13 December 1937, Japanese aircraft attacked and sank the American gunboat *Panay* in the Yangtse river. Unwilling to mobilise the Pacific Fleet, as the British suggested, the Americans accepted a grudging apology from Japan and took no action. Congress was so scared that the incident might have led to war that Representative Louis Ludlow from Indiana at last found a majority willing to debate the proposal he had first made in 1935 that war could only be declared after a popular referendum, and not by the President in Congress. The Ludlow Amendment was only narrowly defeated after frantic political activity from the White House, but it showed how anxious American opinion still was to avoid war at all costs. Even America's Ambassador in Tokyo, Joseph Grew, encouraged Roosevelt to adopt 'a sympathetic, co-operative and helpful attitude towards Japan'. Isolation and appeasement were two sides of the same coin.[26]

Roosevelt himself was certainly sympathetic to the victims of aggression and hostile to fascism and dictatorship. So too was Cordell Hull, who later wrote that the isolationists reminded him 'of the somnambulist who walks within an inch of a thousand-foot

Franklin Delano Roosevelt, 1938, the hoped-for paladin of Western democracy but still a politician needing re-election.

precipice without batting an eye'.[27] Yet Roosevelt remained trapped in the dilemma of recognising the dangerous nature of international developments on the one hand, and the deep political hostility at home among broad sections of American opinion against foreign intervention of any kind. Though frustrated by this contradiction, Roosevelt hesitated to do anything that threatened his own political security. The balance between foreign danger and political survival haunted Roosevelt throughout the four years that led to war. On 5 October 1937 he tested the water of opinion in a speech at Chicago in which he publicly stated his hostility to the powers disturbing peace. He called for a 'quarantine' to be operated by all peace-loving states against those preaching violence. 'I am inclined to think', he wrote to Endicott Peabody a few days later, 'that this is more Christian, as well as more practical, than that we should go to war with them.'[28] The speech brought a storm of protest from the isolationist press, which scrutinised everything the President said in order to check his foreign policy credentials. Aware of this hostility Roosevelt did nothing to follow up the speech. He had tested the water and found it too hot. Two weeks later he wrote to Colonel House that the process of educating American opinion was a slow and frustrating one: 'I believe that as time goes on we can slowly but surely make people realize that war will be a greater danger to us if we close all the doors and windows than if we go out in the street and use our influence to curb the riot.'[29]

Roosevelt was disillusioned by the impact of his 'quarantine' speech. He found himself 'fighting against a psychology of long-standing which comes very close to saying "Peace at any price."'[30] His attempt to educate opinion was not helped by what Americans perceived as European efforts to pass the buck. The threats to peace condemned by Roosevelt were more directly the concern of Britain and France. They had the most to lose, if the international order collapsed; Americans thought they should make greater efforts on their own behalf. They could not understand why Britain and France would not do more; it was assumed that both states were much stronger militarily and financially than they claimed, and that they appeased out of mere self-interest. There was much American sympathy for the views of Winston Churchill, and a strong suspicion that Britain had 'deserted her cause', that France showed 'complete bewilderment and bankruptcy of policy' and that neither power could be entirely trusted. 'What the British need today', Roosevelt wrote later in February 1939, 'is a good stiff grog, inducing not only the desire to save civilization but the continuing belief that they can do it.'[31] Under no circumstances would the New World again be duped into doing the work of the Old.

Hard on the heels of crisis in the Far East came crisis in Europe. Hitler, secure in power, rapidly rearming, was now in a position to put the Versailles system to the test. In March 1938 he occupied Austria. In May he began to threaten Czechoslovakia. By the end of the summer Europe seemed close to war. America stood and watched. Roosevelt was under strong pressure to avoid any American involvement in the crisis, even to join forces with the appeasers. 'They would really like me to be a Neville Chamberlain,' he complained to a friend. He was aware that Americans as ever sympathised with the victims of bullying and aggression, but as ever wanted no part in protecting them. He wrote to the American Ambassador in Rome in September that it would probably be America's role 'to pick up the pieces of European civilisation'. He would encourage sympathy 'while at the same time avoiding any thought of sending troops to Europe'.[32]

Two days before the meeting at Munich to decide the fate of the Czechs, Roosevelt finally sent an appeal to all the states involved urging them to continue talking: 'there is no problem so pressing for solution that it cannot be justly solved by the resort to reason than by the resort to force', a view, in fact, not very different from Chamberlain's. But he made it clear that 'The United States has no political entanglements. It is caught in no mesh of hatred.' At a meeting of his Cabinet two days before, Roosevelt had assured them that he wanted to avoid 'any embroilment in European quarrels'.[33] Still, he could not conceal his contempt for Britain and France for perpetrating what he saw as an international outrage; they were guilty powers who would 'wash the blood from their Judas Iscariot hands'.[34]

But once the deed was done American leaders recognised what little room for manoeuvre existed. 'What would the United States have done if we had had to face the terrible issue?', wrote Secretary of the Interior Harold Ickes in his diary. Roosevelt's private answer was disarmingly unrealistic: if it were up to him Germany would be bottled up by an economic blockade mounted by all her neighbours, while Britain, France and the Soviet Union pounded Germany from the air with a hail of bombs until German morale collapsed. His Cabinet took the more sensible view that Munich had produced a 'universal sigh of relief and pleasure'. There was optimism in Washington that the Munich agreement might make possible real moves towards international settlement, in particular a restoration of a liberal economic system, through which lay, it was still believed, the real road to peace. The health of the American economy could not be ignored, whatever was happening elsewhere. The threat of war had rocked European business. It was Roosevelt's view that 'economically the United States will fare well whether Europe goes to war or not.'[35] Gold was flowing in from Europe's capitals; orders were mounting daily for equipment and supplies of all kinds; America was building a battleship for Stalin, aero-engines for France.[36] As fresh blood flowed into the arteries of industry, America became absorbed once again with recovering the prosperity it had forfeited in 1929.

It is tempting to look at United States policy as a cynical expression of economic selfishness. But from the outset in 1933 Roosevelt had pursued economic recovery as the only cure for social crisis and political uncertainty. America had always pursued an *economic* foreign policy, as long as it did not involve political commitments. Economic expansion was its own justification; its morality was quite separate from the issues of diplomacy. For most of the 1930s America traded as openly with Germany and Japan as with any other power. Japan relied on fuel oil and scrap iron from the United States through to 1941. Germany was one of the United

States' most important markets during the 1930s. American investment in Germany increased by 40 per cent between 1936 and 1940. A series of cartel agreements reached between German and American firms – Standard Oil and Du Pont were the most famous – gave Germany access to markets and to new technologies essential for her war preparations. The Ethyl Gasoline Corporation built tetraethyl lead plants in both Germany and Italy before the war, which were vital for the Axis air forces after 1939. When the activities of American firms in Germany were officially investigated later in the war a whole series of similar arrangements was unearthed. The view of American business was summed up by the chairman of General Motors, Alfred Sloan Jr, in 1939, defending the operation of the GM subsidiary, Opel, in Germany: 'an international business operating throughout the world should conduct its operations in strictly business terms, without regard to the political beliefs of the country in which it is operating.'[37]

The real concern of American business was not the rights or wrongs of trading with fascism, but the fear that commercial rivals, particularly Britain and France, might reach a separate agreement with either Japan or Germany to exclude American goods from Europe and Asia altogether. Economic co-operation with all powers was one way of ensuring access for American exports. In questions of commercial rivalry America trusted no one. American business abroad looked to the White House to keep American foreign policy free of any tensions likely to damage America's long-term economic interests. Economic appeasement was the New Deal applied to foreign policy. It was only when Japan in China and Germany in Latin America began to encroach seriously on American trading and investing interests that the business community, as well as the politicians, started to choose their friends abroad more carefully.

Between Munich and the outbreak of the European war America made this choice. It amounted in essence to a choice between Britain and Germany. Japan was still not seen as a major military threat, though there was strong popular hostility to the Japanese. France had for some time been regarded as a power in decline, dependent on British initiatives. There was never much doubt about how the choice would turn out. If Americans had a preference it was clearly for democracy and against fascism. This did not mean that Roosevelt was now able to embark on an active foreign policy, for the mood of isolation was still too strong for that. The position of American strategy was summed up by Adolf Berle, Roosevelt's Assistant Secretary of State, in a memorandum of April 1939 on the future course of American strategy:

> Await that climax [world war], nominally on the side-lines, but actually giving strong intimations of sympathy to one side or the other – actually, to the British and French, since it is unthinkable that we could find any ground to sympathize with the German or Italian governments as now constituted.[38]

This in effect became the core of American foreign policy until the German victory fifteen months later.

Though this now seems an obvious choice, the relationship between Britain and the United States was by no means straightforward. For much of the period between the wars Britain was a major trading rival, and a naval competitor. American forces based their annual manoeuvres on the hypothesis of a British invasion from Canada. Neither state liked the international conduct of the other. Britain thought America should help more and not simply indulge in grand talk; Americans thought Britain should expect to take a greater share in sorting out the problems of the world, and not expect to be bailed out by everyone else. But the British were very wary about what sort of help America should give, for they did not want to have to make concessions on colonialism or trade to pay for it, and they did not want to be supplanted by America in world affairs. It was never clear that either party had very much to offer the other, and Americans could never rid themselves of the suspicion that Britain would sell out world democracy if the deal were good enough.

The ambiguity of Anglo-American relations was highlighted by the poor personal relations between Chamberlain and Roosevelt. The British Prime Minister had his own views on how best to keep the peace. He regarded Roosevelt's proposals as 'drivel', 'stark staring madness'. Chamberlain, uncharacteristically, reserved his most intemperate language for Americans. Congress he dismissed as populated by 'pig-headed and self-righteous nobodies'.[39] Roosevelt knew that Chamberlain was a major cause of the poor relations between the two states. 'As long as Neville Chamberlain is there,' he complained to Henry Morgenthau, his Treasury Secretary, 'we must recognise that fundamentally he thoroughly dislikes America.'[40] The two men were far apart politically. Chamberlain, the Conservative imperialist who disliked labour and fought for empire tariffs, occupied a quite different ideological position from the American Democrat, committed to labour legislation and state intervention at home, liberal trade and colonial reforms abroad. Chamberlain was typical of the establishment politics that Roosevelt most distrusted. 'He lives and breathes', an aide reported, 'only in the atmosphere of the money-changers in the City.' Appeasement was their policy, the world of financial deals, backstairs diplomacy, naked self-interest, the world of 'British Tories . . . who want peace at a great price'. If Churchill became an American hero, Chamberlain was, and remains, for many Americans what Ickes called him: 'the evil genius not only of Great Britain, but also of western civilisation'.[41] The only men Roosevelt liked were Eden and Churchill, both at loggerheads with Chamberlain. Not until 1940 and Churchill's premiership was a sound personal relationship introduced into Anglo-American affairs.

Nonetheless personal antipathy could not disguise the very real common ground between the two democracies. After Munich Chamberlain swallowed hard and sought economic help from America for British rearmament. A stream of machinery, raw materials and even armaments began to flow across the Atlantic, to both Britain and France. American public opinion, which had until recently regarded the European powers as all as bad as each other, began to move towards sympathy for Britain. There was no question yet of intervention, or of ending neutrality if war came, but in the summer of 1939 relations between the two states were closer than at any time in the 1930s, not least because Britain at last appeared to be facing up to responsibilities in Europe.

To put a seal on improved relations Roosevelt invited the King and Queen to visit America on the occasion of the World's Fair, the first time that a British monarch had visited the 'lost dominion'. Their reception was tumultuous. In Canada it was estimated that six million out of eleven million Canadians turned out to greet the royal visitors. On 7 June the royal couple entered the United States at Niagara Falls. Everywhere they went they were welcomed by enthusiastic, flag-waving crowds. The parade to the White House was described as 'one of the most impressive demonstrations ever seen in Washington'. When the royal couple visited the World's Fair in New York, three and a half million Americans turned out to greet them with cries of 'Hello King!' The Roosevelts laid on a lavish reception, including a popular musical cabaret in which the Coon Creek Girls sang 'How Many Biscuits Can You Eat?' The King and Queen performed their role as ambassadors for democratic Europe to everyone's satisfaction. At a final picnic of hotdogs and beer in the grounds of the Roosevelt's home at Hyde Park the President, in emotional mood, told the King that if the Nazis bombed London, America would 'come in'.[42] Chamberlain had not quite anticipated this (nor did America do so), but he was happy to exploit America's evident willingness to play the part of a rich, friendly neutral – a substantial improvement on relations a year earlier. Chamberlain had, in fact, no desire for direct American intervention. 'Heaven knows,' he exclaimed in January 1940, 'I don't want the Americans to fight for us. We should have to pay for that too dearly.'[43] But he was well aware of the shift in the moral climate; America would be supportive, but would not interfere.

Relations with Nazi Germany were understandably much cooler. The principles underlying the Nazi movement were abhorrent to most Americans. American Jews regularly lobbied for a boycott of German goods. American labour held a rally in Madison Square Gardens as early as March 1934, where an effigy of Hitler was burned after a mock trial attended by 20,000 spectators. In the same year Congress approved the setting up of the House Committee on Un-American Activities to investigate the pro-Nazi groups in America. Throughout the 1930s popular fears were aroused of German fifth columnists in America, a secret fascist underground bent on subverting American life. Hollywood kept alive a strong prejudice against German militarism, in films like *Hell's Angels* with its classic stereotype of the cruel but dumb German major: or *Confessions of a Nazi Spy*, which parodied with great effect the activities of America's own Nazi movement. Roosevelt himself, who had spent some of his childhood at school in Baden, kept his boyhood dislike of German regimentation and 'arrogance'.[44]

The Nazi movement did little to dispel these fears. Hitler's view of America was provincial and ill-informed. He saw America as nothing more than a melting-pot of other races, a decadent, gaudy society whose weaknesses were fully exposed by the depression. 'What is America', he asked, 'but millionaires, beauty queens, stupid records and Hollywood?' It was a society weakened biologically, 'half-Judaized, half-negrified, with everything built on the dollar'. America would, according to Hitler, never again interfere in European affairs, for it was consumed by its own domestic crisis: 'America is permanently on the brink of revolution,' led by a man Hitler called 'an imbecile'. Most important of all, American isolation had just the effect on Hitler that its American critics feared: it gave him a freer hand to seek the domination of Europe. In the summer of 1939 he was confident that America would do nothing to stop him: 'Because of its Neutrality Laws, America is not dangerous to us.' Roosevelt's regular appeals for peace he dismissed as mere 'Bluffpolitik' – so much hot air, a mere pretence to win domestic approval. American isolation convinced Hitler that 1917 would not happen again.[45]

Instead Germany began to encroach more and more on the

Western hemisphere. As early as 1934 Hitler talked of 'incorporating the United States in the German world empire'. In Latin America Germany undertook through trade and economic assistance to undermine American interests there. Nazi agitators were active in every state from Argentina to Mexico. Hitler was drawn particularly to Brazil, which he thought could be turned within a few years from 'a corrupt *mestizo* state into a German dominion'.[46] In America itself Hitler hoped to mobilise the hundreds of thousands of German immigrants as a vanguard for the plans to Nazify America. This particular plan backfired. The American Nazi movement did more than anything else to alienate Americans from Germany, so much so that Hitler withdrew official support from the movement in 1937; but by then the American *Führer*, Fritz Julius Kuhn, war veteran and ex-Freikorps fighter, had created a broad fascist front, the *Volksbund*, with 20,000 followers. The American Nazis set up special camps – Siegfried on Long Island, Nordland in New Jersey, Hindenburg in Wisconsin – where they trained young recruits in military tactics and fed them Nazi propaganda. The movement reached its peak when it organised a mass rally of 22,000 people in Madison Square Gardens on the night of 20 February 1939. Fights broke out in the crowd, and an attempt was made on Kuhn's life by a young Jewish protester. The result was a police investigation of the whole movement. The Bund was broken up, and Kuhn sentenced to two and a half years in jail on charges of embezzlement.[47]

In the Reich Göring authorised work on the 'Amerika-bomber', the first intercontinental bomber, designed to fly the 3000 miles to New York with a bombload of 3000 pounds. Messerschmitt was well on the way to developing it when war broke out. German rocket research, the 'America Project', had the same ultimate target in mind; Germany's 'Z-Plan' for navy rearmament included the heavy ocean-going submarines to challenge American naval power. Hitler began to talk openly of the final struggle with America, once the war in Europe was over.[48] Americans knew little of this, though wild rumours circulated in Washington in the summer of 1939 that Germany had invented a stratospheric bomber that could stay aloft for three days and a gas bomb that could destroy every living thing on Manhattan Island.[49] What they could see happening in Germany, they disliked. In November 1938 the American Ambassador was recalled in protest at 'Kristallnacht', the attacks on German Jews; in March 1939, in retaliation for the occupation of Prague, a 25 per cent tax was placed on all German imports. None of this deflected Hitler. 'Hopelessly weak' was his judgement of America as the Polish crisis deepened.[50] American feebleness was further insurance in Hitler's eyes that the West would not dare to fight; America mattered only to the extent that it promoted this conviction.

The United States made little difference to the outbreak of war in Europe. There was never any question that Roosevelt could have defeated the isolationists and non-interventionists together in Congress, or that he could have mobilised public support for an armed crusade in Europe. If Roosevelt needed convincing of this, he had the evidence of the Gallup Polls, recently established as the popular guide to American opinion and almost all of which were shown directly to the President. In April 1939 95 per cent of those polled favoured non-intervention in any European war; 66 per cent were against giving material assistance to either side. During 1939 the number of those opposed to American intervention against Germany actually increased.[51]

Q. Should America send its forces to Europe to fight Germany?

	Yes	*No*
March 1939	17	83
May 1939	16	84
August 1939	8	92
September 1939	6	94

Roosevelt himself would certainly have answered no if he had been polled in 1939. He was more like Chamberlain than he would have wished. When the new Italian Ambassador, Prince Colonna, called on him in April 1939, he jotted down a few notes for his meeting beforehand: 'sit around a table and work it out. . . . Get nothing in *end* by war. Save peace – save dom[ination] of Europe by Germany'.[52]* Like Chamberlain, Roosevelt hoped that an alliance of the peaceful against aggressors would act as a sufficient deterrent, and like the British he was persuaded by reports from Berlin that the Nazi regime was 'in bad shape'. At the same time he was increasingly sure that war would break out in Europe in the near future. He was convinced that the United States would not be able to hide behind neutrality for ever. What the American public would accept was a limited programme of rearmament. In a world bristling with heavily armed powers it made no sense to ignore America's military weakness any longer. In December 1938 Roosevelt and his advisers

* Italics in original.

drew up the proposals for expansion of all three services, a large naval building programme, and a commitment to the strategic bomber, the famous 'Flying Fortress'. In January Congress gave its approval for an extra $500 million of military spending. Some of these programmes, shielded from full public scrutiny, anticipated action at some future date outside America, but the main motive was to ensure that when peace collapsed abroad America would have the means to protect herself against any threat to the New World. Roosevelt, like Chamberlain, also hoped that extensive American military spending would act as a deterrent. He saw rearmament as 'an alternative to war' rather than 'a preparation for' it.[53] There even existed the attractive possibility that American arms could be used by other powers fighting as America's proxy against the common threat to peace. With this in mind Roosevelt tried to loosen the binding legislation on neutrality so that he could give greater military assistance to the Allies.

If anything were needed to demonstrate to Roosevelt how difficult it was going to be to get the United States committed to intervention abroad, the struggle to repeal the mandatory arms embargo across the summer of 1939 was enough. Roosevelt wanted to remove the embargo and introduce a cash-and-carry policy for military equipment. He knew this favoured Britain and France, since their naval power could prevent German traffic across the Atlantic. After months of lobbying individual Senators, Roosevelt's proposals were defeated in the Senate by a hostile coalition of isolationists and anti-New Dealers. When he revived the proposal again in September, after war had broken out in Europe, the White House was deluged with one million letters in three days protesting by a margin of 100 to 1 against the attempt to lift the arms embargo. Even his political friends were anxious about the proposals, in case they weakened the chances of electing a Democrat in 1940.

While Roosevelt made the first tentative assault on isolationism the crisis in Europe moved closer to war. Americans who cared were uncertain and anxious about the outcome. They were unsure about British and French firmness over Poland. American intelligence withheld information on Nazi–Soviet negotiations, in case it weakened their resolve. Roosevelt sent the usual appeals for peace, but was anxious to avoid any sense that he was looking for a second Munich. The appeals, Berle noted acidly, 'will have about the same effect as a valentine sent to somebody's mother-in-law out of season'. The European states ignored them. The most alarming thing of all when it came was the Nazi–Soviet Pact, the nightmare of a totalitarian bloc 'running from the Pacific clear to the Rhine'.[54]

These were moves that transformed the balance of power; for the first time many Americans could see how the fate of American democracy might rest on the outcome of the European war. The stark evidence of German ambition and violence in September 1939 began the slow erosion of America's commitment to isolationism. Roosevelt received the news of war in the small hours of the morning in Washington. By 7.30 a.m. on 3 September, American time, his staff began to gather at the State Department. 'A very gloomy meeting', noted one of them; 'it was really the last meeting of the death watch over Europe. There was really not very much to be done, save to watch the game play itself out.'[55]

The President declared formal neutrality. Unlike his Cabinet he was much more confident of the outcome. He believed that 'the French and English have more stamina than the Germans and that if the war goes its normal course, German morale will crack.'[56] Not until the German victory in the summer of 1940 did Americans fully wake up to the military threat Germany posed. Nonetheless the German victory in Poland, and the growing military strength of Japan in China and the Pacific, gave Roosevelt the opportunity to push on against isolationism and pacifism. Despite a nationwide campaign against any change to the neutrality laws, led, among others, by his Republican predecessor Herbert Hoover, Roosevelt found Congress willing in November to lift the embargo on arms sales. Now Britain and France could be reinforced with American munitions. By the summer of 1940 Britain had on order 14,000 aircraft and 25,000 aero-engines from American factories. These had to be paid for cash-in-hand. By 1941 Britain had liquidated almost all her assets in the United States to pay for them. American assistance did, as Chamberlain realised, have its price.

Roosevelt, boosted by his victory over the embargo issue, began a number of initiatives to dent isolationism further. The United States gave vital financial help to the Chinese nationalist cause under Chiang Kai-shek. In January 1940 she refused to renew the long-standing commercial treaty with Japan, first signed in 1911. Roosevelt and Hull hoped to be able to restrict the flow of iron and oil to the Japanese war machine through informal, moral pressure on American exporters. But when that failed the first restrictions on high-quality fuel-oil and steel-scrap exports were introduced in July, and a full embargo of scrap iron in September. In the European theatre Roosevelt sent Sumner Welles, from the State Department, on a tour of the major capitals of Europe in March 1940 to see what grounds there were for securing a lasting peace. Though Welles could not say so openly, Roosevelt still hoped to play the part of honest broker, if the powers would grasp at his ideal of real face-to-face co-operation. Ribbentrop in Berlin would consider nothing before German victory – 'very stupid' Welles thought him – and neither the French nor British governments could really understand what Welles had been sent for. There was no prospect of appeasement now. Welles confirmed what Roosevelt himself already knew. When Germany invaded Scandinavia and the Low Countries a month later the President was convinced that sooner or later America would find herself at war with powers who wished 'to dominate and enslave the human race'.[57]

At home he launched a campaign of propaganda to convince Americans that the issues at stake in Europe were America's issues too. He established a Non-Partisan Committee for Peace through Revision of the Neutrality Law under William Allen White, a curiously clumsy title for an agency designed to galvanise American opinion to support the worldwide contest for democracy. Roosevelt was a pastmaster at using the media to promote his own policies, and had done so to great effect during the New Deal. In 1940 he won the co-operation of the bulk of the national press, radio, newsreels and film-makers to present his side of the picture. The *March of Time* documentaries brought home to Americans everywhere the nature of the conflict in Europe and the Far East and the perils of ignoring it. Hollywood promoted films that showed in more indirect ways the virtues of standing out against tyranny, and defending freedom. A major radio series about Britain at war was made into an epic film: *From Oxford Pacifist to Fighter Pilot*. Its central, less than subtle, message was the possibility of making an honest transition from hatred of war to defence of liberty. Only a handful of national media figures stood out against the regime's foreign policy. By 1941 five times as much air time went to interventionist as to non-interventionist programmes.[58]

Important though the propaganda campaign was it needed more than that to turn opinion to a more active foreign policy after years of isolationism. Roosevelt's critics hit back through their own organisation, the 'America First' campaign, which united a broad church of opponents to war. Some of this propaganda was paid for with funds channelled from the German Embassy in Washington. The literacy agency William C. Lengel took $20,000 from Ribbentrop to fund the publication and distribution of speeches and books hostile to intervention. The New York publishers Howell & Soskin printed 100,000 copies of 'the German White Paper' containing documents purporting to link Roosevelt with active promotion of the European war, again paid for with German funds. And the same source contributed to the 'Keep America Out of the War' lobby which campaigned at the Republican Convention in June 1940 for an isolationist candidate for the forthcoming election.[59]

Roosevelt had to tread as warily as he had done since 1936. His position in 1940 was to offer Britain and France 'aid-short-of-war'. This was acceptable to a majority of Americans. The opinion polls showed large majorities against intervention, but equally large majorities in favour of helping the democracies with war supplies. This shift of opinion was reflected in the Republican nomination of a staunch pro-British candidate, Wendell Wilkie, despite the efforts of 'America First' and the opposition of powerful isolationists. Yet Roosevelt was reluctant to do more than this. He was standing for an unprecedented third term and he continued to pose as a firm opponent of intervention, on prudential as much as moral grounds. 'What worries me', he confessed to his old friend William Bullitt, then in Paris, 'is that public opinion over here is patting itself on the back every morning and thanking God for the Atlantic Ocean. . . . People are also saying "Thank God for Roosevelt and Hull" – no matter what happens, they will keep us out of war".' Roosevelt was trapped in a political snare of his own making. As the Presidential contest drew to a climax he had to distance himself as far as possible from any prospect of intervention, while making it clear where his sympathies lay: 'my problem', he continued to Bullitt, 'is to get the American people to think of conceivable consequences without scaring the American people into thinking they are going to be dragged into war.'[60]

Discretion proved the better part of valour; from September 1940 Roosevelt moved to reassure voters that he was as hostile to war as anyone. In a major speech in the Midwest he reiterated: 'I hate war, now more than ever.' At Boston a few weeks later he assured an audience of Irish–Americans: 'Your boys are not going to be sent into any foreign wars.'[61] Roosevelt won the election by a much narrower margin than in 1936, losing ground in the Midwest isolationist belt, but winning the North-east, the South and the seaboard states. This pattern reflected a shift in Roosevelt's own power-base which had been going on since the collapse of the New Deal in 1937–8. He was forging a closer alliance with business and the conservative Democrats and labour, moving away from the small townsmen and homesteaders who had voted for his social programmes in the depression. Businessmen were hostile to much of the New Deal, with its open dislike of corporate power. By 1940 Roosevelt needed them to build America's weapons, while they needed the President to safeguard America's economic interests abroad. By the end of 1940 he had the political alliance that would produce America's war effort.

It was still a long way from electoral victory and vigorous propaganda to actual conflict. Roosevelt certainly favoured a much more active foreign policy, but he was not a warmonger. Electoral victory did allow him to continue the momentum of rearmament. There was no disguising the dangers America was exposed to and Congress agreed to very high levels of military spending in peacetime to buy domestic security. Budget appropriations for the army and navy in 1941 were four times the level of 1940, outlays for military equipment were nearly seven times greater.[62] America was preparing the sinews of superpower status. Roosevelt also moved to staff his Cabinet and the Washington bureaucracy with those more sympathetic to active foreign policy. Secretary for War Harold Woodring was sacked and replaced by the Republican hawk Henry Stimson. The strength of the isolationist lobby ebbed away in Washington. By April 1941 Moffat found 'the interventionists in the saddle' in the capital.[63] The army Chief of Staff, General George Marshall, and his naval counterpart, Admiral Stark, both favoured greater action. Bit by bit Roosevelt was able to construct a consensus among the American establishment hostile to isolationism.

It was less clear exactly what the alternative to isolation was. After an initial optimism about British and French prospects against Germany, the defeat of France forced Washington to accept that on her own Britain was unlikely to be able to subdue the continent. 'The English are not going to win this war without our help,' argued the Secretary for the Navy, Frank Knox, in October 1940.[64] This was a genuine shock for American opinion, which had continued to regard Britain as the major world military power long after the reality had faded. A few weeks after the election Admiral Stark drew up a memorandum which laid out America's strategic options. He strongly favoured a policy of confronting Germany first, as the greatest risk to American security, in the hope that Japan would then remain neutral. He argued that in the long run Germany could only be defeated by sending a large American army and air force overseas. Roosevelt agreed; Stark's 'Plan Dog' formed the basis of American strategic planning thereafter. The planning was kept secret, but it governed the development of American military production and aid to Britain.

What Roosevelt could do was to step up the economic assistance to the powers opposing the Axis. On 29 December, in a famous fireside chat, he told his audience that the United States now had to accept a special role, to be 'the arsenal of democracy', providing the sinews of war for the British Empire, 'the spearhead of resistance to world conquest'. He painted a lurid prospect for his listeners: 'If Great Britain goes down, the Axis powers will control the continents of Europe, Asia, Africa and Australia, and the high seas.' The speech marked a personal turning point for the President. It was the moment at which he publicly committed America to the very greatest economic efforts in support of the Allied cause. At the same time he turned his back finally on any prospect of a negotiated settlement with Hitlerism: 'no nation can appease the Nazis. No man can tame a tiger into a kitten by stroking it.'[65]

The promise to become the arsenal of democracy was prompted by another alarming revelation. To the surprise and consternation of American leaders, Britain was forced to confess that she had reached the end of her foreign resources and was close to international bankruptcy. Roosevelt suspected that Britain was trying to pass the responsibility for paying for war on to the United States as she had done in 1917. But closer examination showed that Britain was right. Roosevelt promised to provide the aid whether Britain could afford to pay cash on the nail or not. This was a major violation of the cash-and-carry concession wrung out of Congress almost two years before. A fierce debate followed in Congress. By March 1941 the legislation was through; Britain's battle was clearly America's too. Giving Britain the tools to fight it made good political and economic sense. It destroyed any remaining vestige of 'neutrality', but it avoided actual fighting. Berle observed in March that the United States was experiencing 'a steady drift into a deep gray stage in which precise difference between war and peace is impossible to discern'.[66] The Lend–Lease Act was a logical extension of thc initial decision to sell arms taken in 1939, but it was not an act of war. Roosevelt was determined not to be cast in the role of warmonger in Europe or the Far East. 'We have no intention', he wrote to a friend shortly after the 'arsenal' speech, 'of being "sucked into" a war with Germany. Whether there will come to us war with either or both of those countries, will depend far more upon what they do. . . .'[67]

During 1941 American strategy pulled in two opposing directions, reflecting the ambiguity of Roosevelt's own position. Material help from the United States kept the British war effort afloat, and, after June 1941, the Soviet one as well. At the same time Roosevelt made every effort to ensure that the United States avoided war for as long as possible, and that her enemies should fire the first shot. The first of these made the second more likely. In order to supply goods to Britain, the United States navy found itself gradually absorbed into the battle of the Atlantic in defence of American lives and ships. By

February there were 159 ships in the Atlantic Fleet, and Roosevelt was under pressure to move more of the navy from the Pacific. Gradually over the course of the year American naval forces moved further and further into the Atlantic sea-lanes, while American troops were stationed in Greenland and then Iceland. But Roosevelt would only move at a slow pace, step by step, each encroachment preparing the ground with American opinion for the next one. In April he refused to sanction the convoying of merchant ships across the Atlantic because 'public opinion was not yet ready'. By July more than 50 per cent of opinion was in favour of convoys, but Roosevelt was not sure of Congress. Thomas Lamont observed that Roosevelt was 'moving just about as rapidly as he can considering the fact that he must keep a united country and a not-too-divided Congress'. Not until September, when domestic opinion was much more strongly anti-German, did he agree to allow convoying of British ships. Even then he found the opposition to the proposal in Congress, including a number of Democrats, difficult to swallow.[68]

Roosevelt's greatest fear was that war would break out in 1941 long before either American rearmament or American opinion was ready. There were also more personal reasons. Roosevelt did not want, genuinely enough, to be branded as the President that took America into war. In May 1941 his confidant Harry Hopkins noted that 'the President is loath to get us into this war'. When war finally did come in December Roosevelt recalled with regret 'his earnest desire to complete his administration without war'.[69] He was determined that at all costs America should never appear as the aggressor. 'I am waiting to be pushed into this,' he told Morgenthau in May.[70] If war had to come, then it must come through some deliberate assault on American interests. This might take the form of armed conflict in the Atlantic, 'the accidental shot of some irresponsible captain'.[71] Roosevelt was also convinced that his cautious, step-by-step politics at home was the only way to get American opinion to swallow the inevitable clash with Germany and Japan. The Conscription Act was renewed in August by the narrow margin of one vote, 203 to 202. Yet there was evidence that Roosevelt was now hiding behind the fear of opinion to avoid taking firmer action. Gallup Polls released privately to the President in May showed that only 19 per cent thought he had gone too far in helping Britain, and that 75 per cent favoured continued aid even if the United States ended up in war. Digests of press opinion forwarded by Morgenthau in the same month showed that 'the impact of events abroad has produced a mass migration in American opinion. . . . Today's isolationist follows the precepts of yesterday's interventionist.'[72]

Roosevelt's excessive caution frustrated his colleagues. In May there was strong pressure from within the Cabinet for a declaration of war on Germany. When Stimson was pressed on the issue he responded angrily: 'Go see the isolationist over in the White House.'[73] During the summer American foreign policy began to drift. Roosevelt was ill for some weeks with a debilitating influenza; Hull ignored the European crisis and spent his time trying to win peace in the Far East. Roosevelt stuck to his guns on the issue of war: it would have to be declared on America, not by America. To be fair, there were other factors at work which made Roosevelt's caution more understandable. In 1941 American rearmament was still in its very early stages. Even by September 1941 there was virtually no expeditionary force to send overseas, while the air force had hardly begun to create the great bomber force of the later war years. There were real fears for America's own security. American intelligence services produced alarming reports that Germany was building vast air fleets in 1941 – 42,000 aircraft altogether, with 12,000 long-range bombers (the real figures were 11,700 and 2800).[74] To challenge both Germany and Japan openly in 1941 would expose the real limitations of American military strength. The spring or summer of 1942 was the point at which America might safely contemplate war.

American production was also aimed at the possibility of defeating Germany without American intervention. Supplies to Britain had to be maintained in order to keep a foothold in Europe. Defeat of Britain would make America's situation even more difficult, yet an American declaration of war would immediately divert American production away from Lend–Lease to the supply of America's own forces. This was a strong argument for not pushing Japan to war as well. A Japanese–American war would make it almost impossible to pursue the 'Germany first' strategy agreed in December 1940. Opinion would expect maximum effort against Japan at the expense of Europe and even of British survival. The German attack on the Soviet Union made American strategy more complicated. The attack raised the prospect that Japan would now move southward against British or American possessions, freed from the threat from Russia. This called for renewed efforts to avoid any confrontation in the Pacific. At the same time Roosevelt authorised military supplies for the Soviet Union too, in the hope that a combination of British bombing, in which he had very great confidence as a potential war-winning weapon, and Soviet resistance would defeat Hitler.

It is small wonder that American policy in the summer and autumn of 1941, faced with such an array of imponderable factors, displayed a hesitancy and incoherence that frustrated the British and the hawks in Washington, while it gave heart to the Axis powers that America would be too feeble to obstruct their building of a New Order. On one thing all were agreed in Washington. No one wanted war with Japan in 1941. As American rearmament began to develop in 1941 the hawks found it hard to believe that Japan would dare to go to war with a state so evidently more powerful. But to reduce the risk Washington practised a dual policy of firmness towards Japan, while keeping open the prospect of a negotiated settlement of outstanding issues in the Far East. From January to November Secretary of State Hull was engaged in the thankless task of finding a formula which the Japanese would accept for negotiation, while sticking to the American demands for an end to the war in China and open trade in Asia.[75] Some moderate opinion in Tokyo favoured discussion of the American position but the military would not accept abandoning the Asian conquests on any grounds. What Tokyo did not know was that American intelligence with its 'Magic' equipment had broken the diplomatic code and could follow the agonies of Japanese decision-making as it developed over the summer.

The intercepts showed that Japan hoped to keep the discussions going while it continued the slow march into southern Asia. By July it was clear that the militarists were in the ascendant. To keep up the pressure on Japan the economic noose was tightened further. A complete embargo was placed on iron exports and then oil, and on 25 July all Japanese assets in America were frozen. The effect was to push the Japanese Cabinet to the brink. Prince Konoye, the Japanese premier, made one last attempt to maintain a dialogue on Japanese terms. In August he proposed a face-to-face meeting with Roosevelt to thrash out the issues between the two states. Roosevelt was attracted immediately; this was his style of politics. He had just returned from a successful conference with Churchill where an Atlantic Charter for the post-war settlement of Europe had been agreed between them. The prospect of a Charter for the Pacific was one too good to miss. Only when it became clear via 'Magic' that Konoye would not agree to any of the principles for discussion proposed by Washington for the meeting did the Americans finally abandon any real hope for a negotiated agreement. The prospect for a peaceful outcome had effectively disappeared by November 1941. Roosevelt and his commanders found it hard to believe that Japan would attack the United States in cold blood, even when the evidence was plain to see. But as in the Atlantic Roosevelt did everything to avoid deliberate conflict, and authorised American forces in the Pacific to ensure 'that Japan commits the first overt act'.[76]

At the end of November the United States stood poised to face war in either or both major oceans. Roosevelt did nothing to hurry the process on, and continued to deflect all calls for belligerency on the grounds that the United States was only acting 'in self-defense'. The latest polls still showed less than half the population in favour of sending troops to Europe, and only one-third in favour of war with Japan in the near future.[77] Until American interests were directly threatened, and American opinion united by the threat, Roosevelt hesitated to push the button. We cannot be certain that without the Japanese attack on Pearl Harbor on 7 December 1941 America would have fought in 1942. On the following day Roosevelt argued that the attack 'had given us an opportunity'. Congress approved the declaration of war with only one dissenting voice. Eleanor Roosevelt noted that the effect of the Japanese attack was to release her husband from months of pent-up tension and anxiety: 'Franklin was in a way more serene than he had appeared in a long time.'[78] It is tempting to see Pearl Harbor as the crisis Roosevelt was waiting for and did nothing to prevent. America's most vital interest, defence of American soil, had been challenged. The American people rose to the challenge, after decades of isolation, with a great anger and determination to wage war with all the strength at their disposal.

It is certainly true that by November 1941 the Roosevelt administration knew that a crisis was imminent in the Pacific. A warning was sent out to all commanders on 26 November. 'Magic' revealed that the Japanese had set a final deadline for a peaceful settlement on 29 November. 'After that things are definitely going to happen,' warned Roosevelt; 'we must be prepared for real trouble.'[79] The most likely place was not Hawaii, which Roosevelt for one believed to be reasonably immune to attack from the sea, and where substantial air and naval forces were assumed to be on alert, but Thailand or the Dutch East Indies. After intelligence reports that a large task force was steaming south, Thailand seemed the most likely. After some difficulty the British Ambassador in Washington, Lord Halifax, got Roosevelt to agree that both their states would defend Thai independence militarily, though it was by no means clear that American forces could do very much to help or that Roosevelt would honour his word. The Philippines was a possible target, but was so distant from Japanese airbases that it was thought reasonable warning would precede any attack. Washington suffered during the few days before Pearl Harbor from an excess of intelligence information, like the Russians before Barbarossa. Information indicating Pearl Harbor as a target was lost under piles of 'Magic' intercepts; when it finally surfaced it was hard to distinguish from other intelligence on Japanese spying, and was ignored. The great merit of the Japanese plan was its secrecy and its boldness. The timing of the attack and the place were both successfully concealed; or almost so. On 6 December a telegram to the Japanese Embassy in Washington was intercepted. It contained a detailed fourteen-point rejection of all American grounds for further discussion, which Hull had sent as a final gesture to Tokyo on 26 November. The first thirteen were decoded that same day. The last point indicated a severing of diplomatic relations at 1.00 p.m. the following morning, Washington time. This part of the message was not finally communicated until the middle of the morning of the 7th. It was a Sunday and officials were difficult to track down; General Marshall was out riding. A final warning was sent far too late to help either Hawaii or the Philippines.[80]

Much has been made of the final débâcle, but the evidence suggests not some Machiavellian ploy on Roosevelt's part but a genuine strategic miscalculation, compounded with sloppy intelligence. Roosevelt was certainly much relieved in the end to be fighting a war with clear aims and a united people. The Japanese action removed the last nagging doubts about the morality of a democratic, internationalist President taking his country into war. But to suggest that Pearl Harbour was knowingly left to face the Japanese in the hope that it would shock opinion into supporting war makes little sense historically. Roosevelt did not want to wage war if it could be avoided until America was armed; if possible, not at all. The American defence effort was concentrated in the Atlantic, and a Pacific war would have seriously compromised that priority. Nor is it likely that any commander-in-chief, and his military, could conspire to lose eight ships and 2000 men to calm domestic public opinion. Roosevelt was not the kind of man to sacrifice American lives for the sake of a diplomatic gambit. Losing eight capital ships on purpose made no strategic sense at all. In the end American miscalculation about intention and capability had much in common with Stalin's misjudgement in June of German plans: Americans could not bring themselves to believe that Japan would attack the United States head on. These views were conditioned by a genuine belief that Japan lacked the military means to launch attacks with such precision and devastation over long tracks of ocean with small numbers of trained pilots. Japan, for once, profited from the persistent American habit of underestimating Japanese potential.

Roosevelt was immediately faced, as he had feared, with the problem of persuading his countrymen to keep to the 'Germany First' strategy. 'Magic' intercepts showed that Germany had agreed with Japan on 4 December to fight America if Japan found herself at war with her, and that after Pearl Harbour the pledge would be fulfilled. Once again Roosevelt was released from the difficulty of declaring war on America's behalf. On 11 December Hitler and Mussolini declared war on the United States. Hitler's exact motives remain obscure. But by December the Axis powers were at their apogee; the Soviet Union was close to defeat – or seemed so – Britain strangled by the submarine. Japan had crippled the Pacific Fleet. A few weeks earlier Hitler talked of the change in the balance of power brought about by his conquest of Europe: 'we will be four hundred million compared with one hundred and thirty million Americans.'[81] The United States was an enemy Hitler knew he would fight eventually; a state of near-belligerency had existed in the Atlantic for almost a year. By December 1941 the risk of fighting America appeared much reduced. Neither the Japanese nor the Germans could guess at how rapidly the United States could create and supply forces so vast that the prospects of Axis victory receded decisively within months of American entry.

The United States was the last of the world's great powers to start down the road to war and the last one to fight. During the 1930s America did not use her very great economic and political weight to reverse the expansion of the three aggressor states but instead withdrew into the isolation of the Western hemisphere. Yet the war demonstrated that America's military potential was vast. Only a few years separated determined non-intervention from the exercise of world leadership.

America's withdrawal from world affairs mattered a great deal in the background to war in 1939. American neutrality and the evident strength of isolationism among the American public gave additional encouragement to Japan and Germany to embark on local programmes of expansion which Britain and France were too feeble to reverse on their own. Hitler convinced himself that America had declined in the 1930s because of social crisis and 'degenerate' materialism, and that the balance in world affairs was swinging towards the Axis powers. This perception, false though it proved to be, contributed to Hitler's decision to attack Poland, confident that the West would do nothing serious. The same misconception fuelled Japan's growing determination to confront the United States in 1941.

Though it might now be argued that it would have served American interests better in the long run to have kept up the progressive climb to 'globalism' after Versailles, it is essential to see that American leaders were faced with overwhelming pressures against war and intervention. Above all American society had to recover from the self-inflicted wounds of the Great Crash, which damaged not only American finance but social confidence and political consensus. 'America First' was the only political strategy that made sense to Americans in the 1930s. Nor should we assume that the United States were committed to shoring up the existing international system, dominated by what they saw as greedy imperial powers, old and new. When America did re-enter world politics, it resulted in a transformation of the system. Until at least 1939 most Americans thought the European powers were all as bad as each other, and should clean up the international mess themselves. American isolation meant the defence of American concepts of liberty and democracy, and fear of contamination from Europe with the twin evils of communism and fascism. Only when it was self-evident that liberty could only be preserved by entering and transforming that world in America's image was isolation finally abandoned. In 1944 Walter Lippmann urged his countrymen to see that the age of innocence was past; now was the age of responsibility.[82]

CONCLUSION

'A WAR OF GREAT PROPORTIONS'

Towards the end of the Second World War, in February 1945, Hitler instructed Goebbels to begin publishing long articles on the Punic Wars in the German press. The struggle of Germany against the rest of the world was for Hitler the struggle of Rome against Carthage, of a new world against the old. The Punic Wars, Goebbels reflected in his diary, were 'decisive in a world-historical sense'. The victory of one side over the other had been felt 'over several centuries'; the fate of Europe, like the fate of those ancient states, was 'not settled by a single war' but in a number of wars, culminating in what Göring had called a 'war of great proportions' now being fought out on Germany's battered territories.[1]

Hitler's mistake was to see Germany as the new Rome; Germany was Carthage. The complete defeat in 1945 of Germany and her allies brought decisively to an end centuries of European domination. It marked a break in world history more complete and permanent than 1918. The change was not just the substitution of one world order for another, the rise of new powers and the decline of old. There was also a change in ideas, in the assumptions and attitudes that underlie political behaviour, a transformation of the mental world which marks off the long peace since 1945 from the age of violent crisis that preceded it.

If we are to understand clearly what brought the great powers into conflict between 1939 and 1945 something of that distant age must be recaptured. Nothing reveals the gulf between the two ages more strikingly than simple questions of geography and communication. In the 1930s distance still was a barrier. Air travel was in its infancy; it took days rather than hours to reach the Far East or Southern Africa even by aircraft. Links between the United States and Europe or Asia were by ship. Travel was restricted to a small minority who could afford it. For most of the world's population mobility was very restricted; the overwhelming bulk of that population was composed of peasants or farmers, even in Europe. Knowledge of the world was limited too. The earth's surface was only finally mapped completely in the 1930s by airship and aircraft; some of it was still unexplored. There existed a genuine ignorance of the way of life of other peoples, and only limited contact between them. This was true even in Europe where the population was richer and the railway an accessible artery of contact. Hitler's entire spatial world was made up of a triangle between Austria, where he was born, the Western Front where he served as a soldier, and Berlin where he became Chancellor. He had not visited any other country; nor did he do so during his period in power before 1939 except for two brief trips to Italy. Stalin's world was similarly enclosed. Even the 'cosmopolitan' Roosevelt only visited Europe once as an adult before American entry into the war. No leading statesman visited Japan during the 1930s. The excitement caused by Chamberlain's visit to see Hitler in 1938 was not just the result of his decision to fly for the first time in his life at the age of nearly seventy, but because this kind of shuttle-diplomacy, face to face between the leaders of great powers, was almost unheard of in the 1930s.

The inhibiting effects of distance and poor communication profoundly affected the perception of what other people were like, or how other states in the world system, with values very different from each other, might behave in a crisis. Towards the end of the war Walter Lippmann recalled his own experience:

> When I attempt to compare the America in which I was reared with the America of today, I am struck by how unconcerned I was as a young man with the hard questions which are the subject matter of history. I did not think about the security of the Republic and how to defend it. I did not think about intercourse with the rest of the world, and how to maintain it.[2]

This kind of isolation was not confined to the United States. An involuntary isolation separated the major states from each other before 1939. Chamberlain's claim in 1938 that Czechoslovakia was a 'far-away country of which we know nothing' would not have struck his listeners as oddly as it does now in an age of jet travel and satellite communications; and the British were, of all the people engaged in the crisis of the 1930s, the most cosmopolitan, thanks to a far-flung empire.

To an involuntary isolation was added deliberate restriction. In Nazi Germany or Fascist Italy close control over the press, radio and cinema reduced knowledge of the outside world and presented a distorted and selected version of it. After years of propaganda and censorship it was difficult even for the most sceptical spirit to distinguish clearly between official news and the truth. William

Shirer was struck forcibly by this when he arrived to report the Danzig crisis in August 1939:

> How completely isolated a world the German people live in. A glance at the newspapers . . . reminds you of it. Whereas all the rest of the world considers that the peace is about to be broken by Germany, that it is Germany that is threatening to attack Poland over Danzig, here in Germany, in the world the local newspapers create, the very reverse is being maintained. . . . You ask: But the German people can't possibly believe these lies? Then you talk to them. So many do.[3]

In the Soviet Union the situation was similar, though here knowledge of the outside world, or even the next province, had always been restricted through geographical isolation and ignorance. Now it was limited by the deliberate suppression and selection of news. Soviet propaganda was manipulative, creating a view of the world, full of imperial and fascist demons, which most Soviet citizens were in no position to challenge, and which was even exported abroad with more success than it deserved.

The gulf of understanding was not only confined to the totalitarian powers, and was not simply a consequence of ideological rifts. A great degree of prejudice and illusion fuelled the perception each power had of the others in the 1930s, whether German views of British decadence, or British views of French unreliability, or American views of Japanese inferiority. The habit of cultural stereotyping was a substitute for real knowledge and understanding of other people, and it was shared not only by popular opinion but even by politicians and officials, who might have known better. Prejudice and misjudgement of this kind permeated the crises of the pre-war years; but it was not entirely without foundation. There *were* very profound differences between the communities in conflict in the 1930s, more pronounced in a great many respects than they are a half-century later. A distance much greater than geography separated Japan from Europe and America; the divide between Britain and the Soviet Union, at opposite points on the spectrum of social structure and cultural attitudes, was almost unbridgeable in the 1930s, but it was no more remarkable than the cultural distance between Britain and the Midwestern United States. Mongolia and Montana were both 5000 miles from London. Even within Europe these differences were striking. 'You come from a world', Hitler told Burckhardt, the Swiss historian who was League Commissioner in Danzig, 'which is alien to me.'[4] Hitler, the ill-educated Austrian provincial, did not speak the same language, did not share the same cultural background or moral world, of the educated, liberal upper classes which still dominated Western diplomacy between the wars. Part of the failure of British appeasement lay in the gulf between these two worlds. British statesmen expected Germany to conform at least to some extent with 'modern' diplomatic practice, with negotiation and reasonable concession. Hitler worked on very different assumptions, and the mutual incomprehension that resulted, the parallel universes of international discourse, made appeasement appear more feeble and foolish than its champions intended.

Only reliable political and military intelligence might have made good some of the deficiencies of understanding. But in the 1930s the intelligence communities were in their infancy. The United States obtained little systematic intelligence on other countries. In Europe intelligence-gathering was more advanced and more institutionalised, but it was still in most cases rudimentary by the standards of today. Partial information, often assessed and communicated by officials with little professional experience of intelligence, contributed to the process of distorting the strengths and weaknesses, the political attitudes and strategic assumptions of other states. Many of the politicians who had to make choices about foreign policy were unaccustomed to using intelligence information systematically and doubted its usefulness. Even the Soviet Union, gathering extensive intelligence through the recruitment of foreign communist sympathisers, could make fundamental misjudgements. Both the German attack in June 1941 and the Japanese attack six months later enjoyed the element of complete surprise. The war witnessed a great mushrooming of intelligence activity, which continued on into the post-war world. But up to 1939 personal judgement, intuition or impression were just as likely to carry the day.[5]

For all these differences, there were shared assumptions too. Most of the statesmen who played a part in the international crisis were born before 1900, in an age of European expansion and imperialism. Chamberlain, the oldest of the world leaders in 1939, was born in 1869, before the Scramble for Africa, before Queen Victoria was enthroned as Empress of India. The domination of European values and institutions was taken for granted; empire was seen as a defining characteristic of the status of being a great power. Powers outside Europe sought to emulate Europe's example. Japanese expansion in Asia was deliberately modelled on British colonial practice. Even the United States joined halfheartedly in the imperial scramble by seizing the decaying Spanish colonies in 1898. Though empire was as much a source of weakness as of strength by the 1920s, it was assumed by states which possessed large empires, as much as by those which did not, that empires were well worth having. The instability of the inter-war years owed a great deal to the prevailing climate of geopolitical and social-darwinist thinking that saw the world in terms of the endless contest of empires and for empire. Stanley Baldwin captured this view in his Empire Message in 1925:

> The Empire is not only our master hope; it is our greatest heritage, the widest opportunity for patriotic service. It is something infinitely precious which we hold in trust from our forefathers and for our children. To be worthy of that trust, we cannot be merely passive admirers of its achievement and its promise. We must all, in our several degrees, be active learners in the school of Empire.[6]

There were no more eager pupils than the imperialists in Italy, Germany and Japan. Mussolini recalled the legacy of the great Roman empire. Hitler was an avid imperialist, who sought a new German imperium across the expanse of Eurasia. He saw empire in terms of living-space; Britain and France had theirs in the under-populated overseas possessions, Germany deserved the same. Even the British openly admitted that these were the terms of the contest: 'We have got most of the world already, or the best parts of it, and we only want to keep what we have got and prevent others from taking it away from us.'[7] Japanese ruling circles in the 1930s were united in their view that Japanese power and future prosperity rested on carving out a similar area for themselves in Asia, reproducing in the Far East what they saw as the dominant features of Western international behaviour: 'Since Great Britain itself has a self-sufficient empire and the United States is assured of a similar position in the American continents, these Powers should not object to recognising for Japan the right of attaining a self dependent status in East Asia. . . .'[8] By the time these views were written, in 1941, the age of empire was almost over, but imperialism was still the idiom within which international conflict was expressed.

A second assumption closely related to imperial endeavour was racial superiority. Most statesmen in the inter-war years were the product of cultures where, consciously or unconsciously, concepts of racial hierarchy and racial conflict were widespread and obtrusive. The biological view of the world, that there were races fitted to rule and races fitted only to obey, that racial conflict was at the root of national rivalries, was not confined to Nazi Germany, though Hitler certainly gave the idea of race a central and violent place in German strategy. German anti-Semitism carried racial intolerance to the very limit, but it grew out of the intellectual milieu of the late nineteenth century in Europe which sought to give a scientific foundation to racialism through eugenic theory, ideas on degeneration, and racial explanations for empire. During the inter-war years these ideas were the stock-in-trade of a great many populist and nationalist politicians, stoking the fires of national rivalry and overt racism. This kind of conflict was regarded as perfectly natural, perhaps necessary, and even Western, liberal, politicians were not inhibited from expressing their opinions in racial terms. Attitudes to Japan, for example, were overtly racist. Eden talked of reimposing 'white-man authority' in Asia; Americans dismissed Japan's military threat on the grounds that the Japanese were bow-legged and shortsighted, biologically unfitted for conquest. In turn, Japanese nationalists saw Westerners as inferior racially to Japan, and regarded Koreans or Manchurians as even worse. At the end of the war Hitler warned the West in his 'political testament' of the dangers they faced from the 'yellow race', a danger that could be met only by the revival of the 'white peoples'.[9] This kind of cultural pessimism was widespread after the First World War. Imperial and racial conflict, the rise and fall of civilisations, the constant ebb-and-flow of national fortunes were taken for granted not just among the intellectual radicals of Central Europe, but among the political classes of the liberal West as well.

These views of a shifting, uncertain world were also the product of three great landmarks which dominated the skyline of the 1930s: the experience of the First World War, the Russian revolution of 1917, and the Great Depression of 1929–32. In different ways these were the events that dominated the attitudes and choices made by statesmen in the years before 1939. They were reference points of great significance, cataclysmic events eclipsed only by what was to happen between 1939 and 1945. The First World War was a fundamental shock to the comfortable, ordered, prosperous life of bourgeois Europe. In one stroke it destroyed the confidence in Progress, the liberal conviction that, given time, reason, peace and free trade would triumph everywhere. The war brutalised a whole generation of young Europeans, sharpened national antagonisms, and, for young soldiers like Hitler, excited the view that violent struggle, the contest for sheer survival, was, after all, at the root of national existence. After four years of struggle the victors imposed on the vanquished a humiliating and vindictive peace. In the terms in which the contest had been played out this was hardly surprising. But the Versailles Settlement seemed to the losers a great hypocrisy, preaching universal peace and national justice while creating all the conditions for national vendetta. Even Italy, one of the victors, felt cheated. Nothing about the outcome of the war arrested the conviction widely held that the old liberal conception of the world had been replaced by one derived from Darwin.

This was not the only reaction to the conflict, though it was a powerful ingredient in the popular, radical nationalism of the inter-war years. The war also produced a widespread revulsion against military conflict which was institutionalised in the idealist side of the peace, in the League of Nations and the commitment, unfulfilled, to general disarmament. Side by side with talk of revenge and cultural decline, there arose an optimism that the experience of war was so grotesque that no reasonable state would ever contemplate it again. 'Modern war is so beastly,' wrote Hankey to a friend, 'so drab, so devoid of the old "joie de guerre" . . . that everyone hates it.'[10] The revulsion against war expressed often and openly by Western statesmen was utterly sincere. No statesman could lightly contemplate at any point in the twenty years after 1918 taking a population into total war again. 'When I think of the 7 million of young men who were cut off in their prime,' said Chamberlain, 'the 13 million who were maimed and mutilated, the misery and the sufferings of the mothers and the fathers . . . in war there are no winners, but all are losers.'[11] Chamberlain was not a pacifist, though thousands of his fellow countrymen were. He expressed an understandable horror at the thought of war, and could not comprehend those whose experience of the war was the reverse, that war was the real school of nationhood, and military endeavour the mark of a vigorous people.

No aspect of warfare was dreaded more than aerial bombardment. At the very end of the First World War the Allies were on the point of launching an independent bombing offensive against German towns. London and other British and French cities had already been bombed. Most German towns within range of the Western Front had been attacked at some time in 1917 and 1918. What had been science-fiction before the war became horrible fact by its end. Air power, ruthlessly and systematically employed, could bring war home to the civilian population; it could, so the new generation of air strategists argued, bring the war to an end on its own, through a 'knock-out blow' so terrible that popular morale would crack and governments sue for peace. During the inter-war years public imagination far outran the technical development of air power. 'I have often uttered the truism', said Baldwin in a speech in April 1936, 'that the next war will be the end of civilisation in Europe.' By the 1930s it was widely assumed that any future war between great powers might be settled within days by bombers pounding enemy cities to pulp or gassing their populations. 'I believe that if such a thing were done,' continued Baldwin, '. . . the raging peoples of every country, torn with passion, suffering and horror, would wipe out every Government in Europe and you would have a state of anarchy from end to end.'[12] Even in Berlin, in early September 1939, the inhabitants kept asking where the Polish bombers were. Almost as soon as war was declared the air-raid sirens went off and gasmasks went on in London and Berlin; they were false alarms, for neither power had the means to launch an effective bombing campaign by the end of the 1930s. But no state could be certain of this. The Japanese bombing in China and the German bombing of Guernica in the Spanish Civil War were the images that stuck in people's minds. 'We thought of air warfare in 1938', wrote Harold Macmillan later, 'rather as people think of nuclear warfare today.'[13]

The prospect of general war brought with it another threat, that the next war would complete the social revolution begun in the first war, in Russia, in 1917. Communists everywhere shared Trotsky's view of war as the 'locomotive of history'. Though formally committed to peaceful coexistence, communism waited for the next armed clash of the capitalist powers which would complete the social emancipation of the working classes. The impact of the revolution on the old world order was well understood by Stalin:

> the October Revolution inflicted a mortal wound on world capitalism from which the latter will never recover. . . . Capitalism may become partly stabilised, it may rationalise production, turn over the administration of the country to fascism, temporarily hold down the working class; but it will never recover the 'tranquillity', the 'assurance', the 'equilibrium' and the 'stability' that it flaunted before; for the crisis of world capitalism has reached the stage of development where the flames of revolution must inevitably break out. . . .[14]

After 1917 a new kind of social crisis was placed on the agenda. The international repercussion of the Russian revolution was like that of the French revolution. 'Just as the word "Jacobin" evoked horror and loathing among the aristocrats of all countries,' continued Stalin, 'so now . . . the word "Bolshevik" evokes horror and loathing among the bourgeois of all countries.' Communism was indeed feared and detested by the ruling circles of every country outside the Soviet Union in the 1930s. The fear of social revolution contributed substantially to the triumph of Mussolini in Italy and Hitler in Germany. Working-class parties everywhere, even the moderate parliamentary parties, invited distrust. The social question was reduced to a simple formula: how to avert the triumph of communism. This view exaggerated the strength and distorted the purpose of working-class radicalism. There was little more prospect of a social 'knock-out blow' in the 1930s than there was of one from the air. But in the 1930s the ruling classes could not be sure of this either, and fear of the left dominated domestic politics and affected foreign policy choices. Daladier complained to the American Ambassador just before Munich in 1938: 'Germany would be defeated in the war. France would win; but the only gainers would be the Bolsheviks as there would be social revolutions in every country of Europe and communist regimes. The prediction that Napoleon had made at St Helena was about to come true: "Cossacks will rule Europe".'[15]

It is against this background fear of social revolution that the impact of the third great crisis, the economic catastrophe of 1929, must be measured. The depression that followed the Wall Street Crash was the worst in the history of the industrial world. It struck at a time when confidence in the long-term survival of the social order and world peace was already in the balance. Communism preached the imminent collapse of capitalism; 1929 heralded that collapse. As the crisis deepened governments struggled to protect the established order and prevent social revolution. The slump was a shock to the world system. In 1936 Paul Reynaud described it in vivid terms:

> The oceans were deserted, the ships laid up in the silent ports, the factory smoke-stacks dead, long files of workless in the towns, poverty throughout the countryside. . . . Then came the stage when wealth was destroyed. The Brazilians threw their sacks of coffee into the sea, and the Canadians burned their corn in railway engines. . . . Men questioned the value of what they had learned to admire and respect. Women became less fertile. . . . The crisis was even more general and prolonged than the war. Nations were economically cut off from one another, but they shared in common the lot of poverty.[16]

The international economic order broke down; 'beggar my neighbour' policies replaced co-operation. Britain and Germany came close to the point of national bankruptcy in 1931. American politicians thought their Republic was closer to revolution in 1932 than at any time in its history. Throughout the 1930s politicians looked back to the years of recession as a benchmark to measure economic recovery and political stability. But domestic recovery, protected by tariffs, quotas and controls, was bought at the cost of a revival of the international economic prosperity of the 1920s. Economic nationalism became the order of the day; economic considerations openly trespassed into foreign policy, so that economic rivalry was expressed in terms of sharper political conflict. It was no mere chance that economic recovery at the end of the 1930s was fuelled by high levels of rearmament. The 'have-not' nations were determined to improve their economic share of the cake by force.

It is tempting to see all these things, war, revolution, economic collapse, as symptoms of a broader crisis, the death throes of an age of liberal empire, ruling-class politics and bourgeois social order which was mortally wounded by the First World War. People could not fail to be aware that they were living in an age of rapid transition, of profound changes. It was a disorientating, alarming experience for some. Hitler expressed the disquiet of his anxious constituency in his own words:

> Nothing is anchored any more, nothing is rooted in our spiritual life any more. Everything is superficial, flees past us. Restlessness and haste mark the thinking of our people. The whole of life is being torn completely apart.[17]

In the inter-war years the sense of *fin de siècle*, of the impending collapse or decline of the European world order, and of social order at home, was widespread: 'This sick, decadent continent', Shirer called it.[18] It produced a deep cultural pessimism among intellectual circles haunted by the self-destructive violence of the war and the prospect of proletarian victory. The certainties, moral, intellectual, even material, of the pre-war world dissolved in the crisis that followed. Various prescriptions were suggested: moral rearmament, racial hygiene, corporative politics, dictatorship. But the most powerful was the pursuit of a New Order, a restructuring of the world system, a consolidation along very different lines from the world of 1914.

Yet many of the problems of the post-war world stemmed from the attempt to restore the old order. In the 1920s Europe was still at the centre of world affairs, and was dominated by the traditional great powers, France and Britain, whose empires survived the war, enlarged. The economic order of free-trade, gold-standard economics was patchily recovered too. Parliamentary democracy dominated by the bourgeois parties was the rule in the Europe of 1920; by 1939 it was the exception. The attempt to stabilise the liberal order after 1919 was doomed to failure. Even without the slump of 1929, there were forces at work that could no longer be contained within the old system. British and French politicians recognised this as well as anyone, but they were committed to the status quo. For almost entirely fortuitous reasons that status quo survived in the 1920s. The United States, on the very brink of being a world power when it came to the rescue of the Old World in 1917, retreated into sulky isolation. The Soviet Union withdrew to save the revolution and build 'socialism in one country'. Germany was defeated and disarmed.

The forces that challenged this system were already in evidence well before 1914. Nationalism contributed to the outbreak of war in 1914. Its force was recognised at Versailles in the principle of national self-determination which the peacemakers so inexpertly applied. In the inter-war years nationalism challenged the survival of the overseas empires; Britain and France were faced with nationalist crisis almost permanently. In Ireland, India, Indo-China, Palestine, Syria, Egypt, Iraq, nationalist movements fought the colonial powers, often violently, and were encouraged in their contest by critics of empire in the United States and the Soviet Union. Britain and France lacked the military resources, even the political will, to repair their decline as imperial powers until the very end of the 1930s, when the mother countries themselves were under threat. By the 1930s it was impossible to ignore the fact that the balance of world power was now very different from the structure that Britain and France were trying to preserve. The rise of Japan, the development of an independent China, the sheer economic weight of the United States, and a Soviet state rapidly overtaking both imperial powers in industrial muscle and military capability put Europe's position into a different perspective. The desire to change the system was expressed in increasingly violent nationalist language. The growing sense of a world out of balance encouraged the search for a New Order among those states with a grudge against the arrogance of Western Europe.

This was a change that would have taken place fascism or not, though it would not necessarily have produced world war. For at the back of the shift in the balance of power was the rapid social and economic modernisation begun in the British Industrial Revolution two centuries before, and now spreading out inexorably to embrace the entire world. After 1918 Britain and France faced a steep relative decline in their share of world trade and production, already apparent well before then with the rise of the German and American industrial economies. The long march of economic modernisation inevitably shifted power to those states with larger populations, greater resources or more efficient production. In this sense Germany could never be contained within the structure set up by Versailles without partition or deliberate economic strangulation. The whole conflict over reparations can be seen as part of a wider effort to find ways of reining the German economy back, a strategy that fell apart in the 1930s when Hitler increased Germany's national product by two-thirds in four years. Nor, ultimately, could the Soviet Union be contained, though the Western powers were less aware of the shift brought about by Stalinist industrialisation than of that achieved by Nazi recovery. Hitler was all too aware of it:[19]

> Against this decay in continental Europe stands the extraordinary development of Soviet power. . . . we see ourselves in a position which is extremely dangerous. Pictures of distraught insecure governments on the one side, and the gigantic Soviet bloc, which is territorially, militarily and economically enormously strong on the other side. The dangers which arise from this are perhaps at the moment not clearly recognised by all. . . . But if this evolution goes any further, if the decomposition of Europe becomes more pronounced, and the strengthening of Soviet power continues at the same rate as hitherto, what will the position be in ten, twenty, or thirty years?[19]

For Hitler the 1930s were 'the decisive years', the years when Europe finally 'forfeited its leading position' to rising new powers.[20]

Industrial growth trailed in its wake the rise of mass politics, which challenged the monopoly of power enjoyed by the alliance of traditional ruling class and bourgeoisie for much of the previous century. In Italy and Germany the rapid spread of political awareness among groups previously poorly organised and politically powerless generated a backlash against the old political elite that produced fascism. In Russia popular politics overthrew the parliamentary regime set up in February 1917, and established an authoritarian communist state. The rise of mass participation did not lead automatically to democracy, but to bitter class conflict and extreme nationalism. In much of Europe the argument was reduced by the 1930s to the two extremes, fascism or communism. Ideology and propaganda were the hallmarks of the new politics, a means to mobilise allegiance in an age of rapid change, social crisis and economic stagnation, of creating certainty in a world in the process of dissolution and reformation. The 1930s was the great age of causes and enthusiasms – for social justice, against fascism, against communism, against war, for the nation. Politics became a crusade, violent and righteous.

This was a style of politics which profoundly threatened parliamentary democracy. By the 1930s confidence in democracy, like confidence in capitalism, had worn thin. The new states challenging the status quo were anything but democratic. There was every evidence that any New Order, whether right or left, would bring with it an authoritarian, single-party politics. By the late 1930s even political circles in the United States feared the imminent collapse of democracy everywhere outside America. 'We may be on the eve of the breaking up of the British and French empires,' wrote Harold Ickes in his diary in 1939. 'We may be about to pass over the crest of the civilization we have built up, headed for a decline of fifty or one hundred years, or even longer, during which our descendants will lose many of the gains that we have made.'[21] Under such circumstances war in the 1930s was a great risk for any democratic power. It was not a question of a democratic world bringing fascist troublemakers to heel, but of a democratic retreat in the face of fanatical nationalism, military rule and communist dictatorship. Not only the status quo abroad, but political freedom at home was at stake. The decision to use force in its defence was not as easy as it now looks from the perspective of German defeat. Fears for internal political stability, the urgent search for consensus, the pursuit of economic security were not mere excuses for democratic inaction, but were the product of a very real anxiety. Only the massive military power of the United States preserved democracy after 1939.

In the course of the 1930s the process of dissolution of the old international order became manifest. First Japan, then Italy, then Germany tore up the rules for international conduct drawn up at Versailles and confirmed again in the Washington system in the Pacific and the Locarno system in Europe. They were pushed in that direction by militant nationalists at home, and by what they perceived as economic necessity in the impoverished, protectionist world after the slump; but they were also pulled by opportunity. Japan was faced with a China in chaos, an isolationist America and enfeebled European empires with tiny Far Eastern forces. Mussolini hesitantly, then with growing confidence, exploited the weaknesses of the Western position in the Mediterranean and Middle East. Finally Germany began after 1936, with almost no resistance, to reassert what many Germans, even non-Nazis, saw as her natural right to establish domination in Central and Eastern Europe. The effect of all this was cumulative; there was no decisive turning point. By 1938 there was no system of security that could be made to work in any of these three areas. More rearmament would have made the weak Western position a little less explicit, but could hardly have postponed the reality of the shift in the balance of power for very long. Both powers lacked the resources to rearm to the necessary extent to guarantee a real and lasting security. To assume otherwise is wishful thinking. Even a rearmament effort on the greatest scale would not have sufficed to keep every revisionist power at bay, including, eventually, the Soviet Union; and it would have produced economic and political chaos at home. As it was, the effort produced in 1938 and 1939 was a once-and-for-all drive to produce the short-term military means of defending not only the far-flung empires but the mother countries as well and the economic cost was prodigious.

There were already signs of severe economic strain in 1939. By 1941 Britain was virtually bankrupt, dependent on the financial goodwill of the United States to continue the war. France was defeated and declined into the violent political conflicts that had threatened to break to the surface throughout the last years of peace.

It is easier to date the point at which the aggressor powers sensed a real opportunity to embark seriously on the New Order. That year was 1938. Japanese leaders narrowed down the policy choices of the empire by declaring a New Order in Asia and fighting their way across eastern China to achieve it. In Europe the Western powers failed to stop German advances in Austria or Czechoslovakia, and convinced Hitler that they would give him the free hand he wanted in the east. Whether he later struck westwards or eastwards depended on circumstances; but the expansion into Central and Eastern Europe and the drive for giant military power were both confirmed in 1938. There was another factor of great importance for Hitler: the neutrality of the United States and the isolation of the Soviet Union. Both Japan and Germany were aware of these two potentially dangerous colossi which flanked them both. The issue all three aggressor states faced was whether they could exploit a temporary or regional advantage in time before the declining global powers were replaced by two new ones.

The war with Poland was a direct consequence of the German decision, Hitler's decision, to press on with creating the resource base for the bid for world power. German demands might not have led to war, and German leaders assumed that if the great Western empires would not face up to them, Poland certainly would not. When Poland resisted, Hitler opted for a quick military campaign to annihilate Polish resistance, the last barrier to German domination of the whole European area from the Baltic to the Aegean. On his southern flank Mussolini flexed muscles of his own. Albania was occupied in April 1939; arrogant demands for the 'return' of Corsica, Savoy and Tunisia were directed at France. Franco's victory in Spain in May 1939 did not bring Hitler an ally, but at the least a benevolent neutral. The only problem was the Soviet Union, and here Hitler benefited from the impact that Western diplomacy in 1938 had on Soviet strategy. Soviet leaders up to 1938 still held both the Western empires in some respect internationally. But the effect of Munich, when the Soviet Union was deliberately ignored by the Western states as a serious factor, drove Soviet leaders away from the existing order and back to the idea of revision. The Nazi–Soviet Pact was a recognition by Soviet leaders too that there had occurred a fundamental shift in the balance of power in the late 1930s, and it was no longer in their interest to support the West if that meant facing a hostile Germany. Stalin told Churchill in 1942: 'We formed the impression that the British and French Governments were not resolved to go to war if Poland were attacked, but that they hoped the diplomatic line-up of Britain, France and Russia would deter Hitler. We were sure it would not.'[22] Stalin had no master-plan in 1939, but he could see that the old equilibrium could not be sustained without war and the self-interest of the Soviet state would not be promoted by involvement.

For France and Britain the only way to reverse the sharp decline in their international position after 1938 was to find allies willing to uphold the existing system without asking questions. This was always a forlorn expectation. They were the main beneficiaries of the status quo. They could hardly expect other powers to share that interest with enthusiasm. There was very little that they could offer; appeasement had very clear limits. British leaders deeply distrusted both the United States and the Soviet Union. 'Pray God', wrote Cadogan, Permanent Under-Secretary at the British Foreign Office, 'that we shall never have to depend on the Soviet, or Poland, or on the United States.'[23] The price of American help was known to be major concessions on colonies and tariffs which the British government could not tolerate; Soviet help involved the risk of giving Stalin the free hand in Eastern Europe that they were trying to deny to Germany. Close dependence on either power would not necessarily prevent the decline in British and French security or prestige, which was the only real justification for an alliance in the first place. In the end the matter was decided for them. The United States had no intention of entering any foreign alliance; the Soviet Union would do so only on terms unacceptable to the West, and preferred a German alliance. The outcome was a logical one: Britain and France allied with each other.

This was hardly an auspicious marriage, certainly not one strong enough to achieve the ambition Chamberlain stated after Munich, 'to achieve a stabilisation of Europe'.[24] But it was an alliance that made sound sense. Without co-operation the status quo would hardly survive Hitler's next move; it was already a tattered garment by 1939. Both states were rapidly rearming, and though in decline were not negligible military powers. Both enjoyed considerable economic strength, though much more brittle than they pretended. And they enjoyed the temporary benefit that in the absence of any better alternative many smaller powers – the British dominions, Greece, Turkey, Egypt, Belgium, Holland – sought shelter with the West. Both powers were helped in securing international goodwill and popular support at home by the nature of the enemy states. Fascism was for Western populations by 1939 a demonstrably evil cause. The war was not simply one set of self-interested powers against another, but right against might, good against evil. In practice, of course, both the British and French governments pursued the strategy that they judged to be in the interest of the empires they guided. The ideological divide helped to create a greater degree of political unity and enthusiasm for confrontation in the democracies than could possibly have been expected from the evidence of a year before, but the conflict at the end of the 1930s was really about national rivalry and great-power status as much as it was about ideology. It was the threat of German domination, and everything that would flow from that for the political future of the decaying imperial structures, that impelled them, reluctantly, to choose a fight if Hitler insisted on it.

Seen in these terms, 1939 was almost certainly the best moment to fight. There was no ideal time, and both powers would gladly have accepted any solution that would have kept their status and the peace at the same time. But in 1939 the transition was delicately poised. Hitler had embarked on his drive for world power, but was not yet ready to fight his big war. He calculated that the West would back down. The Western powers for their part calculated that on the balance of risks the defence of the old order was worth while. A few more years and it might, they argued, be incapable of serious defence, while the economic power they counted on would have been undermined by high rearmament, and the political consensus at home blown open by the failure to act. The view expressed by the military chiefs was that the Allies should not lose the war, though it might be more difficult to win it. Chamberlain explained to Roosevelt in October 1939 that Britain would not win 'by a complete and spectacular victory, but by convincing the Germans that they cannot win'.[25] These two convictions were the crucial components that made a general war in 1939 impossible to prevent. The Western powers were convinced that the time had come to make a stand in defence of their vital interests and that there was still sufficient strength in the old system to act as a real deterrent. Germany was convinced that the West would not act, and so would not be deterred.

Poland had only an auxiliary role to play in all this. Hitler's war to punish the obstinate Poles was not supposed to turn into general war. Britain and France were not interested in Poland as such, but used the issue as a way to force Hitler to conform to a system that could protect what was still vital in the status quo. It is an obvious but important truth that no established structure of imperial power has ever voluntarily co-operated in its disintegration but has, in the end, fought to reverse its decline. It is a real irony that an Austrian, of all people, should have made the mistake of misjudging the actions of empires in peril.

The immediate outcome of the war was not predictable. Germany found herself without help from Italy or Japan; the military balance slightly favoured the Allies. The United States supplied economic resources to the West; Russia supplied them to Hitler. After the rapid destruction of Polish resistance, Hitler still hoped that the West would sue for peace and accept the shift in the balance. In October 1939 he discussed these prospects with the Swedish explorer Sven Hedin:

> Why do they fight, they have nothing to gain? They have no definite objectives. We want nothing from Great Britain or France. I have not a single aspiration in the west. I want England to retain her Empire and her command of the seas unimpaired. But I must have the continent. A new age is dawning in Europe. England's control over the mainland of Europe has had its day. It is over now.[26]

What Hitler would not admit to himself was that it was precisely to prevent the dawning of the new age that Britain and France had fought in the first place. When it became clear that the West was serious Hitler ordered an immediate attack, beside himself with rage that the West would not see sense. His sceptical generals and early autumn weather prevented a premature offensive. But when German troops did go into action in the spring the outcome was a disaster for the Allied strategy of blockade and defence. The Maginot Line was pierced at its weakest and most unlikely point in the deep wooded gorges of the Ardennes forest. The Line was turned and German forces exploited the high fighting quality of officers and men to achieve a rapid and devastating defeat of French and British armies. In six weeks everything the Allies had staked on the war in September was gone. German hegemony was established and Western decline open for all to see.

The startling victory of 1940 accelerated the building of the Axis New Order, an international structure with different leaders, and new rules of conduct, dominated by self-consciously 'new' and aggressive states, imbued with the values of a post-liberal age. Germany occupied and controlled by the summer of 1940 nine European states that had been independent before 1938. German victory brought Italy and Japan to the point where their revisionism could be embarked on with little risk. But more significantly from

Hitler's point of view the Soviet Union also used the defeat of the West to share uninvited in the restructuring. This was no part of Hitler's agreement with Stalin. In September 1940 Germany signed a Tripartite Pact with Japan and Italy which announced their joint determination to seize the opportunity presented in 1940 to build a different world order: 'it is their prime purpose', ran the agreement, 'to establish a new order of things,'[27] Germany and Italy in Europe and the Mediterranean, Japan in the Far East. For a period of twelve months the gap Hitler had perceived between the failing Western empires and the rise of the superpowers opened up. The bid for the Axis order reached its peak in 1941. The United States was rapidly rearming but was not ready to declare war. Britain was, Hitler thought, effectively finished and could be brought to surrender at German leisure. The only hope Britain had was the Soviet Union. In the summer of 1940 Hitler recognised that his bid for world power, which had come sooner than he expected and by a rather different route, would sooner or later be obstructed by Soviet power. Defeat of the Soviet Union in a great military blow would free vast resources in Eurasia to fuel the German war effort and would make the Continent impregnable. Then Germany could produce the aircraft and naval power to challenge the Anglo-Saxons. In November 1940, when it was clear enough that Stalin could not easily be restrained in Eastern Europe without conflict, Hitler finalised his plan of attack.

By December 1941 the bid for world power was closer than ever. The Soviet Union was thought to be on the point of defeat. The British were facing mounting losses in the Atlantic sea-lanes which brought them vital food and supplies. Japan attacked and destroyed the American Pacific Fleet at Pearl Harbor. Hitler was right that an acute moment of crisis did occur in the years 1939–41 in which the old order collapsed in ruins. But he always underestimated American and Soviet power. This was a curious misjudgement, since Hitler at other times was all too aware of the rise of a new Soviet threat and the great potential of American economic strength. He also underestimated the British will-to-resist. Britain had the advantages of considerable international political skill, an unexpectedly united empire, and sufficient military resources and strategic grasp to avoid defeat until powerful allies could be secured. None of this could be taken for granted on Britain's part; and if Soviet forces had sued for an armistice in December 1941 little could have saved Britain in the long run. British leaders knew well that things would never be the same again after the defeat of Hitler, but by then it was simply a question of survival at all costs, not any longer of saving British world power.

After 1941 United States power transformed the prospects for both sides. Roosevelt was already committed to the survival of democracy, to 'the kind of world we want to live in'. Some of his colleagues saw more clearly what American entry would mean in the long run: 'the only possible effect of this war', wrote Adolf Berle in his diary, 'would be that the United States would emerge with an imperial power greater than the world has ever seen.'[28] The injection of relatively modest forces into the Pacific and North Africa was sufficient to secure both theatres for the Western Allies. The American plans for invasion of Europe and American air power ended any real hope of the New Order surviving to argue about the post-war world with the enemy. Soviet military strength proved just enough to blunt the operationally skilled and technically advanced German armies. What German forces lacked everywhere was military equipment in sufficient quantities to exploit that operational competence to the full, and this deficiency was largely due to the Allied decision to declare war in 1939, and not when Hitler wanted it in 1943–5. By comparison Italian and Japanese ambitions were always more modest and less likely of success divorced from German triumphs. Italy surrendered in 1943; Japan survived only two years longer because of the British and American priority in the European theatre. With the final defeat of Japan in August 1945 the brief Axis order, which grew by opportunism out of the crisis of the old, was over. There were few mourners.

As the German New Order dissolved around him Hitler saw plainly where the reality of the new power constellation lay:

> After a collapse of the Reich, and until the arrival of nationalist striving in Asia, in Africa and perhaps even in Latin America, there will now only be two powers in the world: the United States and Soviet Russia. Through the laws of history and geographical position these two colossi are destined to measure each other's strength either in the military sphere, or in the sphere of economics and ideology.[29]

Within the space of six years the two great powers that had stood aside from the conflict over Poland, anxious for their different reasons to avoid war, found themselves slowly but surely defining a new world order of their own.

APPENDIX

COMPARATIVE MILITARY EXPENDITURE AND MILITARY STRENGTH

The following figures on government military expenditure for the period 1931–40 are expressed in the different national currencies. The value of military expenditure is thus not directly comparable. What can be compared is the scale and pace of change of the military effort. Military expenditure is only a very rough guide to rearmament levels, partly because different countries classified military spending in different ways, partly because military outlays in some countries represented the building up of the military infrastructure as well as arms and equipment (for example in the Soviet Union or Germany), and in others was primarily expenditure on weapons, training and military expansion on top of an existing infrastructure. These differences must be borne in mind when German and Soviet spending is compared with that of Britain and France, which were both more heavily armed and militarily prepared in the early 1930s. (See Table I.)

The same care must be taken with comparative air and naval strength. Most navies had a large number of over-age, obsolete ships on their naval strength in the early to mid-1930s. Many of these were taken out of commission during the period of naval rearmament and were replaced by more modern vessels. In 1932, for example, out of the 267 destroyers in the US navy only 69 were not over-age or obsolescent. A great number were removed from service, explaining the apparent decline in the size of the US destroyer force over the course of the 1930s. Aircraft figures also disguise the major differences between the powers in the technical standards and performance of their aircraft. Up to 1937 German aircraft production was concentrated on trainer aircraft (58 per cent of all production) and only a fraction (18 per cent) were bomber and fighter aircraft. British and French production was lower, but had a higher combat-aircraft ratio. The quality of aircraft also varied widely, German and British fighter aircraft by the late 1930s leading the field, with France rapidly catching up, and the other powers several years behind. German medium bombers were of very high quality, but the United States by 1940 was the closest to producing, in the B-17, the best multi-engined bomber. The figures for both air and naval strength

Table I
Government Expenditure for Defence in the Major Powers, 1931–40

Fiscal year[a]	*Britain (m.£ sterling)*	*France (m. francs)*	*Germany (m. RM)*	*Italy (m. lire)*	*USSR (m. roubles)*	*USA (m. dollars)*	*Japan (m. yen)*
1931	107.5	13,800	610	4,890	1,404	733	434
1932	103.3	13,800	720	4,880	1,412	703	733
1933	107.6	13,400	740	4,300	1,547	648	873
1934	113.9	11,600	4,190	5,590	5,000	540	955
1935	137.0	12,800	5,480	12,624	8,200	711	1,032
1936	185.9	15,100	10,270	16,573	14,800	914	1,105
1937	256.3	21,500	10,960	13,272	17,480	937	3,953
1938	397.4	29,100	17,240	15,028	27,044	1,030	6,097
1939	719.0	93,600	38,000	27,732	40,885	1,075	6,417
1940	2,600.0	–	55,900	58,899	56,800	1,498	7,266

Note
(a) The US fiscal year ran from 1 July to 30 June.

Sources
R. Shay, *British Rearmament in the Thirties* (Princeton, 1977); R. Frankenstein, *Le Prix du réarmament français, 1935–39* (Paris, 1982); W. Boelcke, *Die Kosten von Hitlers Krieg* (Paderborn, 1985); M. Knox, *Mussolini Unleashed 1939–1941* (Cambridge, 1982); J. B. Cohen, *Japan's Economy in War and Reconstruction* (1949); League of Nations, *Armaments Year Book* (Geneva, annually 1932–9); *Historical Statistics of the United States from Colonial Times to 1957* (Washington DC, 1960).

give an approximate indication of the size of the rearmament effort and the alignment of forces in 1939 (Tables II and III), but again the figures are not directly comparable.

Table II
Military Aircraft Production of the Major Powers 1935–41

	Great Britain	*France*	*Germany*	*Italy*[a]	*USSR*	*USA*	*Japan*
1935	1,440	785	3,183[c]		2,529	459	952
1936	1,877	890	5,112		3,770	1,141	1,181
1937	2,153	743	5,606		4,435	949	1,511
1938	2,825	1,382	5,235	1,850	5,467	1,800	3,201
1939	7,940	3,163	8,295	1,800	10,382	5,846	4,467
1940	15,049	2,441[b]	10,247	1,800	10,565	12,804	4,768
1941	20,094	–	11,776	2,400	15,735	26,277	5,088

Notes

(a) There are no reliable figures for Italian production. The figures for 1938–41 are estimates.

(b) January–June only.

(c) A high proportion of the aircraft in 1935–8 were trainers. Combat-aircraft figures are: 1935, 1,823; 1936, 1,530; 1937, 2,651; 1938, 3,350; 1939, 4,733.

Sources

R. J. Overy, *The Air War 1939–1945* (London, 1980); M. Harrison, *Soviet Planning in Peace and War 1938–1945* (Cambridge, 1985).

Table III
The Naval Strength of the Major Powers 1932, 1936 and 1939

		Battleships	*Aircraft-Carriers*	*Cruisers*	*Destroyers*	*Submarines*	*Total*
1932	Britain	15	6	46	148	55	270
	France	9	1	21	70	84	196
	Germany	5	–	8	28	–	41
	Italy	4	1	20	114	53	192
	USSR	4	–	7	29	14	54
	Japan	10	3	34	98	57	202
	USA	15	4	28	267	84	398
1936	Britain	15	6	48	163	52	284
	France	9	1	14	60	72	156
	Germany	6	–	6	19	20	51
	Italy	4	1	23	103	62	193
	USSR	4	–	7	35	26	72
	Japan	10	4	40	112	64	230
	USA	15	4	25	199	88	331
1939	Britain	15	6	54	145	54	274
	France	7	1	18	72	80	178
	Germany	5	–	8	50	57	120
	Italy	2	–	22	126	105	255
	USSR	3	1	7	51	146	208
	Japan	10	6	37	122	62	237
	USA	15	5	37	221	94	372

Sources
League of Nations, *Armaments Year Book* (Geneva, annually 1932–40); N. Gibbs, *Grand Strategy*, vol. I: *Rearmament Policy* (London, 1976).

REFERENCES

Preface

1 Fritz Fischer, *Krieg der Illusionen* (Düsseldorf, 1969), translated as *War of Illusions: German Policies from 1911 to 1914* (London, 1975).

Introduction: 'Who Will Die for Danzig?'

1 H. S. Levine, *Hitler's Free City: A History of the Nazi Party in Danzig 1925–1939* (Chicago, 1973), pp. 6–9.
2 C. M. Kimmich, *The Free City: Danzig and German Foreign Policy 1919–1934* (New Haven, 1968), pp. 3–9.
3 Ibid., pp. 11, 32–4.
4 J. Beck, *Dernier Rapport: politique polonaise 1926–1939* (Paris, 1955), p. 187.
5 J. Hochman, *The Soviet Union and the Failure of Collective Security 1934–1938* (Ithaca, NY, 1984), p. 165.
6 M. Laffan, 'Weimar and Versailles: German Foreign Policy 1919–1933', in M. Laffan (ed.), *The Burden of German History 1919–1945* (London, 1988), p. 86.
7 R. Leslie et al., *History of Poland since 1863* (Cambridge, 1980), pp. 193–5; J. Karski, *The Great Powers and Poland* (Lanham, Maryland, 1985), pp. 231–4.
8 F. R. Nicosia, *The Third Reich and the Palestine Question* (London, 1985), p. 165.
9 A. Polonsky, *Politics in Independent Poland 1921–1939* (Oxford, 1972), p. 448.
10 Leslie, pp. 203–4; Karski, pp. 322–3.
11 Karski, pp. 241–2.
12 Ibid., p. 243.
13 Beck, p. 182.
14 Karski, p. 244.
15 'Weisung Adolf Hitlers an die Wehrmacht von 3 April 1939 (Fall Weiss)' in *Ursachen und Folgen von deutschen Zusammenbruch 1918 und 1945*, vol. 13 (Berlin, 1967), p. 212.
16 R. Young, *In Command of France: French Foreign Policy and Military Planning 1933–1940* (Cambridge, Mass., 1978), p. 242.
17 O. H. Bullitt (ed.), *For the President. Personal and Secret. Correspondence between Franklin D. Roosevelt and William C. Bullitt* (London, 1973), entry for 26 September 1938, p. 291.
18 Karski, pp. 236–7; W. Jedrzejewicz (ed.), *Diplomat in Paris 1936–1939: Papers and Memoirs of Juliusz Lukasiewicz* (New York, 1970), p. 176; E. Raczynski, *In Allied London* (London, 1962), p. 29.
19 B. B. Budurowycz, *Polish–Soviet Relations 1932–1939* (New York, 1963), pp. 127–30.

20 Polonsky, p. 477.
21 Levine, pp. 121–5, 127–38, 152.
22 G. Gafencu, *The Last Days of Europe: A Diplomatic Journey* (London, 1947), p. 28.
23 Beck, p. 184; 'The Biddle Report, Oct. 1939', in P. V. Cannistraro, E. D. Wynot and T. P. Kovaleff (eds), *Poland and the Coming of the Second World War: The Diplomatic Papers of J. Drexel Biddle Jr, 1937–1939* (Columbus, Ohio, 1976), p. 53.
24 J. E. Davies, *Mission in Moscow* (London, 1942), Journal 26 May 1939, p. 293; A. Prazmowska, *Britain, Poland and the Eastern Front, 1939* (Cambridge, 1987), p. 48.
25 Karski, p. 247.
26 *Biddle Papers*, pp. 48–53.
27 Beck, pp. 183–4.
28 W. Shirer, *Berlin Diary* (London, 1941), entry for 13 August 1939, p. 143.
29 Polonsky, p. 465; Beck, p. 184.
30 Gafencu, p. 45; Raczinski, p. 12; Jedrzejewicz, pp. 180–7.
31 Prazmowska, pp. 94–5; Karski, p. 330.
32 S. Newman, *March 1939: The British Guarantee to Poland* (Oxford, 1976), p. 152.
33 Karski, p. 333.
34 R. Debecki, *Foreign Policy of Poland 1919–1939* (London, 1963), p. 144; Prazmowska, pp. 186–7.
35 *Documents on British Foreign Policy*, 3rd Ser., vol. 7, p. 198.
36 Beck, p. 193; P. Reynaud, *In the Thick of the Fight 1930–1945* (London, 1955), p. 53.
37 R. Macleod (ed.), *The Ironside Diaries 1937–1940* (London, 1962), pp. 81–2.
38 *Documents on German Foreign Policy*, Ser. D, vol. 6, 'Führer's conference with the heads of the armed forces, 23rd May 1939', pp. 575–6.
39 Karski, p. 245.
40 Shirer, entry for 11 August 1939, p. 141.
41 *Biddle Papers*, p. 63.
42 G. Weinberg, *World in the Balance* (Hanover, New England, 1981), p. 43.
43 Details in Levine, pp. 152–3.

Chapter One: Germany

Epigraph: F. von Bernhardi, *Germany and the Next War* (London, 1914), p. 21.; H. Rauschning, *Hitler Speaks* (London, 1939) p. 48.

1 *Letters of Thomas Mann 1889–1955* (London, 1970), vol. 1, letter to Gustav Blume, 5 July 1919, p. 97.
2 O. Friedrichs, *Before the Deluge* (London, 1974), pp. 53–4.
3 M. Laffan, 'Weimar and Versailles: German Foreign Policy 1918–1933', in M. Laffan (ed.), *The Burden of German History 1919–1945* (London, 1988), p. 85.
4 Ibid., p. 86.
5 A. Kolnai, *The War Against the West* (London, 1938), pp. 514, 525–6; G. Mosse, *The Crisis of German Ideology* (London, 1964), pp. 281–2.
6 R. J. Overy, *The Nazi Economic Recovery 1932–1938* (London, 1982), pp. 13–27;

D. Petzina, 'The Extent and Causes of Unemployment in the Weimar Republic', in P. Stachura (ed.), *Unemployment and the Great Depression in Weimar Germany* (London, 1986), pp. 29–48.
7 A. Speer, *Inside the Third Reich* (London, 1970), p. 18.
8 F. von Papen, *Memoirs* (London, 1952), p. 251.
9 A. Crozier, 'Imperial Decline and the Colonial Question in Anglo-German Relations 1919–1939', *European Studies Review*, 11 (1981), p. 224.
10 J. Killen, *The Luftwaffe: A History* (London, 1967), pp. 72–3.
11 Speer, p. 72.
12 M. Kater, 'Hitler in a Social Context', *Central European History*, 14 (1981), pp. 247, 250–1; H. Hoffmann, *Hitler Was My Friend* (London, 1955), pp. 187–96.
13 W. Schellenberg, *The Schellenberg Memoirs* (London, 1956), p. 111.
14 E. W. D. Tennant, *True Account* (London, 1957), p. 226.
15 E. O. Lorimer, *What Hitler Wants* (London, 1939), pp. 90–1; H. Rauschning, *Hitler Speaks* (London, 1939), p. 128.
16 M. Michaelis, 'World Power Status or World Dominion?', *Historical Journal*, 15 (1972), p. 348.
17 Rauschning, pp. 126–7.
18 G. Stoakes, '"More Unfinished Business?" Some Comments on the Evolution of the Nazi Foreign Policy Programme 1918–1924', *European Studies Review*, 8 (1978), p. 431; Rauschning, p. 137.
19 J. Thies, 'Hitler's European Building Programme', *Journal of Contemporary History*, 13 (1978).
20 E. Jäckel, 'Hitler's Foreign Policy Aims', in H. A. Turner (ed.), *Nazism and the Third Reich* (New York, 1972), p. 204.
21 Rauschning, p. 38.
22 General W. Groener, 'Bedeutung der modernen Wirtschaft für die Strategie', reprinted in *Zeitschrift für Geschichtswissenschaft*, 19 (1971), pp. 1167–77; B. A. Carroll, *Design for Total War: Arms and Economics in the Third Reich* (The Hague, 1968), p. 40.
23 K.-H. Minuth (ed.), *Akten der Reichskanzlei: Regierung Hitler 1933–1938. Band I* (Boppard a R., 1983), p. 62.
24 R. J. Overy, 'German Air Strength 1933–1939: A Note', *Historical Journal*, 27 (1984), p. 469.
25 W. Treue, 'Der Denkschrift Hitlers über die Aufgaben eines Vierjahresplan', *Vierteljahrshefte für Zeitgeschichte*, 3 (1954), pp. 184–91.
26 R. J. Overy, *Goering: The 'Iron Man'* (London, 1984), pp. 46–7.
27 M. Riedel, *Eisen und Kohle für das Deutsche Reich* (Göttingen, 1973); D. Petzina, *Autarkiepolitik im Dritten Reich* (Stuttgart, 1968).
28 F. Leith Ross, *Money Talks: Fifty Years of International Finance* (London, 1968), p. 255.
29 W. Shirer, *Berlin Diary* (London, 1941), p. 74.
30 G. Weinberg, *World in the Balance* (1981), p. 63.
31 J. P. Fox, *Germany and the Far Eastern Crisis 1931–1938* (Oxford, 1982), p. 190.
32 Ibid., p. 200.
33 Jäckel, p. 213.
34 Rauschning, p. 127.
35 Jäckel, p. 213.

36 Christie Papers, Churchill College, Cambridge, 180 1/5, Notes from a conversation with Göring, 3 February 1937, p. 52.
37 Lord Gladwyn, *The Memoirs of Lord Gladwyn* (London, 1972), p. 66. The remarks were made to Lady Stanley.
38 The Earl of Halifax, *Fulness of Days* (London, 1957), p. 189.
39 Minutes of the conference in the Reich Chancellery, 5 November 1937, *Documents on German Foreign Policy*, Ser. D., vol. 1, pp. 29–39 (cited *DGFP*). The most recent discussion of the 'Hossbach Memorandum' meeting is in B.-J. Wendt, *Grossdeutschland: Aussenpolitik und Kriegsvorbereitung des Hitler-Regimes* (Munich, 1987) pp. 11–37.
40 E. Frölich (ed.), *Die Tagebücher von Joseph Goebbels; sämtliche Fragmente* (Munich, 1987), part I, vol. 3, p. 55.
41 *DGFP*, ser. D, vol. 2, p. 357, 'Directive for Operation "Green" from Hitler to his Commanders-in-Chief, 30th May, 1938'; p. 473, 'General strategic directive by the General Staff, June 18th 1938'.
42 J. Lipski, *Diplomat in Berlin 1933–1939*, ed. W. Jedrzejewicz (New York, 1968), Lipski to Beck 19 June 1938, p. 369.
43 J. von Herwarth, *Against Two Evils* (London, 1981), pp. 122–3; Lipski, pp. 374–5, 377–9.
44 H. Gisevius, *To the Bitter End* (London, 1948), p. 323.
45 Ibid., p. 325.
46 G. Engel, *Heeresadjutant bei Hitler 1938–1943: Aufzeichnungen des Majors Engel* (Stuttgart, 1974), entry for 28 September 1938, p. 39.
47 I. Kirkpatrick, *The Inner Circle* (London, 1959), p. 135.
48 Speer, p. 111.
49 W. Michalka, 'Conflicts within the German Leadership on the Objectives and Tactics of German Foreign Policy 1933–1939', in W. Mommsen and L. Kettenacker (eds), *The Fascist Challenge and the Policy of Appeasement* (London, 1983), p. 57; Conference between Göring and Durčansky, October 1938, *DGFP*, Ser. D, vol. 4, pp. 82–3.
50 *Hitlers politisches Testament: die Bormann Diktate vom Februar und April 1945* (Hamburg, 1981), pp. 100–1, entry for 21 February 1945.
51 Speer, p. 107.
52 Overy, *Goering*, pp. 84–7; J. Dülffer, *Weimar, Hitler und die Marine: Reichspolitik und Flottenbau 1920–1939* (Düsseldorf, 1973), pp. 471 ff.
53 Gisevius, p. 325.
54 J. Heyl, 'The Construction of the *Westwall* 1938: An Example of National Socialist Policy-making', *Central European History*, 14 (1981), p. 77; Overy, *Goering*, p. 84.
55 Herwarth, p. 134.
56 Goebbels, *Tagebücher*, vol. 3, p. 595, entry for 15 April 1939; Shirer, p. 149, entry for 26 August 1939.
57 J. de Courcy, *Searchlight on Europe* (London, 1940), pp. 109–14.
58 D. Eichholtz and W. Schumann (eds), *Anatomie des Krieges* (Berlin, 1969), doc. 88, Bericht von Wilhelm Keppler über die Rede Adolf Hitlers am 8 März 1939, p. 204.
59 On Czech supplies W. Deist, *The Wehrmacht and German Rearmament* (London, 1981), pp. 88–9; Goebbels, *Tagebücher*, vol. 3, p. 577, entry for 16 March 1939.

60 Herwarth, p. 170.
61 Engel, p. 40.
62 Rauschning, p. 123.
63 Minutes of a conference on 23 May 1939, *DGFP*, Ser. D., vol. 6, pp. 575–6.
64 Ibid., pp. 576–80.
65 M. Muggeridge (ed.), *Ciano's Diplomatic Papers* (London, 1948), conversation with the Reich Foreign Minister, 6 May 1939, p. 284; First Conversation with the Führer, 12 August 1939, pp. 201–2.
66 Führer's speech to the Commanders-in-Chief, 22 August 1939, in International Military Tribunal, *Nazi Conspiracy and Aggression* (Washington, 1947), vol. 3, doc. 789-PS, p. 582 (cited as *NCA*).
67 Carroll, p. 191.
68 Tennant, p. 215.
69 G. Craig and F. Gilbert (eds), *The Diplomats 1919–1939* (Princeton, 1953), pp. 482–3; see too E. von Weizsäcker, *Memoirs* (London, 1951), p. 203.
70 Tennant, p. 222.
71 *NCA*, vol. 3, p. 584; S. Friedländer, *Prelude to Downfall* (London, 1967), pp. 15–25.
72 *NCA*, vol. 3, p. 585; O. Dietrich, *The Hitler I Knew* (London, 1955), p. 42; Heyl, pp. 64–77.
73 Tennant, p. 222.
74 Rauschning, p. 136; A. Ulam, *Expansion and Coexistence: A History of Soviet Foreign Policy 1917–1967* (London, 1968), p. 272.
75 Speer, p. 161.
76 Engel, entry for 22 August 1939, p. 58.
77 Ibid., entry for 24 August 1939, p. 59; on the mobilisation order, Imperial War Museum, EDS, Mi 14/328(d), OKW minutes of meeting of war economy inspectors, 21 August 1939.
78 Engel, entry for 25 August 1939, p. 59; P. Schmidt, *Hitler's Interpreter* (London, 1951), p. 15.
79 Overy, *Goering*, p. 92; B. Dahlerus, *The Last Attempt* (London, 1948).
80 *NCA*, vol. 3, p. 584; Speer, p. 162.
81 Dietrich, pp. 43–4.
82 Schmidt, pp. 157–8.
83 L. E. Hill (ed.), *Die Weizsäcker-Papiere 1933–1950* (Frankfurt a M., 1974), entry for 7 September 1939, p. 164; Dietrich, p. 47; Speer, p. 165.
84 Dietrich, p. 44.
85 Gisevius, p. 372.
86 Papen, p. 453.

Chapter Two: Great Britain

Epigraph: R. Taylor, *Lord Salisbury* (London, 1975), p. 133.
K. Feiling, *The Life of Neville Chamberlain* (London, 1946).

1 R. Tamchina, 'In Search of Common Causes: The Imperial Conference of 1937', *Journal of Imperial and Commonwealth History*, 1 (1972), p. 100; Royal Institute of International Affairs, *Survey of International Affairs, 1937* (Oxford, 1938), p. 1.

2 K. Feiling, *The Life of Neville Chamberlain* (London, 1946), p. 336.
3 P. Kennedy, 'The Tradition of Appeasement in British Foreign Policy 1865–1939', *British Journal of International Studies*, 2 (1976), p. 205.
4 R. Douglas, 'Chamberlain and Appeasement', in W. Mommsen and L. Kettenacker (eds), *The Fascist Challenge and the Policy of Appeasement* (London, 1983), p. 79.
5 S. Baldwin, *On England* (London, 1926), speech in the House of Commons, 23 July 1923, p. 234.
6 A. Crozier, 'Imperial Decline and the Colonial Question in Anglo-German Relations 1919–1939', *European Studies Review*, 11 (1981), pp. 208, 225.
7 W. D. Gruner, 'The British Political, Social and Economic System and the Decision for Peace or War', *British Journal of International Studies*, 6 (1980), p. 212.
8 M. Howard, *The Continental Commitment* (London, 1972), p. 95.
9 B. Powers, *Strategy Without Slide-Rule: British Air Strategy 1914–1918* (London, 1976), pp. 170–3.
10 F. Coghlan, 'Armaments, Economic Policy and Appeasement: Background to British Foreign Policy 1931–7', *History*, 57 (1972), p. 207.
11 L. R. Pratt, *East of Malta, West of Suez: Britain's Mediterranean Crisis 1936–1939* (Cambridge, 1975), p. 5
12 G. Schmidt, 'The Domestic Background to British Appeasement Policy', in Mommsen and Kettenacker, p. 121.
13 D. C. Watt, *Too Serious a Business* (London, 1975), p. 89.
14 Schmidt, in Mommsen and Kettenacker, p. 119.
15 N. Forbes, 'London Banks, the German Standstill Agreements, and "Economic Appeasement" in the 1930s', *Economic History Review*, 2nd Ser., 40 (1987), pp. 580–5.
16 L. Fuchser, *Neville Chamberlain and Appeasement* (New York, 1982), p. 35.
17 Pratt, p. 3.
18 D. Dilks, 'The Unnecessary War? Military Advice and Foreign Policy in Great Britain 1931–1939', in A. Preston (ed.), *General Staffs and Diplomacy before the Second World War* (London, 1978), p. 115.
19 Pratt, p. 4.
20 Ibid., p. 10.
21 J. Dunbabin, 'The British Military Establishment and the Policy of Appeasement', in Mommsen and Kettenacker, p. 177.
22 W. R. Louis, *British Strategy in the Far East 1919–1939* (Oxford, 1971), pp. 205, 235.
23 Crozier, p. 225.
24 A. Parker, 'British Rearmament 1936–39: Treasury, Trade Unions and Skilled Labour', *English Historical Review*, 96 (1981); G. Peden, *British Rearmament and the Treasury 1932–1939* (Edinburgh, 1979).
25 G. C. Peden, 'Keynes, the Economics of Rearmament and Appeasement', in Mommsen and Kettenacker, p. 153.
26 R. Shay, *British Rearmament in the Thirties* (Princeton, 1977), p. 159.
27 Ibid., p. 85.
28 New Fabian Research Bureau, *The Road to War, Being an Analysis of the National Government's Foreign Policy* (London, 1937), pp. 96, 148; Shay, pp. 85–6.

29 Schmidt, in Mommsen and Kettenacker, p. 103.
30 G. C. Peden, 'Sir Warren Fisher and British Rearmament against Germany', *English Historical Review*, 94 (1979), p. 43.
31 Feiling, pp. 347, 350.
32 J. Hermann, 'Soviet Peace Efforts on the Eve of World War II', *Journal of Contemporary History*, 15 (1980), p. 585.
33 Fuchser, p. 34; *Documents on International Affairs 1937* (Oxford, 1938), Chamberlain's speech in the House of Commons, 21 December 1937, pp. 73, 77.
34 Ibid., Chamberlain in the House of Commons, 21 October 1937, p. 58.
35 Ibid., Speech by Chamberlain at Edinburgh, 12 November 1937, p. 72.
36 R. Ovendale, *'Appeasement' and the English-Speaking World 1937–1939* (Cardiff, 1975), p. 36.
37 Fuchser, p. 32.
38 Feiling, p. 252.
39 N. Chamberlain, *The Struggle for Peace* (London, 1939), National Broadcast, 27 September 1938, p. 276.
40 Pratt, pp. 102–3.
41 A. Parker, 'The Pound Sterling, the American Treasury and British Preparations for War', *English Historical Review*, 98 (1983), pp. 261–70.
42 S. Newman, *March 1939: The British Guarantee to Poland* (Oxford, 1976), p. 41.
43 Ibid., pp. 28–9.
44 Crozier, p. 231.
45 A. Crozier, *Appeasement and Germany's Last Bid for Colonies* (London, 1988) pp. 239–40.
46 He was referring to his period of office as Viceroy of India.
47 The Earl of Halifax, *Fulness of Days* (London, 1957), p. 189.
48 Fuchser, p. 112.
49 Viscount Simon, *Retrospect* (London, 1952), p. 240; Howard, p. 121.
50 Newman, pp. 33–4.
51 Dilks, p. 124.
52 H. Aulach, 'Britain and the Sudeten Issue, 1938: The Evolution of a Policy', *Journal of Contemporary History*, 18 (1983), p. 246.
53 Simon, p. 244.
54 Feiling, pp. 366–8.
55 Aulach, p. 251.
56 Simon, p. 249.
57 S. Roskill, *Hankey: Man of Secrets*, vol. 3: *1931–1963* (London, 1974), p. 386; Simon, p. 249.
58 D. C. Watt, *Succeeding John Bull: America in Britain's Place* (Cambridge, 1984), pp. 80–1.
59 B. Bond (ed.), *Chief of Staff: The Diaries of Lieutenant-General Sir Henry Pownall*, vol. 1: *1933–1940* (London, 1972), p. 161, entry for 25 September 1938.
60 R. A. Butler, *The Art of the Possible: The Memoirs of Lord Butler* (London, 1971), p. 63; Dunbabin, in Mommsen and Kettenacker, p. 181.
61 M. Gilbert, *Winston S. Churchill*, vol. 5: *1922–1939* (London, 1976), pp. 996–1001.
62 P. Williams, *Hugh Gaitskell* (Oxford, 1982), p. 85.
63 D. C. Watt, *Personalities and Policies* (London, 1965), Essay 8, 'The

Influence of the Commonwealth on British Foreign Policy: The Case of the Munich Crisis', pp. 169–73.
64 Dilks, p. 125.
65 Ovendale, p. 316.
66 Shay, p. 233.
67 *Pownall Diaries*, entries for 21 November, 26 December 1938, pp. 171, 175; Roskill, p. 394.
68 A. Maurois, *Memoirs 1885–1967* (London, 1970), p. 201.
69 M. Muggeridge (ed.), *Ciano's Diary 1939–1943* (London, 1947), entry for 11 January 1939, p. 10.
70 Newman, p. 43.
71 A. P. Young, *The 'X' Documents* (London, 1974), pp. 78–82, 'Conversation with Carl Goerdeler Sept. 11th 1938', doc. 2.
72 F. H. Hinsley, *British Intelligence in the Second World War* (London, 1979), vol. 1, p. 69.
73 D. Reynolds, *The Creation of the Anglo-American Alliance 1937–1941* (London, 1981), p. 40.
74 Ibid., p. 48.
75 Public Record Office (PRO) AIR9/105, Chief of Staff, 'British Strategical Memorandum, Mar. 20th 1939', pp. 6–7.
76 D. C. Watt, 'British Domestic Politics and the Onset of War', in Comité d'Histoire de la 2ème Guerre Mondiale, *Les relations franco-brittaniques de 1935 à 1939* (Paris, 1975), pp. 257–8.
77 Butler, p. 77.
78 *Documents Concerning German–Polish relations*, Cmd 6106 (London, 1939), Speech by the Prime Minister at Birmingham, 17 March 1939, pp. 5–10.
79 Newman, pp. 152–3.
80 S. Hedin, *German Diary* (Dublin, 1951), p. 32.
81 Watt, *John Bull*, p. 85.
82 S. Aster, *1939: The Making of the Second World War* (London, 1973), pp. 260–1.
83 Ibid., p. 261.
84 *Pownall Diaries*, p. 219. On the Anglo-Soviet talks see R. Manne, 'Some British Light on the Nazi–Soviet Pact', *European Studies Review*, 11 (1981); J. Haslam, *The Soviet Union and the Struggle for Collective Security in Europe 1933–1939* (London, 1984), pp. 213–24.
85 Shay, pp. 162–3.
86 Ibid., pp. 276–7.
87 Ibid., p. 280.
88 G. Orwell, *Coming Up for Air* (London, 1939), p. 193.
89 *Pownall Diary*, entry for 29 August 1939, p. 221.
90 Roskill, p. 417.
91 Ovendale, pp. 4, 300–11.
92 Feiling, pp. 416–17.
93 Halifax, p. 210.
94 R. Rhodes James (ed.), *Chips: The Diaries of Sir Henry Channon* (London, 1967), p. 181.
95 Feiling, p. 415.
96 *Documents on International Affairs, 1937*, speech at Edinburgh, p. 72.
97 Harold Nicolson, *Diaries and Letters 1930–1964*, ed. S. Olson (New York,

1980), p. 152, Diary 14 June 1939.
98 Orwell, p. 158.

Chapter Three: France

Epigraph: L. Schwarzschild, World in Trance (London, 1943), p. 256.

1 L. Schwarzschild, *World in Trance* (London, 1943), p. 50.
2 K. M. Wilson (ed.), *George Saunders on Germany 1919–1920* (Leeds, 1987), letter from Saunders to J. Headlam-Morley, 7 April 1919, pp. 24–5.
3 J. Cairns, 'A Nation of Shopkeepers in Search of a Suitable France', *American Historical Review*, 79 (1974), p. 727.
4 Ibid., p. 725.
5 A. Horne, *The French Army and Politics 1870–1970* (London, 1984), p. 45.
6 A. Adamthwaite, *France and the Coming of the Second World War* (London, 1977), pp. 6–8.
7 *The Treaty of Peace, June 28th 1919* (London, 1919), p. 116.
8 Cairns, p. 718.
9 W. Manchester, *The Arms of Krupp* (London, 1968), pp. 368–70.
10 Cairns, pp. 722–3.
11 S. Schuker, *The End of French Predominance in Europe: The Financial Crisis of 1924 and the Adoption of the Dawes Plan* (Chapel Hill, North Carolina, 1976), pp. 388–9.
12 Schwarzschild, p. 164.
13 Public Record Office (PRO), AIR 9/8, Air Ministry memorandum, 2 May 1929, plans for a 'Locarno' war.
14 A. Kemp, *The Maginot Line: Myth and Reality* (London, 1981), pp. 11–21.
15 Ibid., pp. 27–31, 113–14; V. Rowe, *The Great Wall of France: The Triumph of the Maginot Line* (London, 1959), pp. 38, 66–5; R. J. Young, *In Command of France: French Foreign Policy and Military Planning 1933–40* (Cambridge, Mass., 1978), pp. 15–16.
16 R. J. Young, 'La Guerre de longue durée: Some Reflections on French Strategy and Diplomacy in the 1930s', in A. Preston (ed.), *General Staffs and Diplomacy before the Second World War* (London, 1978).
17 T. Kemp, *The French Economy 1913–1939* (London, 1972), pp. 99–145; A. Sauvy, 'The Economic Crisis of the 1930s in France', *Journal of Contemporary History*, 4 (1969), pp. 21–35.
18 M. Adereth, *The French Communist Party: A Critical History 1920–1984* (Manchester, 1984), pp. 60–75.
19 G. Wright, *Rural Revolution in France* (Oxford, 1964), pp. 49–51.
20 R. Rémond, *The Right Wing in France from 1815 to de Gaulle* (Philadelphia, Pennsylvania, 1969), pp. 281–9; R. J. Soucy, 'France', in D. Mühlberger (ed.), *The Social Bases of European Fascist Movements* (London, 1987), pp. 192–9, 203–6.
21 M. Vaïsse, 'Against Appeasement: French Advocates of Firmness 1933–38', in W. Mommsen and L. Kettenacker (eds), *The Fascist Challenge and the Policy of Appeasement* (London, 1983), p. 231.
22 G. Warner, *Pierre Laval and the Eclipse of France* (London, 1968), pp. 12–29.
23 P. Reynaud, *In the Thick of the Fight 1930–1945* (London, 1955), p. 155.
24 Ibid., pp. 49–50; details in W. E. Scott, *Alliance against Hitler: The Origins of*

the Franco-Soviet Pact (Durham, North Carolina, 1962).
25 J. Jackson, *The Popular Front in France Defending Democracy 1934–1938* (Cambridge, 1988), pp. 42–51; Blum quotation in Schwarzschild, p. 258.
26 R. Frankenstein, *Le prix du réarmament français 1935–1939* (Paris, 1982), pp. 290–1, 303–4.
27 Jackson, p. 191.
28 A. Werth, *The Destiny of France* (London, 1937), pp. 292–314.
29 Jackson, p. 250; J. E. Dreifort, 'The French Popular Front and the Franco-Soviet Pact 1936–37', *Journal of Contemporary History*, 11 (1976), pp. 217–36.
30 Warner, p. 129.
31 J. Jackson, *The Politics of Depression in France 1932–1936* (Cambridge, 1985), p. 207.
32 Adamthwaite, p. 15.
33 Jackson, *Politics of Depression*, p. 202.
34 M. Wolfe, *The French Franc between the Wars 1919–1939* (New York, 1951), pp. 120–2, 213. The franc was worth 15 to the dollar in June 1936, but only 36 to the dollar two years later.
35 Reynaud, p. 36.
36 S. Weil, *Écrits historiques et politiques* (Paris, 1960), p. 290.
37 Adamthwaite, p. 125.
38 Young, *Command*, p. 201.
39 Adamthwaite, p. 199.
40 Young, pp. 193–8, 210.
41 O. H. Bullitt (ed.), *For the President. Personal and Secret. Correspondence between Franklin D. Roosevelt and William C. Bullitt* (London, 1973), entry for 28 September 1938, pp. 297–8.
42 Young, p. 4; on domestic politics S. Butterworth, 'Daladier and the Munich Crisis; A Reappraisal', *Journal of Contemporary History*, 9 (1974), pp. 191–205.
43 Vaïsse, in Mommsen and Kettenacker, p. 232.
44 J. P. Sartre, *The Reprieve* (London, 1947), p. 353.
45 Adamthwaite, pp. 217–18.
46 J. Duroselle, *La décadence 1932–1939* (Paris, 1979), p. 352.
47 A. Gide, *The Journals*, vol. 3: *1928–1939* (London, 1949), p. 405; Schwarzschild, p. 268.
48 A. Werth, *France and Munich* (London, 1939), pp. 344–5.
49 A. Adamthwaite, 'France and the Coming of War', in Mommsen and Kettenacker, p. 247.
50 Werth, *Munich*, p. 364.
51 Ibid., p. 366.
52 Ibid., loc. cit.
53 Adamthwaite, 'France and Coming of War', p. 251; R. Girault, 'La décision gouvernmentale en politique extérieure', in R. Rémond (ed.), *Édouard Daladier* (Paris, 1977), p. 226.
54 Weil, 'Fragment 2, 1939', p. 292.
55 Werth, *Munich*, p. 379.
56 H. de Kérellis, *Kérellis and the Causes of the War* (London, 1939), pp. 88–114.
57 Bullitt, *Correspondence*, pp. 309–10.
58 K. Feiling, *The Life of Neville Chamberlain* (London, 1946), p. 322.
59 Young, p. 22.

60 J. Duroselle, '*Entente* and *Mésentente*' in D. Johnson, F. Crouzet and F. Bédarida (eds), *Britain and France: Ten Centuries* (Folkestone, 1980), p. 279.
61 H. Michel, 'France, Grande-Bretagne et Pologne', in Comité d'Histoire de la 2ème Guerre Mondiale, *Les relations franco-brittaniques de 1935 à 1939* (Paris, 1975), pp. 384–6.
62 Reynaud, p. 215.
63 J. Sherwood, 'The Tiger's Cub: The Last Years of Georges Mandel', in J. Joll (ed.), *The Decline of the Third Republic* (London, 1959), pp. 97–9.
64 J. Mc. Haight, 'Les Négociations relatives aux achats d'avions américains par la France pendant la période qui précéda immédiatement la guerre', *Revue d'histoire de la deuxième guerre mondiale*, 15 (1965).
65 F. R. Kirkland, 'The French Air Force in 1940', *Air University Review*, 36 (1985), pp. 101–17; R. Stolfi, 'Equipment for Victory in France in 1940', *History*, 55 (1970), pp. 1–20.
66 R. Genebrier, *Septembre 1939: La France entre en guerre: le témoignage du chef de cabinet de Daladier* (Paris, 1982), p. 91.
67 Bullitt, *Correspondence*, p. 360
68 P. R. Stafford, 'The French Government and the Danzig Crisis: The Italian Dimension', *International History Review*, 6 (1984), pp. 62–4, 68.
69 Ministère des Affaires Etrangères, *The French Yellow Book* (London, 1940).
70 Genebrier, pp. 87–91; Reynaud, pp. 236–9; *Yellow Book*.
71 F. Steegmuller, *Cocteau* (London, 1970), p. 436.
72 Weil, p. 291.
73 Bullitt, *Correspondence*, p. 369.

Chapter Four: Italy

Epigraph: E. Ludwig, *Talks with Mussolini* (London, 1933), p. 61.

1 M. Gilbert, *Winston S. Churchill*, vol. 6: *Finest Hour* (London, 1983), p. 345.
2 W. S. Churchill, *The Second World War*, vol. 2: *Their Finest Hour* (London, 1949), p. 107.
3 R. J. B. Bosworth, *Italy, the Least of the Great Powers: Italian Foreign Policy before the First World War* (Cambridge, 1979), pp. 8–9.
4 C. J. Lowe and F. Marzari, *Italian Foreign Policy 1870–1940* (London, 1975), p. 57.
5 R. J. Bosworth, 'Italy and the End of the Ottoman Empire', in M. Kent (ed.), *The Great Powers and the End of the Ottoman Empire* (London, 1984), p. 68
6 M. Dockrill and J. D. Goold, *Peace without Promise: Britain and the Peace Conferences 1919–1923* (London, 1981), p. 110.
7 L. Schwarzschild, *World in Trance* (London, 1943), pp. 78–9.
8 J. Macdonald, *A Political Escapade: The Story of Fiume and D'Annunzio* (London, 1921).
9 T. Koon, *Believe–Obey–Fight: Political Socialization in Fascist Italy 1922–1943* (Chapel Hill, North Carolina, 1985), p. 8.
10 A. Lyttleton, *The Seizure of Power: Fascism in Italy 1919–1929* (2nd edn, London, 1987), p. 95.
11 I. Kirkpatrick, *Mussolini: Study of a Demagogue* (London, 1964), p. 275.
12 J. Joll, *Intellectuals in Politics* (London, 1960), p. 181.

13 D. Mack Smith, *Mussolini* (London, 1982), p. 160.
14 R. de Felice, *Mussolini il duce: I, gli anni del consenso 1929–1936* (Turin, 1974), pp. 597–604.
15 A. Cassels, *Mussolini's Early Diplomacy* (Princeton, 1970), pp. 118–26.
16 E. Robertson, *Mussolini as Empire-Builder* (London, 1977), pp. 38–40.
17 Lyttleton, pp. 178, 384.
18 Koon, pp. 18–30.
19 E. Ludwig, *Talks with Mussolini* (London, 1933), p. 89.
20 Ludwig, pp. 153, 204.
21 Kirkpatrick, p. 88.
22 Mack Smith, p. 115.
23 Ludwig, pp. 61, 200.
24 G. Baer, *The Coming of the Italo-Ethiopian War* (Cambridge, Mass., 1967), p. 29.
25 D. Schmitz, *The United States and Fascist Italy 1922–1940* (Chapel Hill, North Carolina, 1988), p. 148.
26 Ludwig, p 153.
27 C. de Cambrun, *Traditions et souvenirs* (Paris, 1952), p. 169.
28 Baer, pp. 373–4; D. Mack Smith, *Mussolini's Roman Empire* (London, 1976), p. 33.
29 Robertson, pp. 95–6.
30 R. Quartararo, *Roma tra Londra e Berlino: La politica estera fascista dal 1930 al 1940* (Rome, 1980), ch. 4, passim.
31 Ibid., p. 98; E. Santarelli, 'The Economic and Political Background of Fascist Imperialism', in R. Sarti (ed.), *The Ax Within: Italian Fascism in Action* (New York, 1974), pp. 168–70.
32 C. Macdonald, 'Radio Bari: Italian Wireless Propaganda in the Middle East and British Countermeasures', *Middle Eastern Studies*, 13 (1977), pp. 195–207.
33 Robertson, p. 33.
34 Ibid., pp. 114–16.
35 Baer, p. 237.
36 Robertson, pp. 182–3.
37 A. J. Barker, *The Civilizing Mission: The Italo-Ethiopian War 1935–6* (London, 1968), pp. 152–6.
38 Schmitz, pp. 162–6; on oil supplies see R. Quartararo, 'Imperial Defence in the Mediterranean on the Eve of the Ethiopian Crisis', *Historical Journal*, 20 (1977), pp. 185–220.
39 R. Macgregor-Hastie, *The Day of the Lion* (London, 1963), p. 228.
40 M. Muggeridge (ed.), *Ciano's Diary 1937–1938* (London, 1952), p. 24.
41 Ibid., entry for 22 October 1937, p. 24.
42 Santorelli, p. 177.
43 A. Sbacchi, *Ethiopia under Mussolini: Fascism and the Colonial Experience* (London, 1985), p. 178; Santarelli, p. 178; H. Thomas, *The Spanish Civil War* (London, 1961), p. 634; Mack Smith, *Roman Empire*, p. 105.
44 *Documents on German Foreign Policy*, Ser. D, vol. 8, 'Observations on German–Italian Relations', 3 January 1940, p. 610 (cited as *DGFP*).
45 Christie Papers, Churchill College, Cambridge, 180/1 5, conversation with Göring, 28 July 1937.
46 Lowe, pp. 303–4.

47 A. L. Goldman, 'Sir Robert Vansittart's Search for Italian Co-operation against Hitler 1933–1936', *Journal of Contemporary History*, 9 (1974), p. 130.
48 Ciano, *Diaries*, p. 167.
49 Lowe, p. 320.
50 M. Muggeridge (ed.), *Ciano's Diary 1939–1943* (London, 1947), entry for 11 January 1939, pp. 9–10.
51 *Documents on International Affairs, 1938*, vol. 1 (Oxford, 1942), Mussolini speech, 14 May 1938, p. 240.
52 M. Knox, *Mussolini Unleashed 1939–1941: Politics and Strategy in Fascist Italy's Last War* (Cambridge, 1984), p. 40.
53 Ciano, *Diary 1939–1943*, p. 9.
54 Ibid., entry for 16 March 1939, p. 47.
55 Ibid., entry for 30 November 1938, p. 201; Lowe, p. 327.
56 A. Aquarone, 'Public Opinion in Italy before the Outbreak of World War II', in Sarti, pp. 214, 217.
57 Lowe, p. 314.
58 F. Deakin, *The Brutal Friendship* (London, 1962), pp. 1–2.
59 M. Toscano, *The Origins of the Pact of Steel* (Baltimore, 1967), pp. 377–8.
60 Ciano, *Diary 1939–1943*, pp. 114, 116, 119.
61 Ibid., entry for 10 August 1939, p. 123.
62 Ibid., entry for 13 August 1939, p. 125.
63 Ibid., pp. 138–41.
64 Lowe, pp. 367–8; Knox, p. 56.
65 M. H. Macartney, *One Man Alone: The History of Mussolini and the Axis* (London, 1944), speech of 21 February 1941, p. 54.
66 Ciano, *Diary 1939–1943*, entry for 3 September 1939, p. 144.
67 Lowe, p. 366.
68 Aquarone, p. 219.
69 Lowe, p. 349.
70 *DGFP*, Ser. D, vol. 8, the Duce to the Führer, 3 January 1940, p. 608.
71 Ibid., 'Observations', p. 612.
72 Knox, pp. 61–2.
73 See for example Quartararo, *Roma tra Londra e Berlino*, p. 616, and R. de Felice, *Mussolini il duce: II. Lo Stato Totalitario 1936–1940* (Turin, 1981), pp. 828–9, for details on British and French negotiations with Italy.
74 *DGFP*, Ser. D, vol. 8, p. 608; Lowe, p. 368.
75 Ibid., Conversation between the Reich Foreign Minister and the Duce, 11 March 1940, p. 902.
76 H. Cliadakis, 'Neutrality and War in Italian Policy 1939–1940', *Journal of Contemporary History*, 8 (1974), pp. 176–81.
77 *DGFP*, Ser. D, vol. 9, Conversation between the Führer and the Duce, 18 March 1940, p. 11.
78 Macartney, p. 54.
79 *DGFP*, Ser. D, vol. 8, p. 907.
80 Cliadakis, p. 181.
81 Lowe, p. 369; Knox, pp. 99–100.
82 Knox, p. 118.
83 Ibid., pp. 124, 128–9.
84 J. Lukacs, *The Last European War* (London, 1976), p. 88.

85 F. Halder, *Kriegstagebuch. Tägliche Aufzeichnungen des Chefs des Generalstabes des Heeres 1939–1942* (Stuttgart, 1962–4), vol. 2, p. 212.
86 Ciano, *Diary 1939–1943*, entry for 10 June 1940, p. 263.
87 Ludwig, p. 86.

Chapter Five: The Soviet Union

Epigraph: J. Hochman, *The Soviet Union and the Failure of Collective Security 1934–1938* (Ithaca, New York, 1984), p. 164.
Documents on International Affairs 1939–1945 (Oxford, 1951), pp. 440–1.

1 A. Ulam, *Expansion and Co-Existence: A History of Soviet Foreign Policy 1917–1967* (London, 1968), p. 78.
2 T. J. Uldricks, 'Russia and Europe: Diplomacy, Revolution and Economic Development in the 1920s', *International History Review*, 1 (1979), p. 58.
3 Ulam, p. 79.
4 E. R. Goodman, *The Soviet Design for a World State* (New York, 1960), pp. 30–2.
5 J. Stalin, *Problems of Leninism* (Moscow, 1947), p. 160.
6 Ibid., p. 159.
7 Ulam, p. 135.
8 Ibid., p. 134; Uldricks, pp. 66–8.
9 W. Laqueur, *Russia and Germany: A Century of Conflict* (London, 1965), p. 131; N. Tolstoy, *Stalin's Secret War* (London, 1981), p. 81.
10 R. Garrett, *Motoring and the Mighty* (London, 1970), pp. 66–8; M. Wilkins, *American Business Abroad: Ford in Six Continents* (Detroit, 1964), pp. 215–25.
11 Uldricks, p. 73.
12 Ulam, p. 129.
13 Uldricks, p. 75.
14 R. Schiness, 'The Conservative Party and Anglo-Soviet Relations 1925–7', *European Studies Review*, 7 (1977), pp. 385–8; G. Gorodetsky, *The Precarious Truce: Anglo-Soviet Relations 1924–1927* (Cambridge, 1977), pp. 222–34.
15 A. Amba, *I was Stalin's Bodyguard* (London, 1952), p. 69.
16 Stalin, *Problems of Leninism*, speech to the First All-Union Conference of Managers, 4 February 1931, p. 356.
17 M. Harrison, *Soviet Planning in Peace and War 1938–1945* (Cambridge, 1985), pp. 46–51; S. Wheatcroft, R. W. Davies and J. M. Cooper, 'Soviet Industrialisation Reconsidered', *Economic History Review*, 2nd Ser., 39 (1986), pp. 264–94.
18 Harrison, pp. 250–3.
19 For a first-hand account see M. Hindus, *Red Bread* (London, 1934).
20 R. B. Day, *The 'Crisis' and the 'Crash': Soviet Studies of the West 1917–1939* (London, 1981), pp. 202–11.
21 Report by M. Molotov to the 7th All-Union Soviet Congress, 28 June 1934 in *Documents on International Affairs, 1934* (Oxford, 1935), p. 413.
22 Report of Stalin to the 17th Congress of the CPSU, 26 January 1934 in J. Degras (ed.), *Soviet Documents on Foreign Policy* (Oxford, 1953), vol. 3, p. 68.
23 Ulam, pp. 218–19.
24 J. Hochman, *The Soviet Union and the Failure of Collective Security 1934–1938* (Ithaca, NY, 1984), pp. 29, 32.

25 E. M. Bennett, *Franklin D. Roosevelt and the Search for Security* (Wilmington, Delaware, 1985), p. 20.
26 Hochman, p. 29.
27 K. E. McKenzie, *Comintern and World Revolution* (New York, 1964), pp. 143–5; F. W. Deakin, H. Shukman and H. T. Willett, *A History of World Communism* (London, 1975), pp. 119–21.
28 McKenzie, p. 157.
29 Ibid., pp. 150–4.
30 A. C. Brown and C. B. Macdonald, *The Communist International and the Coming of World War II* (New York, 1981), pp. 467–73.
31 Ibid., pp. 456–60.
32 G. Warner, *Pierre Laval and the Eclipse of France* (London, 1968), pp. 80–2, 92–3.
33 J. Haslam, *The Soviet Union and the Struggle for Collective Security in Europe 1933–1939* (London, 1984), p. 133.
34 This paragraph and the following, J. A. Getty, *Origins of the Great Purges: The Soviet Communist Party Reconsidered 1933–38* (Cambridge, 1985), pp. 116–17, 172–89.
35 E. O'Ballance, *The Red Army* (London, 1964), pp. 129–31.
36 R. Medvedev, *Let History Judge: The Origins and Consequences of Stalinism* (London, 1971), p. 375; Hochman, pp. 132–4.
37 J. J. Stephan, *The Russian Fascists: Tragedy and Farce in Exile 1925–1945* (London, 1978).
38 Haslam, p. 153.
39 Hochman, pp. 137–46.
40 K. Feiling, *The Life of Neville Chamberlain* (London, 1946), p. 347.
41 Molotov, speech before the Supreme Council of the USSR, 19 January 1938 in *Documents on International Affairs* (Oxford, 1939), p. 313.
42 J. E. Davies, *Mission to Moscow* (London, 1942), Davies to Hull, 9 June 1938, p. 223.
43 Hochman, p. 152.
44 Haslam, p. 146.
45 Hochman, p. 146.
46 Speech by Litvinov at Leningrad, 23 June 1938, in *Documents on International Affairs, 1938*, p. 319.
47 Hochman, p. 158.
48 Ibid., p. 149.
49 Davies, *Mission*, Davies to Sumner Welles, 20 March 1938, p. 194.
50 Haslam, p. 189. There were alleged to be thirty rifle and cavalry divisions, seven tank, motorised rifle and aviation brigades.
51 Hochman, pp. 166–7; see too J. von Herwarth, *Against Two Evils* (London, 1981), pp. 122–3.
52 Davies, *Mission*, Davies to Sumner Welles, 22 August 1939, p. 290.
53 Haslam, pp. 196–7.
54 J. Hermann, 'Soviet Peace Efforts on the Eve of World War II: A Review of the Soviet Documents', *Journal of Contemporary History*, 15 (1980), p. 583.
55 Ibid., p. 584.
56 Ibid., p. 586.
57 Stalin, *Problems of Leninism*, Report to the 18th Congress of the CPSU, 10 March 1939, p. 606.

58 Ibid., p. 602.
59 R. Manne, 'Some British Light on the Nazi–Soviet Pact', *European Studies Review*, 11 (1981), p. 88.
60 Ibid., pp. 89–90; Hermann, p. 597.
61 D. C. Watt, 'The Initiation of Negotiations Leading to the Nazi–Soviet Pact: A Historical Problem', in C. Abramsky (ed.), *Essays in Honour of E. H. Carr* (London, 1974), pp. 162–3.
62 Ulam, p. 272.
63 Manne, p. 87.
64 Hermann, pp. 594, 597.
65 Speech by M. Molotov to the 4th Special Session of the Supreme Soviet, 31 August 1939, in *Documents on International Affairs 1939–1945* (Oxford, 1951), p. 439; J. R. Dukes, 'The Soviet Union and Britain: The Alliance Negotiations of March–August 1939', *Eastern European Quarterly*, 19 (1985), pp. 311–15.
66 Laqueur, p. 22; G. Weinberg, *Germany and the Soviet Union 1939–1941* (Leiden, 1972), pp. 33–50.
67 L. Namier, *Europe in Decay: A Study in Disintegration* (London, 1950), p. 246.
68 Davies, *Mission*, Davies to Welles, 26 March 1938, p. 194.
69 Ulam, p. 209.
70 Feiling, p. 403; Dukes, p. 310.
71 Namier, p. 242.
72 Stalin, *Problems of Leninism*, Speech, 10 March 1939, p. 604.
73 P. Reynaud, *In the Thick of the Fight 1930–1945* (London, 1950), pp. 255–6.
74 Polish Ambassador in Moscow, Final Report, 6 November 1939 in *Documents on International Affairs 1939–45*, p. 437.
75 G. Kennan, *Soviet Foreign Policy 1917–1941* (New York, 1960), doc. 32, Soviet statement to Poland, 17 September 1939, p. 179.
76 Medvedev, p. 442.
77 E. Browder, *The Second Imperialist War* (New York, 1940), p. 70; McKenzie, p. 171; A. Rossi, *The Russo-German Alliance 1939–1941* (London, 1950), pp. 163–5.
78 C. R. Richardson, 'French Plans for Allied Attacks on the Caucasus Oilfields, Jan–Apr 1940', *French Historical Studies*, 8 (1973); D. J. Dallin, *Soviet Russia's Foreign Policy 1939–1942* (New Haven, 1942), pp. 166–72.
79 G. Zhukov, *The Memoirs of Marshal Zhukov* (London, 1971), pp. 197–201.
80 R. J. Overy, 'Mobilization for Total War in Germany 1939–1941', *English Historical Review*, 103 (1988), p. 624.
81 B. Leach, *German Strategy against Russia* (Oxford, 1973), p. 78.
82 Ulam, p. 302.
83 B. Whaley, *Codeword Barbarossa* (Massachusetts, 1973), p. 211.
84 F. W. Deakin and G. A. Storry, *The Case of Richard Sorge* (London, 1966), pp. 227–30.
85 Ulam, p. 312; F. H. Hinsley, *British Intelligence in the Second World War*, vol. 1 (London, 1979), pp. 451–81.
86 Whaley, p. 209.
87 Medvedev, p. 450.
88 Amba, p. 37.
89 P. G. Grigorenko, *Memoirs* (London, 1983), pp. 115–19; Zhukov, *Memoirs*, pp. 217–29.

90 B. Bromage, *Molotov: The Story of an Era* (London, 1956), pp. 191, 196.
91 Herwarth, p. 174.
92 G. R. Gorodetsky, *Stafford Cripps' Mission to Moscow 1940–42* (Cambridge, 1984), p. 161.
93 Uldricks, p. 58.
94 G. Weinberg, *World in the Balance* (Hanover, New England, 1981), p. 7.

Chapter Six: Japan

Epigraph: W. H. Chamberlin, *Japan over Asia* (London, 1938) p. 18.
T. Ishimura, *Japan must fight Britain* (London, 1936) p. 319.

1 See Nobutaka Ike, *Japan's Decision for War: Records of the 1941 Policy Conferences* (Stanford, 1967), pp. 263–80.
2 The Japanese described this antagonism as 'Taiheyo-no-gan' – 'Cancer of the Pacific'. See Gordon V. Prange, *At Dawn We Slept: The Untold Story of Pearl Harbor* (London, 1981), pp. 5 ff.
3 See Akio Watanabe, *The Okinawa Problem* (Melbourne, 1970), p. 9.
4 See Akira Iriye (ed.), *Mutual Images: Essays on American–Japanese Relations* (Cambridge, Massachusetts, 1975), p. 237.
5 Ibid., p. 11.
6 See Akira Iriye, *Pacific Estrangement: Japanese and American Expansion 1897–1911* (Cambridge, Massachusetts, 1972), pp. 126–9.
7 See James Winter, *Rebuilding London* (forthcoming).
8 Cited in Togo Minoru, p. 132.
9 Cited in John Dower, *War without Mercy: Race and Power in the Pacific War* (New York, 1986), p. 156.
10 See R. M. Connaughton, *The War of the Rising Sun and the Tumbling Bear: A Military History of the Russo-Japanese War 1904–5* (London, 1989), pp. 276–7.
11 See Akira Iriye, *Mutual Images*, p. 73.
12 Cited in W. J. Macpherson, *The Economic Development of Japan c.1868–1941* (London, 1987), p. 33.
13 Figures cited in P. Kennedy, *The Rise and Fall of the Great Powers* (London, 1988), p. 203.
14 J. T. Walton Newbold, *How Europe Armed for War 1871–1914* (London, 1917), p. 77.
15 See H. C. Engelbrecht and F. C. Hanighen, *Merchants of Death: A Study of the International Armament Industry* (London, 1934), pp. 219–36.
16 See Shigemitsu Mamoru, *Japan and Her Destiny* (London, 1958), p. 49.
17 Akira Iriye, *Mutual Images*, p. 11.
18 See Richard Storry, *The Double Patriots: A Study of Japanese Nationalism* (Boston, Massachusetts, 1957), p. 21.
19 See Appendix VIII in David James, *The Rise and Fall of the Japanese Empire* (London, 1951).
20 See M. Maruyama, *Nippon Fasshizmu no Shiso to Undo* ('The Movement and Thought of Japanese Fascism'), cited in Storry, p. 99.
21 See Hosoya Chihiro, 'Britain and the United States in Japan's View of the International System 1919–37', I. Nish (ed.), *Anglo-Japanese Alienation 1919–1952* (Cambridge, Massachusetts, 1982), pp. 7 ff.

22 See Peter Duus and Daniel I. Okimoto, 'Fascism and the History of Pre-War Japan: The Failure of A Concept', *Journal of Asian Studies*, 39(1) (November 1979), pp. 70–1.
23 See James B. Crowley, 'Japanese Army Factionalism in the Early 1930s', *Journal of Asian Studies*, 21 (1962), pp. 311–14.
24 For the contrast between the two types of officer, see Hillis, *Japan's Military Masters* (London, 1947), pp. 177–9.
25 See Kungtu C. Sun, *The Economic Development of Manchuria* (Cambridge, Massachusetts, 1969).
26 See Michael J. Barnhart, *Japan Prepares for Total War* (Ithaca, NY, 1987), pp. 73–4.
27 See Borg, p. 235.
28 Cited in Storry, p. 85, translating from the memoirs of Baron Harada.
29 Cited in C. Thorne, *The Limits of Foreign Policy: The West, the League and the Far Eastern Crisis of 1931–1933* (London, 1972), p. 158.
30 Ibid., p. 177.
31 Ibid., pp. 247, 255.
32 Ibid., p. 42.
33 Ibid. The figures are for 1931–2.
34 Chiefs of Staff Annual Review. 1932, cited in Thorne, p. 266.
35 'Plan Orange', which was the US navy war plan against Japan, was known to be unworkable.
36 See Shunsuke Tsurumi, *An Intellectual History of Wartime Japan 1931–45* (London, 1986), pp. 37–8.
37 Cited in Thorne, p. 283.
38 See Akira Iriye, *The Origins of the Second World War in Asia and the Pacific* (London, 1987), pp. 9–11.
39 See *Foreign Relations of the United States 1933* (Washington DC, 1949), vol. 3, p. 165.
40 See Usui Katsumi, 'A Consideration of Anglo-Japanese Relations: Japanese Views of Britain 1937–41', in Nish, p. 95.
41 Cited in Hosaya Chihiro, p. 59.
42 See Dower, pp. 282–4.
43 'Land Disposal Plan in the Gt. Asia Co-Prosperity Sphere', in International Military Tribunal Far East, Exhibit 1334, transcript, pp. 11969–73, cited in part in Storry, pp. 317–19.
44 See Akira Iriye, *Pacific Estrangement*, p. 132.
45 Cited in J. Toland, *The Rising Sun: The Decline and Fall of the Japanese Empire 1936–45* (London, 1971), p. 18.
46 Harada memoirs, 18 November 1937, cited in Storry, p. 214.
47 See Toland, p. 47.
48 See Michael Barnhart, 'Japan's Economic Security and the Origins of the Pacific War', *Journal of Strategic Studies*, vol. 4(2) (1981), pp. 113–15.
49 See Dower, pp. 286–7.
50 See Thorne, p. 68.
51 Ickes description, cited in R. Dallek, *Franklin Roosevelt and American Foreign Policy* (New York, 1979), p. 274.
52 Cited in Prange, p. 209.
53 See Borg, p. 256.

54 See Akira Iriye, *Mutual Images*, p. 134.

Chapter Seven: The United States

Epigraph: W. Lippman, *U.S. Foreign Policy* (London, 1943), p. 99.
R. Dallek, *Franklin D. Roosevelt and American Foreign Policy 1932–1945* (New York, 1979), p. 129.

1 N. H. Hooker (ed.), *The Moffat Papers: Selections from the Diplomatic Journals of Jay Pierrepoint Moffat 1919–1943* (Cambridge, Massachusetts, 1956), p. 262.
2 J. W. Pratt, *America and World Leadership 1900–1921* (London, 1967), p. 120.
3 Ibid., p. 195.
4 W. S. Cole, *Roosevelt and the Isolationists 1932–1945* (Lincoln, Nebraska, 1983), pp. 190–2; BBC Radio 3, 'The Voice from the Shrine', January 1987.
5 Cole, p. 54.
6 Cordell Hull, *Memoirs* (London, 1948), vol. 2, p. 587.
7 E. M. Bennett, *Franklin D. Roosevelt and the Search for Security* (Wilmington, Delaware, 1985), p. 21.
8 A. W. Schatz, 'The Anglo-American Trade Agreement and Cordell Hull's Search for Peace 1936–1938', *Journal of American History*, 57 (1970/1), pp. 86–9.
9 R. Dallek, *Franklin D. Roosevelt and American Foreign Policy 1932–1945* (New York, 1979), pp. 85–6.
10 R. T. Goldberg, *The Making of Franklin D. Roosevelt: Triumph over Disability* (Cambridge, Massachusetts, 1981), p. 169.
11 *The Public Papers and Addresses of Franklin D. Roosevelt 1936* (New York, 1938), p. 289, 'Address at Chautauqua, New York, Aug. 14th 1936'.
12 D. C. Watt, *Succeeding John Bull: America in Britain's Place 1900–1975* (Cambridge, 1984), pp. 80–1.
13 Cole, p. 38.
14 R. Moley, *The First New Deal* (New York 1966), p. 228.
15 Cole, pp. 8–9, 190–201.
16 H. U. Faulkner, *American Economic History* (New York, 1960), pp. 685–90.
17 J. E. Wiltz, *In Search of Peace: The Senate Munitions Inquiry 1934–1936* (Baton Rouge, Louisiana, 1963), pp. 9–20.
18 Dallek, p. 95.
19 *Public Papers, 1936*, p. 289.
20 R. W. Steele, 'The Pulse of the People: Franklin D. Roosevelt and the Gauging of American Public Opinion', *Journal of Contemporary History*, 9 (1974), pp. 197–202.
21 R. A. Harrison, 'A Presidential Démarche: Franklin D. Roosevelt's Personal Diplomacy and Great Britain 1936–1937', *Diplomatic History*, vol. 5 (1981), p. 24; A. A. Offner, 'Appeasement Revisited: The United States, Great Britain and Germany 1933–1940', *Journal of American History*, 64 (1977), p. 380.
22 Harrison, pp. 262–3.
23 Ibid., p. 250; C. Macdonald, *The United States, Britain and Appeasement 1936–1939* (London, 1981), p. 20.
24 P. Brendon, *Ike: His Life and Times* (London, 1986), p. 64.

25 S. Ambrose, *Rise to Globalism: American Foreign Policy since 1918* (London, 1971), p. 11; J. L. Cate and W. F. Craven, *The Army Air Forces in World War II* (Chicago, 1948), vol. 1, pp. 188–9; J. Rae, *Climb to Greatness* (Cambridge, Massachusetts, 1968), pp. 171–5.
26 A. A. Offner, *The Origins of the Second World War: American Foreign Policy and World Politics 1917–1941* (New York, 1975), p. 151.
27 Hull, *Memoirs*, vol. 1, p. 667.
28 E. Roosevelt (ed.), *The Roosevelt Letters*, vol. 3: *1928–1945* (London, 1952), Roosevelt to Peabody, 16 October 1937, p. 220; *Public Papers, 1937* (London, 1941), Address at Chicago, 5 October 1937, pp. 406–11.
29 *Roosevelt Letters*, 19 October 1937, Roosevelt to House, p. 221.
30 Ibid., p. 220.
31 D. Reynolds, *The Creation of the Anglo-American Alliance 1937–1941* (London, 1981), p. 43; *Moffat Papers*, p. 191.
32 *Roosevelt Letters*, Roosevelt to John Cudahy, 16 April 1938, pp. 233–4; Roosevelt to William Phillips, 15 September 1938, p. 241.
33 *Public Papers, 1938* (London, 1941), President's Message to Czechoslovakia, Germany, Great Britain and France, 26 September 1938, pp. 531–2.
34 H. Ickes, *The Secret Diary of Harold L. Ickes* (London, 1955), vol. 2, p. 468.
35 Ibid., p. 469; *Moffat Papers*, p. 219.
36 M. Muir, 'American Warship Construction for Stalin's Navy Prior to World War II', *Diplomatic History* 5 (1981), pp. 337–51.
37 G. Kolko, 'American Business and Germany 1930–1941', *Western Political Quarterly*, 15 (1962), p. 725.
38 B. B. Berle and T. B. Jacobs (eds), *Navigating the Rapids 1918–1971: From the Papers of Adolf A. Berle* (New York, 1973), 'Mémoire: Foreign Policy of the United States, 2nd Apr. 1939', p. 206.
39 Watt, pp. 80–1, 88; Offner, 'Appeasement', p. 380.
40 Ickes, *Diary*, vol. 3, p. 171; Watt, p. 81.
41 Harrison, p. 271; Ickes, *Diary*, vol. 3, p. 171.
42 B. D. Rhodes, 'The British Royal Visit of 1939 and the Psychological Approach to the United States', *Diplomatic History*, 2 (1978), pp. 204–11.
43 Watt, p. 85.
44 M. Jonas, *The United States and Germany: A Diplomatic History* (Ithaca, NY, 1984), p. 216; B. von Everen, 'Franklin D. Roosevelt and the Problem of Nazi Germany', in C. L. Egan and A. W. Knott (eds), *Essays in Twentieth Century American International History* (Lanham, Maryland, 1982), pp. 138–9.
45 H. Gatzke, *Germany and the United States* (Cambridge, Massachusetts, 1980), p. 113; J. Compton, *The Swastika and the Eagle: Hitler, the United States and the Origins of the Second World War* (London, 1968), pp. 15–32; G. Weinberg, *World in the Balance* (Hanover, New England, 1981), p. 63.
46 H. Rauschning, *Hitler Speaks* (London, 1939), pp. 69–72, 77–9.
47 S. A. Diamond, *The Nazi Movement in the United States 1924–1941* (Ithaca, NY, 1974), pp. 289–304, 326.
48 W. Green, *Warplanes of the Third Reich* (London, 1970), pp. 519–20, 640–1. The aircraft were the Ju 390, which was not completed until 1942, when it won the design competition with its rival, and the Me 264, first designed in 1940 and flown in 1942.
49 Ickes, *Diary*, vol. 3, p. 37.

50 Compton, p. 181.
51 M. Leighton, *Mobilizing Consent: Public Opinion and American Foreign Policy 1937–1948* (London, 1976), pp. 41–7.
52 *Roosevelt Letters*, FDR Memorandum, 3 April 1939, p. 259.
53 Reynolds, p. 212.
54 *Berle Papers*, pp. 242–3.
55 Ibid., p. 248.
56 Ickes, *Diary*, vol. 3, p. 37.
57 S. E. Hilton, 'The Welles Mission to Europe, February–March 1940: Illusion or Realism?', *Journal of American History*, 68 (1971), pp. 93–120; Offner, 'Appeasement', p. 387.
58 R. W. Steele, 'The Great Debate: Roosevelt, the Media and the Coming of War 1940–1941', *Journal of American History*, 81 (1984), pp. 69–92.
59 A. Frye, *Nazi Germany and the American Hemisphere 1939–1941* (New Haven, 1967), pp. 131–6.
60 *Roosevelt Letters*, Roosevelt to Bullitt, 14 December 1939, pp. 292–4.
61 *Public Papers, 1940* (London, 1940). Address to the Teamsters Union Convention, Washington, 11 September 1940, p. 415; Campaign Address at Boston, 30 October 1940, p. 517.
62 H. G. Vatter, *The U.S. Economy in World War II* (New York, 1985), p. 8.
63 P. Hearden, *Roosevelt Confronts Hitler* (Dekalb, Illinois, 1987), p. 191.
64 Ibid., loc. cit.
65 *Public Papers, 1940*, White House 'Fireside Chat', 29 December 1940, pp. 640–3.
66 Hearden, pp. 133–4; W. Kimball, 'Beggar-My-Neighbour: America and the British Interim Finance Crisis 1940–1941', *Journal of Economic History*, 29 (1969), pp. 758–72.
67 *Roosevelt Letters*, Roosevelt to Francis B. Sayre, 31 December 1940, pp. 342–3.
68 Hearden, pp. 194–200; J. G. Utley, *Going to War with Japan* (Knoxville, Tennessee, 1985), pp. 138, 148.
69 Reynolds, p. 218.
70 Offner, *Origins*, p. 204.
71 Hearden, p. 196.
72 *Roosevelt Letters*, Gen. E. M. Watson for the President, 16 May 1941, pp. 369–70.
73 Goldberg, p. 177.
74 Library of Congress, Arnold Papers, Box 246, 'Estimates of German Air Strength', 21 January 1941.
75 Utley, pp. 139–43, 159–68.
76 Hearden, p. 220.
77 Dallek, pp. 310–11.
78 Hearden, pp. 220–1.
79 Utley, p. 174.
80 G. W. Prange, *At Dawn We Slept: The Untold Story of Pearl Harbor* (London, 1982), pp. 474–92; F. C. Pogue, *George C. Marshall: Ordeal and Hope* (London, 1968), pp. 220–9.
81 Frye, p. 193.
82 W. Lippmann, *U.S. War Aims* (Boston, 1944), pp. 196–210.

Conclusion: 'A War of Great Proportions'

1 H. Trevor-Roper (ed.), *The Goebbels Diaries: The Last Days* (London, 1978), entry for 28 February 1945, pp. 11–12.
2 W. Lippmann, *U.S. War Aims* (Boston, 1944), p. 196.
3 W. Shirer, *Berlin Diary* (London, 1941), entry for 10 August 1939, pp. 140–1.
4 C. J. Burckhardt, *Meine Danziger Mission 1937–1939* (Munich, 1960), p. 346.
5 See for example D. C. Watt, 'Introduction' to D. Irving (ed.), *Breach of Security: The German Secret Intelligence File on Events Leading to the Second World War* (London, 1968), pp. 15–42.
6 'Empire Day Message', 1925, in S. Baldwin, *On England* (London, 1926), p. 216.
7 L. R. Pratt, *East of Malta, West of Suez: Britain's Mediterranean Crisis 1936–1939* (Cambridge, 1975), p. 3.
8 J. C. Lebra (ed.), *Japan's Greater East Asian Co-Prosperity Sphere in World War II: Selected Readings and Documents* (Oxford, 1975), p. 76.
9 *Hitlers politisches Testament: die Bormann Diktate vom Februar und April 1945* (Hamburg, 1981), p. 125.
10 S. Roskill, *Hankey: Man of Secrets*, vol. 3: *1931–1967* (London, 1974), p. 394.
11 L. W. Fuchser, *Neville Chamberlain and Appeasement* (New York, 1982), pp. 33–4.
12 New Fabian Research Bureau, *The Road to War, Being an Analysis of the National Government's Foreign Policy* (London, 1937), pp. 177–8, speech delivered at Bewdley, 20 April 1936.
13 U. Bialer, 'Elite Opinion and Defence Policy: Air Power Advocacy and British Rearmament during the 1930s', *British Journal of International Studies*, 6 (1980), p. 37.
14 Stalin's speech on the Tenth Anniversary of the October Revolution, in J. Stalin, *Problems of Leninism* (Moscow, 1947), pp. 202–3.
15 O. H. Bullitt (ed.), *For the President. Personal and Secret. Correspondence between Franklin D. Roosevelt and William C. Bullitt* (London, 1973), entry for 27 September 1938, p. 292.
16 P. Reynaud, *In the Thick of the Fight 1930–1945* (London, 1955), p. 8.
17 E. Nolte, *Three Faces of Fascism* (New York, 1969), p. 510.
18 Shirer, p. 120.
19 S. Hedin, *German Diary* (Dublin, 1951), p. 29. The remarks were allegedly made by Hitler to Lord Londonderry.
20 *Hitlers politisches Testament*, entry for 4 February 1945, p. 44.
21 H. Ickes, *The Secret Diary of Harold L. Ickes* (London, 1955), vol. 3, entry for 14 October 1939, p. 37.
22 L. Namier, *Europe in Decay: A Study in Disintegration* (London, 1950), p. 242.
23 G. Weinberg, *World in the Balance* (Hanover, New England, 1981), p. 49.
24 Pratt, p. 152.
25 A. A. Offner, *The Origins of the Second World War: American Foreign Policy and World Politics 1917–1941* (New York, 1975), p. 165.
26 Hedin, p. 43.
27 F. C. Jones, *Japan's New Order in East Asia* (Oxford, 1954), p. 469.
28 P. J. Hearden, *Roosevelt Confronts Hitler: America's Entry into World War II* (Dekalb, Illinois, 1987), p. 244.
29 *Hitlers politisches Testament*, entry for 2 April 1945, p. 124.

SELECT BIBLIOGRAPHY

The following list is not intended to be an exhaustive one. It is broken down country by country and includes most of the books consulted directly in the writing of *The Road to War*. Where possible it includes translations or English editions of foreign-language works.

General

A. Adamthwaite, *The Making of the Second World War* (London, 1977).
P. Bell, *The Origins of the Second World War in Europe* (London, 1987).
E. H. Carr, *International Relations between the Two World Wars* (London, 1947).
G. Craig and F. Gilbert (eds), *The Diplomats 1919–1939* (Princeton, 1953).
G. Gafencu, *The Last Days of Europe: A Diplomatic Journey* (London, 1947).
D. Kaiser, *Economic Diplomacy and the Origins of the Second World War* (Princeton, 1980).
P. Kennedy, *The Rise and Fall of the Great Powers* (London, 1988).
C. Kindleberger, *The World in Depression 1929–1939* (London, 1973).
F. Leith Ross, *Money Talks: Fifty Years of International Finance* (London, 1968).
W. Mommsen and L. Kettenacker (eds), *The Fascist Challenge and the Policy of Appeasement* (London, 1983).
W. Murray, *The Change in the European Balance of Power 1938–1939* (Princeton, 1984).
L. Namier, *Europe in Decay: A Study in Disintegration* (London, 1950).
R. J. Overy, *The Origins of the Second World War* (London, 1987).
A. Preston (ed.), *General Staffs and Diplomacy before the Second World War* (London, 1978).
E. M. Robertson, *The Origins of the Second World War* (London, 1971).
A. J. P. Taylor, *The Origins of the Second World War* (London, 1961).
C. Thorne, *The Approach of War 1938–1939* (London, 1967).
D. C. Watt, *Personalities and Politics* (London, 1965).
D. C. Watt, *Too Serious a Business* (London, 1975).
G. Weinberg, *World in the Balance* (Hanover, New England, 1981).

Poland

J. Beck, *Dernier rapport: politique polonaise 1926–1939* (Paris, 1955).
B. B. Budurowycz, *Polish–Soviet Relations 1932–1939* (New York, 1963).
C. J. Burckhardt, *Meine Danziger Mission 1937–1939* (Munich, 1960).
P. V. Cannistraro, E. D. Wynot and T. P. Kovaleff (eds), *Poland and the Coming of the Second World War: The Diplomatic Papers of J. Drexel Biddle Jr 1937–1939*

(1976).
A. Cienciala, *Poland and the Western Powers 1938–1939* (London, 1968).
A. Cienciala, 'Polish Foreign Policy 1926–1939. "Equilibrium": Stereotype and Reality', *Polish Review*, 20 (1975).
N. Davies, *God's Playground: A History of Poland* (2 vols, Oxford, 1981).
R. Debecki, *Foreign Policy of Poland 1919–1939* (London, 1963).
T. Gromada, *Essays on Poland's Foreign Policy 1918–1939* (New York, 1970).
W. Jedrzejewicz (ed.), *Diplomat in Paris 1936–1939: Papers and Memoirs of Juliusz Lukasiewicz* (New York, 1970).
J. Karski, *The Great Powers and Poland* (Lanham, Maryland, 1985).
C. M. Kimmich, *The Free City: Danzig and German Foreign Policy 1925–1939* (New Haven, 1968).
R. Leslie et al., *History of Poland since 1863* (Cambridge, 1980).
H. S. Levine, *Hitler's Free City: A History of the Nazi Party in Danzig 1925–1939* (Chicago, 1973).
J. Lipski, *Diplomat in Berlin 1933–1939*, ed. W. Jedrzejewicz (New York, 1968).
S. Newman, *March 1939: The British Guarantee to Poland* (Oxford, 1976).
A. Polonsky, *Politics in Independent Poland 1921–1939* (Oxford, 1972).
A. Prazmowska, *Britain, Poland and the Eastern Front 1939* (Cambridge, 1987).
E. Raczynski, *In Allied London* (London, 1962).
G. Weinberg, 'German Policy and Poland 1937–1938', *Polish Review*, 20 (1975).
E. D. Wynot, *Polish Politics in Transition* (Athens, Georgia, 1974).

Germany

A. Bagel-Bohlan, *Hitlers industrielle Kriegsvorbereitung 1936–1939* (Koblenz, 1975).
V. Berghahn (ed.), *Germany in the Age of Total War* (London, 1981).
A. Bullock, 'Hitler and the Origins of the Second World War', *Proceedings of the British Academy*, 53 (1967).
W. Carr, *Arms, Autarky and Aggression* (London, 1972).
W. Carr, *Hitler: A Study in Personality and Politics* (London, 1978).
B. A. Carroll, *Design for Total War: Arms and Economics in the Third Reich* (The Hague, 1968).
A. Crozier, *Appeasement and Germany's Last Bid for Colonies* (London, 1988).
B. Dahlerus, *The Last Attempt* (London, 1948).
W. Deist, *The Wehrmacht and German Rearmament* (London, 1981).
W. Deist, M. Messerschmidt, H.-G. Volkmann, W. Wette, *Ursachen und Voraussetzungen der deutschen Kriegspolitik* (Stuttgart, 1979).
O. Dietrich, *The Hitler I Knew* (London, 1955).
H. von Dirksen, *Moscow, Tokyo, London: Twenty Years of German Foreign Policy* (London, 1951).
J. Dülffer, 'Der Beginn des Krieges 1939: Hitler, die innere Krise und das Mächtesystem', *Geschichte und Gesellschaft*, 2 (1976).
J. Dülffer, *Weimar, Hitler und die Marine: Reichspolitik und Flottenbau* (Düsseldorf, 1973).
G. Engel, *Heeresadjutant bei Hitler 1938–1943: Aufzeichnungen des Majors Engel* (Stuttgart, 1974).
J. Fest, *Hitler* (London, 1974).
J. P. Fox, *Germany and the Far Eastern Crisis 1931–1938* (Oxford, 1982).

S. Friedländer, *Prelude to Downfall: Hitler and the United States 1939–1941* (London, 1967).
E. Fröhlich (ed.), *Die Tagebücher von Joseph Goebbels; sämtliche Fragmente* (4 vols, Munich, 1987).
H. Gisevius, *To the Bitter End* (London, 1948).
S. Hedin, *German Diary* (Dublin, 1951).
J. L. Heinemann, *Hitler's First Foreign Minister* (Berkeley, 1979).
J. von Herwarth, *Against Two Evils* (London, 1981).
F. Hesse, *Hitler and the English* (London, 1954).
J. Heyl, 'The Construction of the *Westwall*: An Example of National Socialist Policy-making', *Central European History*, 14 (1981).
A. Hillgruber, *Die gescheiterte Grossmacht: eine Skizze des deutschen Reiches 1871–1945* (Düsseldorf, 1981).
Hitlers politisches Testament: die Bormann Diktate vom Februar und April 1945 (Hamburg, 1981).
H. Hoffmann, *Hitler Was My Friend* (London, 1955).
E. Jäckel, *Hitler's Weltanschauung* (Middletown, Connecticut, 1972).
M. Kater, 'Hitler in a Social Context', *Central European History*, 14 (1981).
I. Kershaw, *The 'Hitler Myth'* (Oxford, 1987).
A. Kolnai, *The War against the West* (London, 1938).
A. Kuhn, *Hitlers aussenpolitisches Programm* (Stuttgart, 1970).
M. Laffan (ed.), *The Burden of German History 1919–1945* (London, 1988).
W. Manchester, *The Arms of Krupp* (London, 1968).
M. Michaelis, 'World Power Status or World Dominion?', *Historical Journal*, 15 (1972).
W. Michalka, *Ribbentrop und die deutsche Weltpolitik 1933–1940* (Munich, 1980).
G. Mosse, *The Crisis of German Ideology* (London, 1964).
R. J. Overy, 'Germany, "Domestic Crisis" and War in 1939', *Past & Present*, 116 (1987).
R. J. Overy, *The Nazi Economic Recovery 1932–1938* (London, 1982).
R. J. Overy, *Goering: The 'Iron Man'* (London, 1984).
F. von Papen, *Memoirs* (London, 1952).
D. Petzina, *Autarkiepolitik im Dritten Reich* (Stuttgart, 1968).
H. Rauschning, *Hitler Speaks* (London, 1939).
J. von Ribbentrop, *The Ribbentrop Memoirs* (London, 1954).
M. Riedel, *Eisen und Kohle für das Deutsche Reich* (Göttingen, 1973).
E. M. Robertson, *Hitler's Pre-War Policy and Military Plans* (London, 1963).
H. Schacht, *Account Settled* (London, 1949).
W. Schellenberg, *The Schellenberg Memoirs* (London, 1956).
P. Schmidt, *Hitler's Interpreter* (London, 1951).
W. Shirer, *Berlin Diary* (London, 1941).
A. Speer, *Inside the Third Reich* (London, 1970).
A. Speer, *Spandau: The Secret Diaries* (London, 1976).
P. Stachura (ed.), *Unemployment and the Great Depression in Weimar Germany* (London, 1986).
T. Taylor (ed.), *Hitler's Secret Book* (New York, 1961).
J. Thies, *Architekt der Weltherrschaft: die Endziele Hitlers* (Düsseldorf, 1976).
J. Thies, 'Hitler's European Building Programme', *Journal of Contemporary History*, 13 (1978).

J. Toland, *Adolf Hitler* (New York, 1976).
H. A. Turner (ed.), *Nazism and the Third Reich* (New York, 1972).
G. Weinberg, *The Foreign Policy of Hitler's Germany 1933–1936* (London, 1970).
G. Weinberg, *Hitler's Foreign Policy 1937–1939* (Chicago, 1980).
E. von Weizsäcker, *Memoirs* (London, 1951).
B.-J. Wendt, *Grossdeutschland: Aussenpolitik und Kriegsvorbereitung des Hitler-Regimes* (Munich, 1987).

Great Britain

S. Aster, *1939: The Making of the Second World War* (London, 1973).
H. Aulach, 'Britain and the Sudeten Issue 1938: the Evolution of a Policy', *Journal of Contemporary History*, 18 (1983).
C. Barnett, *The Collapse of British Power* (London, 1972).
U. Bialer, 'Elite Opinion and Defence Policy: Air Power Advocacy and British Rearmament during the 1930s', *British Journal of International Studies*, 6 (1980).
B. Bond, *British Military Policy between the Wars* (Oxford, 1980).
B. Bond (ed.), *Chief of Staff: The Diaries of Lieutenant-General Sir Henry Pownall*, vol. 1: *1933–1940* (London, 1972).
T. D. Burridge, *British Labour and Hitler's War* (London, 1976).
R. A. Butler, *The Art of the Possible: The Memoirs of Lord Butler* (London, 1971).
F. Coghlan, 'Armaments, Economic Policy and Appeasement: Background to British Foreign Policy 1931–7', *History*, 57 (1972).
D. Cooper, *Old Men Forget* (London, 1954).
M. Cowling, *The Impact of Hitler* (Cambridge, 1976).
A. Crozier, 'Imperial Decline and the Colonial Question in Anglo-German Relations 1919–1939', *European Studies Review*, 11 (1981).
D. Dilks (ed.), *The Diaries of Sir Alexander Cadogan* (London, 1971).
D. Dilks (ed.), *Retreat from Power: Studies in Britain's Foreign Policy of the Twentieth Century* (2 vols, London, 1981).
A. Eden, *The Eden Memoirs: Facing the Dictators* (London, 1962).
K. Feiling, *The Life of Neville Chamberlain* (London, 1946).
N. Forbes, 'London Banks, the German Standstill Agreements, and "Economic Appeasement" in the 1930s', *Economic History Review*, 2nd Ser., 40 (1987).
L. Fuchser, *Neville Chamberlain and Appeasement* (New York, 1982).
N. Gibbs, *Grand Strategy*, vol. 1: *Rearmament Policy* (London, 1976).
M. Gilbert, *The Roots of Appeasement* (London, 1966).
M. Gilbert, *Winston S. Churchill*, vol. 5: *1922–1939* (London, 1976).
M. Gilbert and R. Gott, *The Appeasers* (London, 1963).
W. D. Gruner, 'The British Political, Social and Economic System and the Decision for War and Peace', *British Journal of International Studies*, 6 (1980).
Earl of Halifax, *Fulness of Days* (London, 1957).
J. Harvey (ed.), *The Diplomatic Diaries of Oliver Harvey 1937–1940* (London, 1970).
N. Henderson, *Failure of a Mission* (London, 1940).
F. H. Hinsley, *British Intelligence in the Second World War*, vol. 1 (London, 1979).
M. Howard, *The Continental Commitment* (London, 1972).
P. Kennedy, *Realities behind Diplomacy* (London, 1981).
P. Kennedy, 'The Tradition of Appeasement in British Foreign Policy 1865–1939', *British Journal of International Studies*, 2 (1976).

W. R. Louis, *British Strategy in the Far East 1919–1939* (Oxford, 1971).
C. Macdonald, 'Economic Appeasement and the German "Moderates" 1937–39', *Past & Present*, 56 (1972).
J. M. MacKenzie, *Propaganda and Empire: The Manipulation of British Public Opinion 1880–1960* (Manchester, 1984).
H. Macmillan, *Winds of Change 1914–1939* (London, 1966).
R. Manne, 'Some British Light on the Nazi–Soviet Pact', *European Studies Review*, 11 (1981).
Viscount Maugham, *The Truth about the Munich Crisis* (London, 1944).
S. Newman, *March 1939: The British Guarantee to Poland* (Oxford, 1976).
H. Nicolson, *Diaries and Letters 1930–1964* (New York, 1980).
F. S. Northedge, *The Troubled Giant: Britain among the Great Powers 1916–1939* (London, 1966).
R. Ovendale, *'Appeasement' and the English-speaking World 1937–1939* (Cardiff, 1979).
A. Parker, 'British Rearmament 1936–1939: Treasury, Trade Unions and Skilled Labour', *English Historical Review*, 96 (1981).
A. Parker, 'The Pound Sterling, the American Treasury and British Preparations for War', *English Historical Review*, 98 (1983).
G. Peden, *British Rearmament and the Treasury 1932–1939* (Edinburgh, 1979).
G. Peden, 'A Matter of Timing: The Economic Background to British Foreign Policy 1938–1939', *History*, 69 (1984).
G. Peden, 'Sir Warren Fisher and British Rearmament against Germany', *English Historical Review*, 94 (1979).
B. Porter, *The Lion's Share: A Short History of British Imperialism 1850–1970* (London, 1975).
L. R. Pratt, *East of Malta, West of Suez: Britain's Mediterranean Crisis 1936–1939* (Cambridge, 1975).
D. Reynolds, *The Creation of the Anglo-American Alliance 1937–1941* (London, 1981).
R. Rhodes James (ed.), *Chips: The Diaries of Sir Henry Channon* (London, 1967).
W. Rock, *British Appeasement in the 1930s* (London, 1977).
S. Roskill, *Hankey: Man of Secrets*, vol. 3: *1931–1963* (London, 1974).
G. Schmidt, *England in der Krise: Grundzüge und Grundlagen der Britischen Appeasement-Politik* (Opladen, 1981).
R. Shay, *British Rearmament in the Thirties* (Princeton, 1977).
Viscount Simon, *Retrospect* (London, 1952).
R. Tamchina, 'In Search of Common Cause: The Imperial Conference of 1937', *Journal of Imperial and Commonwealth History*, 1 (1972).
D. C. Watt, *Succeeding John Bull: America in Britain's Place* (Cambridge, 1984).
B.-J. Wendt, *'Economic Appeasement': Handel und Finanz in der Britischen Deutschlandpolitik* (Düsseldorf, 1971).

France

A. Adamthwaite, *France and the Coming of the Second World War* (London, 1977).
M. Adereth, *The French Communist Party: A Critical History 1920–1984* (Manchester, 1984).
R. Albrecht-Carrié, *France, Europe and Two World Wars* (Paris, 1960).

C. Andrew and A. Kanya-Forstner, *France Overseas: The Great War and S. H.the Climax of French Imperial Expansion* (London, 1981).
M. Bloch, *Strange Defeat: A Statement of Evidence Written in 1940* (Oxford, 1949).
O. H. Bullitt (ed.), *For the President. Personal and Secret. Correspondence between Franklin D. Roosevelt and William C. Bullitt* (London, 1973).
S. Butterworth, 'Daladier and the Munich Crisis: A Reappraisal', *Journal of Contemporary History*, 9 (1974).
J. Cairns, 'A Nation of Shopkeepers in Search of a Suitable France', *American Historical Review*, 79 (1974).
Comité d'Histoire de la 2ème Guerre Mondiale, *Les relations franco-brittaniques de 1935 à 1939* (Paris, 1975).
J. E. Dreifort, 'The French Popular Front and the Franco-Soviet Pact 1936–1937', *Journal of Contemporary History*, 11 (1976).
J. Duroselle, *La décadence 1932–1939* (Paris, 1979).
A. François Poncet, *The Fateful Years* (London, 1949).
R. Frankenstein, *Le prix du réarmament français 1935–1939* (Paris, 1982).
E. M. Gates, *The End of the Affair: The Collapse of the Anglo-French Alliance 1939–1940* (London, 1981).
R. Genebrier, *Septembre 1939: La France entre en guerre: le témoignage du chef de cabinet de Daladier* (Paris, 1982).
A. Gide, *The Journals* vol. 3 *1928–1939* (London, 1949).
J. M. Haight, *American Aid to France 1938–1940* (New York, 1970).
A. Horne, *The French Army and Politics 1870–1970* (London, 1984).
J. Jackson, *The Politics of Depression in France 1932–1936* (Cambridge, 1985).
J. Jackson, *The Popular Front in France: Defending Democracy 1934–1938* (Cambridge, 1988).
D. Johnson, F. Crouzet and F. Bedérida (eds), *Britain and France: Ten Centuries* (Folkestone, 1980).
J. Joll (ed.), *The Decline of the Third Republic* (London, 1959).
A. Kemp, *The Maginot Line: Myth and Reality* (London, 1981).
T. Kemp, *The French Economy 1913–1939: The History of a Decline* (London, 1972).
H. de Kérellis, *Kérellis and the Causes of the War* (London, 1939).
F. R. Kirkland, 'The French Air Force in 1940', *Air University Review*, 36 (1985).
P. J. Larmour, *The French Radical Party in the 1930s* (London, 1984).
A. Maurois, *Memoirs 1885–1967* (London, 1970).
J. Néré, *The Foreign Policy of France from 1914 to 1945* (London, 1975).
S. H. Osgood, 'Le mythe de "la perfide Albion" en France 1919–1940', *Cahiers d'histoire*, 20 (1975).
R. Rémond (ed.), *Édouard Daladier* (Paris, 1977).
R. Rémond, *The Right Wing in France from 1815 to de Gaulle* (Philadelphia, Pennsylvania, 1969).
P. Réynaud, *In the Thick of the Fight 1930–1945* (London, 1955).
V. Rowe, *The Great Wall of France: The Triumph of the Maginot Line* (London, 1959).
A. Sauvy, 'The Economic Crisis of the 1930s in France', *Journal of Contemporary History*, 4 (1969).
S. Schuker, *The End of French Predominance in Europe: The Financial Crisis of 1924 and the Adoption of the Dawes Plan* (Chapel Hill, North Carolina, 1976).
W. E. Scott, *Alliance against Hitler: The Origins of the Franco-Soviet Pact* (Durham, North Carolina, 1962).

P. R. Stafford, 'The French Government and the Danzig Crisis: The Italian Dimension', *International History Review*, 6 (1984).
E. R. Tannenbaum, *The Action Française: Die-Hard Reactionaries in Twentieth Century France* (New York, 1962).
N. Waites (ed.), *Troubled Neighbours: Franco-British Relations in the Twentieth Century* (London, 1971).
G. Warner, *Pierre Laval and the Eclipse of France* (London, 1968).
S. Weil, *Écrits historiques et politiques* (Paris, 1960).
A. Werth, *France and Munich* (London, 1939).
A. Werth, *France in Ferment* (London, 1934).
A. Werth, *The Destiny of France* (London, 1937).
M. Wolfe, *The French Franc between the Wars 1919–1939* (New York, 1951).
G. Wright, *Rural Revolution in France* (Oxford, 1964).
R. Young, *In Command of France: French Foreign Policy and Military Planning 1933–1940* (Cambridge, Massachusetts, 1978).
R. Young, 'La guerre de longue durée: More Reflections on French Strategy and Diplomacy in the 1930s', in A. Preston (ed.), *General Staffs and Diplomacy before the Second World War* (London, 1978).
R. Young, 'The Strategic Dream: French Air Doctrine in the Inter-war Period 1919–1939', *Journal of Contemporary History*, 9 (1974).

Italy

G. Baer, *The Coming of the Italo-Ethiopian War* (Cambridge, Massachusetts, 1967).
G. S. Barclay, *The Rise and Fall of the New Roman Empire* (London, 1973).
A. J. Barker, *The Civilising Mission: The Italo-Ethiopian War 1935–6* (London, 1968).
R. J. B. Bosworth, *Italy, the Least of the Great Powers: Italian Foreign Policy before the First World War* (Cambridge, 1979).
A. Cassels, *Fascist Italy* (London, 1969).
H. Cliadakis, 'Neutrality and War in Italian Policy 1939–1940', *Journal of Contemporary History*, 8 (1974).
J. Coverdale, *Italian Intervention in the Spanish Civil War* (Princeton, 1975).
F. Deakin, *The Brutal Friendship* (London, 1962).
E. Faldella, *L'Italia e la seconda guerra mondiale* (Bologna, 1960).
R. De Felice, *Mussolini il duce: I, gli anni del consenso 1929–1936* (Turin, 1974).
R. De Felice, *Mussolini il duce: II. Lo stato Totalitario 1936–1940* (Turin, 1980).
M. Gallo, *Mussolini's Italy* (London, 1974).
A. de Grand, *Italian Fascism: Its Origins and Development* (London, 1982).
F. Hardie, *The Abysinnian Crisis* (London, 1974).
R. Katz, *The Fall of the House of Savoy* (London, 1972).
I. Kirkpatrick, *Mussolini: Study of a Demagogue* (London, 1964).
M. Knox, *Mussolini Unleashed 1939–1941* (Cambridge, 1983).
T. Koon, *Believe–Obey–Fight: Political Socialization in Fascist Italy 1922–1943* (Chapel Hill, North Carolina, 1985).
C. J. Lowe and F. Marzari, *Italian Foreign Policy 1870–1940* (London, 1975).
E. Ludwig, *Talks with Mussolini* (London, 1933).
A. Lyttleton, *The Seizure of Power: Fascism in Italy 1919–1929* (2nd edn, London, 1987).

M. H. Macartney, *One Man Alone: The History of Mussolini and the Axis* (London, 1944).
C. Macdonald, 'Radio Bari: Italian Wireless Propaganda in the Middle East and British Countermeasures', *Middle Eastern Studies*, 13 (1977).
J. Macdonald, *A Political Escapade: The Story of Fiume and D'Annunzio* (London, 1921).
R. Macgregor-Hastie, *The Day of the Lion* (London, 1963).
D. Mack Smith, *Mussolini* (London, 1981).
D. Mack Smith, *Mussolini's Roman Empire* (London, 1976).
M. Muggeridge (ed.), *Ciano's Diary 1939–1943* (London, 1947).
M. Muggeridge (ed.), *Ciano's Diary 1937–1938* (London, 1952).
R. Quartararo, *Roma fra Londra e Berlino: la politica estera fascista dal 1930 al 1940* (Rome, 1980).
R. Quartararo, 'Imperial Defence in the Mediterranean on the Eve of the Ethiopian Crisis', *Historical Journal*, 20 (1977).
E. M. Robertson, *Mussolini as Empire-Builder* (London, 1977).
R. Sarti (ed.), *The Ax Within: Italian Fascism in Action* (New York, 1974).
A. Sbacchi, *Ethiopia under Mussolini: Fascism and the Colonial Experience* (London, 1985).
D. Schmitz, *The United States and Fascist Italy 1922–1940* (Chapel Hill, North Carolina, 1988).
M. Toscano, *The Origins of the Pact of Steel* (Baltimore, 1967).
G. Waterfield, *Professional Diplomat: Sir Percy Loraine* (London, 1973).
J. Whittam, *The Politics of the Italian Army* (London, 1977).

The Soviet Union

A. Amba, *I Was Stalin's Bodyguard* (London, 1952).
G. Bilainkin, *Maisky: Ten Years Ambassador* (London, 1944).
B. Bromage, *Molotov: The Story of an Era* (London, 1956).
A. C. Brown and C. B. Macdonald, *The Communist International and the Coming of World War II* (New York, 1981).
S. Cohen, *Rethinking the Soviet Experience: Politics and History since 1917* (Oxford, 1985).
D. J. Dallin, *Soviet Russia's Foreign Policy 1939–1942* (New Haven, 1942).
J. E. Davies, *Mission to Moscow* (London, 1942).
R. B. Day, *The 'Crisis' and the 'Crash': Soviet Studies of the West 1917–1939* (Ithaca, NY, 1984).
F. W. Deakin, H. Shukman and H. T. Willett, *A History of World Communism* (London, 1975).
F. W. Deakin and G. A. Storry, *The Case of Richard Sorge* (London, 1966).
J. Degras (ed.), *Soviet Documents on Foreign Policy* (3 vols, Oxford, 1953).
J. R. Dukes, 'The Soviet Union and Britain: The Alliance Negotiations of March–August 1939', *Eastern European Quarterly*, 19 (1985).
J. Elleinstein, *Staline* (Paris, 1984).
J. Erickson, *The Road to Stalingrad* (London, 1975).
J. A. Getty, *Origins of the Great Purges: The Soviet Communist Party Reconsidered 1933–1938* (Cambridge, 1985).
E. R. Goodman, *The Soviet Design for a World State* (New York, 1960).

G. R. Gorodetsky, *Stafford Cripps' Mission to Moscow 1940–1942* (Cambridge, 1984).
G. R. Gorodetsky, *The Precarious Truce: Anglo-Soviet Relations 1925–27* (Cambridge, 1977).
P. G. Grigorenko, *Memoirs* (London, 1983).
M. Harrison, *Soviet Planning in Peace and War 1938–1945* (Cambridge, 1985).
J. Haslam, *Soviet Foreign Policy 1930–1933: Impact of the Depression* (London, 1983).
J. Haslam, 'The Soviet Union and the Czech Crisis', *Journal of Contemporary History*, 14 (1979).
J. Haslam, *The Soviet Union and the Struggle for Collective Security 1933–1939* (London, 1984).
J. Herman, 'Soviet Peace Efforts on the Eve of World War II: A Review of the Soviet Documents', *Journal of Contemporary History*, 15 (1980).
M. Hindus, *Red Bread* (London, 1934).
J. Hochman, *The Soviet Union and the Failure of Collective Security 1934–1938* (Ithaca, NY, 1984).
G. Kennan, *Soviet Foreign Policy 1917–1941* (New York, 1960).
W. Laqueur, *Russia and Germany: A Century of Conflict* (London, 1965).
B. Leach, *German Strategy against Russia* (Oxford, 1973).
K. E. McKenzie, *Comintern and World Revolution* (New York, 1964).
I. Maisky, *Journey into the Past* (London, 1962).
R. Medvedev, *Let History Judge: The Origins and Consequences of Stalinism* (London, 1971).
E. O'Ballance, *The Red Army* (London, 1964).
A. U. Pope, *Maxim Litvinoff* (London, 1943).
A. Read and D. Fisher, *The Deadly Embrace: Hitler, Stalin and the Nazi–Soviet Pact 1939–1941* (London, 1988).
C. R. Richardson, 'French Plans for Allied Attacks on the Caucasus Oilfields Jan–Apr 1940', *French Historical Studies*, 8 (1973).
A. Rossi, *The Russo-German Alliance 1939–1941* (London, 1950).
R. Schinness, 'The Conservative Party and Anglo-Soviet Relations 1925–1927', *European Studies Review*, 7 (1977).
J. Stalin, *Problems of Leninism* (Moscow, 1947).
J. J. Stephan, *The Russian Fascists: Tragedy and Farce in Exile 1925–1945* (London, 1978).
N. Tolstoy, *Stalin's Secret War* (London, 1981).
E. Topitsch, *Stalins Krieg: die sowjetische Langzeitstrategie gegen den Westen als rationale Machtpolitik* (Munich, 1985).
A. Ulam, *Expansion and Co-Existence: A History of Soviet Foreign Policy 1917–1967* (London, 1968).
A. Ulam, *Stalin: The Man and His Era* (London, 1973).
T. J. Uldricks, 'Russia and Europe: Diplomacy, Revolution and Economic Development in the 1920s', *International History Review*, 1 (1979).
B. Whaley, *Codeword Barbarossa* (Massachusetts, 1973).
S. Wheatcroft, R. W. Davies and J. M. Cooper, 'Soviet Industrialisation Reconsidered', *Economic History Review*, 2nd Ser., 39 (1986).
G. Zhukov, *The Memoirs of Marshal Zhukov* (London, 1971).

Japan

M. Barnhart, 'Japan's Economic Security and the Origins of the Pacific War', *Journal of Strategic Studies*, 4 (1981).
M. J. Barnhart, *Japan Prepares for Total War* (New York, 1987).
R. Benedict, *The Chrysanthemum and the Sword* (London, 1967).
D. Borg and O. Shumpei (eds), *Pearl Harbor as History: Japanese–American Relations 1931–1941* (New York, 1973).
R. J. Butow, *Tojo and the Coming of the War* (Princeton, 1961).
R. M. Connaughton, *The War of the Rising Sun and the Tumbling Bear: A Military History of the Russo-Japanese War 1904–5* (London, 1989).
J. B. Crowley, *Japan's Quest for Autonomy: National Security and Foreign Policy 1930–1938* (Princeton, 1966).
J. Dower, *War without Mercy: Race and Power in the Pacific War* (New York, 1986).
T. Fukatake, *The Japanese Social Structure: 20th century Development* (Tokyo, 1982).
E. P. Hoyt, *Japan's War: The Great Pacific Conflict* (London, 1986).
M. Hyoe, *Japan: The Years of Trial 1919–1952* (Tokyo, 1982).
S. Ienaga, *Japan's Last War: World War II and the Japanese 1931–1945* (Oxford, 1979).
N. Ike (ed.), *Japan's Decision for War: Records of the 1941 Policy Conferences* (Stanford, 1967).
A. Iriye (ed.), *Mutual Images: Essays on American–Japanese Relations* (Cambridge, Massachusetts, 1975).
A. Iriye, *Pacific Estrangement: Japanese and American Expansion 1897–1911* (Cambridge, Massachusetts, 1972).
A. Iriye, *The Chinese and the Japanese: Essays in Political and Cultural Interaction* (Princeton, 1980).
A. Iriye, *The Origins of the Second World War in the Pacific* (London, 1987).
D. James, *The Rise and Fall of the Japanese Empire* (London, 1951).
M. B. Jansen, *Changing Japanese Attitudes to Modernisation* (Princeton, 1965).
M. B. Jansen, *Japan and China: From War to Peace 1894–1972* (Chicago, 1975).
F. C. Jones, *Japan's New Order in East Asia* (Oxford, 1954).
M. Kajima, *The Emergence of Japan as a World Power 1895–1925* (Tokyo, 1968).
G. J. Kasza, 'Fascism from Below? A Comparative Perspective on the Japanese Right 1931–36', *Journal of Contemporary History*, 19 (1984).
J. C. Lebra (ed.), *Japan's Greater East Asia Co-Prosperity Sphere in World War II: Selected Readings and Documents* (Oxford, 1975).
B. A. Lee, *Britain and the Sino-Japanese War* (Stanford, 1973).
P. Lowe, *Great Britain and the Origins of the Pacific War 1937–1941* (Oxford, 1977).
W. J. Macpherson, *The Economic Development of Japan c. 1868–1941* (London, 1987).
S. Mamoru, *Japan and Her Destiny* (London, 1958).
M. Maruyama, *Thought and Behaviour in Modern Japanese Politics* (London, 1963).
J. W. Morley, *Deterrent Diplomacy: Japan, Germany and the USSR 1935–1940* (New York, 1977).
J. W. Morley (ed.), *Dilemmas of Growth in Pre-war Japan* (Princeton, 1971).
R. H. Myers and M. R. Peattie, *The Japanese Colonial Empire 1895–1945* (Princeton, 1984).
I. Nish, *Anglo-Japanese Alienation 1919–1952* (Cambridge, 1982).

I. Nish, *Japanese Foreign Policy 1869–1942* (London, 1977).
S. A. Shillony, *Politics and Culture in Wartime Japan* (Oxford, 1981).
R. Smethurst, *A Social Basis for Prewar Japanese Militarism* (Berkeley, 1974).
R. H. Spector, *Eagle against the Sun: The American War with Japan* (New York, 1984).
R. Storry, *The Double Patriots: A Study of Japanese Nationalism* (Boston, 1957).
C. K. Sun, *The Economic Development of Manchuria* (Cambridge, Massachusetts, 1969).
C. Thorne, *Allies of a Kind: The United States, Britain and the War Against Japan 1941–1945* (Oxford, 1978).
C. Thorne, *The Limits of Foreign Policy: The West, the League and the Far Eastern Crisis of 1931–1933* (London, 1972).
S. Tsurumi, *An Intellectual History of Wartime Japan 1931–1945* (London, 1986).
E. Wilkinson, *Japan versus Europe: A History of Misunderstanding* (London, 1983).

The United States

S. Adler, *The Uncertain Giant: American Foreign Policy 1921–41* (London, 1965).
S. Ambrose, *Rise to Globalism: American Foreign Policy since 1918* (London, 1971).
E. M. Bennett, *Franklin D. Roosevelt and the Search for Security* (Wilmington, Delaware, 1985).
B. B. Berle and T. B. Jacobs (eds), *Navigating the Rapids 1918–1971: From the Papers of Adolf A. Berle* (New York, 1973).
P. Brendon, *Ike: His Life and Times* (London, 1986).
R. Burns and E. Bennett (eds), *Diplomats in Crisis: United States–Chinese–Japanese Relations 1919–1941* (Oxford, 1974).
M. L. Chadwin, *The Warhawks: American Interventionists before Pearl Harbor* (New York, 1970).
W. S. Cole, *Roosevelt and the Isolationists 1932–1945* (Lincoln, Nebraska, 1983).
J. Compton, *The Swastika and the Eagle: Hitler, the United States and the Origins of the Second World War* (London, 1968).
R. Dallek, *Franklin D. Roosevelt and American Foreign Policy 1932–1945* (New York, 1979).
S. A. Diamond, *The Nazi Movement in the United States 1924–1941* (Ithaca, NY, 1974).
R. A. Divine, *The Reluctant Belligerent: American Entry into World War II* (New York, 1965).
A. Frye, *Nazi Germany and the American Hemisphere 1933–1941* (New Haven, 1967).
L. C. Gardner, *Economic Aspects of New Deal Diplomacy* (Boston, 1971).
H. Gatzke, *Germany and the United States* (Cambridge, Massachusetts, 1980).
R. T. Goldberg, *The Making of Franklin D. Roosevelt: Triumph over Disability* (Cambridge, Massachusetts, 1981).
J. C. Grew, *Ten Years in Japan* (London, 1944).
R. A. Harrison, 'A Presidential Démarche: Franklin D. Roosevelt's Personal Diplomacy and Great Britain 1936–1937', *Diplomatic History*, 5 (1981).
P. Hearden, *Roosevelt Confronts Hitler* (Dekalb, Illinois, 1987).
S. E. Hilton, 'The Welles Mission to Europe, February–March 1940: Illusion or Realism?', *Journal of American History*, 68 (1971).
N. H. Hooker (ed.), *The Moffat Papers: Selections from the Diplomatic Journals of Jay*

Pierrepoint Moffat 1919–1943 (Cambridge, Massachusetts, 1956).
C. Hull, *Memoirs* (2 vols, London, 1948).
H. Ickes, *The Secret Diary of Harold L. Ickes* (2 vols, London, 1955).
M. Jonas, *The United States and Germany: A Diplomatic History* (Ithaca, NY, 1984).
K. P. Jones, *U.S. Diplomats in Europe 1919–1941* (Oxford, 1981).
G. Kolko, 'American Business and Germany 1930–1941', *Western Political Quarterly*, 15 (1962).
M. Leighton, *Mobilizing Consent: Public Opinion and American Foreign Policy 1937–1948* (London, 1976).
W. Leuchtenberg, *Franklin D. Roosevelt and the New Deal 1932–1940* (New York, 1963).
W. Lippmann, *U.S. Foreign Policy* (London, 1943).
W. Lippmann, *U.S. War Aims* (Boston, 1944).
C. Macdonald, *The United States, Britain and Appeasement 1936–1939* (London, 1981).
R. Moley, *The First New Deal* (New York, 1966).
M. Muir, 'American Warship Construction for Stalin's Navy Prior to World War II', *Diplomatic History*, 5 (1981).
A. A. Offner, 'Appeasement Revisited: The United States, Great Britain and Germany 1933–1940', *Journal of American History*, 64 (1977).
A. A. Offner, *The Origins of the Second World War: American Foreign Policy and World Politics 1917–1941* (New York, 1975).
F. C. Pogue, *George C. Marshall: Ordeal and Hope* (London, 1968).
D. L. Porter, *The Seventy-sixth Congress and World War II, 1939–1940* (New York, 1979).
G. W. Prange, *At Dawn We Slept: The Untold Story of Pearl Harbor* (London, 1982).
J. W. Pratt, *America and World Leadership 1900–1921* (London, 1967).
D. Reynolds and D. Dimbleby, *Oceans Apart* (London, 1988).
B. D. Rhodes, 'The British Royal Visit of 1939 and the Psychological Approach to the United States', *Diplomatic History*, 2 (1978).
E. Roosevelt (ed.), *The Roosevelt Letters*, vol. 3: *1928–1945* (London, 1952).
A. W. Schatz, 'The Anglo-American Trade Agreement and Cordell Hull's Search for Peace 1936–1938', *Journal of American History*, 57 (1970/1).
R. W. Steele, 'The Great Debate: Roosevelt, the Media and the Coming of War 1940–1941', *Journal of American History*, 81 (1984).
R. W. Steele, 'The Pulse of the People: Franklin D. Roosevelt and the Gauging of American Public Opinion', *Journal of Contemporary History*, 9 (1974).
J. G. Utley, *Going to War with Japan* (Knoxville, Tennessee, 1985).
H. G. Vatter, *The U.S. Economy in World War II* (New York, 1985).
M. Wilkins, *American Business Abroad: Ford in Six Continents* (Detroit, 1964).
W. Williams, *The Tragedy of American Diplomacy* (2nd edn, New York, 1970).
J. E. Wiltz, *In Search of Peace: The Senate Munitions Inquiry 1934–1936* (Baton Rouge, Louisiana, 1963).

INDEX

PICTURE ACKNOWLEDGEMENTS

Hoffmann Collection, Imperial War Museum: pages 1, 2 above and below. Hulton Picture Company: pages 5, 9, 10 above, 11 above, 12 below. Imperial War Museum: pages 8 above, 23, 25. National Archives, Washington DC: pages 4 above and below, 7 below, 8 below, 16 below left, 20, 22 above, 26 above and below, 27, 29, 30 above, 31 below, 32. Private Collection: page 24. Topham Picture Library: pages 3 above and below, 6, 7 above, 10 below, 11 below, 12 above, 16 below right, 31 above. Roger Viollet, Paris: pages 13, 14 above and below, 15 above and below, 16 above, 17, 18 above and below, 19, 21, 22 below, 28, 30 below.